UNIFORM FANTASIES

Soldiers, Sex, and Queer Emanci
Imperial Germany

Starting in the nineteenth century in Germany, colourful military uniforms became a locus for various queer male fantasies, fostering an underground sexual economy of male prostitution as well as a political project to exploit the army's prestige for queer emancipation. In the first decade of the twentieth century, however, a series of scandals derailed this emancipatory project. Simultaneously, public debates began to invoke homosexuality, sadism, transvestism, and other sexological concepts to criticize military policies and practices.

In pursuing the threads with which queer authors and activists stitched their fantasies about uniforms, Jeffrey Schneider offers fresh perspectives on key debates over military secrecy, disciplinary abuses in the army, and German militarism. Drawing on a vast trove of materials ranging from sexological case studies, trial transcripts, and parliamentary debates to queer activist tracts, autobiographies, and literary texts, *Uniform Fantasies* uncovers a particularly modern set of concerns about such topics as outing closeted homosexuals, the presence of gay men in the military, and whether men in uniform are more masculine or more insecure about their sexual identity.

(German and European Studies)

JEFFREY SCHNEIDER is an associate professor of German studies at Vassar College.

GERMAN AND EUROPEAN STUDIES

General Editor: James Retallack

Uniform Fantasies

Soldiers, Sex, and Queer Emancipation in Imperial Germany

JEFFREY SCHNEIDER

UNIVERSITY OF TORONTO PRESS
Toronto Buffalo London

© University of Toronto Press 2023
Toronto Buffalo London
utorontopress.com

ISBN 978-1-4875-4868-1 (cloth) ISBN 978-1-4875-4962-6 (EPUB)
ISBN 978-1-4875-4961-9 (paper) ISBN 978-1-4875-4963-3 (PDF)

German and European Studies

Library and Archives Canada Cataloguing in Publication

Title: Uniform fantasies : soldiers, sex, and queer emancipation in Imperial
   Germany / Jeffrey Schneider.
Names: Schneider, Jeffrey (Lecturer in German studies), author.
Series: German and European studies ; 51.
Description: Series statement: German and European studies ; 51 | Includes
   bibliographical references and index.
Identifiers: Canadiana (print) 20230192572 | Canadiana (ebook) 20230192688 |
   ISBN 9781487548681 (cloth) | ISBN 9781487549619 (paper) |
   ISBN 9781487549633 (PDF) | ISBN 9781487549626 (EPUB)
Subjects: LCSH: Gay military personnel – Sexual behavior – Germany. | LCSH:
   Germany. Heer – Uniforms – Social aspects. | LCSH: Closeted gays – Germany. |
   LCSH: Coming out (Sexual orientation) – Germany. | LCSH: Masculinity –
   Germany. | LCSH: Gender identity – Germany. | LCSH: Germany – Military policy.
Classification: LCC HQ76.2.G4 S36 2023 | DDC 306.76/620943 – dc23

Cover design: Will Brown
Cover image: The New York Public Library

We wish to acknowledge the land on which the University of Toronto Press
operates. This land is the traditional territory of the Wendat, the Anishnaabeg, the
Haudenosaunee, the Métis, and the Mississaugas of the Credit First Nation.

The German and European Studies series is funded by the DAAD with funds from
the German Federal Foreign Office.

 Deutscher Akademischer Austauschdienst
German Academic Exchange Service

University of Toronto Press acknowledges the financial support of the Government
of Canada, the Canada Council for the Arts, and the Ontario Arts Council, an agency
of the Government of Ontario, for its publishing activities.

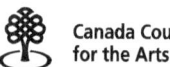   

For Karl, Susan, and Pascal

Contents

List of Illustrations ix

Preface xi

Acknowledgments xvii

Introduction 3

1 Outing Officers: Queer Activism, Melodrama, and the Harden-Moltke Trial 28
 The Military Melodrama of Homosexual Activism 31
 "Gutter Melodramatics": The Harden-Moltke Trial 45
 Conclusion 60

2 Disciplinary Abuses: From Military Secrecy to Sadism in the Army 64
 Ars Erotica: *From Administrative Secrecy to Secret Society* 67
 Scientia Sexualis: *Sadism in the Army* 78
 Conclusion 94

3 The Obscure Object of Desire: Uniform Fetishism, Male Prostitution, and German Soldiers 96
 Sparse Facts and Plentiful Fantasies: The Discursive Twists and Turns of Soldatenprostitution 100
 In/appropriate Desire: The Queer Fetish for Military Uniforms 120
 Conclusion 135

4 Camping in His Own Private Militarism: Thomas
   Mann's Queer Art of Failure and the Fantasies
   of Military Service   138
   The Volunteer Conscript   141
   The Literary Draft Dodger   151
   A Writer Goes to War   162
   Conclusion   171

5 Perversions of Fantasy: Parody and the Left-Liberal
   Critique of German Militarism in Heinrich Mann's
   The Loyal Subject   174
   Psychopathia Homosexualis   179
   Psychopathia Masochismus   188
   Psychopathia Transvestitis   196
   Conclusion   204

Epilogue: The War on Fantasy   208

Notes   225

Bibliography   281

Index   307

Illustrations

0.1   Uniforms of the Cavalry Guard of the Kingdom of Prussia   7
0.2   Commemorative image of Private Friedrich Werz galloping on horseback while holding the regimental flag   15
1.1   Magnus Hirschfeld   39
1.2   Kuno von Moltke   47
1.3   Maximilian Harden   49
2.1   "Villa-Adler," caricature produced in response to testimony by Johann Bollhardt at the first Harden-Moltke libel trial   89
2.2   "Military Innovations," caricature produced in response to testimony by Johann Bollhardt at the first Harden-Moltke libel trial   90
3.1   "Nightlife in Potsdam," caricature produced in response to testimony by Johann Bollhardt at the first Harden-Moltke libel trial   116
3.2   "Hero Worship," caricature produced in response to testimony by Johann Bollhardt at the first Harden-Moltke libel trial   121
4.1   Thomas Mann and Paul Ehrenberg in a field with their bicycles   145
5.1   Heinrich Mann and Thomas Mann   178
5.2   "Tête-à-tête," caricature produced in response to testimony by Lily von Elbe at the first Harden-Moltke libel trial   185
E.1   *The Warriors*, oil painting by Marsden Hartley   213
E.2   Postcard photograph of Karl von Freyburg on horseback   216
E.3   *Portrait of a German Officer*, oil painting by Marsden Hartley   218

Preface

"It is the omnipresent soldiery of Berlin that first catches the American visitor's attention," W.E.B. Du Bois observed at the beginning of an essay on German politics, which he drafted in the summer of 1893 while on a two-year academic fellowship in the German capital.[1] According to the young African American scholar, "[t]he whole city seems to have a half military stride, all Prussia rushes pell-mell to the window to see the ever-passing regiment, and German ideals from king to lover appear at first sight to be clad in spurs and shoulder-strap." Moreover, he explained, "[t]he military spirit appears not to be confined to the army, but largely to permeate society. The American sees it in the stiff bow of the students, in the perfect rage for uniforms in all classes, which enables both footman and chancellor to carry their histories on their backs." Finally, this military spirit also infused the operations of the state, which, he noted, "works about and around the new-comer, with a military precision and careful attention to trifles which is calculated to make a Bostonian uncomfortable, and take a New Yorker's breath away."

Du Bois's opening gambit no doubt conveyed his own initial astonishment at the ubiquity of military uniforms in Berlin.[2] But while their omnipresence seemed to symbolize a widespread adoption of martial values at all levels of state and society, the future civil rights advocate – himself a dapper dresser and life-long admirer of Imperial Germany – also discouraged readers from jumping to any premature conclusions.[3] For example, rather than penning his portrait of German militarism in indelible ink, the Massachusetts native drew it with a string of tentative verbs and adverbs: soldiery is what the outsider sees "first," Imperial Berlin's pace "seems" half-military, ideal German men "appear at first sight" to wear only uniforms. This emphasis on first impressions suggests that military uniforms may have been a surface phenomenon, obscuring a number of potentially less visible but no less important forces. In fact, by bringing "his ears to aid his eyes," Du Bois detected a vibrant and self-consciously modern society that chafed "under the restraints" of this martial ethos.[4] According to the budding social scientist, Germany's emergence as a modern nation – its advanced industry, its intellectual and scientific achievements, and its "growing radicalism" in politics and social reform – had "set into motion a democratic movement in the land" that, he optimistically predicted, would likely prove "fatal to monarchy and militarism alike."[5]

Du Bois characterized this tension between the country's authoritarian military state and its bustling modernity as the "political paradox of Germany" – one "so well-known that it is apt easily to be forgotten."[6] Yet his opening description suggests these two realms were neither separate nor entirely in opposition to each other, but rather deeply enmeshed. After all, if marching regiments had "all Prussia" dashing "pell-mell" to the windows for a glimpse, then the "military spirit" that infused government operations with "military precision" inevitably contributed to a certain dynamism, even chaos, in civil society. Likewise, while military discipline supposedly led students to bow stiffly, it also ignited an irrational and exuberant "rage" for uniforms that extended from the German emperor and his chancellor to the lowliest servant. And with the soldier embodying the ideal "lover," this American visitor recognized that Germany's reverence for military dress had an erotic dimension as well.

Du Bois's rich, multilayered reflections offer a useful springboard for my own (twenty-first-century American) exploration of the dynamic role that uniforms, soldiers, and military politics played in and around Imperial Germany's queer emancipation movement. Though the early 1890s marked a brief caesura in queer activism, the queer scene in Berlin was already flourishing, thanks to the Berlin police department's decision in the late 1880s to end its practice of raiding bars and most other venues catering to a queer clientele.[7] There is, of course, now a large and ever-growing body of excellent scholarship on Germany's early queer emancipation movement, already too vast to cite in one footnote.[8] In addition to important monographs and articles on many of the leading figures in this project,[9] much of this work has contextualized the phenomenon of queer emancipation within the major political movements of the day (nationalism, socialism, feminism, and far-right activism),[10] the lively panoply of German bourgeois life reform movements (clothing reform, nudism, homeopathy, etc.),[11] the rise of the scientific study of sexuality (psychiatry, sexology, psychoanalysis, etc.),[12] the criminal legal system (policing, criminology, and high-profile trials and scandals),[13] the high-decibel debates and pitched activism around sexual mores and diseases (blackmail, prostitution, venereal disease, Christian morality movements),[14] and the systems of racial oppression (anti-Semitism, colonialism, orientalism, eugenics, etc.).[15] However, despite the military's outsized role in public life in this period, the scholarly exploration of entanglements between military Germany and queer Germany has largely been limited to the series of sex scandals in 1907 involving high-ranking army officers.[16] Though, as I claim, these scandals were even more important than has hitherto been recognized, my investigation also focuses on a range of queer and queerphobic discourses about uniforms and soldiers – as ideal exemplars of hegemonic masculinity, as fetishistic objects of desire and clandestine sexual partners, as "innocent victims" of homophobic witch-hunts or, conversely, "helpless victims" of homosexual aggression – that all played a foundational and multifaceted role in the articulation of queer identities and desires in Imperial Germany as well as their broad dissemination throughout the country and other parts of the world.[17]

To the extent that these discourses revolved around sexual desires or involved sensationalism, exaggeration, or dissimulation, *Uniform Fantasies* approaches its sources through the concept of fantasy. My title, of course, is a play on *Male Fantasies*, Klaus Theweleit's iconoclastic two-volume study devoted to the writings of men active in the paramilitary *Freikorps* units after the First World War.[18] *Uniform Fantasies*, however, charts a very different course, not only because it deals with an earlier period in German history, but because it also starts from very different premises. Thus, while Theweleit's inquiry tended to blur historical distinctions between *Freikorps* volunteers, Nazi Party members, and *male* identity more generally, my project uses the military *uniforms* of the Imperial German Army as a specific locus for exploring the tensions between military service and male desire in the decades leading up to the First World War.[19] Similarly, Theweleit's primary objects of analysis were the sexual fantasies of his protofascist authors, which he essentially traced back to sexual repression.[20] Foucault's work, however, has raised important doubts about the primacy of repression in explaining modern sexuality, arguing instead that sexuality was constituted through a "regime of power-knowledge-pleasure" that produced the very desires and identities it was ostensibly seeking to prevent or cure.[21] Still, like Theweleit and some of the queer theorists and historians I draw on, I too find it useful to employ psychoanalytic tools, particularly its rich approach to fantasy.

In order to fully explore the complex entanglements between queer emancipation and military politics in Imperial Germany, I have had to make some difficult decisions about the materials and timeframe for this study. For example, most of the debates in this investigation rotate almost exclusively around men, masculinities, and male (sexual) identity. Despite the centrality of women and the women's movement in the larger project of emancipation in the nineteenth century, there are several reasons for this singular focus. First, because sexual relations between women were not criminalized in Germany, women's involvement (and inclusion) in the broader queer emancipation movement came late and haltingly, primarily in response to the accusations of homosexuality levelled against the leaders of the women's movement as well as the lack of attention to the issues of women-loving-women within the feminist movements, which were largely committed to a politics of respectability.[22] Moreover, while men's citizenship was grounded in the principle of their required military service, women's participation in politics were, as German feminists knew only too well, highly constrained by law and custom. Yet as Georg Simmel argued in a prescient 1894 essay on militarism and the position of women in society, "wherever war is the main interest [*Hauptinteresse*], those who are not in a position to participate are automatically degraded [*deklassiert*]. For that reason we find in those decidedly militant peoples [*kriegerischen Völkern*] a surprisingly high social position of women as soon as these take an active share in military affairs."[23] While a few women did begin to exert a public interest in military affairs over the second half of the nineteenth century – through nursing the war wounded (à la Florence Nightingale), founding a pacifist movement (à la Bertha von Suttner), or writing themselves into the narrative of German colonialist expansion and other nationalist projects (à la Frieda von Bülow) – it took the First World War for women's military service to become a popular and widespread phenomenon.[24]

Moreover, my study is focused primarily on Imperial Germany between 1890 and 1914, roughly the period after Bismarck's dismissal as chancellor, when entirely new forms of politics and social experimentation began in earnest, and before the First World War radically changed German society and politics. Though the world war's impact on queer activism in the 1920s and 1930s is certainly fascinating, there is fortunately already good scholarship on both masculinity and homosexuality during the war, the Weimar Republic, and the rise of National Socialism, some of which I discuss briefly in the book's epilogue.[25] Instead of focusing on subsequent developments into these later periods, I have been persuaded by Volker Berghahn's insistence that the "more immediate task" for historians of Imperial Germany is "to explain not how Germany landed itself in the Third Reich in 1933, but how the country got into the 'great war' in 1914 that – all are agreed – was nothing less than catastrophic for Germans and the rest of Europe."[26] Though the goals of my study are different and more modest than the one proposed by Berghahn, *Uniform Fantasies* does offer new insights into how the queer fascination with uniforms contributed to the initial support for the war among queer individuals and leaders of the queer emancipation movement. At the same time, war was by no means an inevitable outcome of Imperial Germany's military politics, let alone the military politics of queer emancipation. In fact, the queer emancipation movement was an exemplary actor in what Geoff Eley, Jennifer Jenkins, and Tracie Matysik call Germany's "modernities," in which "[g]rasping the future meant actively shaping 'the political' and 'the social' of the present tense, the ideas of citizen and the subject, their material and intellectual worlds."[27]

For this reason, many of the issues I explore will likely strike readers as rather similar to recent or contemporary phenomena in the United States and elsewhere, including debates about "outing" closeted homosexuals, the presence of gays in the military, and whether men in uniform are more masculine or more insecure about their sexual identity. These similarities are surely not accidental. But though I draw on some of these contemporary debates in a few instances to help decipher turn-of-the-century German practices and discourses, my focus is squarely on this earlier period. Thus, while David Halperin has called for a genealogical approach to queer history – one that by providing "a calculated encounter with the otherness of the past" would produce "an altered understanding of the present," in particular, of our "own non-identity to ourselves" – I am persuaded by Laura Doan's concern that such an approach tends to limit a full engagement with the past – especially "those aspects of the sexual past that resist explanation" with our current concepts.[28] Instead, she advocates combining the theoretically informed and self-reflective practices of critical history (which includes an abiding interest in the methodologies of psychoanalysis) with the theoretical insights of queer theory – "queerness-as-method" – to 'look through' the archive to see what is unknown at the present moment."[29]

The emerging queer theory of Imperial Germany also seems to have had an impact on Du Bois's own work. To be sure, as someone strongly attracted to women, he seems not to have noticed Berlin's lively queer scene – or returned to America prepared to offer much sympathy or support for queer African Americans or non-normative cultural expressions.[30] Yet even as most scholars now agree that the social-scientific methodologies he encountered during his two-year fellowship at the University of Berlin had a profound impact on his development as a scholar and civil rights activist, Seth Clark Silberman has argued that key concepts in Du Bois's groundbreaking *The Souls of Black Folk* (1903) – "the veil" and "double consciousness" – were also indebted to "the burgeoning method and theory of psychoanalysis" as well as "the racial metaphors in sexology that helped bring 'the homosexual' into language as such."[31] Of course, perhaps one of the most surprising legacies of his two-year immersion in Imperial Germany was his abiding "strong affection" for the country, for despite an awareness of growing anti-Semitism and Germany's recent colonization of parts of Africa, he claims that Germany "was the land where I first met white folk who treated me as a human being."[32]

Though I have only "visited" Imperial Germany through its texts, I share Du Bois's critical fascination with this dynamic and complex period. And like Du Bois, it is my modest hope to have also "returned" with some unexpected insights into not only German militarism but also the connections and clashes between military politics and queer sexual politics. While some of the incidents I discuss may no doubt sound a familiar chord, others will, I trust, still have the capacity to once again "make a Bostonian uncomfortable" or "take a New Yorker's breath away."

Acknowledgments

Writing can be a long, arduous, and lonely process, but the final product is never the work of just one person. It thus gives me great pleasure to acknowledge all the encouragement, financial support, and feedback without which this book would not have seen the light of day. Initial impulses for my approach to this topic came from a German Academic Exchange Service (DAAD) fellowship to participate in a faculty seminar on gender and sexuality at Cornell University led by Biddy Martin in the summer of 1999. During that summer, Randall Halle, Dagmar Herzog, Brad Prager, and other workshop participants gave me much food for thought. Additional research in Germany was provided by two Louise Boyd Dale Research Grants from Vassar College.

I benefited early on from a number of superb teachers and mentors, in particular Craig Decker†, Peter Uwe Hohendahl, Isabel Hull, Biddy Martin, and George Mosse†, who also first directed me to the work of Ernst Wildenbruch.

Many thanks are due to the many librarians and archivists who helped me find the sources I needed for this project: the Staatsbibliothek zu Berlin, the libraries of the Humboldt University and Free University of Berlin, the Universitätsbibliothek Heidelberg, the Klassik Stiftung Weimar, the Österreichische Nationalbibliothek, the Schwules Museum, and the amazing staff in the interlibrary loan department of the Vassar College Libraries.

Parts of this work have appeared earlier, and I wish to acknowledge those prior publications here: a shorter version of chapter 3 was published as "Soliciting Fantasies: Knowing and Not-Knowing About Male Prostitution by Soldiers in Imperial Germany," in *After the History of Sexuality: German Interventions*, ed. Dagmar Herzog, Helmut Puff, and Scott Spector (Oxford: Berghahn, 2012), 124–38. A very early version of the third part of chapter 5 was published as "'The Pleasure of the Uniform!': Masculinity, Transvestism and Militarism in Heinrich Mann's *Der Untertan* and Magnus Hirschfeld's *Die Transvestiten*," *The Germanic Review* 72, no. 3 (1997): 183–200.

Several colleagues gave me welcome opportunities over the years to present parts of this manuscript on their conference panels or campuses. Special thanks to Friederike Bruehofener, Jennifer Evans, Geoffrey Giles, Dagmar Herzog, Helmut Puff, Alex Sager, Scott Spector, James Steakley, Lynn Tatlock, and Clayton Whisnant.

I am extremely grateful to have wonderful colleagues at Vassar College. A particularly heartfelt thanks to Silke von der Emde, Elliott Schreiber, Lioba Gerhardi, and a number of visiting faculty who have made the Department of German Studies such a welcoming and vibrant intellectual home over these many years. My colleagues in three of Vassar's multidisciplinary programs – International Studies; Women, Feminist, and Queer Studies; and Global Nineteenth Century Studies – have also offered me an intellectually stimulating space to grow as an interdisciplinary scholar. Many, many thanks are also due to my students at Vassar who have made teaching such a pleasure over the years. Among these, I want to especially thank the Posse veterans I have had the honour of working with at Vassar, including Francisco Andrade, Devon Arceneaux, Luis Arguello, Rebekah Graham, Priscilla Kendall, Daniel Reyes, Mark, Savarese, Kyle Trumble, and Eduardo De La Torre.

This manuscript benefited from many colleagues over the past decade or more who offered generous and honest feedback. I particularly want to thank Mona Ali, Mita Choudhary, Colleen Cohen, Wendy Graham, Pascal Grosse, William Hoynes, Jean Kane, Susan Kassouf, Timothy Koechlin, Barbara Mennel, Himadeep Muppidi, Lydia Murdoch, Elliott Schreiber, Scott Spector, Vinay Swamy, Denise Walen, and Susan Zlotnick. I owe a special debt of gratitude for insightful and timely advice from Beth Bouloukos and Emily Andrew. A big shout out is due to Katherine Hite for feedback on various iterations of my manuscript, sage advice on publishing, and a few swift kicks in the butt. Finally, I can't thank enough the members of my writing group, who read multiple versions of every part of this manuscript over many long years: Sophia Harvey, Susan Hiner, Joshua Schreier, Silke von der Emde, and Eva Woods. I couldn't have finished this without you.

It is also a pleasure to extend my thanks to the people at the University of Toronto Press who shepherded this book to its completion: Stephen Shapiro, my patient and reliable editor; Jennifer Jenkins and James Retallack, for accepting the book into their series; and Janice Evans for guiding the book through the production process. Also thanks to Beth McAuley of The Editing Company for her expert editing, and to

Michel Pharand for creating such an excellent index. I especially owe a heartfelt debt of thanks to the three anonymous reviewers who offered extensive and constructive feedback for significantly improving this manuscript in its final stages. Though I may not have been able to integrate all their excellent suggestions, I hope they will be gratified to see the fruits of their generous labour in these pages.

In addition to the many people who contributed to the refinements of my ideas, I also want to acknowledge the many others who sustained my soul and gave me other forms of support. In addition to my parents, Thomas and Patricia Schneider†, who instilled in me a strong work ethic, I would like to thank my extended family of siblings, aunts, uncles, nieces, nephews, cousins, and in-laws for their patience and sense of humour over the many years. I am also grateful to the members of End the New Jim Crow Action Network for their fellowship and abiding commitment to social justice for more than a decade. For providing nourishment in both spiritual and material ways, I am extremely grateful to the friends and fellow members of my weekly Thursday night "Stammtisch": Cathy Baer and Heather Whitefield, Steve and Pat Duane Lichtenberg, Barbara Page and Judith Dollenmayer, Robert Pounder, and Karl Kruszynski. Many thanks, too, to the best neighbours I could hope for, especially Sophia Harvey and Katherine Hite. Finally, for their long-standing friendship and abiding love, I want to give my deepest thanks to Pascal Grosse, Susan Kassouf, and, most especially, Karl Kruszynski. Over the years, you cooked, listened, encouraged, humoured, celebrated, cajoled, and, perhaps most importantly, demonstrated the patience of Job. I dedicate this book to you!

UNIFORM FANTASIES

Introduction

In his 1868 pamphlet *Memnon: The Sexual Nature of the Male-Loving Urning*, the seventh in his twelve-volume opus *The Riddle of "Man-Manly" Love*, the former civil servant turned activist and sexual theorist Karl Heinrich Ulrichs (1825–95) offered up his own experience as evidence that same-sex desire was a natural, inborn trait rather than a perversion caused by masturbation, seduction, or a wanton lifestyle.[1] For example, he noted that more than one full year before his first nocturnal emission at the age of fifteen years and ten-and-a-half months, his chaste younger self had already begun to feel the initial vague stirrings of sensual longing for various male figures. In addition to a fascination with "a nude image of a Greek god or hero" in a book on architecture, Ulrichs recalled the particularly intense experience of being beset by a "thought" that "often arose suddenly and could not be suppressed" just as he was about to fall asleep: "What if now a soldier were to climb up through the window and come to me in my room!" As he explained, his "imagination [*Phantasie*] always painted some splendid [*prachtvolle*] military specimen, 20–22 years of age, and then it burned in me like a fire."[2] Despite the specificity of the erotic image, Ulrichs insisted he had as of yet "never come into any kind of contact with a soldier" nor "exchanged even one word" with one.[3] Thus, unlike one of his Viennese confidants, who at the age of fourteen had gone to request a leave for his older brother, a cadet in a Hussar regiment, only to be caressed and kissed by the unit's thirty-year-old captain in the latter's office, Ulrichs was consigned to his solitary fantasies: "If my picture had come to life and walked over to me in flesh and blood: how I would have also shuddered with the thrills of ecstasy."[4]

Though Ulrichs stressed that his prepubescent fantasies about a soldier entering his room were "completely without a goal" and "not in the least directed toward any particular pleasure," it is nevertheless curious form of militarism "from above" was challenged by far-right populist militarisms "from below" that sought a radical social transformation of the status quo as part of a path to world domination.[14] Importantly, historians have begun to demonstrate that even this bifurcation is too neat, documenting the various "ways in which different groups of stakeholders appropriated the prestige of the military for their own purposes and with their own meanings."[15] The queer emancipation movement was very much part of this broader process of drawing on the military's cachet, even as it encountered considerable resistance at times from the army leadership, its political supporters in the Reichstag, and the many segments of the public who saw it as an incursion on their own efforts to exploit the army's prestige.

But beneath or alongside the strategic value of the German Army for queer politics was, as Ulrichs's own biography makes clear, the persistent queer attraction to men in uniform. Yet despite their designation as uniforms, the clothes worn by army personnel in this period in Europe were hardly consistent in terms of colour, cut, or cloth – even within any one national army. And the relatively late unification of Germany under Prussian hegemony in 1871 made its military dress a particularly fragmented affair. Though Article 63 of the constitution stipulated, among other things, that "the principal colors and cut of the Royal Prussian Army uniforms shall prevail (*maßgebend*)" throughout the land, there were substantial regional differences that in some cases persisted until 1914, with, for instance, Bavarian troops retaining their traditional light-blue colours.[16] Just as significant, however, were the extensive variations within Prussia's own army, Imperial Germany's largest, with infantry and artillery regiments sporting dark blue coats and both the *Leibgendarmerie* (life guards) and the *Jäger* and *Schützen* units (light infantry) clad in forest green ones.[17] Meanwhile, the differences in attire among the Prussian Cavalry units (*Kürassiere, Ulanen, Husaren, Dragoner*) were even greater, with Guard-Cuirassiers clad in all-white and Hussars sporting elaborately braided red jackets. Finally, to make matters more complicated, there were seasonal variations (such as, in some cases, light-coloured pants for warmer weather and dark-coloured pants for colder days) as well as separate work, guard, dress, and parade uniforms. Officers also had an additional uniform for business at the royal court as well as a gala uniform for balls. A lithograph by Georg Krickel, completed for an official compendium on German military uniforms, nicely illustrates this astonishing variety of dress uniforms for both officers and rank-and-file soldiers (Figure 0.1). Just this small cross-section of parade, gala, court, and winter uniforms from the Prussian Royal Guards' four main cavalry contingents features

Figure 0.1. Uniforms of the Cavalry Guard of the Kingdom of Prussia. From G. Krickel und G. Lange, *Das deutsche Reichsheer in seiner neuesten Bekleidung und Ausrüstung*, Berlin (H. Toussaint & Cie.) (1888–92), Blatt 8. Privatsammlung. Photo: akg-images.

four different colours of coats, five different varieties of pants, three different kinds of boots, and four different forms of headgear, not to mention the different breastplates (cuirass), collars, cuffs, epaulettes, sashes, belts, buttons, braids, trims, and other insignias!

At the same time that Prussian militarism and its policy of universal conscription ensured the pervasive presence of military uniforms in German society, German-speaking Europe also became a hotbed of ambitious theorizing, experimentation, and political organizing around sexuality – unleashing debates that, according to Dagmar Herzog, were "more raucous and open" than anywhere else in Europe at this time.[18] It is no surprise, then, that the causes and consequences of these sexual disputes have been rancorously debated by historians of this period, with the first volume of Michel Foucault's *The History of Sexuality* serving as a lightening rod. Rather than accepting the biological origins of sexual behaviour, Foucault argued that the operations for exacting knowledge about sex – the "truth" of the individual's "hidden" sexuality – in fact elicited, linked, and solidified those very desires and identities that such fields thought they were merely describing. For example, Foucault contended that in their efforts to understand and prevent "abnormal" same-sex relations between men, the disciplinary operations of criminology, forensic psychiatry, and sexology inadvertently produced "the homosexual": while "sodomy was a category of forbidden acts [and] their perpetrator was nothing more than the juridical subject of them, ... the nineteenth-century homosexual became a personage, a past, a case history, and a childhood, in addition to being a type of life, a life form, and a morphology, with an indiscreet anatomy and possibly a mysterious physiology."[19] In Foucault's famous formulation, "the sodomite had been a temporary aberration; the homosexual was now a species."

While Foucault's conception of sexuality as "an especially dense transfer point for relations of power" informs my approach to sexuality more generally and to same-sex desires and identities in particular, it is not without its limitations.[20] To be sure, historians of same-sex activism in Germany have taken the French philosopher to task for various methodological problems. For example, Robert Beachy criticizes Foucault for failing "to consider the German context of his own observations," in particular "the urban context that gave rise to the neologism."[21] Likewise, other historians have attacked Foucault – or those who use him – for ignoring the dimensions of bodies and subjective agency in favour of a singular focus on discourse and language.[22] And even as *The History of Sexuality* helped establish the field of Queer Studies before the term was established, queer theorists have raised additional conceptual concerns.[23] For instance, while Foucault claims to have uncovered the birth of "the homosexual," Eve Sedgwick has pointed out that the very conceptualization of homosexuality from the late nineteenth century to today has been structured by a number of epistemological problems rooted in conflicting and contradictory accounts of its causes and nature.[24] Subsequently, David Halperin has identified "at least four different but simultaneous categories or traditions of discourse pertaining to aspects of what we now define as homosexuality," including effeminacy, sodomy, friendship, and inversion.[25] Finally, Judith Butler has criticized Foucault's concept of discourse for treating the psyche as merely "a malleable surface for the unilateral effects of disciplinary power."[26]

While *Uniform Fantasies* incorporates these concerns into how it approaches the history of queer emancipation, it also addresses an additional lacuna in Foucault's *History of Sexuality*: the absence of a concept of fantasy. Not only does fantasy operate as an important location for the expression of sexual desire, but as a form of linguistic and visual expression fantasy is also as a particularly productive contribution to the discourses that Foucault's theory describes. In fact, Foucault himself acknowledged that the texts of *scientia sexualis* often exhibited "systematic blindnesses," though he never pursued this line of inquiry.[27] But even as fantasy inheres in all efforts to "produce knowledge, multiply discourse, induce pleasure, and generate power" as well as resist it, fantasies also operate quite differently than the knowledge discourses that concerned Foucault.[28] As products of desire, they are not only noticeably resistant to knowledge claims but also often escape our attempts to even recognize them as fantasies. Rather than assuming the status of truth claims (though we often mistake fantasies for truth and knowledge), they tend to exhibit instead the features of narrative fiction or filmic and theatrical scenarios. And rather than operating according to logic or reason, fantasy instead works according to displacement, misrecognition, and even denial.

Queer Studies has often been attuned to the operations of fantasy – particularly in its homophobic and heteronormative varieties. In *Gender Trouble*, for instance, Butler famously argued that the performative nature of gender – the "acts, gestures, enactments" of masculinity and femininity – made "true gender" merely "a fantasy instituted and inscribed on the surface of bodies."[29] Yet the theoretical concern with fantasy is not merely an arcane matter confined to post-structuralist queer theory, but is in fact central to the historiography of gender and sexuality. For example, in her methodological reflections on studying the persecutions of witches in baroque Germany, Lyndal Roper has argued that "unless we have a way of analyzing why particular fantasies have power and attraction, we can't explain their historical effectiveness. This is why we need to think of fantasy as a historical force, and we need to include the unconscious as part of the territory."[30] Thus, not only do fantasies constitute an important material archive for historical investigation, but determining their impact on individuals and groups also requires a model of the human psyche in which the unconscious plays a prominent role. Similarly, Joan Scott, has argued forcefully for seeing fantasy as "a critically useful tool for historical analysis."[31] And like Butler, who supplements Foucault's silence on the psyche with concepts drawn from psychoanalysis, both Roper and Scott draw variously on psychoanalytic approaches – not just for the tools they offer, but, in Scott's case, for the way that psychoanalysis productively challenges conventional historiography: by conceiving of the past as non-linear, by troubling clear lines of causality with the distortions caused by the unconscious, and by calling into question the rational subjectivity of historical actors. For Scott, the radical "incommensurability" between psychoanalysis and history opens up a "conversation and debate" in which "a rethinking" of the discipline of history can occur.[32] In drawing on concepts from psychoanalysis, *Uniform Fantasies* seeks to participate in that ongoing conversation, too.

Within Queer Studies, of course, the prevalence of psychoanalysis continues to rival the popularity of Foucault's work.[33] In addition to Butler's own engagement with psychoanalytic concepts, Lee Edelman's work is perhaps the most prominent.[34] Drawing on Lacanian psychoanalysis, Edelman conceives social reality as "a network of signifying relations" – that is, language as a system of signs and endless signifying chains – in which "we experience social reality, but only insofar as it compels us to experience that reality in the form of a fantasy."[35] To escape this enmeshment in fantasy and enjoin Lacan's theoretical apparatus to queer theory's suspicions of all forms of norms and normativity, Edelman advocates for "an impossible project of a queer oppositionality," one that perversely embraces the negativity that the heterosexual social order ascribes to queerness – social abjection, reproductive barrenness, a dangerous threat to "the family" and especially "the Child" – and which, in turn, enables "the queer … [to] insist on disturbing, on queering, social organization as such."[36] Within the psychoanalytic terms of Edelman's work, this negativity ascribed to queerness marks the death drive, which can never be grasped directly in the signifying chains but which promises access to an unbearable pleasure (what Lacan calls *jouissance*).

Though Edelman's contributions offer a compelling queer application of Lacanian theory, this approach – along with other celebrations of queer antinormativity – has also come in for a great deal of criticism. For example, Robyn Wiegman and Elizabeth A. Wilson point out the potential misunderstanding behind using "norm" only as a "synonym for what is constricting or controlling or tyrannical"; they also see the rhetorical lure of negativity as ironically akin to the repressive hypothesis that Foucault targets in *The History of Sexuality*.[37] Moreover, as Elizabeth Freeman points out, "'queer' cannot signal a purely deconstructive move or position of pure negativity," for whatever momentary access to the unsettling force of jouissance that the death drive might offer, all "subjects must relatively quickly rebound into fantasies, or … perish after only one release of energy."[38] While these criticisms are valid, my concern with Edelman's otherwise compelling deployment of psychoanalysis is different. Whereas he calls for embracing the negativity of the death drive to avoid the trap of fantasy, I am more interested in the fantasies themselves. As Freeman notes, while fantasies "may be false," they are also "often beautiful and weird."[39]

Thus, to unpack the uniform fantasies circulating in Imperial Germany, I follow Joan Scott in frequently drawing on the Lacanian-inflected philosophy of Slavoj Žižek.[40] Far from tracing fantasies back exclusively to individual psyches (though they remain important), Žižek's writings are primarily concerned with their political function as ideological formations – militarism, for example, but also homosexual identity – that mask deep structural conflicts in society over the distribution of resources, the allocation of power, or the kinds of sexual practices that should be permitted. Though Žižek hardly qualifies as a "queer theorist" in any conventional sense of the term, his analysis of the ideological fantasies behind oppressive social formations can be enormously useful for Queer Studies. Moreover, his style of writing, argumentation, and penchant for pop cultural references also express a kind of impish perversity that strikes me as, if not exactly queer, then at least queer-adjacent. Yet as Kadji Amin contends, what constitutes queer theory ultimately has less to do with the text or its author than "the fact that it is taken up as such and used to found bodies of queer scholarship."[41] My "promiscuous" borrowing from psychoanalysis, however, is not to leave behind Foucault's insights into sexuality, but rather, as Charles Shepardson puts it, to think "Foucault with Lacan" (if in my case primarily via Žižek, Butler, Edelman, and other theorists who have studied Lacan's works more fully).[42]

That fantasies are not just "beautiful and weird" but also, in Foucault's sense, unpredictably productive becomes apparent when we turn our attention back to nineteenth-century military uniforms, for these elaborate and colourful forms of dress incited a plethora of conscious and unconscious fantasies with very real dimensions. Of course, many inside and outside of the army sought to harness those psychic responses that either reaffirmed normative gender roles for men or supported the military's ongoing pre-eminence in German society. For instance, educators regularly extolled the way that colourful military uniforms fired the imagination of boys, who often indulged their passion for different forms of military dress with picture books, toys, and games.[43] Tin and lead soldiers – remembered as a boy's "most beloved game" and one of the largest segments of the German toy market – were manufactured with precise attention to uniforms, since "children often see and observe more sharply than adults."[44] Many middle-class men at this time not only recalled "playing soldier" or engaging in war games "with enormous enthusiasm" as children but also receiving army and navy outfits that, according to one authority of the day, were "so carefully and exquisitely executed that they can only be distinguished from real uniforms by their smaller size."[45] Meanwhile, one pedagogue who grew up in a city frequented by soldiers from around the world proudly recalled that he "not only acquired a great knowledge of uniforms [*Uniformkenntnis*] but also eventually studied them in such depth that [he] was capable of immediately recognizing each foreign uniform" – a skill he hoped to promote among all boys.[46]

By the end of the nineteenth century, however, several factors led to growing concerns about the tradition of colourful uniforms – and many of the other unintended and less socially acceptable fantasies they elicited. Most apparent to contemporaries was their escalating departure from civilian norms for male dress, which by this time had become rather "inconspicuous, practical and simple, perhaps boring," dominated by drab palettes – grays, browns, and especially black – in relatively forgiving cuts.[47] Most alarming for military experts, though, was their inadequacy for the new conditions of modern combat. Originally, of course, brightly coloured dress served an important function when black gunpowder filled battlefields with dense smoke and inaccurate weapons often led to combat at close range, making it essential to be able to quickly distinguish friend from foe. But with the invention of smokeless gunpowder and the manufacture of increasingly accurate rifles, battlefield visibility was transformed into a lethal liability in the late nineteenth century.[48] Finally, with the dramatic growth in the size of European armies during this period, outfitting troops had become an expensive enterprise for national governments struggling to meet a variety of competing needs. In light of these factors, a growing number of critics – inside the army, but especially in Parliament and in the press – began to take aim at these colourful outfits.[49] Yet even as the British Army introduced its khaki uniform during the Boer War in 1899, extending it to all troops in 1902, the Imperial German Army only started adopting its field grey uniform in 1910 – and even then restricted its use to manoeuvres and actual warfare.

Thus, while pedagogues might praise the effect of colourful uniforms on boys' imaginations, the German word *Phantasie* (fantasy, imagination) was also repeatedly invoked during this period to castigate the uniforms' impractical, ornamental, and self-consciously visible nature, all of which were hallmarks of *female* fashion at the time. Indeed, the parallels between nineteenth-century military dress and "frivolous" forms of *la mode* for women are structurally apparent in the uncanny similarities between nineteenth-century fashion plates and the illustrations found in the numerous works devoted to contemporary and historical uniforms.⁵⁰ For instance, like the images that populated women's fashion journals, the soldiers and officers in Georg Krickel's chromolithograph (Figure 0.1) adopt stances that conveniently offer frontal, profile, and posterior perspectives of the eight uniforms pictured. And, as in fashion plates, the similarity of the individuals, all of equal height and all sporting more or less the same facial hair and expressions, de-emphasize the wearer in favour of the clothes, encouraging viewers to linger over the intricate differences of dress among the eight men – an activity further facilitated by the neutral background, empty of all distractions. Finally, Krickel's image also mirrors the fashion plate by placing the figures into various groupings that vaguely suggest that they are not merely posing to be looked at, but rather in the midst of some meaningful activity, such as discussing army business, giving and taking orders (one soldier stands at attention) or viewing something happening just out of the frame. As scholars of the female fashion plate have been arguing for some time, such images of idealized figures vaguely "about to complete a motion" do not just convey information about clothing but in fact stoke the viewers' fantasies – by spurring them to concoct stories about the images or by evoking desires "that are fantasmatic in the sense that they can never be fully realized."⁵¹

Even more unsettling for a modern bourgeois world organized around ensuring clear gender differences, colourful uniforms did not merely resemble women's fashion but also competed with female dress for public attention. In effect, the colourful dress uniforms that officers and soldiers wore out in public transformed military personnel into dandies, a social performance through clothing that while initially tied to long-standing monarchical and aristocratic practices of representation, had by the end of the nineteenth century, following Oscar Wilde's arrest in 1895, become inextricably linked to effeminacy and queerness.⁵² Especially among the upper Prussian nobility, many of whom were expected to take up careers in the army regardless of their own personal interests and inclinations, regulation dress sometimes took on foppish dimensions. For instance, Count Robert Zedlitz-Trützschler, a long-serving controller of the imperial household under Wilhelm II, began the first chapter of his memoirs with various anecdotes from his earlier military career, when he served as an adjutant to Prince Friedrich Leopold of Prussia, a member of the extended Hohenzollern dynasty and commander of the 2nd Battalion of the First Guard Regiment of the Infantry. According to the future controller, "the Prince had so little real interest in the service that he allowed the plan for drill to be written down for him; and what he preferred was to read out the orders, line for line as they stood," sometimes losing his place in the text until Zedlitz-Trützschler "whispered to him what the next word of command in the programme was."[53] But where the prince was negligent in the details of his command, he was meticulous in the details of his uniform: "His toilet was fearful and wonderful. It took an incredible time and he spent fantastic sums on it. Once when he fainted on parade, because his clothes were too tight, it was discovered that nothing could be undone, since he was sewn in from head to foot. Once he mounted his horse and his breeches were so tight that they split. The same thing happened with four successive pairs; it was only the fifth that held fast, and even then he had to mount with the utmost circumspection."[54] For such officers, the military uniform (and military life) had little to do with the army's stated peacetime mission – to prepare troops for the eventuality of war or civil unrest – and more to do with strategies of self-presentation.

But cultural practices of the day enveloped even the self-consciously masculine conscript within a fantasy tableau that was far removed from battlefield preparedness. For instance, photography ateliers offered individualized keepsakes for conscripts eager to represent their time in the "king's coat," as the uniform was often called. In one such image, for example, Private Friedrich Werz, appears in full regalia as he gallops on a horse while holding the regimental flag in his right hand, with the rest of the regiment riding in attack formation in the background (Figure 0.2). What is most unusual, though, is that the entire image consists of a lithographic watercolour in which Werz's photographed head has clearly been superimposed onto a generic and idealized body. Though such images seem ridiculous and almost amateurish today, viewers then would have appreciated, according to the art historian Elizabeth Otto, the combination of "the accuracy of photography and the naturalistic and much-admired coloration of lithographic prints."[55] This romanticized mélange of real and fake serves as a particularly arresting illustration of Alfred Vagts's famous formulation of militarism: "The general, and other officers, are eager to live up to, and perhaps to die for, a largely fictitious convention established around them, for them, and finally by them. The soldier is, therefore, to be regarded as an *imaginary individual* in a social scene."[56] Though Vagts was more interested in warning readers of the dangerous political consequences of illusions than in understanding how they operated, Otto points out that these kinds of visual mementos "created a powerful fiction of military masculinity" with real value for current and former soldiers in Wilhelmine Germany's "social scene."

The element of fantasy, however, did not just reside in these remarkable images, but was also, in effect, woven into the uniforms themselves.

Introduction 15

Figure 0.2. Commemorative image of Private Friedrich Werz galloping on horseback while holding the regimental flag in his right hand, with the rest of the regiment riding in attack formation in the background. Landesarchiv Baden-Württemberg, Hauptstaatsarchiv Stuttgart, M 703 R788N5 Bild 1.

Much as corsets shaped women's bodies, the tightly tailored cut of the uniform forced the soldier's body into particular poses. According to the clothing historian Kerstin Flintrop, Imperial German Army uniforms compelled their wearers to adopt an especially erect posture, with a straight back and stretched neck, to ensure that the jacket material lay flat on the body.[57] This upright carriage was reinforced by high, stiff collars, which lay directly on the neck and obliged men to hold their heads in a rigid position, while narrow openings for the arms and shoulder seams that were placed much further in the back of the coat than today's suit jackets also significantly constrained movement of the upper body. Moreover, uniforms did not just shape and display a disciplined male body but also guided and excited the gazing eye in particular ways. While epaulettes gave the impression of broad shoulders, which is one of the key features of men's suitcoats today, the cut of the Imperial German jacket, which in some cases also included padding – not on top of the shoulders (where we expect it today) but running from top to bottom inside the front – directed the viewer's attention to the chest and made it seem like the chest was thrust forward. And in many coats, buttons were laid in slightly diagonal rows (wider at the top than at the bottom), which further accentuated the chest while also making the waist appear narrower.[58] All this tailoring suggests that military dress did not so much reveal a masculine body as cloak it in an erotically charged illusion. As the fashion historian Colin McDowell puts it: "Chests were padded, waists whittled, thighs encased in skintight breeches and calves in shiny leather boots," all of which transformed soldiers into "the sex objects of the nineteenth century."[59] It is no wonder that Ulrichs and many of his fellow Urnings and homosexuals were so powerfully drawn to soldiers in their uniforms.

And yet the deep and abiding queer male attraction to soldiers not only incited the queer emancipation movement, but often proved a stumbling block to reaching its goals. It's helpful to illustrate this paradoxical dimension by briefly returning to Ulrichs. While he traced his conception of the Urning as a congenital, natural phenomenon back to the sudden appearance of his desire for uniformed soldiers, his later activism was spurred by his sense of injustice when an investigation into rumours that he practised "unnatural lust with other men" (quite possibly soldiers) led him to pre-emptively resign from his position as court assistant (*Gerichtsassessor*) in the government of the Kingdom of Hanover.[60] Though Hanover's criminal code did not contain a "notion of the crime of unnatural lust," the investigation report asked: "Can there remain even only a doubt about whether actions (otherwise corresponding to the law) have been undertaken in circumstances that give public offense or grounds for concern?"[61] Since the answer was a predetermined yes, Ulrichs was eventually moved to start his own studies into the phenomenon as part of his campaign to change public opinion and the expansive application of "public offense." His studies, of course, began at the same time that forensic medicine was also taking up the matter with increasing earnestness, and he in fact sought to encourage this development, establishing contact around 1866 with Richard von Krafft-Ebing, whom he initially viewed as an ally.[62] But around this time Ulrichs's political and public education efforts were forced to begin responding to the ensuing new legal challenges that resulted from Prussia's war against Austria and its German allies. Prussia, for instance, militarily occupied and then annexed the Kingdom of Hanover while also forcing other smaller states into a North German Confederation with, among other things, a common legal code. Since the Prussian criminal code outlawed "indecent conduct contrary to nature" (*widernatürliche Unzucht*) between men, one consequence of the imminent unification of Germany under Prussian hegemony was the likely extension of that law to all of Germany.[63] Thus, in both Ulrichs's lifelong attraction to soldiers and its eventual criminalization thanks to Prussian battlefield victories, military politics was deeply embedded in the very project of queer emancipation from the start.

I designate this German political project as "queer emancipation" for a number of reasons. Though "queer" emerged as a critical idiom in the early 1990s, it in fact became originally linked, if homophobically so, to same-sex desire in England in the 1890s, primarily in relation to the political scandals unleashed by the Marquess of Queensbury against then prime minister Lord Rosebery and, more spectacularly, Oscar Wilde.[64] Meanwhile, as Siobhan Somerville notes, "queer" functions today as "an umbrella term for a range of sexual and gender identities that are not 'straight,' or at least not normative."[65] This feature is important for the context of Imperial Germany, where multiple terms for same-sex behaviour not only existed but also quickly proliferated. For example, in response to entrenched religious and legal conceptions of male same-sex behaviour as sodomy, pederasty, or unnatural fornication, Ulrichs developed his own theory complete with new terms: *Urning* for men attracted to other men, *Dioning* for men attracted to women, among many other neologisms.[66] These efforts were quickly followed by others, with the Austrian writer Karl Maria Kertbeny (a rival activist residing in Germany at the time) coining the neologisms *Homosexualismus* (homosexualism) and *Homosexualität* (homosexuality) in 1869.[67]

Meanwhile, in 1870, the Berlin neurologist Carl Westphal used the label *konträre Sexualempfindung* (contrary sexual feeling or sexual inversion), which was then adopted, along with homosexuality, as medical terminology by Krafft-Ebing and Albert Moll, among others.[68] By the end of the nineteenth century, these concepts were joined by a host of others that originated within the medical-scientific wing of the queer emancipation movement, such as *sexuelle Zwischenstufen* (sexual intermediaries), featured in the name of the academically oriented journal of the Scientific-Humanitarian Committee (*das Wissenschaftlich-humanitäre Komitee* or WhK), *Das Jahrbuch für sexuelle Zwischenstufen* (Yearbook of sexual intermediaries), and *das dritte Geschlecht* (the third sex), which was used in publications oriented towards the general public.[69] All these terms, often used synonymously, not only adopted some form of gender inversion as the primary model for both men and women, but, in general, conceived of those who had same-sex desires in what Eve Sedgwick has helpfully called a minoritizing view: "that there is a distinct population of persons who 'really are' gay," that is, who are more or less born that way.[70]

In reaction to these medical-based notions that also connoted disease, abnormality, and inferiority, other male activists of the period coined their own terms – *Lieblingminne* (love of a favourite) and *Freundesliebe* (love of a friend) – in order to link male-male desire back to the age-differentiated practices of same-sex love in Ancient Greece as well as with more traditional notions of masculinity.[71] And if the minoritizing view was popular among activists who subscribed to the scientific discourse on same-sex desire, these masculinists used a universalizing lens that saw sexual relations between men as a cultural practice that could – and should – be taken up by many if not all men. By positing an inherent bisexuality, such views also shared some similarities to the psychoanalytic conception of same-sex desire held by Freud, who, in fact, also criticized the minoritizing models offered by sexology and seems to have preferred Ancient Greek examples in his own theorizing about same-sex desire.[72] Thus, while some of these terms were used as synonyms, other designations carried their own divergent etiologies, descriptions, and social valuations of same-sex desire and identity. All also competed against vernacular slang, such as *warme Brüder* (warm brothers), already in use in the eighteenth century, and *schwul*, a word of nineteenth-century origin that has come to carry similar connotations to gay.[73] And yet even as the "riddle of man-manly love" provided fertile ground for the emergence of new scientific disciplines devoted to the study of sex (sexology and psychoanalysis, to name just two), this development, as Foucault pointed out, also unleashed a plethora of new sexual categories, including ones particularly relevant for this study: fetishism (coined by Albert Binet in 1877), sadism, and masochism (coined by Krafft-Ebing in 1890), and transvestism (coined by Magnus Hirschfeld in 1910).

In addition to its function as a convenient catch-all for these disparate desires and practices, "queer," as I use it, also helps to keep our understanding of same-sex desire and identity as inherently open, contested, and internally contradictory as it was back then. For despite the identarian thrust of the different facets of the queer emancipation movement, and their seeming coalescence into homosexuality "as we know it today," it is important – for both historiographic and conceptual reasons – to avoid the tendency, as Sedgwick warned, "to *re*familiarize, *re*naturalize, [and] damagingly reify" same-sex desires and identities.⁷⁴ In order to prevent those mistakes, we also need to read texts queerly, that is, with an eye and ear open to the contradictions, ruptures, incomprehensibilities in their theories, stories, and activist practices.

Likewise, the various conceptual incoherencies and divisions within the queer emancipation movement also suggest that we need to have a pliable, even pluralistic understanding of the term movement – and, for that matter, emancipation. As a political project, emancipation movements emerged out of the European Enlightenment. In Immanuel Kant's famous formulation, *"Enlightenment is the human being's emancipation from its self-incurred immaturity,"* for which "nothing but *freedom* is required."⁷⁵ In Germany, the legal abolition of serfdom – a slow process achieved in 1807 in Prussia and in 1815 in other German states – was certainly an important precedent, as was the legal emancipation of Jews in Germany, which also began in the Kingdom of Prussia in 1812 (and proceeded very unevenly in other German states).

Gender and sexuality were also important components of emancipation in the German-speaking world, a move accelerated by Napoleon's conquest in the early 1800s. As Isabel Hull has masterfully demonstrated, the sex-gender system that emerged through the creation of Germany's civil society "emancipated" men by investing them with sexual autonomy while placing women "in fetters" by stripping them of economic and personal autonomy and by defining their sexual nature as "derivative." As Hull explains, "not independent, emancipated, or a citizen, she could not be sexually self-determining, she could not 'posit' her own desire, will it, and act upon it."⁷⁶ This state of legal dependency on men certainly informed the emancipation efforts undertaken by women over the course of the nineteenth century as well as their involvement in the scientific discourse on sexuality.⁷⁷ According to Marti Lybeck, "seeking autonomy was the core animating motivation for new women" at the end of the nineteenth century.⁷⁸ Meanwhile, in light of Hull's work, it is possible to see the divisions within the queer emancipation movement between the masculinist wing and the sexological wing as two different responses to the place of male same-sex desire within this Enlightenment project, with the masculinists seeking to expand male sexual autonomy against feminist, socialist, and Jewish emancipation by extending it to German men's sexual relations with other (consenting) men and adolescents, while the sexological wing (some of whose leaders were social democratic and Jewish) aligned queer emancipation – sometimes more loosely, sometimes more explicitly – with these other emancipation struggles.⁷⁹

Ulrichs certainly understood his own project in terms of emancipation rooted in the Enlightenment. While his first two pamphlets sought to educate an uninformed public about "the ideal nature of Uranian love" as well as the harm caused by the prevailing moral tenets and the criminalization of Uranian love in parts of Germany, his third pamphlet, *Vindicta*, focused on the "battle for freedom from persecution" (as the subtitle read), announcing at the outset "I am an insurgent. I decline to accept what exists if I believe it is unjust. I am fighting for a life free from prosecution and scorn. I urge the general public and the state to recognize Uranian love as equal to congenital Dionian love."[80] Inspired by letters of support from both Urnings and Dionings, the pamphlet also included a new category – "Uranian Platform" – under which he invited collaboration from like-minded individuals, regardless of their sexual orientation.[81] By the summer of 1865, he imagined forming an "Urning Union" (*Urningsbund*), even going so far as drafting by-laws.[82] But though he received financial support from other Urnings for a trip to Munich to introduce a resolution at the Sixth Congress of German Jurists in 1867, the union never came to be.[83] Following the 1869 decision to retain Prussia's paragraph outlawing consensual sexual behaviour between men in the North German Penal Code (extended to all of Germany in 1872 as Paragraph 175), he eventually abandoned his homeland and his Urning campaign in 1880 for self-exile in Italy.[84]

After Ulrichs's departure from the scene, the effort to organize for same-sex rights emerged with renewed vigour through the founding of the Scientific-Humanitarian Committee (WhK) in Berlin in 1897. Under the motto "justice through science" (*per scientiam ad justiatiam*), the WhK sought to marry scientific research with a self-assured if not altogether unruly queer politics. Led by the medical doctor and sexologist Magnus Hirschfeld, the WhK became a multifaceted organization that fought for the rights and social acceptance of same-sex-loving individuals and cross-dressers through a combination of scientific study, public education, and political activism.[85] But while Hirschfeld drew on Ulrichs's theories and even oversaw a revised edition of all twelve volumes of *The Riddle of "Man-Manly" Love* in 1898, albeit with some significant excisions, much had changed in the intervening decades.[86] For instance, while Ulrichs drew a clear dichotomy between the Urning, invariably civilian and effeminate, and the soldier, always imagined as a masculine Dioning, the situation in Imperial Germany was far more complicated. Even as many civilian men continued, like Ulrichs, to pursue sexual contact with military personnel, not all of them, as we have seen, understood themselves as effeminate. Similarly, by the end of the nineteenth century, it was also clear that many members of the armed forces – in particular, a number of officers – were themselves sexually attracted to other men, and a few seem to have become dues-paying members of the WhK. Most importantly, though, even as WhK members were united in their opposition to the criminalization of same-sex relations between men, drafting at its first meeting a petition to the Reichstag calling for the repeal of Paragraph 175, it quickly became clear that there was little consensus among the growing number of members (which included several vocal masculinists) about queer emancipation's other goals, let alone the best strategies to achieve them. Thus, emancipation was not the straightforward, teleological process we sometimes imagine it to be, but rather a movement racked by competing interests and definitions that produced unhappy compromises, ongoing contradictions, and outright ruptures.

In fact, like Du Bois's own perception of the fundamental paradox of German politics, there was a fundamental paradox at the heart of this first queer emancipation movement, for it seems odd that military uniforms – whether literally or metaphorically – would play such a foundational role in both fostering and, in some cases, undermining the goals of the queer emancipation movement. And it is indeed contradictory that the desire for the uniform – as a fantasy of normative, heterosexual masculinity and an agent of the disciplinary and violent power of the state – should play any role in the larger project of queer emancipation, which is generally considered a progressive movement.[87] Nevertheless, as *Uniform Fantasies* shows, both the masculinist and sexological wings of the queer emancipation movement exhibited early forms of what Jasbir Puar has called "homonationalism."[88] As such, *Uniform Fantasies* extends the important and ongoing effort by scholars like Heike Bauer, Laura Marhoefer, and others to critically interrogate the reputation of Imperial Germany's queer activism as an inherently progressive movement.[89]

Unfortunately, any straightforward historical investigation of the intersections between Imperial Germany's sexual politics and military politics is necessarily hampered by the loss of two key archives: the Nazis' 1933 destruction of Hirschfeld's Institute for Sexual Science, which housed the papers of the WhK among other valuable materials, and the allied bombing of the Prussian military archives in the final days of the Second World War.[90] Fortunately, the process whereby sex was "put into discourse" means that there still remains a vast trove of materials for this study.[91] Indeed, in addition to WhK publications, sexological case studies, and guidebooks to queer Berlin, *Uniform Fantasies* draws on military manuals, trial transcripts, newspaper articles, and parliamentary debates as well as personal letters, diaries, autobiographies, plays, and other literary texts. And while this varied collection of documents may not disclose as much as we might wish about the institutional operations of the military or the direct interactions between military personnel and the homosexual emancipation movement, they do offer an ideal set of primary sources for probing the ongoing tensions between military politics and sexual politics as they emerged in what I am calling Imperial Germany's "uniform fantasies."

To get at the many threads stitching the science and politics of queer sexuality to the military uniforms of Imperial Germany, *Uniform Fantasies* examines a variety of incidents and debates – all involving the uniform – in which military politics and sexual politics intersected and, in some cases, erupted into full-blown scandal. It is thus no surprise that the period's most significant political scandal, the Eulenburg Affair (1907–9), is a case in point.[92] This complex and multifaceted debacle is named after the main target, Prince Philipp zu Eulenberg-Hertefeld (1867–1921). Though nominally a middling diplomat who had variously served as the Prussian envoy to Bavaria and the German ambassador in Vienna, Eulenburg had in fact long exercised enormous political influence behind the scenes through his exceptionally close friendship with Kaiser Wilhelm II, essentially orchestrating the latter's controversial system of personal rule in which the monarch took an active but destabilizing role in setting domestic and foreign policy.[93] Eulenburg's success in increasing the power of a quixotic and inconsistent ruler at the expense of legitimate ministers had earned him numerous enemies at court and in the public sphere. None of these were more determined and resourceful than the journalist Maximilian Harden, who edited the influential weekly *Die Zukunft*. Suspecting Eulenburg's hand in the Kaiser's unwillingness to go to war with France over the latter's seizure of Morocco in 1905, Harden sought to secure the prince's permanent retirement from politics, first through cryptically worded accusations that only the former diplomat and his friends would understand, and then – after he perceived Eulenburg reneging on a newly brokered agreement – publishing much more direct references.[94]

But if Eulenburg was the scandal's central figure, the brouhaha initially aimed a more glaring public spotlight on the sexual escapades and identities of high-ranking Prussian officers. Thus, while the prince initially avoided a direct confrontation with Harden, his closest friend, General Kuno Count von Moltke, was not so lucky, for he was forced to file a private libel lawsuit against Harden. In contrast to Eulenburg, Moltke – a lieutenant-general and commander of the Berlin garrisons – was a rather unexceptional figure in Wilhelm's entourage, meddling infrequently in politics and primarily tasked with keeping Eulenburg informed of court machinations when the diplomat was elsewhere. But after interviewing Moltke's former wife, Lily von Elbe, following her divorce from the general, Harden began to view Eulenburg, Moltke, and their friends as a homosexual camarilla. As it happened, this first trial also led to unanticipated public revelations that officers in elite guard units had been organizing "orgies" with subordinates, and that recruits in these and other units had been engaging in male prostitution in and around Berlin. However, rather than treat the military dimensions of the scandal as one coherent entity, my approach disaggregates these facets into three distinct concerns, which I then analyze in relation to long-standing debates about military practices, such as institutional secrecy and episodes involving the abusive treatment of recruits, as well as various strategies of the queer emancipation movement, including outing, melodrama, and the politics of respectability.

The first chapter centres on fantasies about the homosexual officer that emerged out of the melodramatic politics of outing and coming out. Though some active and retired military officers did join the Scientific-Humanitarian Committee (WhK), even assuming leadership roles under well-guarded pseudonyms, Hirschfeld and other proponents recognized early on that closeted officers who were driven to suicide offered ideal victims of homophobic oppression that could be used to garner sympathy and public support for their campaign, especially if presented in the familiar terms of melodrama. While this strategy was often inconsistently pursued in the discourse on officers in official publications of the WhK, suicides by male-loving military figures were featured prominently in melodramatic plays and stories written to serve the emancipatory project. Yet melodrama also animated the homophobic fantasy underlying Harden's outing of Eulenburg and members of his circle. Thus, the chapter's second section analyzes the melodramatic strategies deployed in Moltke's libel trial against Harden. Though the general sought to claim the mantle of innocent victim, a staple in melodrama, Harden, a former actor and fearsome drama critic, proved the more skilful "melodramatist" in convincing much of the public that Moltke's military uniform had been a manly costume hiding the true identity of an effeminate evildoer. Unfortunately, because Hirschfeld participated as a forensic expert on Harden's behalf, the trial led to a crisis for the queer emancipation movement from which it would not fully recover until after the First World War.

While the first chapter concentrates on fantasies that accompanied the period's categories for theorizing same-sex desire, other dimensions of the scandal invoked additional fantasies that were yoked to different sexological categories, in particular sadism and fetishism. Chapter

2 connects the scandal of "homosexual orgies" between officers and their subordinates to long-standing concerns about male bonding and violence, especially devastating cases of physical abuse that many conscripts experienced during their time in uniform. Though the army tried to hide these abuses from the public through various forms of institutional secrecy, the sociologist Georg Simmel argued in 1902 that the nature of secrecy cut both ways – hiding the truth on the one hand, while also heightening fantasies about what was being hidden on the other. In this chapter I examine two competing fantasies related to masculinity, secrecy, and violence in the military. The first section focuses on an older, conservative discourse that esoterically celebrated the clandestine role played by uniforms and violence in fostering an idealized martial camaraderie. Though an atmosphere of military camaraderie was officially prized among officers, the violent and homoerotic underside of these bonds are thematized most succinctly in the novella *Das edle Blut* (Noble blood) (1892) by Ernst von Wildenbruch, one of Wilhelm II's favourite authors as well as one of the first four symbolic signatories of the WhK's petition to the Reichstag. Yet after Social Democrats obtained and published secret orders detailing particularly egregious abuses, this esoteric fantasy faced competition from critics who began turning to sexological concepts like sadism to pathologize this behaviour. Though this sexualization of *Soldatenmisshandlungen* (mistreatment of soldiers) was initially a fringe phenomenon, it received a boost when, at the first Harden-Moltke trial, a former soldier testified that senior officers in the exclusive Guards regiments had been inducing their subordinates to participate in "homosexual orgies," events that were read as a sadistic abuse of an officer's power. As such, this facet of the Eulenburg Affair also expanded the application of sexual discourse to the terrain of military politics.

The third chapter takes up the eroticization of the military uniform, foregrounded in the writings of Ulrichs, by investigating Imperial Germany's queer scene in which civilian men sought – and paid for – sexual contact with uniformed personnel. Again, though same-sex desire was a fundamental feature of the practice, the concept of fetishism was in fact a more salient dimension. Despite the lack of official records that might detail the extent of this a relatively obscure phenomenon, I use the sexological discourse on "soldier love," popular guidebooks, and diaries to reconstruct some of the forms it took, ranging from soldiers who sold their bodies on streets or in parks to brothels that catered to a clientele with a taste for men in uniform. More important than the actual practices, however, were the various fantasies that circulated around what was called *Soldatenprostitution* (prostitution by soldiers).

Though much of this discourse was confined to the margins or embedded in sexology, inadvertent revelations at the first Harden-Moltke trial thrust the practice into the limelight. In response to public outrage, the military leadership produced its own enticing fantasy scenario in which soldiers could hardly defend themselves from the sexual aggressions of homosexual civilians. As a result, the chapter also allows us to explore why some ideological fantasies are capable of exerting more power than others.

Even as the revelations around the Eulenburg Affair offered the most explosive intersections between military service and male-male desire, other entanglements between the two were more mundane, though by no means any less indicative of the sexualization of military politics – or the militarization of male-male desire and identity. To get at these, the final chapters explore the competing efforts of two famous Wilhelmine brothers to theorize the significance of military service and uniforms for male civilians in the wake of the Eulenburg Affair. Taking the younger brother first, chapter 4 focuses on Thomas Mann's efforts to appropriate for himself and his art a militarized notion of masculinity with little connection to the real army or its culture of obedience. In addition to exploring the fantasies that surrounded his failed enlistment in the military as a one-year volunteer (and his imaginative efforts to recast that failure as a success of sorts), I pursue Mann's enduring fascination with military service and the military uniform in his literary production, ranging from *Die Bekenntnisse des Hochstaplers Felix Krull* (The confessions of Felix Krull) to the jingoistic essays he wrote during the First World War. While Mann's biography and writings suggest that he attempted to solve the conundrum of his sexual attractions and feelings of effeminacy through an ironic (even campy) series of fantasies, in which his adoption of a military ethos remained aloof from either actual military service or the military politics of the day, they also expose the extent to which his or any self-proclaimed distance from the armed forces proved a mirage after Germany went to war in 1914.

While Thomas Mann sought accommodation within the status quo of a militarized masculinity, his older brother Heinrich built his literary reputation by savagely attacking Imperial Germany's pretensions, particularly the bourgeoisie's subservient adulation of Wilhelm II. Though many scholars hold up his most famous novel, *Der Untertan* (*The Loyal Subject*) (1914/1919), as the period's most revealing mirror, chapter 5 also exposes the limitations of this work's mode of critique by contextualizing the title figure's fantasies and behaviours within the contemporary discourses of homosexuality, masochism, and transvestism. Though Magnus Hirschfeld's efforts to articulate the concept of transvestism as separate from homosexuality (as well as the persistent conflation of them in Mann's novel) produced an ambivalent picture of the military uniform as a marker of masculinity, *The Loyal Subject*'s efforts to satirize the main character's "uniform pleasures" paradoxically reinscribed the link between masculinity and military uniforms as bourgeois society's own implicit reference point for masculinity.

As these brief summaries indicate, the intersections between military politics and queer politics involved an astonishing array of queer sexual categories, discourses, and narrative modes. While same-sex desires and identities played a central role in the sexualization of military politics, the concepts of sadism, masochism, fetishism, and transvestism also figured in public debates. Moreover, the complex set of discourses that emerged not only involved medical doctors and homosexual activists but also included the participation of journalists, lawyers, sociologists, elected officials, the army leadership, rank-and-file soldiers, creative writers, and artists. These social actors, in turn, produced an array of texts that articulated competing fantasies in different modes, including melodrama, esoteric narrative, satire, and camp. These modes then appeared across a range of literary and non-literary texts.

Though historians of this era are apt to invoke fictional works – especially Heinrich Mann's *The Loyal Subject* – as "illustrations" of the period, the detailed attention that fictional texts receive in *Uniform Fantasies* calls for some explanation. First, my selection of particular literary narratives acknowledges their importance in the German public sphere. For educated men and women of Imperial Germany, literature was a serious enterprise with pretensions of offering readers profound, hard-won insights into "life" as well as all manner of social issues. In his memoirs, for instance, Prince Bernhard von Bülow, who served as German chancellor from 1900–9, insisted that "he who is entering into life learns more from novels than from the study of the most learned compendiums."[95] Second, like fiction, fantasies exhibit the structure of narrative. In Žižek's own methodology, the complex narratives of literary texts and feature films often facilitate his efforts to unveil social fantasy "for the fiction that it is."[96] But literary works are also particularly valuable because they do not merely reflect historical processes but rather are themselves part of the play of discourses.[97] Of course, the way that literary texts circulate in society and get interpreted by individual readers makes it more difficult to specify their significance as historical sources. But fiction also offers unique advantages that are often difficult to come by in more typical archival fare, even when it happens to be available. As the historian Martin J. Wiener observes, "To appreciate literature as simultaneously mobilizing and interrogating fantasies is to accord it a greater capacity to reveal its era than it has usually been granted by historians."[98] And it is by attending to their complex meanings that we can better uncover similar conscious and unconscious fantasies operating in news reports, public debates, and everyday activities.

In focusing on the multiple and often contradictory roles that German soldiers and officers played as sought-after sexual partners, idealized victims of homophobic oppression, and targets of tumultuous sex scandals, *Uniform Fantasies* documents a much deeper and more problematic enmeshment between the military, sexology, and the queer emancipation movement than scholars have previously understood. As a result, we get a more complex picture of queer activism beyond a focus on Hirschfeld and other leaders of the movement or sweeping dismissals of their politics and conceptions of same-sex identities as outdated. In fact, one of the underlying conjectures behind *Uniform Fantasies* is that many of the debates and questions facing contemporary queer theorists and activists were already in play in Imperial Germany. Similarly, by attending to the application of sexological concepts to phenomena involving military personnel, *Uniform Fantasies* offers fresh perspectives on key debates about military policy and German militarism in this era, including political efforts to modernize the institution by making it conform to bourgeois expectations of efficiency, the rule of law, and modern gender and sexual conventions. As a whole, then, I hope that this study will contribute to our understanding of turn-of-the-century Germany as a particularly fascinating, complex, and modern society that still has much to teach queer scholars and activists today.[99]

Chapter One

Outing Officers: Queer Activism, Melodrama, and the Harden-Moltke Trial

Of the many important connections between the organized queer emancipation movement and the German military, the closeted homosexual officer was one of the most fateful. Retired and active military officers played a modest yet noteworthy role in the founding, financing, and operation of the world's first organized movement for homosexual rights, the Scientific Humanitarian Committee (WhK), which was established in 1897 under the leadership of Magnus Hirschfeld, a physician with a practice in the Berlin-Charlottenburg district. More important than their material support, however, was their symbolic value as sympathetic victims of homophobia. As part of its public relations campaign to increase social acceptance for homosexuals and win public support for the decriminalization of sexual acts between men, the WhK regularly reported on the existence and sometimes tragic fates of homosexual officers throughout the movement's first decade, when the WhK grew quickly, reaching close to 700 members in 1907.[1] Yet in the course of this year, its meteoric growth and effectiveness were cut short by two events. In April, a group of masculinists within the organization formally mounted a secession from the WhK after years of simmering tensions over political strategies and competing conceptions of same-sex desire and identity. Even more disastrous, though, was Hirschfeld's subsequent involvement in the Harden-Moltke trial in October, when his testimony played a substantial role in establishing General Kuno von Moltke as an effeminate homosexual during his libel suit against the journalist Maximilian Harden.

The broader debate over homosexual officers revolved around the secrecy of the homosexual closet, which, as Eve Sedgwick argued, has been "inexhaustibly productive of modern Western culture and history at large."[2] In this case, closeted officers became the locus of competing fantasies about the nature of homosexuality and its place in the German

Army (and by extension in state and society). Nevertheless, these fantasies were based less in the impenetrable epistemological mysteries of the closet than in the Klieg lights of stage and film, in particular the genre of melodrama. Melodrama, according to Peter Brooks, originated around the middle of the eighteenth century as a theatrical genre in which extreme emotions made "legible" a set of guiding moral truths for an increasingly secular society.[3] While early melodramas traded in stock characters – the innocent heroine, the brave hero, the dastardly villain – that left little doubt about who was good and evil or what was right and wrong, the subsequent form of melodrama offered up in realist and naturalist theatre revolved around the ethical and epistemological challenges of identifying who was virtuous and who was not.[4]

But even as melodrama remained a prominent fixture of German and European stages and emerged with renewed vigour in early cinema, it also pervaded everyday life as a mode of thinking – what Brooks calls "a certain fictional system for making sense of experience."[5] Indeed, Rohan McWilliams and other historians have confirmed that melodrama "provided a cultural resource, a language and set of themes and narratives that enabled the nineteenth century to understand itself."[6] To be sure, the nineteenth-century sciences of sex were infused with melodramatic dynamics and rhetoric: the anguished individual seeking guidance and salvation from the authoritative sexologist, the psychoanalyst's effort to wrest the sexual truths out of the patient's convoluted personal narrative, and the eugenicist's dire warnings about the burgeoning epidemic of sexual pathologies that threatened the health and very survival of the entire nation.[7] Moreover, because many nineteenth-century stage melodramas often climaxed in trial scenes in which good characters, usually falsely accused, were acquitted while evildoers were unmasked and punished, criminal trials at this time also became deeply infused with melodramatic conventions.[8] Melodrama, however, did not just serve the disciplinary interests of medicine and law but also infused the insurgent efforts of social activists, with Hirschfeld and his compatriots drawing heavily on melodramatic conventions to promote public sympathy with homosexuals as innocent victims of draconian laws and social prejudice.[9]

To get at the liminal role of Imperial Germany's closeted officer in uniform, this chapter is divided into two parts. The first section focuses on the real and symbolic importance of the male-loving military officer for the homosexual emancipation movement. Even as a few active and retired officers did support or participate in the WhK as well as in the smaller group of secessionists, many more homosexual officers were conscripted into the movement as objects of study, debate, and sympathy. While Hirschfeld and his collaborators emphasized the supposed mismatch between the masculine uniform and the effeminate nature of German homosexual officers, the masculinists posited instead a fundamental connection between same-sex desire and warrior masculinity. Yet even as the immense theoretical and political differences between these two factions led to the 1907 split within the movement, both sides shared two important strategies related to the German military. First, each endeavoured to argue that homosexual officers did not pose any threat to the military readiness of the army, but in fact strengthened the camaraderie and training of soldiers – albeit for different reasons. Second, both camps enveloped the officer within a melodramatic metaphysics of excessive suffering. Because, as McWilliam warns, any analysis of melodramatic rhetoric in the public sphere needs to be linked back to the fictional and storytelling conventions of the day, this section also examines two literary works – a short story and a play – that each used melodrama to promote the various political aims of the movement.[10]

Melodrama, however, was not only a strategy of homosexual emancipation. Thus, the second section explores the homophobic melodramatics of the highly public 1907 libel trial between Lt.-General Kuno von Moltke and Maximilian Harden. Despite the thespian credentials of both Harden and his Munich-based lawyer Max Bernstein, scholars have largely ignored the theatricality of the first Harden-Moltke trial. To be sure, both sides borrowed heavily on melodramatic rhetoric to represent themselves as the good or innocent protagonist and to paint their opponent as the villain. But melodramatic conventions played a far greater and more volatile role in this case than the rousing speeches each side delivered to judge and jury, public and press. Even more important was their epistemological function in providing a "system for making sense" of the evidence – much of which, in fact, circulated around Moltke's uniforms or his relationship to other articles of clothing. Melodrama, I argue, proved essential in making Moltke's homosexual identity both legible and incompatible with his position as a Prussian general who moved in close proximity to the German emperor.

Despite the competing efforts to deploy melodramatic conventions both for and against homosexual emancipation, neither Harden nor Hirschfeld and his fellow activists emerged from the trial victorious. As it was, the proceedings – like any piece of theatre – elicited multiple readings from its audience, including ones that ran entirely counter to both Harden's and Hirschfeld's projects. For instance, because testimony at the trial breached the discursive restraints that governed even the most excessive melodramas of the day, members of the public viewed the court case as an unforgivable transgression of their own (sexual) innocence. Most alarmingly, anti-Semitic observers conflated the participation of both Hirschfeld and Harden into a *völkisch* fantasy of evil Jews who sought to destroy German values, authentic masculinity, and the exalted place of the Prussian military. But what all sides of the public did agree upon was the need to retailor the military uniform from a decorative costume donned by Prussian noblemen, including effeminate and closeted ones, into apparel that would henceforth only fit the bodies of authentically masculine and heterosexual soldiers.

The Military Melodrama of Homosexual Activism

Right from the beginning, the military – as the state's and society's most prestigious institution – emerged as an important touchstone in the organized campaign to decriminalize sodomy and foster public acceptance of those with same-sex desires. As the title of his 1905 essay indicates – which translates as "Does the social approval of homosexual intercourse damage the military readiness of the race?" – Benedict Friedlaender believed that the political fate of men who desired other men rested on the answer to that question.[11] But while Friedlaender and other masculinists sought to answer it with an unqualified no, Hirschfeld's theory of sexual intermediaries made the WhK's response distinctly more ambivalent. Yet even as some military officers did support or even participate in the WhK, much more crucial to the movement were those who committed suicide, for they could serve as paradigmatic victims in a metaphysics of melodrama that extended from expository texts to actual plays. And though Friedlaender derided the WhK for a political project that amounted to "begging for pity [*Erbettelung von Mitleid*]," masculinist literature also recognized the melodramatic value of suicides committed by same-sex soldiers.[12]

Before turning to the question of melodrama, though, it is worth looking briefly at the participation of military personnel in the homosexual emancipation movement for the ways they figure into the split between the minority of masculinists and the large majority of WhK members who subscribed to Hirschfeld's gender-inversion model. Admittedly, reconstructing this involvement is difficult, not only because of the 1933 destruction of Hirschfeld's institute and its archive but also because most of the era's homosexuals – including many of the movement's leaders – were necessarily guarded about their sexual identity for professional reasons.[13] This kind of secrecy was especially important for active military officers and those with appointments in the Reserve, since key aspects of their personal lives – whom they married, which organizations they belonged to, which venues they could frequent – were strictly controlled and could lead to the loss of their commissions. Fortunately for historians, after anonymous or pseudonymous supporters died, Hirschfeld often eulogized them using their real names.

A small number of active and retired military officers supported the WhK in a variety of ways. The first was Franz Josef von Bülow, a former Prussian first-lieutenant who had been blinded in the 1890s by a bullet wound suffered during a battle against the Herero people in the colony of German-Southwest Africa. According to Hirschfeld, Bülow attended the founding 1897 meeting of the organization in Hirschfeld's apartment and contributed 200 marks – twice what each of the three others put in – to cover initial operating expenses.[14] Because he moved to Italy shortly after the meeting (in order, as Hirschfeld noted, to avoid Paragraph 175), his active participation in the WhK did not last long – though Hirschfeld claimed that he "remained a steadfast supporter for almost twenty years" until his death in October 1915.[15] While Bülow remained anonymous, the first publication of the committee's petition to the Reichstag in 1899 included twenty individuals with military titles.[16] Significantly, most were either writers or former military doctors – two professions that the WhK had been courting for signatures – and were probably not homosexuals themselves.[17] Meanwhile, at least two other retired officers were members of the WhK during its first decade. In October 1907, for instance, the WhK's monthly newsletter announced "with great sadness" the passing of "our esteemed member Lieutenant a.D. Nicolai."[18] Because his name does not appear elsewhere in the published records, we can assume that his identity was only made public with his death. In contrast, a second retired officer, First-Lieutenant a.D. Erich Moll, was the only individual with a military rank who used his full name and title in the list of WhK donors.[19] Nevertheless, after two years, he apparently signed Friedlaender's secession manifesto and left the organization in 1907.[20] Since he subsequently held elected public office in the Berlin suburb of Wilmersdorf, Moll was probably not a homosexual but rather a liberal ally.[21]

Finally, the WhK enjoyed the support of two highly placed homosexuals with military affiliations. The first was easily the most illustrious: Prince Georg of Prussia (1828–1902), the son of a cousin of Kaiser Wilhelm I and an early anonymous financial sponsor.[22] Like any member of the royal family, the prince held an honorary rank in the German army and necessarily always appeared in uniform. Nevertheless, there was a marked discrepancy between the military uniform and the prince's

Outing Officers: Queer Activism, Melodrama, and the Harden-Moltke Trial 33

effeminate nature. In his encomium, Hirschfeld, who never personally met the prince, cited several remembrances of those who did. While one friend of the deceased observed that "the somewhat tight uniform fit like a glove" (recalling other foppish Hohenzollern princes), another recalled meeting him during an anniversary celebration of a student literary society under the prince's protection: "for this occasion the prince always wore his Ulan uniform with the insignia of a general of the cavalry."[23] Yet this same source also recollected that "the prince's soft, almost faint, and pleasant voice stood in a remarkable contrast to his strapping appearance and his soldierly uniform."

The second was the WhK's most involved military contributor: an apparently active army officer who participated in the organization's leadership under the pseudonym Baron Karl Franz von Leexow, when in 1910 he became a member of the large advisory committee (*Obmänner-Kollegium*) and was also selected as one of the organization's two treasurers (*Kassen-Revisoren*).[24] According to Hirschfeld, Leexow was the scion of "an old aristocratic military family" and "a cavalry officer, body and soul."[25] Unlike the effeminate Prince Georg, Leexow had a distinctly masculine appearance, for Hirschfeld recalled that he "exhibited roughly the opposite of those characteristics that [Berlin police commissioner Hans von] Tresckow ... saw as typical for Urnings, when he wrote 'they have a want of willpower and they like to use the feminine weapons of intrigue, dissimulation [*Heuchelei*] and lies.'"[26] Hirschfeld also noted that Leexow "was seriously wounded shortly after the start of the world war and landed in a Russian camp for prisoners of war, where he remained for the rest of the war."[27] Because he was still alive at the time that Hirschfeld was writing, his actual identity was never revealed and remains a mystery.

Though Prince Georg died in 1902 and Leexow joined the WhK leadership in 1910, after Friedlaender's secession and death, they both illustrate nicely the two opposing conceptions of male homosexuality that eventually split the movement. The emphasis on the effeminacy of male homosexuals, including those who wore the military uniform, was a core tenet of Hirschfeld's descriptive doctrine of sexual intermediaries, which, as Ralf Dose helpfully summarizes, posited that "all human characteristics, whether physical or psychological, occur in feminine or masculine form – or, in exceptional cases, androgynously."[28] In this view, men who were sexually attracted to other men evinced a feminine sex drive, though many, it was claimed, also demonstrated physical signs of femininity, such as wide hips, narrow shoulders and fat deposits in the breast, hips, buttocks, and thighs. As a result, Hirschfeld considered homosexuality to be a congenital condition, with homosexuals representing a fixed minority within the population. The masculinists, meanwhile, viewed an individual's gender, not sexual orientation, as immutable. Like Freud, Friedlaender posited a universal bisexuality in which all men were capable of forming same-sex object choices at least at some point in their lives. Moreover, masculinists viewed men's attractions to other men as an expression of heightened virility, making such men more masculine than those who were attracted exclusively or primarily to women. Indeed, building on the influential work of Heinrich Schurtz, Friedlaender, like Hans Blüher after him, argued that homoerotic bonds among men provided the foundation for all sociality, making them (rather than the private heterosexual family) the backbone of the (patriarchal) state.[29]

While the debate between these two factions was not limited to the representation of uniformed officers, both sides had vested interests in claiming such men for themselves. Characteristic for the approach of the masculinists is Elisarion von Kupffer's influential introduction to his collection of literary celebrations of same-sex love, which was first published in essay form in the masculinist literary journal *Der Eigene* in 1899.[30] Opening with a lament about the "unmanly time" in which he was writing, Kupffer called for a resurgence of manliness and manly culture in which same-sex love between men would once again assume the exalted place it had held in Hellenic Greece. Central to this cultural project was the value of same-sex eroticism to the military preparedness of a nation. To that end, Kupffer argued that the love relationship between male warriors "created a bond of moral responsibility in relation to military efficiency [*Tüchtigkeit*]. And what can be more beneficial to common life than when its individual parts [*Glieder*] feel responsible for one another ... when an attack on one feels like an attack on all [*wo eins sich im anderen angegriffen fühlt*]."[31] For Kupffer, "it was exactly in the hour of danger that the effectiveness of this unity is tested," insisting that "the steely might of these unions has already shown itself to be practical, as in the Sacred Band of Thebes, which fought the victory of Leuktra" and which consisted of 150 pairs of male lovers.[32]

Even as Ancient Greece remained the central reference point among masculinists in the late nineteenth and early twentieth centuries, a few attempted to extend the idea of heroic male warrior-lovers into the present day. In his 1905 essay, for instance, Friedlaender pointed to the example of modern Japan, which had recently defeated the Russian Army and Navy and which, like Ancient Greece, also had an older tradition of pederasty among warriors.[33] Friedlaender's desperate desire to find a modern-day military culture that could demonstrate the value of homosexual readiness becomes apparent in the essay's circumstantial evidence and dubious correlations. For instance, after citing a 1902 article in the WhK's *Jahrbuch*, which claimed that pederasty was much more widespread in the nation's southern provinces, he noticed an item in a newspaper indicating that "some of the most famous men of modern Japan were born in the southern parts of the island nation."[34] Subsequently, he read an article in the journal *Ost-Asien* that named "twenty of the most outstanding Japanese men" – fourteen of them generals, field marshals or admirals – and after contacting its author learned that most came from the southern provinces "where from older times onward pederasty is especially widespread."[35] Despite these tenuous associations, Friedlaender nevertheless insisted that "it seems reasonable to assume a causal connection between the social acceptance of male-male love relationships and the successful cultivation of manly fitness."[36]

But while Friedlaender's conclusions amounted to little more than a flimsy fantasy under the guise of social science, a 1905 short story by Konrad Linke in *Der Eigene* seems to have deployed fantasy more effectively, judging by the positive notice it received in the *Jahrbuch*.[37] More importantly, the story sought to translate the idea of warrior-lovers into a modern German context through the mode of melodrama. Drawing its title from the first line of Germany's most iconic soldier's song, "Ich hatt' einen Kameraden – " (I once had a comrade) opens by posing the question of male intimacy among German soldiers fighting in an unidentified war.[38] As a contingent of marching soldiers hears the far-off melody of "Der gute Kamerad" (The good comrade), it "sent a quiver through the column," leading the soldier-narrator to ask: "Did each man possibly have a comrade?"[39] The emotional effect of the song on battle-worn soldiers who had "learned to sneer at the dear old folk songs" suggests that we are entering the realm of melodrama, which originated as pantomimes set to music.[40] Nevertheless, at this point the narrator quickly retreats from the possibility of deep intimacy between two individual soldiers, suggesting that camaraderie is merely the by-product of the close proximity entailed by military life: "Well, I mean, the comradeship of one's neighbor, as occurs from being together daily."[41]

The tone changes, however, when the narrator suddenly notices "one among us who was particularly gripped" by the song. Though he begins to "observe him intensely [*gespannt*]," he does not have the courage to strike up a conversation with the man. Nevertheless, as the soldier turned to look at him during the song's last stanza, the narrator reports: "I trembled. There was a wild, sad pain that blazed out of his eyes at me. I was captivated by this strange, glimmering look, even though it disappeared in an instant, and my neighbor continued on even more melancholy than before. –"[42] By underscoring both the depth of the man's melancholy and the impression his doleful stare made on the narrator, the excessive number of dashes, twenty-five in all, that concludes the sentence represents what Linda Williams calls "the mute pathos inherent in melodrama."[43]

The mysterious source of the ineffable look is revealed after the battle, when the rest of their fellow soldiers "are sleeping as deeply as the dead around us" and the narrator notices that his "lonely comrade" is missing.[44] Setting out to look for him, he eventually finds the man in the field, kneeling down next to a "young soldier from the artillery who had fought so valiantly" but now lay wounded on the ground, as blood soaked his blue uniform red.[45] After the narrator retreats behind a shot-up cannon, he observes his co-fighter "gently lift the wounded man's head, kiss him quietly on the forehead, mouth, eyes and then hold the pale head in his arm. There he remained lying – long – long. A solemn stillness was all around; the angel of love presided over them with sacred woe; nothing disturbed the noble consecration of this great love. –"[46] While the series of dashes again marks the scene's "mute pathos," what he witnesses in the "long – long" embrace between the two is a tableau, which, according to Williams, offered melodrama audiences "a silent, bodily expression of what words could not fully say."[47] Moreover, the imagined presence of "the angel of love" watching over this "sacred woe" invests the scene with a moral sanctity reminiscent of the "sacred band of Thebes" and which is further emphasized by the "plaintive tone" of "Der gute Kamerad" – a piece of music that, the narrator claims, is even "more beautiful and precious than all the church hymns."[48] After watching the man "bend over and kiss the dying friend, – who gently passes," the narrator sets off again only to hear a shot and runs back to find "my comrade with a shot through his head, his left arm looped around his dead friend next to him."[49] As the narrator and some others bury the two lovers "just as they died, lying arm in arm," the refrains of the "Der gute Kamerad" can be heard once again.

Linke's story offers a paradigmatic example of homosexual melodrama in prose form. Like the original French melodramas, it essentially presents pantomime scenes accompanied to a song that would have been deeply familiar to its readers. Moreover, the story's theatricality is emphasized by the fact that the narrator is neither the object nor subject of such homosexual longing – but rather a surreptitious and voyeuristic witness for whom the homosexual expression of love is staged. Freud, who identifies this kind of voyeurism as a characteristic quality of conscious fantasies or daydreams, suggests that it enables the fantasizer to identify with both subject positions – in this case, the doting and bereaved lover and the dying beloved.[50] In addition, as nameless figures, the two soldiers also serve as allegorical stand-ins for an exemplary idea of selfless heroism. While the dying beloved has demonstrated his heroism with his death, the other soldier has perhaps demonstrated an even more impressive mettle, for the narrator recalls that "in combat he appeared to me as a god, so proud and beautiful in his enthusiasm – missing, as it was, the astuteness of the modern soldier who looks for cover. He seemed to me to match the time of the noble fight of our ancestors."[51] Since the story suggests that the godly heroics stem from his selfless love – that is, his willingness to take risks with his own life if it might ensure the quick victory that would protect his male lover – it serves as a modern illustration of Kupffer's "bond of moral responsibility" that supports military efficiency. Finally, despite the tender kisses, the mute scene of love is innocent of all sexual overtones and even sanctified through the imagined presence of the angel of love.

In contrast to the masculinists' unadulterated military enthusiasm, the WhK's theory of sexual intermediaries often led to ambivalent, even schizophrenic pronouncements about homosexual officers. For instance, in an article on the occupational choices of homosexuals, Georg Merzbach – a Berlin-based physician who served as the WhK's second-in-command until the First World War – provocatively asked whether "anyone in any occupation has ever noticed that a homosexual was not a match for his position [*seinen Platz ausfüllt*], that in the right place even someone with the most feminine tendencies does not stand his ground [*seinen Mann steht*]?"[52] The choice of a military phrase – stand his ground – matched the combative tone of the essay's answer: not only have such "doubts" long since been "eliminated for experts on homosexuality," but "even the most persistent doubters will eventually be persuaded, for wherever they look, ... they encounter in the history and culture of nations homosexual bearers of the most illustrious names."[53] As with the masculinists, the heroic past is called on to vouch for a positive view of homosexuals' contributions to society.

Yet when Merzbach trained his sights on the military profession itself, the effeminacy of male homosexuals inevitably raised some doubts. Though he acknowledged that homosexuals were "not seldom officers," he insisted that this choice of profession was generally forced upon them by families with strong military traditions, since most homosexuals, if given the choice, would "follow their inner inclination [*Neigung*] for feminine activities, such as designing women's dresses, hats or floral arrangements or purely artistic careers like acting, painting, and music."[54] Indeed, he imagined a visible disjuncture between the homosexual and his manly profession such that "the observer must often ask himself: how could this girlish appearing homosexual become an officer?"[55] To reconcile the contradictions, he imagined how such officers found ways to "come to terms" (*Sichabfinden*) with the disjuncture, "which he compensates for in his lonely chamber, hidden from the eyes of the world, by wrapping the rough warrior in the soft garments of a lady of fashion and ruling his small, secret realm like a housewife."[56] In place of sociological facts, Merzbach offered up a fantasy scenario in which the closeted officer can only express his true identity in what amounts to a (clothes) closet, "hidden from the eyes of the world," where he can exchange his masculine uniform for fashionable women's clothes, and his manly career as a soldier for the domestic fiefdom of a housewife.

Despite their effeminacy, however, homosexual officers, so the WhK claimed, did not necessarily undermine military preparedness. For example, Hirschfeld used a lengthy essay based on extensive interviews and questionnaires with approximately 100 homosexuals to suggest that feminine qualities made homosexual officers quite popular with their men.[57] One of his military interlocutors, for instance, insisted "I looked after my recruits in every way, the men [*Leute*] went through fire for me, I avoided excessive drilling, was always in the barracks, since I never found any charm in pubs – thus, the presentation of the troops turned out splendidly and thanks to my good theoretical knowledge I earned the special praise of my commander."[58] Here, the homosexual officer's effeminacy is expressed in his own diligence and his maternal care, which elicited the best from his soldiers.

Inexplicably, however, Hirschfeld also saw some drawbacks. Because of the homosexual officers' maternal concern for the welfare of their subordinates, he concluded that they "are not well suited to being *strict* superiors."[59] Moreover, though Uranian members of the military and other exclusive male societies "are well liked in the beginning because of their polite, agreeable, and self-sacrificing nature [*Wesen*]," the sexologist claimed that "they have difficulties over the years because they cannot submit to the strict etiquette and strike friendly relations with outsiders."[60] More damningly, they lacked the other manly qualities necessary for military success: "they have no understanding for the strict sense of honor," they are "conciliatory" (*versöhnlich*) and "always inclined to forgive," and are "generally incapable of rendering a judgment."[61] Finally, this *mental* effeminacy was often compounded by unmanly *physical* traits. Hirschfeld noted, for instance, that "the muscles of Uranians are weaker than the masculine ones, even if seldom as

Figure 1.1. Magnus Hirschfeld, 1900. Staatsbibliothek zu Berlin – Preußischer Kulturbesitz, Berlin, Germany. Portr. Slg / Med. kl / Hirschfeld, Magnus, Nr. 1.

weak as female muscles."[62] One of his interlocutors also recalled that his "feminine" buttocks meant that his uniform didn't initially fit right and had to be altered.[63] Similarly, an officer "with a 'martial' appearance" (albeit "with somewhat wide hips") told Hirschfeld that "whenever he is agitated [*in Erregung befände*] his very large, blue and dreamy eyes are recognized by completely impartial observers [*von gänzlich unbefangener Seite*] as feminine."[64] Thus, supposedly even a well-fitting military uniform could not completely cover up a homosexual's underlying femininity. Indeed, even though "some homosexual men make a thoroughly masculine impression," Hirschfeld insisted that in examining more than 1,500 homosexuals, he had never met one who did not "physically or psychologically differ from a complete man [*Vollmann*]."[65]

But if homosexuals made questionable officers, the suicide of such officers was unequivocally useful as a melodramatic tactic for winning public support to the homosexual cause. The WhK, for instance, assiduously documented cases in which German, Austrian, British, and Dutch military officers were arrested, blackmailed, or committed suicide on account of their homosexuality. Though German cases consisted largely of reprints of newspaper clippings submitted by WhK members from around the country, these notices remain some of the best surviving documentation about the extent and prosecution of homosexuality in the German Army and Navy in the wake of the destruction of Prussian military archives during the Second World War. And while the first two volumes of the *Jahrbuch* included incidents going back to the 1880s, the *Monatsbericht* covered the cases of at least four navy and thirteen army officers accused of being homosexuals (or sexually harassing their subordinates) between the summer of 1905 and the end of 1907, just as Moltke's libel lawsuit against Harden got underway.

For instance, in September 1905, the *Monatsbericht* reprinted two articles from the *Hannover Anzeiger*, the first a suicide attempt by a one-year volunteer named Sebald who, as he was about to be arrested for repeatedly violating Paragraph 175, asked for permission to return to his apartment to change clothes, where he then shot himself twice and had to be transported to the military infirmary (the second notice announced his death).[66] Though these newspaper articles focused on conveying key details about the incident, including a statement by one of the arresting guards and allegations that the "serious offenses" also involved other suspects, the next issue of the *Monatsbericht* published excerpts from two of the "numerous letters" that Hirschfeld and the WhK had received in the wake of the suicide, one of which read: "The heart of everyone with human feelings bleeds when he sees how a young man is hounded into a horrible death by the responsible severity of the law, even though he perhaps could have otherwise contributed usefully to human society ... May you and the revered committee soon succeed in bringing down this horribly unjust law whose consequences have exacted rivers of blood and unspeakable misery, so that the sun of justice may shine a little on us despised outcasts [*uns Ausgestoßenen und Geächteten*]."[67] While it is understandable that many homosexuals would feel upset by Sebald's death, what is significant here is the melodramatic framing of the suicide: the "rivers of blood" extracted from innocent victims of an unjust law, the bleeding hearts of those who read the notice, the meekness of the request for a small ray of sunshine, and the heroic efforts of Hirschfeld and the WhK in taking on the cause of those unfairly despised by society and driven to kill themselves.

Reprinted in the *Monatsbericht*, which had a run of 1,800 copies, the letter not only offered a paradigmatic reading of the original newspaper's notice, but framed the political fight for the decriminalization of same-sex acts between men as a moral imperative to relieve suffering.[68]

Perhaps the most important officer suicide, however, was the one that appeared in the preface of Hirschfeld's first work on same-sex desire, *Sappho und Sokrates*, which was initially published anonymously in 1896 and which led directly to the founding of the WhK.[69] It too begins with a newspaper notice about the mysterious suicide of an officer who had been Hirschfeld's patient. Though the paper attributed the act to an "inexplicable fit of mental derangement," Hirschfeld's intimate knowledge of his patient – along with the timely arrival of a suicide letter – gave him a different reading of the event. According to the sexologist, this lieutenant was the only child of parents who had pressured him for years to marry a childhood friend, which he finally did. As the closeted officer supposedly wrote to Hirschfeld, he didn't have "the strength" to tell his parents "the truth" about his sexuality – and he hoped that "these good people never learn what pressed so heavily on my heart [*was mir schier das Herz abdrücken wollte*]." He then asked Hirschfeld "to accept this outcry of a miserable wretch, the justification of my act, and simultaneously the salvation of honor for so many individuals who like me live their lives under a double curse – the curse of nature and the curse of the law." Nevertheless, the desperate man closed his letter with the wish that his suffering and death will not have been in vain: "May it be possible that my voice, like those of better champions [*Sachverwalter*], will not fall on deaf ears. The thought that [my voice] could contribute to the German fatherland thinking more justly about us brightens [*verschönen*] my dying hour."[70]

What distinguishes this officer's suicide from the ones that came after it is the existence of a letter, and thus the final words of the victim. But while it is understandable that the farewell letter of a young man about to end his life would be filled with pathos, its melodramatic perfection and suitability to a political project of homosexual emancipation makes it likely that some or all of the passages that Hirschfeld quoted were penned by the sexologist himself, whose first love was and remained literature rather than medicine.[71] Here the realm of melodrama is marked by the needless suffering of an innocent and worthy individual – vouchsafed by his noble profession and his concern for his parents' well-being and honour – who succumbs to unjust laws, prejudice and the heterosexual expectations of his family. At the same time, his wish that his posthumous texts could help change social opinion and thereby prevent other homosexual men from killing themselves also recasts his suicide as a form of heroic self-sacrifice, much like a hero's death (*Heldentod*) on the battlefield. By opening his book with this man's dying wish, Hirschfeld sought to justify the pressing need to speak – if discreetly and scientifically – about the potentially scandalous topic of same-sex desire and to take action: "this case ... commandingly urges us to reach a more just resolution of the law."[72] To this extent, Hirschfeld initially grounded the entire project of homosexual emancipation on the tragic death – recast as a self-sacrifice – of a military officer. As Émile Zola famously, if ironically, quipped in his novel *The Ladies' Paradise*, "it was the mead of blood that every revolution exacted from its martyrs, every step forward was made over the bodies of the dead" – in this case, the dead body of an unnamed Prussian officer.[73]

Though Hirschfeld "reserved the right to return to the story of our patient," *Sappho und Sokrates* strangely never did so. Instead, I want to suggest that this task was taken up by the Austrian writer and playwright Franz Reddi in his 1907 drama *Der fremde Gott* (The strange god), one of several "homosexual problem plays" written between 1899 and 1907 to highlight the plight of homosexuals.[74] In place of Hirschfeld's anonymous officer and his parents, the play presents three generations of the aristocratic Seewald family: the elderly and infirm matriarch Baroness von Seewald, her son-in-law Dr. von Forsbach and his sister Elise, and the doctor's son Gustav, a lieutenant in a Hussar regiment. Set entirely in Dr. von Forsbach's library and study, the play takes place on the afternoon in which Gustav is set to marry his childhood friend Helene, a wealthy orphan who seems to have been raised with him at Seewald estate. In addition to the bride, who is in love with Gustav, the marriage is the last wish of Baroness von Seewald as well as the last hope Gustav's father, Dr. von Forsbach, who confides to his sister that Helene's dowry is the only way to save the estate and fund Gustav's military career – his aristocratic birthright – since the expenses of his profession are not covered by his poor salary and must be supplemented with income from the family. Yet on this unbearably hot and humid wedding day, there is a storm brewing – both literally and figuratively – for Gustav harbours a sexual secret. In melodramatic fashion, this secret is marked by the play's Gothic element: a cursed marble statue of the god Eros – the "strange god" of the title – which a family forefather brought back from Italy and which, according to family folklore, can be seen haunting the woods during moments of crisis (in fact, superstitious servants claim they saw the "white one" walking earlier in the day). Thus, as final preparations are being made and guests are slowly arriving in the main hall, a powerful thunderstorm coincides with Helene's discovery that the Baroness has just died quietly in her chair while her fiancé has committed suicide in his room; she collapses and the curtain falls.

As a "family drama in one act," *Der fremde Gott* exemplifies many of the features of a domestic melodrama: not only its claustrophobic setting, its Gothic element, and the unbearable pressure on Gustav to sacrifice his own desires to save his family but also the young man's decision to apply "cathartic violence" to himself.[75] But whereas the family was left in the dark about the reasons behind the suicide of Hirschfeld's patient, Reddi's drama not only enables its young officer to come out to his father but also foregrounds the numerous tensions around knowing and not-knowing his true sexual identity. The play, for instance, opens with Dr. von Forsbach promising to help the son of his tenant farmer flee to America after he has been outed by some of his co-workers at the factory where he is employed. Just as the man leaves, Dr. von Forsbach's sister arrives, introduced in the text as a "forty-year-old woman with an energetic, almost manly facial expression" (11) who runs the estate for her brother. Much of this first half of the play is taken up with the siblings' discussion, during which Elise professes an "unsatisfied desire" (23) – "something secretly horrible and death-desiring" (22) – to achieve "clarity about herself at any cost" (23). As her brother suggests books she might read, she notices on his desk a monograph by his friend Professor Ebenthal (a blend of Hirschfeld and Krafft-Ebing), upon which Dr. von Forsbach has drawn a skull and crossbones (*Totenkopf*).[76] Though he explains that the image is merely a warning that the book is not for everyone (28), he does admit that the contents deal with "an age-old problem ... that the street of life has sown with countless wounded and dead" (29), including, as we later learn, "the story of the young Brachfeld ... who shot himself a few years ago during the honeymoon after his much envied marriage" (37). As the doctor explains Ebenthal's theories, it slowly dawns on him that his sister is a lesbian, which solves her riddle for her. But while Gustav's impending wedding has reminded Elise of the time long ago when she rejected the advances of a young forester, her brother introduces the discourse of eugenics to insist that homosexuals should never get married, for not only are these marriages unhappy but the offspring are often born disfigured and sick (35).[77]

Though Dr. von Forsbach claims that only doctors can make a determination about whether someone is fit to marry (35), his myopia about his sister extends to his son Gustav, who both siblings agree has been acting strangely in the last few days. The father, who remembers Gustav's "story with the singer," thinks that there must be another woman behind his sour demeanour since "a real Hussar kisses every girl" (18).

Elise, however, is unconvinced since "Gustl has never kept any secrets" from his father. Indeed, even before she recognizes the truth of her own lesbianism, she recognizes all the signs of her nephew's true sexual identity: his artistic streak (15), his tastefully decorated apartment (16), his "sensitive heart" (17), and "a wonderful mixture" of "something soft and at the same time proud, bold, like milk and fire wine" (17). Moreover, as in the discussions by Hirschfeld and Merzbach, Gustav's effeminacy comes across even when he is in uniform. Thus, while the father blindly insists that "the mustache looks good on him" and that "he has become an excellent rider" with "iron muscles" (17), his aunt recalls that even though the "uniform looks good on him ... he always appeared like a disguised girl" (16). Because of the father's wilful ignorance, the play builds to its first melodramatic episode, when Gustav struggles to come out to his father. After he too spies Ebenthal's book, Gustav initially tells his father that he is "not healthy" (50). In response to his father's incomprehension, he finally points to the book and declares "don't you see, Papa, I belong in this book, the one with the skull and crossbones. (*Bitter laughter*.) The skull is quite apt ... yes, the story of the young Brachfeld inside will be my story. (*Makes the gesture of shooting himself*.)" (51).

While Gustav's intimations of suicide are certainly melodramatic, the political function of melodrama lies in the play's attestation of his suffering – and the need to solve it socially. Whereas Hirschfeld's patient gave the task of articulating his truth to his doctor, Reddi's play enables Gustav to explain his plaint to his sympathizing father. He clears up the misunderstanding about the opera singer, who it turns out was a lesbian; both benefited from rumours that they were in a relationship (54). We also learn that Gustav's problems began when he spurned the sexual advances of Frau von Ledinsky, an aggressive widow, who then sought vengeance by sending anonymous letters full of "mean, shameless allegations [and] slander about his friendship with Otto" (52). As a result, Otto put in for a transfer to another regiment, while Gustav consulted with Professor Ebenthal himself, who confirmed that he was homosexual. Yet despite the accusations, Gustav has never indulged in sexual acts, telling his father (and the audience): "You must not believe that these miserable letters had even a shadow of legitimacy to them. Up to now I have fought and conquered my blood – – yes, I have fought against this strange devil or god in me ... But who can vouch for the future! Does your much lauded science there know a way out other than an honorable death?" (57). Because he dreams of finding a life partner, he finds it unfair that he should "have to abstain from the first of all human rights, the right to love" or "suffer a disgrace" (58).

Outing Officers: Queer Activism, Melodrama, and the Harden-Moltke Trial   45

At the end of this heart-to-heart, Gustav ominously announces that he "will go up to my room and don my parade uniform for the last, ceremonial act of my life!" (59).

Though largely unperformable in an era in which theatres were subjected to strict police censorship, Reddi's drama – like other published homosexual plays – were nonetheless reviewed in WhK publications, and some, such as Hanns Heinz Ewers's *Enterbt* (Disinherited), were given public readings at WhK events.[78] As the respected sexologist Albert Eulenburg explained in his preface to *Enterbt*, these playwrights sought "to deliver new munitions [*Kampfmittel*] to the movement" and to tap the stage "as a new [and] perhaps unimaginably effective arena [*Kampfplatz*]" in the fight for homosexual rights.[79] These military metaphors are particularly apt for Reddi's text, which offers an honourable officer as an exemplary victim around which to elicit sympathy, for, as Linda Williams notes, "what counts in melodrama is the feeling of righteousness, achieved through the suffering of the innocent."[80] It was this innocent righteousness, of course, that activists relied on to make their case to the public. Yet while melodrama was an essential weapon in the arsenal of the homosexual emancipation movement, it was also one that could be wielded in homophobic ways, as we will see when we turn to the first Harden-Moltke trial.

"Gutter Melodramatics": The Harden-Moltke Trial

"In the morning, the Moltke-Harden trial; in the evening, Caruso," noted the *Vossische Zeitung* in its coverage of the opening day of the first libel hearing between Maximilian Harden and Count Kuno von Moltke, explaining that "the demand for entrance tickets for the drama in Moabit [the Berlin district in which the courthouse was located] was not any less than for the first performance of the king of tenors in the Berlin opera house."[81] As the paper's opening salvo suggests, the comparison between trials and theatre performances was commonplace by this time. Indeed, in the previous year, the Austrian writer Peter Rosegger had already observed that the ticket-holding public entered the courtroom "as if [it] were being treated to a performance," for despite certain "directorial mistakes" (*Regiefehler*) – by which he meant that the cast of lawyers and defendants stood and spoke with their backs to the audience, while those testifying had not learned to project their voices – the cross-examination of witnesses often led to "dramatic scenes that belong to the best that this genre offers."[82] It is probably for this reason that sensational trials in Germany were often covered in the press by playwrights and theatre critics (including Harden himself) rather than those trained in the law.[83] But while the *Vossische Zeitung* could not predict after opening arguments "whether [this courtroom drama] would be a tragedy or comedy," a consensus quickly emerged on the trial's status as melodrama.[84] After Harden was cleared of slandering Moltke's reputation, for instance, one commentator denounced the trial using the journalist's own words from a similar 1902 scandal: "But the current of our time does not like tragedy, that is, one whose plot proceeds from a character. It prefers gutter melodramatics [*Gassenmelodramatik*] from which cheap philistine wisdom can be drawn."[85]

The Harden-Moltke trial, of course, was the first of several legal battles in the two-year-long Eulenburg Affair (1907–9), Imperial Germany's most important political scandal. But while Kuno von Moltke – a lieutenant-general and commander of Berlin garrisons was supposed to be merely a side casualty in Harden's campaign against Prince Philipp zu Eulenburg und Hertefeld, he nevertheless became the journalist's first legal opponent in the public sphere. And though Harden sought to treat Moltke primarily as a stand-in for Eulenburg, this first trial, which took place over five days in late October 1907, nevertheless emerged as the period's most public scrutiny of the sexuality of a top-ranked Prussian officer.[86] Thus, rather than rehearse the trial's role in the larger Eulenburg Affair, which has been covered in detail elsewhere, I want to explore the legal battle as a spectacular reversal of the melodramatic strategies of the homosexual emancipation movement's investment in closeted military officers as self-sacrificing heroes or innocent victims. As Angus McLaren has pointed out, in the theatricality of courtrooms at this time, male defendants and plaintiffs "tended to follow the conventions of the Victorian melodrama – one was either a hero or a villain," even as the function of the trial revolved around "who had the right to appropriate the role of 'hero' and thereby relegate their antagonist to the position of 'villain.'"[87] Indeed, in addition to supporting the journalist's larger political claims to be uncovering a dangerous camarilla influencing the Kaiser, the conventions of melodrama served as the primary strategy for proving his claims that Moltke was a homosexual. Because Hirschfeld agreed to serve as an expert witness on the journalist's behalf, Harden's image of Moltke corresponded to the WhK's own portraits of homosexual officers as effeminate men in uniform. But while the sexologist tried to distance his diagnosis from Harden's homophobic project, the trial's melodramatics reversed the WhK's ability to cast homosexual officers in the leading role of innocent victim. And even though the court did not entirely accept Harden's homophobic reasoning, it nevertheless applied its own homophobic assessment – a Prussian version of "don't ask, don't tell" – that essentially blamed

Outing Officers: Queer Activism, Melodrama, and the Harden-Moltke Trial   47

Figure 1.2. Kuno von Moltke, no date. Landesarchiv Baden-Würrtemberg, Hauptstaatsarchiv Stuttgart, P 10 Bü 1757.

48   Uniform Fantasies

Moltke for not hiding his homosexual identity sufficiently from others. All these factors led to a conscious effort to tighten the military uniform's fit.

Even before a word was spoken in the courtroom, the nature of the larger political scandal created a series of conditions that encouraged participants and the public to view the trial through the prism of melodrama. For example, Harden's campaign against members of Wilhelm II's entourage mirrored the traditional opening of a melodrama, in which the evildoers operate as respectable figures in powerful state or social positions of authority.[88] In fact, by suing Harden for libel, Moltke played into this melodramatic logic since the move could be interpreted as a case where moral evil was attempting to silence the whistleblower – an impression only strengthened by the plaintiff's unsuccessful request to close the trial to the public. Meanwhile, like the melodramatic heroes in such theatre pieces, Harden stylized his battle as a lifelong and heroic effort to identify the hitherto invisible evil lurking within the Kaiser's personal regime, to articulate it publicly for all to know, and to expunge it and its evil effects from the German nation. Since the trial came months after Harden's initial and enigmatic allegations, the public also expected – and eagerly awaited – the climatic revelations that melodramatic plays invariably delivered in their ubiquitous trial scenes.

That these melodramatic pretensions could be realized so fully was due in part to the advantages and disadvantages of the trial's format as a private criminal prosecution. Initially, Moltke attempted to avoid a public battle with Harden by trying to bring the charges before an internal honour tribunal. But his superiors, eager to get rid of both Eulenburg and his accomplice, prevented this option by insisting that he challenge Harden to a duel (the latter declined) and then take Harden to court for libel. Forced to take a public route, Moltke initially sought (and failed) to get the state prosecutor to accept his case.[89] Out of other options, the general filed a private criminal libel lawsuit against the journalist on 6 June 1907. According to Ann Goldberg, the *Privatklage*, or private prosecution, made it possible for nearly any individual to pursue a *criminal* case for defamation or insult, a legal avenue championed by liberals to "counter arbitrary state power" (since state prosecutors were beholden to the crown) and as an alternative to illegal duelling.[90] Yet private prosecutions also included some potential disadvantages, too, such as prohibiting either party the opportunity to testify under oath on their own behalf.[91] And though melodrama also often imbued trials prosecuted by district attorneys, the format of the private prosecution gave Harden and his attorney significantly more leeway to make their

Outing Officers: Queer Activism, Melodrama, and the Harden-Moltke Trial   49

Figure 1.3. Maximilian Harden, no date. Photo: akg-images / WHA / World History Archive.

case and exploit the trial's inherent melodramatics, especially since the one professional judge in the matter was young and inexperienced.[92]

The conventions of both the domestic melodrama and sexology were also essential to Harden's entire defence against the charges that he had libelled Moltke by claiming he was a homosexual. Unlike a subsequent trial in which Harden located two men who testified to having had sexual relations with Eulenburg, Harden lacked firm evidence that Moltke had committed sexual acts with another man.[93] (Though

Harden and his attorney did introduce testimony from Johann Bollhardt about homosexual orgies in the Potsdam Guards, the former NCO failed to unequivocally identify Moltke as one of the participants.) Instead, Harden's defence rested on an accumulation of testimony about Moltke's behaviour with his wife and male friends, which were then subjected to "scientific" analysis by his forensic expert, Hirschfeld. As a result, the trial closely followed the melodramatic operations that Reddi employed in his drama *Der fremde Gott*. Indeed, the trial played out as an alternative ending for the play – as if Gustav had married and later divorced Helene, with Hirschfeld taking the part of Dr. Ebenthal. But rather than a homosexual problem play, the script followed by the Moabit courtroom adhered instead to the domestic melodrama, in which Moltke's former wife and Harden's star witness, Lily von Elbe, assumed the role of innocent female victim.[94]

A stereotype of nineteenth-century melodramas, the female victim was an enormously effective defendant and witness in nineteenth-century court cases.[95] Lily von Elbe's testimony about the sexual life of her marriage to Moltke offered a litany of her victimization as a loyal, innocent, and long-suffering wife, while also fulfilling the melodramatic compulsion to articulate crucial hidden truths – in this case, the truth of Moltke's homosexuality. She claimed, for instance that her conjugal sexual relations with her former husband ceased against her will after only two days of marriage. She also stated that Moltke had sought to deter her sexual advances by placing a pan of cold water in the bed between them or sleeping with his clothes on. Though the couple continued to sleep in the same room for a period of time to keep up appearances ("because of what people might say," as she said), he eventually insisted on separate bedrooms and social spheres in the house. But the height of her victimization was Moltke's cruel misogyny:

> BERNSTEIN: Did Count Moltke not say to you another time: You are not repugnant to me as a person, but only because you are a woman.
> [ELBE]: That is also true.
> JUSTICE DR. KERN: Did Count Moltke also tell you once that at the performance of the marriage he believed that you would swing in the air next to him like a beautiful fantasy [*Märchen*, literally, fairy tale] in the marriage.
> [ELBE]: Yes, my former spouse said: I did not want to have you as a woman, but rather only view you as a beautiful fantasy in the marriage. By that I understood that I should not demand anything of him as a wife. He explained this to me time and again with fierce scorn.

BERNSTEIN: Did your former spouse also not say repeatedly that he placed friendship between men higher than love for women and everything else?
[ELBE]: Yes, he repeatedly said that to me and gave me other reasons to believe it.[96]

Bernstein's strategy in providing Elbe with yes-no statements was enormously effective, not only because it kept her testimony clear and focused by minimizing, according to Hecht, her "emotional resistance against publicizing an especially unhappy phase of her life," but also because having her tell the stories herself would have further breached the social injunction that wives not air the dirty laundry of their marriage in public.[97] At the very least, Moltke emerges from this testimony as a man who does not view women as sexual objects and as such treats them poorly. But rather than a personalized mistreatment directed at her individual personality, Lily von Elbe claimed that her former husband was disgusted by her gender. (Moltke and his attorney argued that she was prone to hysterical outbursts and was addicted to the sedative Trionol, and thus was intolerable to him.) The concept of the "beautiful" fantasy or fairy tale is particularly revealing – and emphasized by Harden throughout the trial – because it implied Moltke's desire to banish the corporeal reality and sexual aspects of his wife during their marriage. In the picture she paints of Moltke's private life, the bourgeois domestic ideal of marriage was reduced to a lifeless fantasy. In a word, Moltke's marriage was a fake: "Bernstein: Was your marriage ever even once a marriage? [Elbe]: I do not think so!" (3994).

Lily von Elbe's testimony indicated that what should have been the centre of Moltke's private life – his marriage – was empty. But her characterization of his relationship with Eulenburg gave evidence that his friendships with other men were invested with strikingly private, intense, and even erotic emotions. For instance, rather than participating in the "family festivities" during their first Christmas together, Moltke retired to his room to write a long letter to Eulenburg (3992). Since Christmas Eve had become a family-centred holiday in Germany over the nineteenth century, this incident portrays Moltke's attachment to Eulenburg as a profound disruption of the bourgeois household.[98] But she also detailed how Eulenburg's friendship interrupted the married couple's domesticity in even more direct ways. For instance, after the diplomat arranged for his friend to be transferred as a military attaché to Vienna, where he served as the German ambassador to the Austro-Hungarian Empire, Moltke often spent the evening at his friend's apartments rather than return home (3992). Lily von Elbe also testified that

Eulenburg once visited her to demand that she leave Moltke, saying "give me my friend back," and that he was the one who insisted that Moltke cease sexual relations with her after two days (3990).

But the story that captivated the public the most was her account of Moltke's behaviour upon finding a handkerchief that Eulenburg had left behind:

> I did not know then that there could be sexual relations between men. One day after visiting, Count Philipp Eulenburg had forgotten his handkerchief in Count Moltke's room. When Count Moltke found the handkerchief, he pressed it fervently to his lips and said "My soul, my love!" He often spoke enthusiastically of his [male] friends, and was much more tender towards them than to his spouse. He showered Phili Eulenburg with nicknames such as "my sweetheart, my lover-boy, my one and only cuddly-bear." (3989–90)[99]

The handkerchief incident quickly assumed notorious importance. Here, the conventions of melodrama strengthened the story's explanatory power because, as Peter Brooks reminds us, melodrama features an interpretive structure in which "physical signs" and gestures also "make one legible to others."[100] In this case, Moltke's tender treatment of Eulenburg's handkerchief, as a fetish or stand-in for the absent loved one, seemed to offer incontrovertible proof of Moltke's erotic attraction to another man rather than merely an aversion to women. Indeed, by prefacing her story with a claim that she had not previously known about the existence of male homosexuality, Elbe represented her very witnessing of the gesture as an epiphany in which she became aware of the possibility of sexual relations between men, even though she in fact did not witness any explicitly sexual behaviour and only Moltke was in the room. In the end, her story replaced the need for concrete evidence that Moltke had engaged in sexual acts with another man because it embedded this sign of Moltke's deeper psychological constitution within an "aesthetics of astonishment," Brooks's term for "a moment of ethical evidence and recognition."[101]

As Lily von Elbe acknowledged, however, she was not an expert in homosexual relations between men. Thus, the conclusive interpretation of her information fell to Harden's expert witness, Magnus Hirschfeld. Hirschfeld, who had never met Kuno von Moltke, was required to base his expert testimony on the evidence presented at the trial.[102] Relying almost exclusively on Elbe's testimony, he concluded that Moltke was a homosexual: "With Mrs. v. Elbe's portrayal I had the same feeling that I have so often with similar cases: It is the horrible tragedy of the marriage of a person who is unconsciously homosexual."[103] In his affidavit for the court, Hirschfeld laid out the scientific methodology he used to reach his "objective diagnosis of homosexuality" (4050), which rested on three "symptoms" that corresponded with his sexological understanding of homosexuality: the negative and abusive statements that Moltke made about his wife, which indicated aversive behaviour towards the opposite sex; Moltke's "unusually enthusiastic and emotional" behaviour towards members of his own sex, which "departed from the norm" of male relations (4049); and Moltke's sensitivity, artistic streak, and penchant for mysticism, which revealed an "intellectual and physical personhood [*Gesamtpersönlichkeit*] characterized by the presence [*Einschlag*] of feminine qualities" (4051). But while effeminacy and misogyny were widely held signs of homosexuality, Hirschfeld's most important and controversial claim was that Moltke's homosexuality was unconscious even to himself. Though the idea that the psyche harbours unconscious desires was not entirely new in the discourse of sexology, Hirschfeld's affidavit explicitly cites Freud's work on hysteria and implicitly relies on his methodologies in diagnosing Moltke's sexual identity as unconscious.[104] Like the figure of Dr. Ebenthal in *Der fremde Gott* who, though he never appears as a speaking part within the melodrama, is nevertheless given the task of making the ultimate determination of Gustav's homosexuality, Hirschfeld also certifies Elbe's own interpretation of the melodramatic signs of Moltke's true self. Moreover, by developing his diagnosis in opposition to Moltke's own claims, the sexologist also stages the "drama of recognition" that Brooks locates in psychoanalysis: "of finding the place of the 'truth,' of the narrative that explains (and therefore maybe cures), of making the individual and the universe legible."[105]

In addition to being a linchpin in Harden's defence strategy, Hirschfeld's affidavit was epoch-making. According to David Halperin, intense male friendships had functioned historically in opposition to other same-sex practices, in particular sodomy and pederasty, which were based on hierarchal differences – of gender, social status, and age – between partners.[106] By reinterpreting such friendships as evidence of homosexuality, Hirschfeld's testimony applied bourgeois norms of gender and sexuality to forms of behaviour that had largely remained acceptable in rarefied aristocratic circles. As a result, male bonds that surpassed the emotional intensity of husband-wife relations could no longer be taken at face value and required investigation by appropriate fields of knowledge, such as psychiatry, psychology, and sexology. But his testimony's broadest impact was undoubtedly the dissemination of a "modern" definition of homosexuality as a psychological identity independent of an individual's participation in specific sexual acts. As he declared in his affidavit: "Whether [Moltke] acts sexually as a homosexual [*sich dabei homosexuell betätigt*] is secondary [*nebensächlich*] from the standpoint of the natural sciences" (4050). Even Moltke's claim that he had maintained a long-time "relationship" with another woman before his marriage did not alter Hirschfeld's diagnosis, since, for Hirschfeld, homosexuality was a bio-psychological identity one is born with rather than merely a label for someone who had committed sexual acts with a member of the same sex. Though the medicalization of same-sex behaviour had started the process much earlier, whereby "the nineteenth-century homosexual became a personage," as Foucault so famously puts it, the trial's enormous international coverage disseminated these modern ideas beyond the realm of science to the general public.[107] As Scott Spector explains, "the Harden-Moltke scandal, by the sheer magnitude of exposure, did more to bring the existence of actually existing homosexuals into broad public view than all previous prosecutions of Paragraph 175 in Germany and 129(b) in Austria and emancipatory efforts to reform them combined."[108]

Though Hirschfeld seemed to have sought to harness the trial's inevitable publicity to educate the broader German public about homosexuality, his participation backfired spectacularly. Many homosexuals were rightly outraged that the leader of the WhK would participate in what amounted to a homophobic witch-hunt. Yet in agreeing to serve as a forensic witness for the defence, the sexologist may also have felt obligated to Harden for his previous support of the WhK's efforts to repeal Paragraph 175, since he also testified, with prodding from Bernstein, that he did not believe that Harden would attack someone just because he was homosexual (4056).[109] In addition, Hirschfeld also tried to carefully distance his diagnosis of Moltke's homosexuality from Harden's denunciatory project. He emphasized throughout his testimony that homosexuals, while not "similar" (*gleichartig*) to heterosexuals, were still "on the same par" (*gleichwertig*) with them (4053). The sexologist also rejected Harden's claims that homosexuals were necessarily deceptive, countering that their characters were "very diverse" (4058). Nevertheless, his affidavit and testimony effectively supported Harden's politics of denunciation by validating Elbe's testimony with authoritative scientific validity.[110] Moreover, his diagnosis of Moltke's homosexuality clearly contradicted his promise, made in the wake of the 1902 "outing" of the German arms manufacturer Friedrich Alfred Krupp, that homosexuals had "no need to fear indiscretion from the Committee; we will not take the often proposed 'path over corpses,' under any circumstances."[111]

Despite his effort to distance himself from Harden's project, Hirschfeld also inevitably strengthened Harden's political arguments against Moltke by presenting the general's homosexuality as an unconscious state. For example, the general's apparent lack of knowledge about such a fundamental aspect of himself clearly diminished his overall ability to know anything at all, and thus backed up Harden's assertions that homosexuals inevitably give the Kaiser "a false picture of real conditions." Hirschfeld's diagnosis also increased the impression that this form of sexuality is particularly elusive and thus dangerous, since even some homosexuals were apparently unaware of their true sexual identity. And though the sexologist tried to explain that the homosexual's need for secrecy resulted from an unfair lack of social acceptance, he nevertheless underlined a fundamental connection between homosexuality and secrecy: "I have come to the conclusion that the other gentlemen of the circle named here have possibly known to hide their tendencies. Especially a homosexual is always determined to hide his tendency. It is often the case that a homosexual comports himself so that his closest acquaintances notice nothing of his disposition" (4055). According to Hirschfeld, General von Hohenau, one of the officers dismissed in the homosexual Potsdam scandal brought up at the trial, kept his homosexuality "especially carefully hidden" (4057).[112] Thus, when homosexuality is not unconscious but rather a self-aware disposition that leads to (illegal) sexual activities with other men, homosexuals *intentionally* hide their "truth" and actively engage in secrecy and deception.

But if effeminate homosexuals were deceptive, real men and heroes embodied the role of truth teller. In his final remarks, Harden characterized his own campaign as evidence of his courage to articulate the truth: "It is quite clear from the diaries of old [former Chancellor] Chlodwig [zu] Hohenlohe[-Schillingsfürst] what kind of disastrous role Prince Eulenburg played [in national politics]. I had to speak when no one else had the courage to" (4104). Likewise, Bernstein called on the court to affirm Harden's fight for truth as both honourable and masculine: "Yes, strengthen the courage of German men, fortify the courage of those German men who are writers to tell the truth ... If you convict Mr. Harden, you will not embolden German men to participate in politics" (4094). Though Bernstein urged the court to acknowledge and protect the masculinity of writers with unpleasant truths to convey, he also lined up this manly role with the masculinity of uniformed officers, including Moltke's assistant, Major von Hülsen, who had also been called to the witness stand. Though Hülsen had refused to give any information about the contents of specific military orders regarding

Moltke's dismissal, Bernstein explicitly contrasted the major's testimony about the rumours surrounding Eulenburg's homosexuality with Moltke's claims that his military position made it impossible for him to reveal information about his dismissal:

> Count Moltke also said the conscious untruth [*die bewußte Unwahrheit*] in this case. He knows full well that there are no "military-technical" issues here, he just doesn't want to say the word [homosexual]. Now Mr. von Hülsen, who we saw here yesterday, was a true soldier. Believe me, it was not easy for Mr. von Hülsen to vocalize the bitter truth [*das harte Wort*]. As unpleasant as it was for him, he had to say that Prince Eulenburg was dismissed from office because of homosexual things. When Major von Hülsen then answered my question about Count Moltke with "Well, it is because of the same things!" – ah, I said to myself, now everything is settled and the trial is over. (4090)

Bernstein portrayed Moltke's statements about his dismissal not only as cunning dissembling (and thus an extension of his homosexual disposition to lie and distort) but also as a wilful refusal to speak the word "homosexual." In contrast, he held up Hülsen as a "true soldier" for his honesty, which required a manly struggle to articulate the truth. In Bernstein's logic, homosexuality was depicted as so odious that even mentioning the word required overcoming some form of censorship, whether because of social decorum or internalized inhibitions. As a result, merely having an officer speak "the tough word" (*das harte Wort*) lent the very act of articulation a different aura – as if it, like the handkerchief episode, were able to bridge the gap between signifier and signified. Overall, testimony about homosexuality made the very trial itself appear as a victory of articulation: as that which, in Brooks's apt words, "could not be said on an earlier stage, nor still on a 'nobler' stage, nor within the codes of society."[113]

Unfortunately for Moltke, the general and his counsel proved incapable of matching the dramatic eloquence mustered by Harden and Bernstein. Yet perhaps the largest handicap in the general's courtroom strategy was the necessity of appearing at the trial in civilian clothes rather than his military uniform. The right to wear a military uniform in public was a privilege tightly controlled by the military leadership and the Kaiser. While retirement and reserve status usually carried the right to don a military uniform on public holidays and formal events, dishonourable discharges usually revoked that privilege. As a result, Harden and his defence counsel consistently argued that Moltke's civilian dress at the trial proved that the Kaiser and the military leadership were already convinced of his homosexuality. Exploiting the melodramatic conventions of symbols, Harden argued that, stripped of his uniform, the general's mask of virtue had been lifted. Moltke, however, sought to explain to the court that it was the military honour code that prevented him from appearing at the trial in uniform:

> I have taken off my uniform, which I have worn so happily and with such pride for forty-two years, and in which I bled for the fatherland, in order to appear here, for as a soldier I am not allowed to stand here, as a soldier I am not allowed to let myself be insulted. An officer cannot allow himself to be so attacked, and for that reason I first had to take off the uniform. (With a voice almost hoarse from agitation): The rumours, the whisperings that have arisen, the secretive hushing that arises whenever someone sees me, all that confirms I'm right. An officer in uniform cannot let that happen. (4097)

Moltke's attestation lines up with a popular handbook for the officer corps, which exhorted its uniformed reader to avoid situations in which he would "have to listen to utterances of a directly hostile or provocative nature, which he as an officer is not allowed to tolerate and which very often lead to unpleasantries of the most terrible kind."[114] Because such "unpleasantries" were unavoidable at this trial, it would have been more damaging to Moltke's honour if he had worn his uniform, since insults against a uniformed officer were interpreted by the army as insults against the entire officer corps. Yet Moltke's emotional speech also struck its own melodramatic chords. Coming in his closing remarks, the general's words clearly betray the emotional costs of the trial caused by the relentless accusations of being a deceitful homosexual. Though he used the occasion to emphasize his earlier heroism in the Franco-Prussian War, the general was quite literally at pains to explain both the meaning of his uniform to him personally and the requirements of the military honour code. As Moltke's emotional appeal testifies, however, stripping off the uniform did not diminish its psychological and symbolic significance, for the general's repetitious invocation of military dress seems intended – both psychologically and rhetorically – to conjure up a mental image of the uniform in its physical absence. At the very least, this emotionally charged final speech certainly conveyed a melodramatic struggle to find his voice and articulate his innocence, and it was greeted with loud calls of "Bravo!" by his supporters in the courtroom (4096–7).

Especially in the face of charges that he was effeminate and degenerate, Moltke must also have felt the palpable loss of the masculine credentials that military uniforms visually conferred. But Moltke's case was worsened by testimony from his own witnesses that his uniform was not as sacrosanct as it should have been. The public, for instance, was shocked to learn that his former wife, in fits of rage, ripped the epaulettes from his uniform and regularly beat him so "black and blue" that at one point he had to take a temporary leave from his position as commandant of Berlin (3994). Even apart from the claims about his homosexuality, these revelations of his victimhood at the hand of his wife undermined Moltke's claim to masculinity. (At one point in the trial, Harden also accused him of wearing make-up.) And as McLaren's work on trials suggest, men who proclaimed to be innocent or helpless victims of circumstance invariably fared poorly in the courtroom.[115]

The trial's melodramatic structure led to Harden's acquittal. In ruling for the defendant, the court found the testimony of Lily von Elbe and her son to be credible. The court's verdict also relied heavily on Hirschfeld's testimony in determining that Harden's accusations against Moltke were "demonstrably true." Nevertheless, it also used the sexologist's conclusions to steer a path between the competing claims made by Harden and Moltke. On the one hand, the court followed Hirschfeld in finding that Moltke was indeed unconsciously homosexual, which absolved Harden of any libellous wrongdoing. On the other hand, labelling Moltke an unconscious homosexual also allowed the judges to determine that Harden's characterizations of Moltke were wrong and that the general's behaviour as an officer and gentleman was above reproach, that is, he had not engaged in sexual acts nor broken his word of honor. Indeed, they applauded his behaviour as "a man of honour," in particular, his decision to refrain from attacking his wife's testimony (which would have represented a breach of male chivalry), though they also used that honourable silence to conclude that her portrayal of his sexuality was essentially true.

Despite finding "a strong element of truthfulness" (*einen großen Zug von Wahrhaftigkeit*) on the part of the plaintiff, the judges' conclusion that he was a homosexual devastated Moltke, who was visibly crushed as the verdict was read aloud. Even more problematically, the judges overruled Harden's claim (supported by Hirschfeld) that he had not maligned Moltke's honour – while also assigning the blame to the general: "To the question of whether this claim is capable of making the plaintiff contemptible or of degrading him in public opinion, the court is of the opinion that an actual degradation has occurred. As long as the law recognizes Paragraph 175, which in its most extreme form prohibits the practice of homosexuality, then we must expect from a man in the position of the plaintiff to repress his sexual drives to the extent that it is not recognizable to anyone else" (4120). Thus, for all its reliance on Hirschfeld's testimony, the court parted ways with his emancipatory agenda by finding the accusation of homosexuality insulting. But rather than blaming Harden for muckraking, the court determined that Moltke was responsible for not suppressing his homosexuality sufficiently even as they accepted his claim that he had never engaged in illegal sexual acts with other men. Much as Hirschfeld's testimony replaced older notions of sodomite acts with a bio-psychological conception of homosexual identity, so too the court updated its interpretation of Paragraph 175 to ensure that it also condemned this more sophisticated understanding of homosexuality. Though the law merely criminalized certain sexual acts between two men, that is, sodomy, the judges reinterpreted it now as a general prohibition against any homosexual drives and impulses, even if that interpretation was not legally enforceable.[116] From that premise, they reasoned that Moltke was guilty *not* for *being* a homosexual, since that was beyond his control, but for *not suppressing* his homosexuality to the point where others would never able to recognize it. In this sense, then, the court drew the opposite conclusions from Harden. Rather than following Harden's reasoning that homosexuals are de facto dishonest because of their secrecy, the court found that Moltke was not secretive enough. This reasoning – blaming homosexuals for secretiveness and for not being secret enough – is, of course, a classic example of what Sedgwick calls the double bind of the closet.[117]

We might characterize the court's reasoning as a Prussian version of "don't ask, don't tell" – the Clinton-era compromise that allowed gay men and lesbians to serve in the US military to the extent that their sexual identity and behaviour did not lead fellow soldiers to read them as homosexual. Moltke was dishonourable because his behaviour and bearing were such that they "told." In rejecting Harden's claims about the inherent relationship between homosexuality and the subversion of transparent government, the court reaffirmed the traditional liberal distinction between private and public. Assuming that Moltke did experience sexual attractions to other men, that distinction was also, of course, a reaffirmation of the logic of Moltke's life prior to Harden's accusations, that is, an acceptable and necessary disjuncture between his public image as a Prussian officer and his private life, however "lamentable" as it may have been, in so far as he subordinated that private self so that it did not emerge as a disjuncture in public. Yet to the extent that his military uniform provided a heterosexual and masculine cloak for his underlying homosexual effeminacy, Prussian Army officials needed to recut the uniform to fit only healthy, masculine, and heterosexual bodies.

Conclusion

As unexpected as it was, Harden's acquittal did not bring an end to his legal battle with his high-placed opponent. While many Germans outside the courthouse celebrated the journalist as a David who had defeated a Goliath, the verdict did not please everyone, least of all Wilhelm II. In response, the state prosecutor Hugo Isenbiel, who had earlier rejected Moltke's request to bring criminal charges against the journalist, disqualified the first trial on technical grounds and at the end of December mounted his own successful prosecution of Harden, who was sentenced to four months in prison.[118] Though the Leipzig Supreme Court invalidated this second trial in May 1908, the general nevertheless prevailed in their brief third encounter before the bench in April 1909 (even after Harden secured Eulenburg's permanent disgrace in a trial in Bavaria the previous year).[119] Yet despite Moltke's legal victory, the general retired from the military and retreated to his estate.[120] Meanwhile, to prevent Harden from appealing this conviction and prolonging the scandal, representatives of Chancellor Bülow mediated a resolution in which the chancellor's office used a secret fund to cover Harden's 600-mark fine and the staggering 40,000-mark court costs, while also providing the journalist with a written statement acknowledging his "patriotic motives in writing the articles."[121]

Moreover, just as Harden's victory in the first trial proved temporary, so too did the efficacy of his melodramatic strategies in the courtroom. The *Vossische Zeitung*, for instance, rejected the journalist's claim to be uncovering a dangerous villain: "If Count Moltke had been a political evildoer whose activities had to be ended at any price! But what had this man done politically? He said himself: nothing ... Can we deny him, the most harmless of the entire group of accused, our sympathy?"[122] But if some could sympathize with Moltke, Harden's victory also gave free rein to less savoury fantasies. For example, in the *völkisch* revision of Harden's melodrama, the role of evildoer was assigned to the trial's Jewish participants – Harden, Bernstein, and Hirschfeld – who were depicted as a cabal conspiring to besmirch German masculinity and the exalted place of the Prussian military.[123] Similarly, Hirschfeld diagnosed an "epidemic" of homophobia that crossed social classes and political affiliations.[124] Finally, Isenbiel, who personally took over the prosecution in the second trial, used his considerable power to produce an entirely new script. Gone was Harden's domestic melodrama of female victimhood at the hands of a homosexual misogynist; instead, a different melodrama unfolded in which the husband became the victim of a hysterical, oversexed wife who had transformed his home life into a living hell.

Despite Moltke's victory in the second trial, the revelations of the first trial had a decisive effect on both the Prussian military's reputation and the fortunes of the homosexual emancipation movement, pushing both organizations into damage control mode. Just weeks after the verdict in the trial, the war minister Karl von Einem sought to distinguish the army's views about homosexual officers from those espoused by the WhK: "Gentlemen, there is a school of thought, a scientific one, as it calls itself, that asserts that people with these unhappy or unfortunate characteristics be viewed as completely natural, that they are entitled to equal rights [*gleichberechtigt*]. I don't want to analyze that and get involved in this dispute among scientists – for me, these people are disgusting (*Bravo! from the right*) and I despise them!"[125] In addition to parading his own homophobia, he also articulated the army's policy: "one thing is clear: such a man must never be an officer. Wherever such a man with such feelings should dwell in the army, I would like to shout to him: take your leave, remove yourself (*Quite right! from the right*), for you do not belong in our ranks. (*Bravo! from the right.*) Should he be caught, no matter who he is and where he stands, he will be destroyed."[126]

Following Einem's speech, Hirschfeld later reported, various homosexual officers sought him out "to ask what they should now do and whether anyone could tell."[127] According to the sexologist, these officers – none of whom, he parenthetically noted, had ever had sexual contact with a subordinate – were not only wholly devoted to their military careers but also had no other options: "We studied nothing outside of our military careers, our families would reject us, the pain of our mothers and the wrath of our fathers would be boundless," suggesting that suicide would be the only option. In response, Hirschfeld demanded: "*– and a person should voluntarily or willingly submit to such a fate?*"[128] While at least one homosexual officer did commit suicide in the final month of 1907, Hirschfeld's attempt to envelop the homosexual officer in melodramatic tropes fell flat, if only because Moltke and other officers named in the trial seemed to undermine the urgency of such threats through their willingness to endure highly public scandals rather than commit suicide.[129] Moreover, in the face of alleged homosexual misconduct against subordinates by two of them – Major Lynar and General Hohenau – the WhK's construct of an honourable and (sexually) innocent homosexual military officer, driven to suicide by social prejudice,

62 Uniform Fantasies

no longer seemed tenable. For unlike the chaste Gustav in *Der fremde Gott*, whose melodramatic innocence is guaranteed by the duplicitous behaviour of a licentious widow, homosexual officers who pressured their subordinates into sex seemed to provide incontrovertible evidence that such men were in fact a dangerous threat to German morality and military preparedness.

But the scandal did not only end the melodramatic strategies of the WhK, it also damaged the overall efficacy of its political work. As Hirschfeld acknowledged in the opening lines of final edition of the *Monatsberichte* in December 1907, the Scientific-Humanitarian Committee "now faced the most serious crisis since its founding."[130] Alarmed at Hirschfeld's willingness to participate in a homosexual witch-hunt and publicly certify a man's homosexual identity against his will, WhK members fled the organization in droves and funding dried up. Even as late as October 1909, Hirschfeld reported that "the period of decline" in the movement "has continued to progress": not only did the planned effort to replace the *Monatsbericht* with a full-scale academic publication fail in 1908, but the organization lacked the funds to publish its annual yearbook, and instead had to make do with shorter quarterly reports for a while.[131]

Finally, Harden's victory in the first trial hastened the ongoing process of narrowing the contours of the military uniform. Because the Prussian officer corps had largely been the preserve of royal family members and sons of the nobility (until increasing military expansion made it necessary to open the ranks to the bourgeoisie), the military uniform had long functioned as an extension of their representational politics. As such, the uniform was roomy enough to clothe all different sorts of bodies and gendered embodiments, including effeminate figures such as Moltke. However, with the increasing linkage of effeminacy to homosexuality in the diagnostics of Hirschfeld and other sexologists, the officer's uniform was slowly recut to fit only those whose gendered comportment matched the expectations for heterosexual and martial masculinity. For instance, though Einem could still defend the not-yet-guilty General Hohenau in his speech "as a man, entirely a soldier" and "an excellent military aide-de-camp of his majesty, a brilliant regiment commander who kept his regiment in excellent discipline and order, whom his officer corps respected and loved, and who had a happy marriage," he painted Moltke, whom he also knew personally, as "a highly educated man, highly musical, perhaps a little too amiable [*liebenswürdig*], but exceptionally witty [*geistreich*] in conversation."[132] While the supposedly happily married Hohenau cut a manly and soldierly figure, Moltke – despite some positive qualities – seemed better suited to the ladies' salon than to the war room or command staff. Even in his revised affidavit in the second trial, Hirschfeld articulated similar concerns, pointing out that the language of friendship in the letters Moltke wrote to Eulenburg, though "quite common in the time of Goethe and Jean Paul, must be interpreted very differently in our technical and military era."[133] Moreover, the general's "emotional make-up" (*Gefühlskomplex*), in particular, its "especially high sensitivity with strong aesthetic proclivities and a certain tendency toward mysticism" was, as the sexologist explained, "at any rate not typical [*gewöhnlich*] for a soldier."[134] Yet while the masculinization of the uniform – and those who wore it – seemed to solve the military's public relations crisis resulting from Harden's campaign against Moltke, the danger posed by effeminate officers paled in comparison with those who coerced their subordinates into having sex with them. It is to the broader contours of this debate – which revolved around the systematic abuse of soldiers and the army's efforts to cover it up – that we turn to next.

Chapter Two

Disciplinary Abuses: From Military Secrecy to Sadism in the Army

Within the international military community of the day, the Prussian-German Army enjoyed a reputation as the world's most disciplined force. For outside observers like Edward Field, a captain in the US Army writing in 1892, Germany was "the greatest military nation of the world," in part because it achieved "the maximum of discipline with the minimum of punishment."[1] Indeed, as the second European army to ban corporal punishment in 1808 after France, the Prussian Army outpaced most of its competitors, with liberal Bavaria following only in 1848, and the armies of most other nations still much later.[2] But while outside observers professed admiration, many inside Germany nonetheless decried the German Army's excessive inculcation of discipline. For instance, Rudolf Krafft, a former lieutenant in the Bavarian Army and ardent critic of German military policy, complained that "the soldier is forever being commanded about, everything is ordered, every individual initiative [*Regung*] is frowned upon as soon as it is not by chance covered with an order of a higher purpose [*Ansicht*]," that is, an order from above.[3] The result, according to Krafft, was not only a soul-crushing lack of autonomy that critics labelled *Kadavergehorsam* (literarily, the obedience of a cadaver) but also a breeding ground for all sorts of physical and psychological abuse.[4] Yet in light of the frequency with which Social Democrats and other liberal critics of military policy gave speeches on the physical abuse of soldiers by their superiors, commonly referred to as *Soldatenmisshandlungen*, historians have devoted surprisingly little research to the issue.[5]

Because this culture of discipline was underwritten by Prussian military law, the army's legal departures from civilian conventions became a major focus in the public debate on the mistreatment of soldiers. According to critics like August Bebel, the leader of the Social Democratic Party (SPD), military law contributed to Soldatenmisshandlungen since the military criminal code (*Militärstrafgesetzbuch* or MStGB) meted out "punishment of downright brutal severity" for even small acts of insubordination while bestowing "ridiculously minor and mild" sentences on perpetrators of abuse.[6] And since military trials were closed to the public, the element of secrecy proved to be the third and most controversial aspect of the debate. While the Prussian military leadership defended secret trials as essential to maintaining discipline, critics worried aloud about the potential for a miscarriage of justice. In his speech, for instance, Bebel equated Prussian military courts, "from which nothing escapes into the public," with lay Fehmic courts that operated in parts of Germany, particularly in Westphalia, from the middle ages through the eighteenth century and that had a sinister reputation for issuing death sentences in secret sessions.[7]

As it was, the debate over military secrecy extended far beyond questions of justice and discipline. On a grander scale, the secretive nature of military justice was merely part and parcel of the Prussian Army's overall strategy for dealing with the Reichstag and the German public – a bureaucratic practice that Max Weber labelled "administrative secrecy."[8] For while chancellors and war ministers typically withheld information by invoking the Kaiser's "right of command" (*Kommandogewalt*), the military cabinet also successfully diminished the scope of the war minister's office in 1883, in order to drastically reduce his ability to respond to parliamentary interpolations.[9] The army's effort to hide the maltreatment of soldiers was also aided by its own processes of professionalization over the course of the nineteenth century, which had isolated barracks from civilian spaces. As Eugen Richter, a leader of the Freeminded People's Party, noted during the second major Reichstag debate on Soldatenmisshandlungen, "earlier, soldiers were instructed more in public than is the case today. The training grounds lay just off the street. Today it is totally different; now the barracks are secluded; they have been removed from the sight of passers-by through high walls, and thus the oversight [*Kontrolle*] of the public; as much as one may speak of oversight, it is as good as absent."[10] Finally, the military also employed a variety of legal tactics to squelch efforts to disseminate information about abuses, such as court-martialling former military personnel who published personal memoirs or exposés about Soldatenmisshandlungen (as well as other unsavoury details about army life) and prosecuting newspaper editors for libel. As one leader of the military cabinet reportedly said, "The army must remain an isolated [*abgesonderter*] body into which no one dare peer with critical eyes."[11]

But while Weber hypothesized that every form of domination "must in some decisive point be *secret rule*," his friend and colleague Georg

Simmel took the analysis of secrecy even further.[12] In fact, the Prussian Army – especially the officer corps and the upper leadership – exhibited several characteristics that Simmel ascribed to secret societies, such as their strict hierarchical structure, their sense of exclusivity, and their reliance on ritual.[13] Nevertheless, as Simmel pointed out, secrecy was a double-edged weapon that carried risks as well as benefits. In particular, he observed that "the natural impulse to idealization, and the natural timidity of men, operate to one and the same end in the presence of secrecy; viz., to heighten it by phantasy, and to distinguish it by a degree of attention that published reality could not command."[14] Thus, while secrecy may have served as an impediment to actual knowledge about Soldatenmisshandlungen, giving the military an initial advantage over both Parliament and public, it also became a particularly strong catalyst for an array of powerful fantasies about the nature of military discipline as a form of gender and sexual violence within the army.

As might be expected, these fantasies were as divided as the political opinions on Prussian military discipline and jurisprudence. Thus, this chapter focuses on two opposing fantasies about the erotic nature of the violent excesses inherent in the Prussian Army, both of which were anchored in its institutional secrecy. Both, moreover, correspond to Foucault's assertion in the first volume of *The History of Sexuality* that "historically, there have been two great procedures for producing the truth about sex."[15] In the first, which he labelled *ars erotica*, the truth of sex is derived from the practice and accumulated experience of the master, who "can transmit this art in an esoteric manner and as the culmination of an initiation in which he guides the disciple's progress with unfailing skill and severity."[16] In the second, which Foucault labelled *scientia sexualis*, procedures, such as the confession, were developed for telling the truth of sex, with the result that individuals and institutions "dedicated themselves to speaking of [sex] ad infinitum, while exploiting it as *the* secret."[17] While Foucault consigned *ars erotica* to the Orient or the past – "China, Japan, Rome, the Arabo-Muslim societies" – and presented *scientia sexualis* as a modern Western phenomenon, both were in fact present in the German discourse on same-sex desire within the military around roughly the same time at the end of the nineteenth century.[18] And even as *ars erotica* clearly celebrated the army's institutional violence, in part because it redirected male-male desire from a direct expression of sexuality into forms of camaraderie more useful to the military, it did not prevent adherents from supporting the decriminalization of male-male sexual acts under the name of an incipient identity. Conversely, despite its opposition to military secrecy and disciplinary abuses, the framework of *scientia sexualis* had its limits as a political strategy for ending the Prussian military's institutional secrecy. For like in the melodramatic airing of Moltke's private sexual life, revealing sordid details of same-sex behaviour that secretive military courts otherwise kept hidden was itself a violation of the public's sensibilities.

To unpack the various and contradictory fantasies at work in the discourse on the erotic nature of institutional violence in the Prussian Army, this chapter is divided into two parts. The first section focuses on the paradigmatic example of *ars erotica* in Ernst von Wildenbruch's 1892 novella *Das edle Blut* (Noble blood). Far from disavowing the erotic nature of male bonding and violence in the military, Wildenbruch construes them as essential features of the army as a secret society whose truths must be esoterically transmitted from one generation to another, here staged as a civilian narrator's interpretation of a story that a retired officer tells him about his childhood in a Prussian military academy. At the core of the officer's story is an incident involving the mysterious disappearance and reappearance of a important component of the military uniform – a sword-belt – that symbolizes both the social and material differences in class and individual bodies – a lack of uniformity and sameness – that uniforms cannot completely cover and that, in the story, initiates illicit desire and the need for violence.

Though the 1892 novella remained popular – both in Germany and abroad – until well into the 1920s, the appeal of the military as a secret society was dealt a blow in the same year by the SPD's publication of a secret edict from Duke Georg of Saxony, which provided official confirmation that the problem of abuse was in fact even more severe than critics had imagined. As a result, commentators began to deploy the second procedure for producing the truth of sexuality. Thus, the second section pursues the public battle to shape the meaning of Soldatenmisshandlungen as the obscene underside of Prussian-German militarism. Drawing on Reichstag debates, journalistic essays, and medical treatises, I trace the effort to pathologize the maltreatment of soldiers as a form of sadism, especially after it became known through testimony at the first Harden-Moltke trial that high-ranking officers of the elite Guards had been coercing their subordinates to have sex with them.

Ars Erotica: From Administrative Secrecy to Secret Society

Perhaps more than any other text from this period, Ernst von Wildenbruch's novella celebrates the military as a secret society of sorts. A grandson of Prince Louis Ferdinand of Prussia and thus a distant cousin of Kaiser Wilhelm II, the prolific author and his works were largely forgotten after the First World War.[19] Though the historical play

Die Quitzkows is probably his most important work, the novella *Das edle Blut* was easily his most popular story. First published in 1892 in the prestigious *Deutsche Rundschau*, its publication in book form went through 24 editions by 1896, 75 editions by 1905, and 240 by 1969, indicating the story's longevity as a canonical work for German boys.[20] The work also became a staple of reading lists for German programs in the United States, with multiple editions by various editors and presses.[21] Like many German novellas, *Das edle Blut* tells a story within a story and features two narrators: an outer story narrated by a civilian law clerk, who listens to a mysterious story told by a gruff retired colonel and set long ago in the Prussian cadet school. Because the narrative frame of the outer story holds the key for interpreting the mysterious truths of the inner story, *Das edle Blut* dramatizes a fundamental feature of militarism as esoteric practice, that is, as the transmission of military values and knowledge to an audience of civilians.

Violence and secrets – in the form of withheld information as well as seemingly impenetrable mysteries – are at the heart of both inner and outer stories. The novella's opening sentences announce the first of these in the form of a question when, sitting in a deserted wine-tavern one afternoon, the civilian narrator observes the retired colonel looking out the window: "Are there people, I wonder, who are entirely free from curiosity? – People who, when they see someone looking attentively and interestedly at an unknown object, are able to pass by without feeling in the least an itching desire to stop, to follow the direction of the other's gaze and find out what mysterious thing [*Geheimnissvolles*] it is he sees?"[22] As it turns out, "the mysterious thing" happens to be a fight among school boys that apparently takes place every day and invariably plays out the same way: the tall school bully beats up a hapless "short and fat boy" until he is saved by his younger and even smaller brother, who despite his shorter stature overwhelms the bully with his ferocity.

The daily fight between school boys, however, is less of a mystery than the colonel's enthusiasm in watching it. The move from the narrative frame to the inner story occurs after the colonel, faced with the prospect of having to order an entire bottle for himself, silently invites the civilian narrator to join him in imbibing a special vintage, "a noble blood." When, upon taking a sip, the overeager narrator agrees, he receives a look from the gruff and distant colonel "as if he would say: 'What do you know of –'" (132), at which point the elder man slowly launches into a story from long ago that was stirred up by the fight they just witnessed. That the story will convey knowledge from a "master" to an eager candidate is signified by the colonel's initial reluctance: "His gaze wandered over me again as if examining me to see whether I could listen. He did not question, I did not speak, but I looked at him and my glance may have replied: 'Tell me the story'" (133).

As the title of the novella, the concept of "noble blood" serves as the enigmatic symbol whose true meaning can only be unlocked through the civilian narrator's (and by implication, the civilian readers') correct interpretation of the colonel's story. According to Martin Swales, the nineteenth-century German novella created an "intrinsically symbolic constellation," which established "a dual sense of concrete reality on the one hand and of newness of understanding on the other."[23] Such a situation is intricately tied to the dynamics of secrecy itself, since, as Simmel observes, "secrecy secures, so to speak, the possibility of a second world alongside of the obvious world."[24] Within the novella, this secret world is not only represented by the enigmatic symbol of "noble blood" but also, in fact, by the military itself. As Richter noted in connection to Soldatenmisshandlungen, part of the military's secretiveness derived from its architectural isolation. The colonel emphasizes this secretive feature by explaining that the former cadet academy's main building "surrounds a rectangular court called the 'Square Court' which you can't see … from the outside as you pass" (133).[25] But rather than serving as an illicit secret, the hidden grounds and buildings of the cadet school hold a covert and "ancient" knowledge. As our attentive civilian guide announces, "his words made me feel that he knew not only the building but also not a few things that had happened there" (133).

The "few things that happened there" revolve around two brothers, the von Ls, who are strikingly similar to the two brothers involved in the fight that the colonel and civilian narrator have just witnessed: the older one is big, clumsy and ugly, while the younger one is small, strikingly attractive, and, when called upon, ferocious. Because, as the colonel remarks, "such a difference between two brothers I have really never seen since" (135), they themselves constitute a strange mystery of sorts. At the end of their first year in the cadet school, they are involved in the mysterious disappearance of an elegant sword-belt that one of the graduating cadets had specially made for himself. After the younger one returns it, the cadets identify the older brother as the culprit and punish him themselves. Following a brutal and sadistic beating executed by K, a mean-spirited cadet not unlike the bully in the street fight, the cadets agree to never talk about it again. But when K maliciously blurts it out one day, the younger L turns into a ferocious wildcat, mercilessly punching him in the face until the commanding officer pulls him off. However, while K lies defeated and bleeding from the nose, the young L falls into an epileptic fit and dies.

As this synopsis suggests, the violence in the inner story constitutes both a secret means of punishing a crime and a not-so-secret means of enforcing that secret. But both the crime and the desire to keep it secret are inextricably linked to the cadets' bonds, whose fragility is symbolized by the sword-belt (*Koppel*), an accessory for all Prussian officers' uniforms. Like the concept of "noble blood," the sword-belt is an overdetermined symbol. As a component of military dress, it represents the uniform identity of the boys in allegiance to the Prussian monarch. And because it fastens the sword (a classic phallic symbol), it is also deeply resonant of masculinity and the male bonds that underlie military camaraderie. Indeed, the word *Koppel* derives from the Latin word *cōpulāre* (to bind with a band or ribbon) and is related to the English word "couple" – and, for that matter, "copulation."[26] Nevertheless, what should be a symbol of unity and uniformity is in the case of this particular belt a mark of difference and distinction, for "it was of patent leather, narrower, and more elegant than the ordinary belts furnished by the government. He could afford to do things like that, for he used to have money sent [to] him from home. He had shown the sword-belt to everybody, for he was disgracefully proud of it, and the other cadets had admired it" (139). Because such a belt is unattainable for most of the cadets, especially the brothers L, who as sons of a poor major are likely attending the cadet academy on a king's scholarship, it also signifies a class difference that exists within the supposed uniformity of the cadet school – and of the military in general.[27]

Meanwhile, its disappearance rocked the entire school and "remained a mystery [*Geheimnis*] and a foul one at that" (140). Within the conventions around which the nineteenth-century novella is organized, the disappearance of the sword-belt represents the classic enigmatic event that both sets the plot in motion and foregrounds the story's interpretive conundrum. Moreover, its sudden reappearance and return to its rightful owner constitutes an even more unusual incident: "And then something remarkable happened, something that made more of a sensation than what had gone before; all at once the senior got his sword-belt back again" (140). Both mysteries, however, stand in stark contrast to Little L's reputed transparency and character. Though the colonel praises Little L's generosity – he maintains his slovenly brother's uniform, he saves his classmates by calling out the correct answer to questions in class – it is his physical beauty that seals his popularity and power at the cadet school. While Big L "was a thickset fellow with clumsy limbs and a heavy head," Little L "was like a willow-rod [*Weidengerte*], he was so slender and supple. He had a small, narrow head and blond, wavy hair that curled naturally and a little nose, like a young eagle and altogether – he was a boy –" (135). If such a description seems a little too erotically charged, it should, for as the colonel tells his listener "Don't imagine that the cadets were indifferent to these things; on the contrary. The brothers had scarcely come to the military school in Berlin ... before the matter was decided; no one paid any attention to Big L, and Little L was a general favorite" (135).

Though the Colonel extols Little L's good looks as a force that unites all the cadets, the details of his story indicate that they in fact threatened the traditional hierarchy of the military as much as the graduating cadet's sword-belt disrupted the monotonous uniformity of the cadets' dress. In addition to escaping any consequences for calling out answers in class, Little L disrupts the natural hierarchy among the cadets, since he "scarcely got down into the yard before two or three of the other big boys took him by the arm and made him walk with them. And they were seniors too, whereas generally a senior would never have dreamed of walking with a 'knapsack' as they called the boys in the junior class – that was far beneath their dignity. But it was very different when the boy was Little L; they made an exception in his case" (135–6). It may have been Wildenbruch's straightforward acknowledgment of same-sex attraction in this story that led the Scientific Humanitarian Committee (WhK) to ask him to serve as one of the first four symbolic signatures on their 1899 petition to the Reichstag for the decriminalization of homosexuality.[28]

As an object of desire, Little L also plays a pivotal role in the cadets' decision to punish Big L themselves during their secret meeting after lights-out, a gathering that mirrors both the closed military trials and the medieval Fehmic courts that served as a touchpoint for Bebel's critique of the secret trials stipulated by Prussian military law. Though K is opposed to Little L's presence at the meeting, the others quickly overrule him. Similarly, during "the council," K recommends that they "go to the Captain and tell him everything" (142). However, K's proposal is doomed when Little L comes forward out of the corner and tries to speak. Though K initially forbids him from speaking, the cadets are moved by Little L's sobbing and again overrule him. Eventually they rally around a nameless cadet's proposal to let Big L decide if he would rather have his fellow cadets give him "a good flogging and then bury the whole matter" (144) or tell the captain of his crime. Thus, the cadets' feelings for Little L lead them to subvert not only the military's hierarchy (going to the captain) but also the natural order, represented by K, who was "the biggest and strongest" among them and whose words should have carried the most weight. More importantly, it propels them to substitute a more public and official response to Big L's crime with an entirely secretive one based in violence.

The "good flogging" that Big L agrees to submit to is a brutal affair, and not unusual for nineteenth-century military academies, at least in Prussia.[29] After a cadet retrieves one of the canes used to beat the dirt and dust out of clothes, Big L lies face down on a table while four cadets hold down his arms and legs. The task of executing the blows is given to K "because he was the strongest" (145). With each blow, which "sounded through the room," Big L's "body fairly writhed on the table so that the cadets were scarcely able to keep hold of his hands and feet" (145). Meanwhile, in order to keep his brother from screaming – since that would wake the cadets from other classes and then "the whole thing will come out" (145) – Little L "had thrown both arms round his brother's head and hugged it with convulsive strength. His eyes were wide open and staring, his face was like the plaster on the wall, his whole body trembled" (145). Meanwhile, "with all eyes fixed" on Little L, the other cadets find themselves at the limits of what they can tolerate, too (145). As K winds up for a fourth blow, three or four cadets push him out of the way and take the switch from him. To conclude the punishment, one of the cadets announces: "Justice had been done. […] Now the affair is over and buried … every one of us will now shake hands with L-1, and whoever says another word about this matter is a scoundrel" (146).

As the cadets' focus on Little L during the flogging suggests, the secret punishment is deeply connected to the libidinal economy that circulates around the attractive boy. This dimension comes to the surface when the colonel reports what happened next: after shaking hands with Big L, the cadets "as if at a word of command, … rushed at Little L. There was a regular scrimmage around the boy, for every one wanted to shake his hand and press it. Those on the outside of the throng reached in over the others' shoulders. Some of the boys even climbed up on the table to get at him; they stroked his head, patted his shoulders and back, and all the time a general whisper went on: 'Little L, you splendid little chap, you splendid Little L'" (146). Though so sudden that it seemed as if the boys were obeying a military command, the frenzied disorder of boys reaching over other boys and even scrambling onto the table on which Big L was flogged represents an orgiastic eruption of the erotic tension that built up during the punishment scene. In addition to crediting Little L, already equated with a willow rod, for the entire idea for this brutal scene of corporal punishment, they also rush to him as if he had given them permission to experience something akin to excessive enjoyment, Žižek's translation of the Lacanian term jouissance. In contrast to mere pleasure, jouissance marks a form of transgression that, while pleasurable in a hypnotic and nearly irresistible way, has a "properly traumatic character: we are not dealing with simple pleasures, but with a violent intrusion that brings more pain than pleasure."[30] As such, it characterizes not only the hypnotic intensity of the horrific punishment scene itself (the fixation of all eyes on Little L) but also the surge of ecstatic relief at its conclusion, expressed in the excessive rush to touch, pat, and pet the object of desire.

By punishing Big L by themselves in secret, and then swearing to keep what they have done a secret, the cadets have constituted themselves as a secret society within the military cadet academy, itself a secret society of sorts. But whereas the stable hierarchy of the military ensured that the cadets' daily life was "rigorous, simple, and monotonous," the secret society formed by the cadets emerges in opposition to the oppressive regulatory order of the academy.[31] According to Simmel, "whether the secret society, like the *Vehme*, complements the inadequate judicature of the political area; or whether, as in the case of conspiracies or criminal bands, it is an up-rising against the law of that area ... – in either case the apartness [*Heraussonderung*] which characterizes the secret society has the tone of a freedom."[32] Though Simmel emphasizes the experience of freedom, he seems to realize implicitly that the problem is with the law itself, for in his examples the law is either inadequate at securing justice or represents a form of "despotism" and "police control."[33] The freedom that the secret society of cadets enjoys in the novella is both the one-time expression of their desire for Little L – itself an excessive passion prohibited by the law – and the resulting intense camaraderie that arises through their shared knowledge of their secret. As Žižek contends, "a shared lie" (and, we might clarify, a shared secret, including a shared self-deception about the meaning of their desire for Little L) "is an incomparably more effective bond for a group than the truth."[34]

But despite its power to establish bonds, a shared secret is also an unstable binding agent, for secrecy does not just feed its own circuit of silence; secrets also want to be told. Again, Simmel stresses that "secrecy involves a tension which, at the moment of revelation, finds its release [*Lösung*]. This constitutes the climax [*Peripetie*] in the development of the secret; in it the whole charm [*Reiz*] of secrecy concentrates to its highest pitch."[35] Though Simmel's original German is phrased in a matter-of-fact manner, the 1906 translator's rendering of it into English as "release" and "climax" imbues the moment of revelation with a libidinous undercurrent that, at other points in Simmel's essay, is more explicitly present. For example, Simmel writes of "the seductive temptation [*den verführerischen Anreiz*] to break through the barriers [of secrecy] by gossip [*Ausplaudern*] or confession. This temptation accompanies the psychical life of the secret like an overtone."[36] While such acts of revelation may involve a giving in to this kind of temptation, there are more sinister dimensions to the revelation of a secret. As Simmel also points out, secrecy "is sustained by the consciousness that it might be exploited, and therefore confers power to modify the fortunes, to produce surprises, joys, and calamities, even if the latter be only misfortunes to ourselves."[37] A seemingly irresistible temptation that may lead to our own misfortunate is, of course, a pretty exact description of jouissance.

Because of their desire for Little L, most of the cadets seem intent on keeping secret Big L's crime and their decision to punish him on their own. The same, however, cannot be said for K, who either never desired Little L or who, in an identification with the law that also prohibits same-sex relations, transformed his desire into hatred. K's disruption of the erotic group bonds is on display during a demonstration of electricity in a physics class, when all the boys are required to hold hands to form a circuit through which a current can pass. K prevents this symbolic representation of the boys' mutual desires and bonds when he refuses to take Big L's hand (they are seated alphabetically and by age, itself a symbol of order in the military), making "a face as if he were being asked to take hold of a toad" (147). K's decision is in effect a reminder to all the other cadets of Big L's crime, and indeed the latter "sank back in his seat without a word and sat there crimson with shame" (148).

Unsurprisingly, violence once again emerges as the glue that re-establishes the group bonds and enforces the oath of secrecy. In response to K's refusal to touch his brother, Little L "got up from his place, ... squeezed into the latter's place beside tall K, seized his hand and brought it down on the bench with all his strength so that the great bully screamed with the sudden pain" (148). In essence, Little L takes matters into his own hands and enforces K's oath of silence with violence. Though the ensuing fight between the two is broken up by the teacher, the other cadets join in at the end of class. After throwing their books at K's head, "they scrambled across tables and benches to get at tall K, ... tann[ing] the big bully's hide till it fairly smoked" (149). Thus, unlike the caning of Big L, at which the cadets merely looked on, this time they join in on the pummelling. And whereas the first punishment ended with an orgiastic rush to touch Little L, this time the scramble over tables remains at the level of (orgiastic) violence. In a setting that prohibits or severely limits the expression of sexual desire for other males, it may be that they have transformed their desire (for Little L) into violence (towards K). As the only sanctioned form of expressing passion between male subjects, it may explain the colonel's strange delight in witnessing the initial fight between the boys outside the tavern – a kind of ersatz for other proscribed expressions of passionate desire.

In this case, the thrashing that K receives at the hands of Little L and the other cadets succeeds momentarily in ensuring the secret. Nevertheless, the damage to the group bonds has been done, for the electricity experiment never takes place. But the real moment of treacherous revelation occurs shortly thereafter when K encounters the two brothers walking arm in arm through the archway between the inner and outer courtyard, which was forbidden by the rules (149). K – forever cognizant of rules – calls out to them: "What do you mean by walking here arm in arm? Do you want to block the way for decent people, you gang of thieves?" (150). K's verbalization of what all had promised to keep secret draws an even more violent response from Little L. The colonel recalls that "Little L had climbed up tall K just like a wildcat. He was hanging onto the latter's collar with his left hand, so that the tall fellow was half-strangled, and with his right first he was hammering him, smash – smash – smash – right in tall K's face wherever he happened to hit him, so that the blood streamed out of his nose like a waterfall" (150). Even as the authoritarian officer on duty issued booming commands for him to desist, Little L's pounding and animal-like screams persist until the officer has to drag him away by force, after which "Little L rolled his eyes, fell full length on the ground and writhed in convulsions" (151) before dying the next day.

There are several ways to interpret Little L's death. Of course, foreshadowing throughout the story has repeatedly associated Little L's pasty pallor with death. But by being unable to prevent K's revelation of the secret, Little L's presence in the narrative becomes not only superfluous but also, in a psychoanalytic sense, impossible, since the secret of Big L's crime and punishment was only superficially covering up the narrative's acknowledgment of the cadets' desire for Little L. Though the text explicitly concedes the attraction that Little L exerts on all the others, the extent of that desire nevertheless constitutes a psychological secret of sorts whose true libidinal nature must be repressed from the boys' own consciousness. As Simmel – almost in anticipation of Lacan – reminds us, desire itself circulates around mysteries and secrets: "That which we can see through plainly to its last ground shows us therewith the limit of its attraction and forbids our phantasy to do its utmost in adding to the reality. [...] The fact is rather that, if the utmost attractiveness of another person is to be preserved for us, it must be presented to us in part in the form of vagueness or impenetrability."[38] This "vagueness or impenetrability" also emerges in the story's narrative. For instance, while the colonel claims that "Little L couldn't hide anything" (137), why does K refer to *both* brothers as a "gang of thieves" [*ihr Diebsgelichter*]? Should we read K's accusation to mean that he believes Little L was also involved in Big L's crime? Or that Little L's attractiveness to the other cadets is itself implicitly a crime – both as an incipient stage of acts that would be illegal or as a subversion of hierarchical order within the military itself? At the very least, K's choice of words raises questions about the colonel's own reliability as a narrator, suggesting that his own desire for Little L may have distorted his view of the little boy. After all, Little L's goodness and transparency might merely be a fantasy that the colonel holds against indications otherwise.

Of course, the text as a whole discourages such a reading. Within the discursive domain of *ars erotica*, the experienced master is never wrong, and it is up to the pupil or disciple to correctly interpret his words. The civilian narrator who has been listening to the colonel's story thus serves as an ideal model for the reader when at the end of the story he refers to the last beads from the bottle of wine as "a last drop of noble blood" (153). Though the pronouncement repeats the earlier words he uttered brashly after taking his first sip, this time the civilian narrator speaks from a place of knowledge. To be sure, the choice of red wine as a symbol is designed to evoke Christian imagery: the blood of the saviour who has died for our sins. That this blood is noble refers not only to Little L's aristocratic background – he's a *von* L – but to the entire character of the Prussian officer corps. Indeed, the military's expansion in the second half of the nineteenth century had led to a surge of officers from bourgeois backgrounds that threatened to dilute the aristocratic character of the officer corps. In response, Wilhelm II famously recast all officers as constituting "a nobility of character" (*Adel der Gesinnung*) in an 1890 edict.[39] Most importantly, the story implies that for all its institutional secrecy, the Prussian Army carries within it a deeper knowledge about the naturalness and necessity of violence and its fundamental role in binding soldiers to one another: through their shared experience of jouissance in the brutal flogging of Big L and through their shared mourning of the beloved comrade, who stands in for those who have fallen in battle.

However, despite its obvious celebration of violence in the military, the novella ultimately seeks to distinguish any similarities between the acts of violence in the story and real-life incidents of Soldatenmisshandlungen. It achieves that goal by briefly introducing the figure of the "mean lieutenant," who never failed to find problems with the cadets' uniforms at inspection, which he used to cancel the victims' Sunday leave. In contrast, the colonel tells the narrator: "[A]fterward whenever I noticed that any one was setting out to harass and torment the men – there was none of that in my regiment later; they knew that I was there and that I wouldn't have it. To bark at the men once in awhile, even to make it pretty strong at times, to send them to the guard-room, that does no harm – but to torment a man – it takes a mean chap to do that!" (138). The impression is that Soldatenmisshandlungen are caused by bad apples among the NCOs and officers, while those who have learned the ups and downs of camaraderie – especially through the erotic forms of hazing – are committed to upholding a higher ethical standard, one that is fair even if it is, admittedly, severe.

Yet the real distinction the novella seeks to draw is between Little L's thrashing of K and the latter's brutal flogging of Big L. Both boys use violence to punish a wrongdoing that damaged group bonds: while Big L's theft of the sword-belt violated the cadets' sense of trust, K's verbalization of the group's secret undermined those bonds once again (while also threatening to reveal the cadets' forbidden desires for Little L). But whereas Little L's act of violence is portrayed as a selfless act (after all he dies), K's personality and penchant for violence are more enigmatic: "He was not at all popular either, for boys have a tremendously keen instinct, and they probably felt that the fellow had a very mean, cowardly, miserable soul in his big body" (143). Thus, unlike Little L, who is supposedly incapable of hiding his feelings or thoughts, K's strong body hides a weak and nasty soul. Part of what makes him nasty and enigmatic is his inexplicable dislike of Little L. But his fellow cadets also recognize him as a bully: "He was one of those who never dare to attack boys of their own size, but ill-treat smaller and weaker ones" (143).

Though the story goes no further than labelling K a bully, a "coward," and "a revengeful, vindictive, treacherous villain" (149), it tentatively suggests a deeper pathology. On the one hand, K regularly and repeatedly aligns himself with the institution and its hierarchy. He initially argues for reporting Big L to the captain, and after he receives his first thumping from Little L in the physics class, his fellow cadets believe that he would still prefer "to go to the Captain and tell him the whole story from the beginning" (149). But the real indications of K's underlying pathology comes in the punishment scene itself. For unlike the other cadets, who find the ordeal both fascinating and horrifying (the very characteristics of jouissance), K not only delivers the painful blows but also doesn't seem to know when to stop. In Lacanian parlance, K is a sadist, for in executing the punishment he has turned himself into an instrument of the symbolic order of the military, for whose benefit he carries out the task. As Žižek explains, "the sadistic pervert answers the question 'How can the subject be guilty when he merely realizes an objective, externally imposed necessity?' by subjectively assuming this objective necessity, by finding enjoyment in what is imposed on him."[40] That is, rather than partaking of the libidinal desires that cadets harbour for Little L – marked as a kind of freedom over and against the military's disciplinary hierarchy – Big K's passion is thoroughly aligned with that of the natural order (his physical size) and the disciplinary hierarchy of the military (meting out punishment in the name of the law). But what is only incipient in this story and positioned against same-sex attraction, would soon emerge as a specific pathology that, congruent with homosexuality, could be employed politically by critics of Soldatenmisshandlungen more generally, as we will see in the next section.

Scientia Sexualis: Sadism in the Army

The foundations for the pathologization of Soldatenmisshandlungen were also laid at the time that Wildenbruch's story was published, when in the same year the SPD's newspaper *Vorwärts* obtained and published a secret decree by the Duke of Saxony, commander of the XIIth Army Corps. As an edict for officers under Duke Georg's command, the secret order was never intended to be shared with a civilian audience. As a result, its publication undercut government efforts to downplay the nature and extent of abuses by providing official evidence to the contrary: that such abuses were essentially severe, persistent, and pervasive.[41] Indeed, rather than explaining away the problem as the result of momentary lapses, Duke Georg's order offered official confirmation of the seriousness of the crimes, which he described "as a sophisticated form of torture, as the discharge [*Ausfluß*] of a barbarism and brutalization that one could hardly imagine was possible from the pool from which our NCOs and instructors are recruited and which should never be possible under the oversight that should be exerted in the army."[42]

It is perhaps no surprise that just days after *Vorwärts* published the order, the government introduced a new bill to strengthen the law governing military secrecy. Though the Reichstag didn't take up the bill until the following year, many deputies recognized its potential implications for reporting on Soldatenmisshandlungen. In particular, debate revolved around the word *Nachrichten*, which roughly translates not only as intelligence but also as message, announcement, and news. Despite government assurances to the contrary, Carl Ludwig von Bar of the left-liberal German Freeminded Party contended that "information about military discipline, *Soldatenmißhandlungen*, etc. could be construed as

Nachrichten."[43] Adolf Gröber of the Catholic Center Party agreed, warning that "[i]f one can characterize such things as military secrets, then there is hardly anything in Germany that couldn't be characterized as a military secret."[44] Despite the war minister's pleas, the deputies defeated the amendment to restore the word (131 to 97), before ultimately passing the bill minus other key provisions that would have allowed the government to punish efforts to publish military information or confiscate these publications. In light of Duke Georg's secret order, then, the military leadership's adherence to a policy of secrecy inevitably raised suspicions that it was probably hiding a far worse situation – a dimension that Simmel called "the manifold ethical negativeness of secrecy."[45]

But while the government sought to strengthen its administrative secrecy over the abuse of soldiers, the Reichstag demanded sweeping changes to diminish them. In addition to calling for harsher punishments for abusers and making it easier for soldiers to complain about their treatment, representatives focused on opening military trials to the public (and thus to public scrutiny) as the most promising avenue for curbing abuses. In the immediate wake of Duke Georg's order, the Freeminded Party, for instance, introduced a resolution calling on the government to undertake a substantive reform of the Prussian military code of criminal procedures (*Militair-Strafgerichts-Ordnung* or MStGO), the administrative regulations governing the operations of military courts, which were first promulgated in 1845 under Friedrich Wilhelm IV, extended to the North German Federation in 1867, and then reaffirmed in Article 61 of the German constitution of 1871.[46] The Freeminded Party's resolution called for establishing standing military courts, introducing oral arguments and presentation of evidence, and making all trials public. Though the resolution ultimately failed 140 to 103, even some of those who voted "no," such as Wilhelm von Kardorff of the conservative German Reich Party, signalled their dissatisfaction with the current procedures: "I will happily admit that the Prussian procedures, which are in place today in the rest of Germany, raise considerable doubts ... I am an opponent of absolute secrecy as it is handled today in our military code of criminal procedure."[47]

Over the course of the last decade of the nineteenth century, the Reichstag became ever more insistent that the government overhaul the MStGO. In meeting this demand, they found a possible ally in Leo von Caprivi's replacement as chancellor: Prince Chlodwig zu Hohenlohe-Schillingsfürst, who as Bavarian minister-president had overseen that kingdom's modernization of its military criminal procedure in 1869, including making its military trials public (under the new constitution,

Bavaria and Wurttemberg continued to use their own military criminal procedures). Moreover, the new war minister, Walther Bronsart von Schellendorff, also proved to be a willing partner by drafting a new code with exactly such provisions. And when the Prussian ministry approved Bronsart's draft in 1895, it set off a constitutional crisis, for it marked the first time that ministers picked by the Kaiser simply defied his wishes.[48] Though Bronsart was quietly replaced the following year by the more compliant General Heinrich von Goßler, in the end Wilhelm II was forced to allow a new MStGO to be submitted to the Reichstag – albeit with a compromise that granted the Kaiser the right to close military trials to the public under certain conditions.[49] Bebel had predicted back in 1892 that permitting any exceptions for public trials would mean "that 99 cases out of 100 would be conducted behind closed doors, and it will remain by the old state of affairs."[50] As it turns out, even as he authorized Hohenlohe to promise the Reichstag that he would make only limited use of his right to keep certain military trials closed to the public, the Kaiser had already determined to allow public trials only in the southern German states (which already had them) while continuing to forbid them in Prussia.[51] And after 1901, when the law went into effect, Prussian military judges who followed the law and permitted public trials were removed from office.[52]

But while the government and the Reichstag wrangled over the question of the army's administrative secrecy, the details contained in Duke Georg's secret edict authorized an entirely new discursive approach to the problem of Soldatenmisshandlungen. In order to convey to his officers the seriousness of the problem, the 1892 edict listed nine of the most egregious examples of recent cases of abuse in detail. Among them, it records an NCO (a non-commissioned officer) who hit one soldier so hard on his left shoulder that he fractured his collarbone – and then to hide his crime prevented the wounded soldier from calling in sick. Another NCO tormented one mentally limited recruit to the point that he dirtied his pants, after which the NCO forced him to eat his excrement. Meanwhile, yet another NCO became so enraged at one recruit's performance during a drill that he had the soldier lay across a bench and proceeded to whip him thirty times with a leather belt across his behind. When the soldier tried to escape, he ordered his other men to hold him down and cover his mouth while he continued flogging the poor man, who was later admitted to the hospital with severe blisters.[53] For Duke Georg, these cases demonstrated a lack of restraint and oversight with worrisome consequences for morale and following orders; though he noted that some of those who suffered these excesses themselves subsequently meted out abuse to others, his order gave little thought to what led to the illegal behaviour, and instead ordered his officers to be vigilant in preventing such cases in the future. The public, meanwhile, was aghast at the detailed accounts offered in the order. For instance, the Hamburg commentator Otto Ernst Schmidt suggested that the real crimes, richly narrated in the edict, made a mockery of fantasy, for it "shows us that such things can take on real forms in the barracks. It would be folly to avail oneself of fantasy [*Phantasie*] where the reality surpasses all imagination [*Phantasie*]."[54] Even today, as the historian Hartmut Wiedner contends, such extreme forms of violence can only "be explained with the aid of pathological categories."[55]

Of course, exactly such a category emerged in 1890, when Richard von Krafft-Ebing coined the term "sadism."[56] Named after the Marquis de Sade, whose tomes exhaustively recounted stories of sexual cruelty, sadism – along with masochism, fetishism, and contrary sexual feeling (same-sex desire and transgender identity) – represented one of the four primary perversions in Krafft-Ebing's compendium of sexual deviations. Originally laid out in *Neue Forschungen auf dem Gebiet der Psychopathia Sexualis* (New research in the area of sexual pathology), the concept was quickly incorporated into the revised and extended editions of *Psychopathia Sexualis*, his magnum opus, which first appeared in 1886 and was subsequently updated and reissued fourteen times before 1903, the year after he died.[57] It was also taken up by other leading sexologists, including Albert Eulenburg, Iwan Bloch, and Sigmund Freud.[58]

Though there were disagreements among the various theorists – including whether to replace Krafft-Ebing's literary-based terminology of sadism with the Greek-derived term *Algolagnie* proposed by Albert von Schrenck-Notzing – all commentators more or less conceptualized the pathology as an excessive form of masculinity, since, according to Krafft-Ebing, "[i]t is a fact (and may be based in originary or hereditarily bred conditions) that in sexual intercourse the male plays the active, even aggressive role while the female behaves passively, defensively."[59] Indeed, by 1892, he theorized that any man's character could develop into sadism, which he now defined as "nothing else than the pathological increase into excessive and monstrous proportions of – there are possible hints of this under normal conditions – corollary symptoms of the psychological Vita sexualis, especially of the male."[60] But while it was easy for sexologists to identify the emergence of aggression and cruelty in sexual situations, it was harder for them to determine when acts of violence were driven by a pathological sexuality. As Eulenburg noted, some sadists derive such sufficient pleasure from cruelty that their actions never progressed to a sexual act.[61] Nevertheless, he emphasized: "*Naturally not every cruel behaviour is de facto a sadistic act. It becomes one rather whenever it awakens lust* [Wollust] *or whenever it is committed or attempted for the purpose (either intentionally or unintentionally) of exciting lust.*"[62] Thus, even if a sexual act was neither always the outcome nor the sadist's ultimate goal, any experience of pleasure from committing acts of violence amounted to sadism – and hence made it sexual. And because the designation of sadism relied on the subjective experience of lust rather than on the evidence of a sexual act, Eulenburg admitted that any diagnosis "must thus return to the mysterious [*geheimnisvollen*], original interconnection of the elementary feelings of 'pleasure' and 'displeasure' that are rooted in the enigmatic nature of the nervous system."[63] In the absence of direct evidence of a sexual act, then, the determination of sadism pushed the investigation back into the impenetrable mysteries of the individual psyche, where, as Foucault explained, they could be exploited "as *the* secret."[64]

Perhaps because the sexologists drew their material for sadism from criminal forensic cases as well as from individual patients they were treating in their clinical practices or the psychiatric asylums many of them oversaw, the abuse of soldiers did not initially figure into their discussions of sadism. But by the early 1900s, a high-profile criminal case of a tutor torturing two pupils, one of whom died, had put the term sadism into broader circulation.[65] One of those who saw a publishing opportunity was Hans Rau, a young and prolific author of a number of trendy texts on the issue of cruelty and sadism, including a short work with the provocative title *Der Sadismus in der Armee* (Sadism in the army).[66] Not much is known about this author who died following surgery in 1906 at the age of twenty-four.[67] In addition to writing a few manuscripts under the pseudonym A. Sper, he also wrote several works on homosexuality.[68] Because Rau suffered from pecuniary woes as well as physical maladies, his publications seem written to exploit the strong German market for lurid works stamped with an educational or "popular science" imprimatur.

Before turning to Rau's investigation of Soldatenmisshandlungen as a form of sadism, it is important to acknowledge that a few commentators on the issue of abusive tutors and sergeants found it "downright ridiculous to want to trace all these kinds of things ... back to a sexual aberration."[69] Nevertheless, discussions of Soldatenmisshandlungen did begin to invoke the term sadism. Certainly within the German medical community at this time, "sadism in the army" became an acceptable way to refer to the extreme forms of mistreatment of soldiers by their superiors.[70] More importantly, the term was invoked by political critics of militarism in their discussions of Soldatenmisshandlungen. Thus, in a 1905 piece on the topic in the *Sozialistische Monatshefte*, an independent monthly journal that served as a forum for revisionists in the SPD, Ernst Keller wrote that "it is probably not an exaggeration if serious authors consider the acts of cruelty committed by downy bearded boys as the phenomena of sadism."[71] And as a sign of the increasing currency of the term, even the Prussian war minister Karl von Einem spoke of "sadistic tendencies" during a 1906 Reichstag debate on the topic.[72] Though he insisted "that the tendency of people to mistreat soldiers ... is not produced in the barracks but rather in many cases is brought into the barracks ... [by] rough and immoral elements coming into the army," the war minister did acknowledge the role played by military discipline: "Certainly, though, this predilection [*Neigung*], these certain sadistic tendencies [*sadistische Richtungen*] – I must admit – finds in military institutions [*Einrichtungen*], in the basics of military life, a certain fertile soil which in many cases becomes a breeding ground [*Brutstätte*] whenever oversight is missing, which unfortunately also happens."[73]

But while the war minister and others used sadism as a synonym for excessive violence, in *Der Sadismus in der Armee* Rau sought to underscore its pathologically sexual nature. To do so, he cited leading authorities in the field of sexology, including Krafft-Ebing and Eulenburg, even as he quickly dismissed their complex theoretical deliberations as "incomplete and one-sided" in favour of his definition, which was in fact much more simplistic and one-dimensional: "We believe that the explanation of the sexual cruelty drive turns out to be simple when we look at the animal world. It is certain that the sexual activity of animals is almost always connected to acts of violence ... [and] is present in every living organism, even in humans" (7–8). This "popular science" approach is also evident in the book's source material, which lacked first-hand information, and relied instead on published cases, including Duke Georg's secret order, various memoirs, and the scant information about specific incidents that he took from Reichstag debates or newspaper reports.

In spite of this deficiency in scientific seriousness, *Der Sadismus in der Armee* nevertheless demonstrated a solid understanding of sadism – and Soldatenmisshandlungen – as essentially *political* issues. In fact, Rau made his political agenda explicit when at the outset he framed Soldatenmisshandlungen as an effect of militarism: "For only the current structures [*Einrichtungen*], only the spirit of modern militarism can possibly nurture [*Großziehung*] cruel instincts in the army, and only with the elimination of this condition will cruelty disappear from the army" (3–4). Like Einem's later use of the word *Einrichtung*, which suggests conditions of an institutional nature, Rau's choice of words reflected a concern with the structural dimensions of Soldatenmisshandlungen. In this sense, his focus on sadism is fundamentally linked to Sade's own concerns since, as Gilles Deleuze claims, "Sade's secret societies, his societies of libertines, are institutional societies; in a word, Sade thinks in terms of institutions."[74] Indeed, like many in left-leaning parties in the Reichstag, whose debates he cited elsewhere in his monograph, Rau explicitly attributed responsibility for the abuse of soldiers to German military law: "The military criminal code is responsible, ... [for] nothing is punished more severely than the insubordination of a subordinate against his superior" (18). And his manuscript goes on to quote and analyse key components of military law – not only the limitations on soldiers' ability to file a complaint against their superiors but also the forms of class justice that meted out harsh penalties to common soldiers who disobeyed orders while according lighter sentences to superiors – especially officers – who physically abused their subordinates.

One of the attractions of classifying Soldatenmisshandlungen as sadism was that by sexualizing the issue of mistreatment, the clandestine practice became all the more lurid and dangerous. In addition to the immediate harm to those soldiers who experienced violence from their superior officers, many of whom had to be hospitalized or ended up committing suicide to escape the abusive situation, Rau argued that this sadistic mistreatment had long-term consequences. In particular, he argued, sadism produced masochism in those soldiers who suffered disciplinary abuse and sadism in those who witnessed it. Because these men returned to civilian life, they posed a danger to all civilians, either because of the likelihood they would commit sex crimes (like *Lustmord*, a sexually driven act of murder) or because they would pervert others just as they had been perverted by their experience at the hands of a sadist. And since Rau also subscribed to the theory of degeneration, even these former soldiers' return to heterosexual relations did not remove the dangerous consequences of excessive discipline, since, he claimed, these perversions could be passed on to their offspring via reproduction. In essence, Rau's text deployed all the features of what Gayle Rubin calls the "domino theory of sexual peril" and the "fallacy of misplaced scale" in which certain forms of sexuality "are often experienced as cosmic threats."[75]

Yet because cases of abuse occurred in a male-only environment and only in rare cases included explicit sexual contact, Rau's first task was articulating the fundamentally erotic nature of Soldatenmisshandlungen, that is, turning mere acts of cruelty into sexual-pathological expressions of sadism. To be sure, many of the examples he cites, especially those contained in Duke Georg's secret order, were so cruel that they intuitively appeared to be the work of a pathological mind. But his primary means of making them expressions of unconscious sexual desires revolved around the sexual connotations of secrecy. For instance, he focused on scenes of abuse that took place at night in unobserved or seemingly private spaces like sleeping quarters or behind closed doors, places where sexual acts of any nature would presumably take place. He also emphasized examples that involved removing articles of clothing and inflicting physical pain on "private" body parts, such as brutal beatings of soldiers on their bare bottoms, applying a lit cigar to soldiers' exposed penises while they were sleeping, or forcing soldiers to clean the genitals of another soldier using a hard-bristled brush.

Rau's most important piece of evidence, though, revolved around the case of "a non-commissioned officer who was homosexual and who misused his subordinates to gratify his sexual drive countless times" (25). Though he was careful to note that "I do not view homosexuality in and of itself as a criminal phenomenon, as my other writings demonstrate," unwelcome homosexual misconduct had exemplary importance in Rau's argument for, he emphasized, "there cannot be a more horrible abuse of subordinates" (26). Yet despite serving as Rau's only example of actual sexual acts, he insisted that this incident, "which was making the rounds through the press," is not unique because "similar cases are repeatedly becoming known" (26). Nevertheless, because most cases were only uncovered "through some kind of accident, rather than through a direct report made by the victims," he explicitly suggested that the problem was much more pervasive than people thought: "Thus, who can say in reality how large the number of such horrible scenes are that play out in our army!" (26).

Unfortunately, the destruction of the Prussian military archives in the Second World War makes it impossible to answer Rau's question with any precision. Nevertheless, at about this time, the Scientific-Humanitarian Committee (WhK) had begun gathering and republishing press articles from around Germany and elsewhere pertaining to any trials, suicides, and blackmail cases involving homosexuality – including those involving military personnel. Based on these reports, it seems that during the three-year period following the publication of *Der Sadismus in der Armee* at least twelve army officers, four naval officers, and five army NCOs were either under investigation or convicted of physical contact with male subordinates in violation of Paragraph 175 of the German penal code, which prohibited "indecent conduct contrary to nature" (*widernatürliche Unzucht*) between male individuals.[76] A couple of these press items also indicated that some of these officers and NCOs were being prosecuted for abuse of their authority (*Mißbrauch*

86　Uniform Fantasies

der Dienstgewalt), covered by sections 114 to 126 of the military criminal code.[77]

Nevertheless, because military trials were generally closed to the public, the information contained in these reports is often quite sparse. For instance, one item reproduces a sentence from the "Berlin Letter" rubric in the weekly *Der Roland von Berlin*: "The 'mysterious' arrest of a lieutenant that just recently became known proves once again that modern relations [*Verkehr*] are under the sign of § 175 [*im Zeichen steht*]."[78] Here the mystery of the unnamed lieutenant's dismissal from the army is magnified by the vague reference to the anti-sodomy law. Though readers likely understood that the officer had engaged in sexual acts with another man, the lack of details imbued the dismissal with an added air of mystery. Yet even some longer articles emphasized the lack of clarity in particular cases. For instance, the Göppingen (Wurttemberg) newspaper *Der Hohenstaufe* offered a longer report of a case from November 1905 in which a first-lieutenant by the name of Jos. Oppelt and an infantryman named Ludwig Böhm were accused of violating Paragraph 175. The initial tribunal in Ingelstolt acquitted Böhm but sentenced Oppelt to two months confinement in a fortress. The president of the military court, however, appealed the decision to the military court of appeals of the 3rd Bavarian Army Corps in Nuremberg, which met on 19 January 1906, in, as the newspaper emphasized, "a secret session to which even representatives of the press were not admitted."[79] While this second military court concluded that Böhm could not be found guilty of any "moral offence" (*Sittlichkeitsvergehen*) and thus acquitted him again, it determined that Lt. Oppelt was guilty of "moral misconduct" (*sittliche Verfehlungen*), though these "were of such kind that they could not be considered illegal." This conclusion suggests that although the behaviour may have been "under the sign of Paragraph 175," it did not meet the definition of "coitus-like acts" (*beischlafähnliche Handlungen*) which after 1870 became the criteria in court cases for deciding whether Paragraph 175 had been violated and which in practice excluded mutual masturbation.[80] Instead, it found him responsible for "treatment of a subordinate against regulations" (*vorschriftswidrige Behandlung eines Untergebenen*) for which they nullified the lower court's previous ruling and sentenced him to two months in prison and dismissal from the army. The newspaper, however, found the entire outcome "inexplicable" because of the tribunal's secrecy. It noted, on the one hand, that an officer had never before been dismissed and sent to prison for mistreating a subordinate, indicating that the charges against him had to have been serious. On the other hand, the newspaper found it "conspicuous" (*auffallend*) that the Nuremberg court never specified the reasons for its decision. In the newspaper's eyes, both pointed to the likelihood that Oppelt was really guilty of violating Paragraph 175, and the failure to connect the dots "mocked every healthy sense of justice" (*spricht jedem gesunden Rechtsempfinden Hohn*). In this instance, the dearth of sufficient information led public opinion to once again find the secretive military courts untrustworthy.

Against this entrenched pattern of secrecy, it was something of a shock when allegations of sexual transgressions in elite Prussian military units emerged in October 1907 as part of the first Harden-Moltke trial. Because this court case was covered in detail in the previous chapter, I want to focus here on the reception of the testimony by a former NCO in the Cuirassier Guards named Johann Bollhardt, who revealed that a major in the exclusive Garde du Corps, Count Johannes zu Lynar, had used his position of authority to induce him and other enlisted men to attend "homosexual orgies" he organized for friends – including other officers, especially General Wilhelm von Hohenau, who, like Wildenbruch, was related to the Hohenzollern ruling family – at his home in Potsdam.[81] Because of the sexually explicit nature of the testimony, the courtroom was first closed to the public. Even as lawyers and representatives of the press were permitted to remain in the courtroom, the coverage of the testimony was circumspect. Though the press reports make it clear that Bollhardt provided the court with "a detailed account of the love scenes in the Villa," such details were not passed along to the public.[82] Nevertheless, the public did learn that Bollhardt was initially worried that his testimony might incriminate himself (the judge assured him that the statute of limitations had passed) and that the testimony had to do with sexual offences (*Unzucht*) among men.

Even with this scant information, the public's reaction to Bollhardt's testimony was vociferous. During the 28 November 1907 debate, the first Reichstag session devoted to the military budget following the trial, Peter Joseph Spahn of the Catholic Center Party expressed his outrage: "The Moltke-Harden trial ... publicly revealed that an officer used rooms put at his disposal for immoral relations [*unsittlicher Verkehr*] between officers and soldiers."[83] Worse than the misappropriation of government property for illegal activities, however, was the abuse of power, since, he explained "it was emphasized in the trial that these immoral relations were brought about through the misuse of the hierarchical authority [*Dienstgewalt*] that officers have over soldiers."[84] As Spahn went on to clarify, "it may be the case that the relations did not involve the actual invocation of hierarchical authority; [but] discipline and obedience envelop the soldier during his entire time of service, not only when he is on base."[85] In fact, the German articles of war specified

88 Uniform Fantasies

that "the common soldier must respect, obey and promptly execute the orders of every officer and non-commissioned officer … from his own unit as well as every other unit of the army or navy."[86]

In response to the uproar, the Prussian war minister was forced at the next day's session to issue a variety of denials, clarifications, and promises. On the one hand, he raised questions about the trial testimony: "It is impossible that events took place as they were in part portrayed and where one assumes that this villa was like a brothel; for such goings-on could never have been hidden from the police, nor the woman of the house, nor the servants, and it is impossible that they could have escaped the notice of [Lynar's] comrades."[87] Coming from an institution that regularly hid all obscene abuses, this denial failed to convince many deputies. On the other hand, Einem also insisted that there was no evidence of an abuse of authority in Lynar's dismissal in May 1907, but instead the contrary was the case: he had merely inappropriately touched his manservant, who, rather than being cowed by the major's authority, brought it to the attention of the unit's commanding officer: "The crime for which he was dismissed was simply that he had inappropriately touched his manservant. He did nothing more than touch him. I ask you to take this 'nothing more' as the opposite of the much more horrible things that have been assumed."[88] As Einem's words suggest, both the Reichstag and the German public were all too happy to assume the worst, leaving the war minister to fight once again against the common tendency, as Simmel noted, "to heighten" what is secret and unknown "by phantasy."[89]

This process of filling in the gaps of what was unknown "by phantasy" is perhaps most traceable in the caricatures that appeared in the numerous German-language satirical magazines in the month following the trial. As James Steakley notes, caricaturists drew on widespread visual tropes to represent "the political-sensational, erotic-titillating or the grotesquely exaggerated apocalyptic aspects" of the Eulenburg Affair in all its many strands.[90] For example, even before the end of the Harden-Moltke trial, the Munich-based and liberal-oriented *Jugend*, which by 1905 had a print run of 70,000 copies, incorporated into its 28 October issue a drawing to illustrate its understanding of the parties in Adler Villa (see Figure 2.1).[91] It featured an officer dressed in the uniform of the Garde du Corps – signalled by the white pants and coat and the boots that went up over the knee – drinking champagne out of a similar boot. The caption reads: "Formerly one drank from a lady's small shoe – recently, however, one drinks from the cuirassier boot!" Though the image downplays the sexual nature of the events at Lynar's residence by focusing on a single officer in the midst of a romantic gesture, it nevertheless emphasizes the immediate perception of Bollhardt's testimony

Disciplinary Abuses: From Military Secrecy to Sadism in the Army 89

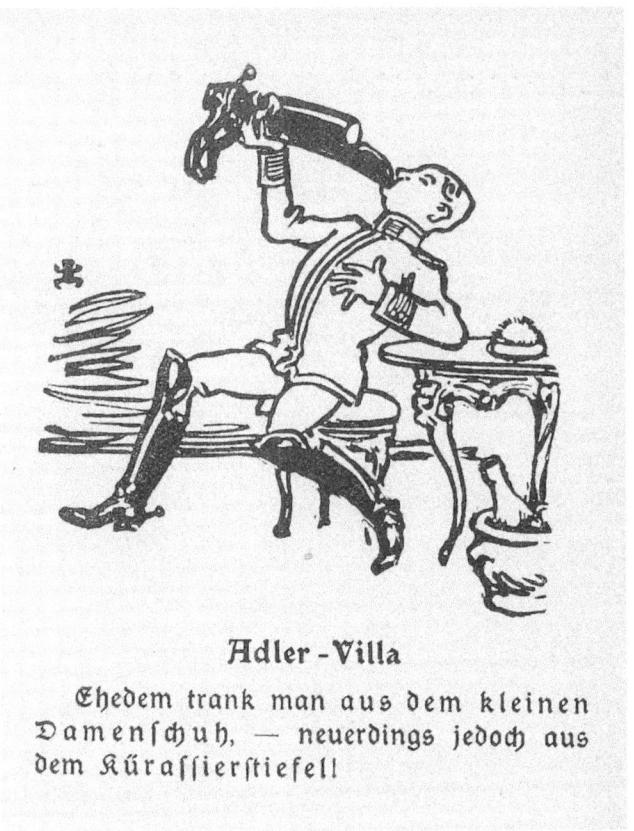

Figure 2.1. "Villa-Adler," caricature produced in response to testimony by Johann Bollhardt at the first Harden-Moltke libel trial. From *Die Jugend. Münchner illustrierte Wochenschrift für Kunst und Leben*, Nr. 45, p. 1027. Universitätsbibliothek Heidelberg.

as a clear reversal of social traditions and hierarchies, as men eschew romantic trysts with women in favour of men, and officers gallantly entertain and pursue their subordinates inside their upper-class homes (referenced by the elegant table and the bottle of champagne) rather than ordering them about outside on the barracks' grounds.

Even more explicit was a drawing published just a few weeks later in *Der Wahre Jacob*, a Stuttgart-based weekly aligned politically with the working class that by 1908 reached a print run of 230,000 copies (see Figure 2.2).[92] Entitled "Military Innovations (from Bollhardt's

90   Uniform Fantasies

Figure 2.2. "Military Innovations (from Bollhart's [sic] Memoirs)," caricature produced in response to testimony by Johann Bollhardt at the first Harden-Moltke libel trial. From *Der Wahre Jacob*, Nr. 557 (26 November 1907), p. 5621. Universitätsbibliothek Heidelberg.

Memoirs)" (*Militärische Neuerungen [Aus Bollhardts Erinnerungen]*), the illustration imagined a troop review taking place in the Garde du Corps regiment in Potsdam. In the background stands a row of soldiers facing backwards, each with their coattails fastened back to prominently expose their buttocks. In the foreground the captain (*Rittmeister*) strides towards an NCO to inquire about the unusual situation: "Since when do we issue the command 'About face!' (*Das ganze kehrt!*) at inspection?" The punchline comes in the NCO's retort: "Yes, sir, Captain! I beg to report that the unit is being inspected today by Count Hohenau." Though the words remain relatively innocuous, the image unmistakably intimates that Hohenau was using his military authority as head of this elite unit to enjoy the sight of attractive men at their expense. In addition, the visual attention paid to the soldiers' backsides, with its insinuation of anal sex, strongly reinforces the sexual intention behind Hohenau's inspection. By foregrounding the conversation between the captain and non-commissioned officer, the cartoon also referenced Bollhardt's testimony at the trial that "in the regiment there was a lot of discussion about the sexual excesses of high-ranking officers."[93] In this case, the "open secret" about Hohenau's predilections within the regiment made his fellow officers and subalterns, like the two men featured here, knowing accomplices in his abuse of authority.

In light of newspapers' coverage of the trial, the litany of criticism in the Reichstag, and the brazen scenarios presented in caricatures like these, the war minister announced in his speech that the army would open an investigation against both Lynar and Hohenau. At the military tribunal held in January 1908, Lynar was sentenced to fifteen months in prison, while Hohenau was acquitted. Perhaps because of its high profile, small parts of the trial were open to the public and were covered to varying degrees by international and German papers.[94] Around Germany, newspapers differed in the amount of information they provided readers. Some conservative papers, like the *Coburger Zeitung*, chose to ignore the trial entirely. Meanwhile, the liberal *Freiburger Zeitung* reported that "the court acquitted Hohenau because his guilt was not proven, but not because his innocence was proven."[95] Lynar, on the other hand, was found guilty of abusing his power on six counts – four in connection with "insulting a subordinate" and three in connection with "moral misconduct" (*sittliche Verfehlungen*). The brief article noted in conclusion that for reasons of military discipline, the court resolved not to share any further details about the trial or its findings (*weitere Begründung*). Unsurprisingly, socialist papers provided their readers with slightly more information. The Magdeburg *Volksstimme*, for instance, knew to report that a total of thirty-seven witnesses had been summoned to testify. It also provided details about the charges against both Hohenau and Lynar. While Hohenau was accused of having sex with an unnamed police official in Berlin in 1906, Lynar's charges included inappropriately touching and passionately embracing his manservant (treated as an insult against a subordinate), asking an orderly to massage one of his legs, and ordering a soldier to lie to a superior (presumably about the sordid events he was trying to hide).[96] And though the *Volksstimme* reported the next day that the hearing "*is being continued behind locked doors,*" it nevertheless recounted the names of several witnesses.[97] Its final report on the convictions included a direct transcript of the public portion of the verdict as well as noting that, for the rest of the court's findings "the public and press had to clear the room."[98]

Hohenau's acquittal and Lynar's conviction and sentencing, however, did little to end public debate. In the Reichstag deliberations on the military budget at the beginning of February 1908, deputies returned again to the scandal. Speaking for the SPD, Gustav Noske used the topic of Soldatenmisshandlungen to address the two-tiered system of justice in the military. After describing how a soldier was sentenced to twenty-two days of hard arrest for not standing at attention while getting boxed on the ears by an NCO, who only received eight days of light arrest, he turned to Lynar: "Count Lynar has been sentenced to one-and-a-quarter years ... I will not indulge in any reflections about whether the decision in itself is harsh or mild; but in comparison with the sentences that are given to soldiers who commit an offence against an officer it is exceptionally mild."[99] In this case, Lynar's sentence – significantly longer than the NCO's above – represented the military's perception that his sexual crimes were especially serious. Yet Noske's sense that his sentence was too short suggests that he shared – or was ready to exploit politically – the belief that, as Rau wrote, "there cannot be a more horrible abuse of subordinates" (26) than homosexual misconduct.

Moreover, because the military trial against Hohenau and Lynar was conducted behind closed doors, it also gave rise once again to the problem of secret trials. Several deputies were moved to introduce resolutions "to request that the chancellor work emphatically to see that the legally guaranteed element of publicity be carried out in all military trials."[100] In response, however, Count Waldemar von Oriola of the National Liberal Party suggested that "there are doubtless cases in which, for reasons of state security, discipline and morality that it is absolutely necessary to exclude the public, and I consider the sad trials that have been talked about so much lately as just such cases."[101] Max Liebermann von Sonnenberg, a leader of the far-right anti-Semitic German-Social Economic Coalition, also insisted – to acclaim from fellow party members – that in the Lynar-Hohenau trial the exclusion of the public "was absolutely correct (*durchaus am Platze*)."[102] The implication was that the public needed to be protected from hearing about such sexual misdeeds. Indeed, such comments exposed the limitations that inhered in using sexological categories and sexual scandal to force the military to open its judicial proceedings, since the public airing of detailed sexual matters was itself a transgression against the norms that the sexual acts had already violated. And to this extent, conservatives in the Reichstag and elsewhere could defend military secrecy if it kept the German public from being further assaulted by detailed discussions of shockingly obscene sexual matters.

Yet despite general consensus about the need for discretion about sexual matters, Noske objected that "in this case the exclusion of the public was taken so far that neither the justification of the sentence nor any other item was publicly communicated. Thus the oversight (*Kontrolle*) – and that should be provided by the public nature of the trial – as to whether the punishment exceeded or fell short of the people's sense of justice (*Rechtsempfinden des Volkes*) was not possible."[103] In response, the Reichstag adopted resolutions calling for full public access to military trials as well as a new code of military law (MStGB). In addition, the body stepped up its criticism of the secrecy of the military cabinet, which it viewed as the main impediment to significant reforms in the military. For example, Ernst Müller of the Freeminded People's Party noted that the secret influence that the military cabinet wielded made a mockery of the war minister: "Then the war minister is, to the best of my belief, nothing more than – to use the old French expression – a 'parliamentary whipping boy.'"[104] In light of the heated discussion of Soldatenmisshandlungen and their connection to sadism, the expression seemed quite apt. Nevertheless, despite these resolutions and verbal attacks, the Reichstag still stopped short of forcing the government to meet its demands. As Noske noted, "The power of the German Reichstag is certainly not big, but it is much bigger than is currently being exercised. The Reichstag could achieve much more if the parties that make such demands wanted to seriously show the administration that they have the intentions to enforce their demands."[105] The implication was that the body could use its budgetary powers to withhold military funding until the government submitted proposed laws that met these demands – and then enforced them.

Conclusion

In addition to serving as a regular feature of parliamentary debates on the military budget, Soldatenmisshandlungen provided plenty of fodder for left-liberal and social democratic newspapers and self-styled popularizers of sexology. But while war ministers and chancellors squared off against liberal and socialist Reichstag deputies over the issue, the one point that all parties could agree on was that the abuse of soldiers was bad. The military, of course, sought to handle the matter in its own characteristic way: through secret orders and secret trials against the perpetrators. Many citizens and their representatives, meanwhile, worried that military policies not only failed to adequately protect soldiers from abusive superiors but also significantly contributed to the culture of abuse through its antiquated judicial system, its valorization of absolute obedience, and its obsession with secrecy.

But as Simmel warned, secrets and secrecy are not merely strategies wielded by government bureaucracies and secret societies, but roadblocks to knowledge that inevitably incite the operations of fantasy. To some extent, supporters of the German military, such as Wildenbruch, constructed elaborate fantasies that, while acknowledging the erotic nature of male bonds, also celebrated the secretive role of violence in establishing those bonds and ensuring that they never developed into illegal acts or a self-conscious identity based on those desires. Yet in light of the larger operations of power-knowledge that Foucault identified in the first volume of *The History of Sexuality*, it was perhaps inevitable that a sexual concept like sadism eventually became the conceptual framework for both critics and government alike to talk about the violent abuse of soldiers. Though some of the acts were indeed so brutal that they could only be seen as evidence of a pathological illness on the part of the perpetrators, it is important to stress that the military's penchant for secrecy inevitably encouraged a reading of Soldatenmisshandlungen as a sexual pathology. Sadism offered a scientific sexual discourse not only for problematizing the abuses themselves but also for pathologizing the very kind of violent masculinity – and male bonding – that Wildenbruch's novella celebrated as an ideal. Of course, the long-term popularity of the novella in Germany and abroad suggests that sexological categories did not entirely root out this form of *ars erotica*. Moreover, to the extent that the sexological concept of sadism also sought to locate the origins for the pathology in the individual mind, army officials like Einem could adopt the terminology of sadism while also downplaying the institutional factors within the military that encouraged it. Perhaps the most fraught dimension of the sexualization of Soldatenmisshandlungen, however, was its reliance on cases of actual sexual abuse – in particular, homosexuality – to brush all forms of disciplinary abuse with a sexual patina. However, the entanglement of military service and homosexuality was in fact much deeper and more complex, as we see when we turn to the next chapter.

Chapter Three

The Obscure Object of Desire: Uniform Fetishism, Male Prostitution, and German Soldiers

Army officers were not, of course, the only men having sex with rank-and-file soldiers. Already in the 1860s, as we saw in the introduction, Karl Heinrich Ulrichs became one of the first queer civilians to write about his own life-long attraction to young men in military uniform, who, he theorized, were natural objects of desire for Urnings like himself. As he acknowledged, however, the reverse could not be said for the soldiers themselves, since they were, in his theory, Dionings (his term for men exclusively attracted to women). As a result, winning their consent to sexual activity that ran against their nature raised a number of thorny ethical questions and practical challenges.[1] Though Ulrichs believed that a Dioning might eventually be moved "to grant favors to a petitioning Urning" out of sympathy or a "bond of love," especially if he were "convinced that what the Urning feels for him is nothing but true and heartfelt love," he also conceded that men like himself "should not be allowed to request sympathy ... without being willing to make compensation for it."[2] Perhaps because of the whiff of prostitution in these liaisons and the possibility that they could often "degenerate into vulgar lust," the public, Ulrichs admitted, scorned "our attraction to soldiers as ignoble."[3]

Ulrichs's pamphlets give some evidence that he was not alone in his pursuit of sexual liaisons with uniformed conscripts. In addition to reproducing news reports about a Parisian male brothel involving "several handsome soldiers" and the trial of a man caught *in flagrante* with a soldier one evening in Vienna, the activist also noted that "a large Uranian coffee social took place in January 1865 in Frankfurt-am-Main" at which several Urnings had brought their lovers, "Austrian and Prussian soldiers."[4] He also published correspondence he received from an anonymous source about male prostitution taking place in larger northern German cities. While this informant reported the existence of organized prostitution featuring "young Dionings with low intentions," he also mentioned the existence of "others, chiefly soldiers" who, he claimed, operated differently, establishing longer-term relations with a single Urning "whose wallet is emptied to defray the costs of 'an extra pair of pants' or some other luxury item."[5]

Yet what may have been a relatively limited, ad hoc practice of paying for sex with soldiers in Ulrichs's day had evolved by the end of the century into a full-blown sexual scene that, in Berlin and other German cities, assumed the character of a systematic underground economy of prostitution. Because German troops were distributed across no less than 150 different cities and towns, it was hypothetically possible for men to pursue sexual contacts with soldiers in almost every part of the country.[6] Yet there are several reasons why Berlin emerged as Imperial Germany's epicentre for *Soldatenprostitution* (prostitution by soldiers). One of the most important was the city's size. Starting with a population of 528,900 in 1860, Berlin's inhabitants more than doubled by 1880, before doubling yet again to more than 2 million residents by 1905.[7] Moreover, the towns and villages abutting the city were growing even faster, such that there were an additional 1.5 million people living in what eventually became known as Greater Berlin.[8] The combination of dense residential districts with large tracts of green space – a feature of the 1862 Hobrecht Plan – afforded a relatively high degree of anonymity while diminishing the ability of authorities to police all areas.[9] Indeed, already by the end of the 1880s, the Berlin police department ceased its practice of raiding homosexual establishments and instead adopted a policy of toleration, which, as Robert Beachy points out, "helps to explain the rapid growth and incredible visibility of Berlin's homosexual scene after 1890."[10]

Most importantly, though, for the phenomenon of Soldatenprostitution was the city's pronounced military character. Even as early as 1860, the census listed 18,027 active duty military personnel in Berlin, which by 1900 had grown to 23,142.[11] Meanwhile, by 1905 there were also an additional 40,187 active duty personnel in nearby Potsdam, Charlottenburg, Lichterfelde, Schöneberg, and Spandau, all of which were either adjacent to the city borders or tightly connected to Berlin by commuter railroad (the latter four municipalities were formerly incorporated into Berlin in 1920).[12] Altogether, then, this Greater Berlin hosted Germany's single largest concentration of soldiers, which – as Prussian Guard units – were also its most prestigious and exclusive. Moreover, unlike the dispersion of garrisons throughout smaller cities, which might host a few different units, the Prussian Guards comprised an entire army corps consisting of two divisions, each with two infantry brigades (with three regiments each); an artillery brigade (consisting of two regiments each); a Prussian Guard cavalry division of four brigades (consisting of one Hussar, two cuirassier, two dragoon, and three uhlan regiments); a railroad brigade; two telegraph battalions; an engineering battalion (*Pionier-Bataillon*); a transport department (*Train-Abteilung*); and a unit each of bodyguards (*Leibgendarmerie*) and palace guards.[13] Each of these regiments had its own distinct uniform. Thus, in his popular 1904 guidebook to queer life in the capital, *Berlins Drittes Geschlecht* (*Berlin's Third Sex*), Magnus Hirschfeld cited an informant who claimed that, with the exception of London, he had never "found such a selection of soldiers of various branches, every evening, except in Berlin."[14]

While Hirschfeld's guide devoted a number of pages to the phenomenon of Soldatenprostitution, and was quickly followed by a few other accounts that all promised readers inside intelligence about male prostitution and other aspects of the city's homosexual subculture, there are nevertheless few reliable sources for accurately reconstructing this underground economy, since neither the extant Berlin police files nor the surviving Prussian military archives apparently contain any records on the matter.[15] Even as some incidents did, as in Ulrichs's time, find their way into newspapers, and from there into publications of the Scientific-Humanitarian Committee (WhK), there are few dependable sources beyond some references in the 1922 memoirs of Hans von Tresckow, who from 1900 until his retirement in 1919 oversaw the unit responsible for homosexual matters in the Berlin police department.[16] Indeed, like many urban subcultures, male prostitution by soldiers might have remained a hidden phenomenon – known only to those who policed, studied, or partook of it – if not for the first Harden-Moltke trial, at which the former NCO Johann Bollhardt inadvertently called attention to recent regulations about military dress enacted in various Guard divisions to disrupt prostitution by conscripts. In addition to threatening the Prussian military's reputation, these revelations also damaged the future prospects of the national queer emancipation movement. And similar to the revelations about Lynar and Hohenau, the resulting public outrage led the Reichstag to devote several days of debate on the issue at which the war minister Karl von Einem was forced to explain the army's position. These attempts at damage control, however, tended to further obscure the actual organizational aspects and dimensions of this underground sexual economy.

But rather than lament the dearth of reliable information, I want to suggest that the significance of Soldatenprostitution lies less in the actual acts themselves than in the heated debates, titillating descriptions, and ambitious theorizing they provoked about the causes and extent of this illicit economy. In fact, the spirited debates about Soldatenprostitution foreground the constitutive role of fantasy not only in eliciting sexual desire but also in attempting to shape the perception of social relations. The first section of this chapter thus focuses on the competing fantasies that circulated in the public pronouncements about male prostitution by soldiers, which were themselves intimately connected to broader ideological debates about military-civil relations and the place of same-sex desire in Imperial German society. Ideology, as Žižek argues, is itself a form of fantasy that emerges in response to social antagonisms and other phenomena that challenge the social order. In the case of Soldatenprostitution, all of the commentators offered their competing responses – replete with fantasy scenarios – to the disturbing knowledge that soldiers were having sex with men, most likely for money. Yet for ideological fantasies to operate, they must remain implicit – that is, not be recognized *as* fantasies by those in their thrall. By reading the published accounts and utterances chronologically from 1904, when Hirschfeld published *Berlins Drittes Geschlecht*, to 1908, when *Das perverse Berlin* (Perverse Berlin) was published anonymously, it is possible to retrace how each publication or pronouncement responds to the insufficiencies in the fantasies that preceded it, either because the scenario offered was too contrived or its author too eager to paper over the rupture and make it usable for his political purposes. But while we need to work back through the articulated fantasies, what we are looking for, in fact, is what remains obscure; that is, the unarticulated fantasies and wishes beneath the articulated ones.

Even more obscure than the ideological fantasies were the erotic fantasies that underwrote the phenomenon of Soldatenprostitution. Thus, the chapter's second section turns to the topic of uniform fetishism. As a theoretical concept, the fetish has a long and complicated history going back to European colonialism. Yet in addition to its long-standing role in anthropology and the study of religion, it took on new importance in the nineteenth century as a term of economic analysis and psychosexual pathology. In 1887 the French psychologist Alfred Binet was the first to articulate fetishism as a sexual dysfunction that beset heterosexual men. It was quickly taken up by Richard von Krafft-Ebing and other German sexologists who also expanded its application beyond heterosexual men to encompass the practices and fantasies of men attracted to other men. Yet while sexologists located the causes of sexual fetishes in the early experiences of individuals (and in Freud's case, an early traumatic realization), I also draw on Marx's concept of the commodity fetish, published in 1864, to trace this uniform fetish back to larger social and material relations. On the one hand, I suggest that homosexuals were not the only ones with a uniform fetish – indeed, that the German military and the broader public also harboured a uniform fetish, which, in turn, offered the coordinates of desire for the erotic economy of Soldatenprostitution. On the other hand, by drawing on a range of texts, including sexological case studies and first-hand accounts by queer uniform enthusiasts like Ulrichs, I reconstruct how the uniform fetish of male homosexuals circulated around two competing but impossible erotic fantasies of illusory fullness: on one side, a queer-affirmative wish-fulfillment in which an Urning or male homosexual could evoke and win the affection of a Dioning or heterosexual man; and, on the other side, a fundamentally self-denigrating erotic utopia in which homosexuals escaped their same-sex identities by accessing a paradise of innocent (but perverse) *heterosexual* male bonds.

Of course, the existence of an illicit underground sexual economy revolving around the erotic fetishization of soldiers and their uniforms proved problematic for the military's leadership. Not only did soldiers engaging in potentially illegal sexual acts symbolize a troubling lack of military discipline within the army but the practice also had the potential to undermine the public's confidence in the military as an institution aligned with its moral values, especially in the case of the vocal Christian morality movement, which had made it its mission to fight both prostitution and homosexual emancipation.[17] Yet even more importantly, Soldatenprostitution signified a nodal point for much larger concerns about the erotic economy of Prussian-German militarism: while the army's own uniform fetishism served to eroticize military masculinity, civilians purchasing sexual services from military personnel also reversed the deference that all civilians were expected to exhibit vis-à-vis even the lowliest soldier. However, despite its threat to the army's discipline and its public reputation, the uniform fetish of homosexual men proved no match for the uniform fetishism shared by the army leadership and the broader German public. In this case, the power of the fetish – to know and simultaneously not know about one's own desires – enabled the latter to place the entire blame for Soldatenprostitution on the homosexuals themselves.

Sparse Facts and Plentiful Fantasies: The Discursive Twists and Turns of Soldatenprostitution

While Ulrichs was convinced that conscripts from the working and peasant classes represented an erotic ideal for almost all Urnings, a claim I examine more fully in the next section, there were also quite practical reasons for bourgeois and even wealthier homosexual civilians to purchase sex from soldiers. As Ulrichs suggested, the Urnings' recourse to male prostitutes merely followed the example of heterosexual relations. In nineteenth-century Germany, the pattern of lowly paid internships and apprenticeships in all professions hampered the ability of most men to achieve sufficient economic independence and social standing to support a family, forcing them to delay marriage until relatively late. Yet as Annette Timm and Joshua Sandborn note, "This late-marriage ... was incompatible with the sexual desires of youth. As a result, premarital sex was common, and many local customs developed to govern it."[18] Because the social conventions of the bourgeoisie and aristocracy prohibited premarital sex for middle-class and upper-class women (who, if they wed, tended to marry much younger), many, if not most, single heterosexual men either pursued temporary relationships with women from the lower-classes or paid female prostitutes for sex. Many married men also visited prostitutes. According to Dagmar Herzog, "for a long time, prostitution had been the 'open secret' supplement to marriage. It had been quietly tolerated as a necessary evil or even a basic good."[19] Because these same moral conventions prohibited bourgeois men from engaging in same-sex desire (itself an insult to a gentleman's honour), many middle-class Urnings adopted similar conventions in seeking out sexual encounters with men from the lower-classes, though intraclass relationships still occurred to a limited extent, particularly in schools and universities.

Though Ulrichs's work pointed to the prevalence of male prostitution in larger cities as early as the 1860s, paying young urban youth for sex also carried its own dangers. According to one of his unnamed informants, "young Dionings with low intentions carry on the business of ordinary prostitution ... [which] is formally organized (procurers, etc.)."[20] And as Ulrichs was only too well aware, these organized forms of prostitution often took the form of organized gangs of blackmailers.[21] As his informant subsequently explained, "often a finely built fellow plays the rowdy (*Rupfer*) without any aid. More often, however, the procedure is carried out by two, which is obviously more practical. In that case, however, the position of the companion varies. He is sometimes only a bystander. Or he could be the fellow's comrade. But even he could also be the leading character, the principal person of the business. For any older, smart gentleman, a fine-looking fellow plays only the part of the bait." In fact, decades later, the pages of the WhK's *Monatsbericht* were filled with reports of prostitutes who blackmailed their victims. Meanwhile, perhaps the most famous case of homosexual blackmail in Imperial Germany was that of August Hasse, a chief judge of the district court in Breslau, who around 1902 was lured into sexually touching a young man – a plant for two blackmailers – while visiting a public toilet. After being financially ruined by the 40,000 marks they extorted from him over the next two years, he attempted to murder one by shooting him on a street in Berlin in 1904 and turning himself into the police.[22]

In contrast to urban youths, with their ties to blackmailers, army conscripts were seen as a relatively safe alternative, especially in Berlin, where there was an abundance of soldiers. While there were a few instances of soldiers blackmailing homosexual civilians, such as two non-commissioned officers in the Berlin Guard cuirassiers in 1900, soldiers were considered much less likely to engage in extortion.[23] First, they were different from urban prostitutes. Because the Prussian military was concerned about potential revolutionary uprisings (especially from the large and well-organized working-class population in Berlin), its recruitment strategies favoured rural conscripts over urban ones.[24] And unlike all other units, which drafted soldiers from one particular region, Guard units recruited nationally.[25] Thus, most Guard conscripts were likely new to Berlin and far less versed in the ways of urban crime. Second, military discipline proved a greater deterrent of crime than the Berlin police. According to the anonymous author of *Das perverse Berlin*, "the soldier is almost never a swindler [*Preller*]. Both he and the homosexual know that blackmail, committed by a member of the military, is punished exceedingly hard. Indeed, that the soldier can already expect trouble [*Ungelegenheiten*] of the most severe sort should his superiors even learn that he has been maintaining abnormal relations with a man. In other words, a homosexual can feel as safe as in Abraham's bosom when engaging with members of the uniformed service."[26]

Despite the known risks for soldiers, many were nonetheless willing to engage in male prostitution during their two-year (for infantry and artillery) or three-year (for cavalry) stints in the army. And while the decisions of individual soldiers were no doubt motivated by varying reasons, nearly all commentators agreed that a lack of money was the universal factor. In fact, soldiers were paid miserably. During the entire period of Imperial Germany's existence, conscripts in the infantry and artillery earned just 22 pfennigs per day, which was paid out every ten days, amounting to 6.60 marks per month for a grand total of 79 marks per year.[27] Cavalry units, which required three years of service, paid slightly better, with soldiers earning 27 pfennigs per day for a total of 8.10 marks a month and 97.20 marks over the course of the year. Guard infantry and artillery units were paid at the general cavalry rate, while Guard cavalry units, such as the cuirassiers (Garde du Corps), earned the most, 32 pfennigs a day (9.60 marks per month for an annual salary of 115.20 marks). But even as soldiers' pay remained the same from 1871 to 1914, real wages rose considerably over these same decades, with the pay for agricultural workers climbing from 444 marks annually on average in 1895 to 682 marks by 1913 (about eight and a half times the annual earnings of a typical conscript).[28] Meanwhile, the differences were even starker for urban industrial workers, who in 1895 were bringing home 768 marks per year on average, which increased to 1,210 marks by 1913 (about fifteen times what most soldiers earned, and fully ten times what even a Guard calvary recruit earned). Though conscripts received furnished lodging in barracks, one daily warm meal (lunch) along with coffee in the morning and evening, for the rest of the day they had to make do with an allotment of 750 grams of bread, leaving many often hungry.[29] (A second warm meal in the evening was added in 1897, which, along with their free lodging, was used by the Reichstag in 1909 to justify maintaining their low wages.)[30]

Yet even with meals and lodging provided, soldiers faced additional expenses and few opportunities to earn extra income. For example, conscripts were responsible for laundry costs and purchasing their own personal grooming supplies as well as shoe polish and other cleaning and maintenance supplies for their uniform, leaving them with even less money for the simplest forms of recreation, such as going to a tavern for beers or a meal in the evening. Though some soldiers earned extra money from polishing the uniform buttons and footwear of officers and one-year volunteers, others sought out additional sources of income. According to Frevert, those lucky enough to find a girlfriend during their military service "seem to have been supported by their 'sweethearts'" whenever they had leave for the night.[31] A number, of course, turned to currying favours from male homosexuals with the financial resources to support them.

Though queer Berlin and military Berlin were worlds apart, the city offered at least three points of intersection. First, homosexual civilians frequented so-called soldier bars that regularly sprang up near the numerous barracks located throughout the city. While often short-lived, these bars made it possible for civilians to gain favour with soldiers by buying them drinks and food. However, as soon as the growing presence of homosexual civilians came to the attention of the police, the locations would be passed on to the local commander who would add them to the list of bars placed off-limits to military personnel. According to Tresckow, "in order to ensure that the ban was adhered to, [the commander] would have patrols conduct checks of the locations" with police accompaniment provided by Tresckow's office.[32] Second, soldiers also canvassed a half-dozen streets as well as certain paths in the Tiergarten in search of customers in the late evening. In a diary entry from 3 July 1907, Tresckow recorded that "the blatant activities of soldiers near the tents and other parts of the Tiergarten had led to complaints. The soldiers are behaving in this area like prostitutes. They offer themselves directly to homosexuals, who mostly belong to the educated classes."[33]

Finally, there was at least one male brothel operating out of a massage parlour in the middle of the city. Again, Tresckow, who raided the operation in the summer of 1907, claimed that it "was known for years as a gathering place for homosexuals who celebrated their orgies with soldiers."[34] While most middle-class men could likely afford to pursue soldiers through the first two options, the brothel was reserved, according to Tresckow, who confiscated the client list, for an exclusive clientele consisting of "illustrious persons, princes, counts, men from the court, and even one crown head [of state]."[35] This male brothel, however, was not the city's first. According to an undated newspaper article reprinted in the 1900 edition of the *Jahrbuch für sexuelle Zwischenstufen*, three waiters (likely in the 1890s) were convicted of running a brothel out of an apartment in which cuirassiers participated, one of whom received a much stiffer sentence than any of the three waiters.[36] Meanwhile, Berlin was not the only German city with male brothels featuring soldiers. In the 1880s and 1890s, Strasbourg, which was located in the territory annexed by Germany after the Franco-Prussian War and thus hosted a disproportionately large number of German military contingents, also harboured a few "soldier bordellos." Unlike the one in Berlin, however, these operations, "mostly located in the vicinity of barracks at the edge of the city, were distinguished – in contrast to bordellos with a bourgeois clientele – by a poorer customers and distinctly lower standards of hygiene."[37]

To the extent that male prostitution by soldiers had become publicly visible in Berlin, it proved a problem for military authorities and police alike. In fact, just months before the first Harden-Moltke trial in October 1907, Tresckow observed in his journal that "the commanders of the Berlin and Potsdam Guard units are coming to me almost daily to ask for advice on how they could combat the pederasty of soldiers that had taken hold in their units."[38] And because of the public outrage it portended, it also carried risks for individuals and organizations striving for queer emancipation. Though Ulrichs had defiantly demanded public acceptance for "the wild Pegasus nature of our love," the strategies pursued by the WhK and its allies were quite different.[39] Despite being inspired by Ulrichs's works and theories, Hirschfeld generally departed from the former's stress on sexual freedom, emphasizing instead that homosexuals had minimal sexual needs and were in fact modest, moral, and socially respectable individuals.[40]

Hirschfeld's first extensive discussion of illicit relations between conscripts and homosexual civilians – and one of the first publications after Ulrichs's pamphlets to treat the matter directly – came in his 1904 book, *Berlin's Third Sex*. Commissioned by Hans Ostwald as the third pamphlet in his series *Großstadt-Dokumente* (Documents of the metropolis), Hirschfeld's book was part anthropological report and part guidebook to Berlin's homosexual subculture.[41] Through its accessible language and affordable price, it represented a significant departure from the efforts of most other sexologists of his day. As one reviewer noted, "In this short work ... the well-known champion for the repeal of Paragraph 175 ... leaves the strict medical-scientific point of view and, in an easily comprehensible manner, turns to address the entire educated German public."[42] Though clearly designed to provide the general (heterosexual) reader with an intriguing, if sympathetic window into the clandestine sexual scenes operating within the German capital, the book was also likely a welcome, perhaps even indispensable resource for first-time homosexual tourists, who could find the names and approximate addresses of establishments catering to homosexuals as well as locations where they might find soldiers or other men willing to have sex in exchange for money.

In dealing with the matter of male prostitution by soldiers, Hirschfeld pursued two strategies to diminish the danger that this illicit underground economy might hold for his political project. On the one hand, he sought to instrumentalize the scandalous nature of Soldatenprostitution as yet another reason for repealing the anti-sodomy laws. Citing his well-travelled informant, Hirschfeld linked the phenomenon to the criminalization of homosexuality, claiming that the "willingness of soldiers to have sex with men [*die Hingabe von Soldaten*], which one should not believe was possible if one didn't see it with one's own eyes, is much more prevalent in all European countries with strict penalties for homosexual relations, while one almost never notices this phenomenon in countries without a sodomy law [*Urningsparagraphen*]."[43] Thus, not only was male prostitution by soldiers so shocking that even a homosexual might doubt its existence if he hadn't see it for himself, but this scandalous and lamentable phenomenon was caused by the legal repression of homosexuality. According to this logic, the only way to get rid of it was to decriminalize same-sex acts between men.

On the other hand, however, Hirschfeld also sought to downplay its scandalous nature. Thus after introducing the term "Soldatenprostitution," which seems to have been the first use of the term in print (even as he explained it was a "customary designation" [*gebräuchliche Bezeichnung*]), he immediately sought to undermine its meaning, noting that "'soldier prostitution' does not conform to the usual definition of prostitution because with the soldiers we are not dealing with 'a professional or commercial sale (*Hingabe*) of the body.'"[44] Hence, because the soldiers were employed by the military and only occasionally exchanged sex for money, it was misleading to label the practice as prostitution. But the sexologist went even further in his effort to diminish the whiff of impropriety: "Here I should like to correct the widespread opinion that relations between soldiers and homosexuals are ordinarily predicated on acts that are punishable in and of themselves. If it should come to the sexual act, and that is not at all so in every case, this usually takes the form of arousal through embrace, pressing against one another and touching of body parts, as is ordinarily the case in homosexual activities."[45] Thus, gone from Hirschfeld's description is any indication of the Urning's "wild Pegasus-like nature" (Ulrichs). Instead, he suggested that homosexual men were largely content with rather restrained and modest forms of sexual expression – or even chaste platonic relationships. (To the extent that two case studies in *Psychopathia Sexualis* reported ejaculating almost immediately after a soldier placed his hand on their genitals, Hirschfeld's claims may not have been entirely inaccurate for at least some of these encounters.)[46]

Though such claims – backed up by Hirschfeld's scientific credentials – were important, a much more critical tool in his arsenal was fantasy. The first fantasy scenario concerned the public space of "soldier taverns" (*Soldatenkneipen*) located close to the barracks. According to the sexologist, in the evening hours before they had to return to their bases "one can see up to 50 soldiers in these establishments, including non-commissioned officers, who have come to seek out a homosexual to pick up their tab, and rarely do they return to their barracks without getting what they came for."[47] In contrast to Ulrichs, who in the 1860s felt obligated to defend the courtship rituals of "the Urning who, while drinking a glass of wine, strikes a match to light the cigar of a handsome soldier," Hirschfeld's account emphasized the soldiers' agency in seeking out homosexuals who would buy them beer and a little dinner or snack. Moreover, the sexologist insisted that "were a sexually normal person to enter such an establishment, he might be puzzled to see so many finely dressed men sitting there with soldiers, though he would find nothing particularly offensive."[48] To prevent readers from imagining a space of seduction or the negotiation of sexual services, Hirschfeld transformed the soldier bars into a scene in which nothing was amiss, a place where soldiers and homosexuals forged friendships "over sausage, salad and beer" that "frequently endure[d] for the full term of service, and often longer," such that even after the soldier returned to his rural home and got married, he occasionally sent his erstwhile admirer freshly slaughtered meats "as a token of friendship."[49]

But if the public setting of a bar was potentially fraught, what transpired between homosexuals and soldiers outside the public purview was even more so. Ulrichs, for example, had protested the 1865 case of a man who was fined for "lewd conduct and *public* indecency" for having "a handsome young soldier follow him into a room to enjoy sensual pleasures *in private*."[50] To dispel any whiff of impropriety when homosexuals and soldiers met outside the bar, Hirschfeld offered the following scenario: "Typically, when his shift is over, the soldier comes to the apartment of his friend, who has prepared his favourite meal with his own hands, which the soldier hastily gulps down in massive quantities. Then the young warrior, his breadth teeming with health, takes a seat on the sofa, while the Urning, humbly perched on a chair, darns the torn laundry [the soldier] has brought with him, or embroiders the Christmas slippers with which he had wanted to surprise his friend, but which considerably exceeded the happy lover's power of self-restraint."[51] It is hard today to take this scene seriously as a representative description of what typically transpired between soldiers and homosexual civilians behind closed doors. Though Hirschfeld's writing usually eschews the ironic in favour of a pedagogical tone, it is possible that he was either parodying heterosexual domesticity or possibly even making fun of what he saw as the self-negating masochism of those who chased after younger, presumably heterosexual men.[52]

Nevertheless, what is clear is that the domestic idyll in this scene served as a double evacuation of sexuality. First, the homosexual situation between the two men is replaced by a heterosexualized one. In response to the effeminizing threat of homosexuality and prostitution, the soldier has all the stereotypical markers of masculinity: his physical size, the space he takes up on the couch, and his healthy appetite. Meanwhile, the feminine role is entirely assumed by the emasculated homosexual who miraculously combines wife, innocent virgin, and even domestic servant into one person, that is, someone who cooks, cleans, darns, knits, and adores – without complaint. Indeed, there is no longer even room for the homosexual to sit on his own sofa in his own home. The implication is that this Urning is so entirely deferential and subservient that he is unlikely to make any demands, sexual or otherwise, upon the soldier. Second, instead of portraying the two men's relationship as some kind of illicit tryst that must necessarily take place out of the purview of military authorities and the policing gaze of the public, the issue of secrecy is recast as an insignificant trifle *between* the two men – where in the end, it was never really much of a secret anyway. The logic seems to be that if the homosexual cannot keep the Christmas slippers he's knitting a harmless secret from his beloved soldier, how can the relations between the two men represent a dangerously illicit secret being kept from the German public?

As these scenarios suggest, Hirschfeld sought to hide the transgressive dimensions of Soldatenprostitution through a fantasy of desexualized "normalcy" that portrayed the phenomenon as largely beneficial to individual conscripts (and Germany's military, indirectly). Though he recognized that soldiers were motivated by a lack of money (without, however, explicitly stating that they were getting paid for sex), he also offered up a lengthy list of reasons that led them into relationships with homosexuals, including a lack of available women (particularly ones that didn't cost the soldier any money), a fear of catching venereal diseases (which was associated with female prostitutes), a promise to remain true to their sweetheart at home (sex with men doesn't count!), and a range of desires for a more comfortable existence, intellectual improvement, and entertainment (the benefits of having young, uneducated men spend time with older men of *Bildung*).[53] Of course, if all this does not sound a lot like prostitution, that's because it's clearly not supposed to. The fantasy that Hirschfeld weaves is not merely that Soldatenprostitution was a necessary (and relatively small) evil that could be eradicated by decriminalizing homosexuality but that also – and much more importantly – it was fundamentally a positive phenomenon. The unarticulated fantasy behind this scenario is that homosexuals could be integrated into the social fabric of Imperial Germany without any substantive changes to the military or the broader German society itself. In this sense, Hirschfeld provided an early, liberal form of what Lisa Duggan has famously labelled "the new homonormativity": "public recognition of a domesticated, depoliticized privacy."[54] As she quips, after integration and assimilation of same-sex identities, "we go home and cook dinner, forever."[55] Moreover, in its efforts to portray a domesticity aligned with the military institution, this "old" homonormativity can also be read as an incipient form of "homonationalism," Jasbir Puar's term for the "political recognition and incorporation" of normative queer or homosexual subjects who become "the temporary recipients of the 'measures of benevolence,'" in turn establishing, among other outcomes, "*convivial* relations between queerness and militarism."[56]

Perhaps in part because of its conciliatory politics, Hirschfeld's book seems to have won general praise from medical colleagues and the general public alike for its accessibility, its "insight into a strange world," its careful avoidance of any "piquancy," and "its cool objectivity and scientific seriousness," which "made the treatment of such delicate matters possible and mitigated the distasteful [*das Unerquickliche*] aspects of the reading even for those who perhaps do not always share the views of the author."[57] Such reviews also suggest that most readers – both scientific and general – accepted Hirschfeld's portrayal of homosexual life in the German capital at face value. Though most of these do not mention the particular topic of Soldatenprostitution, his WhK collaborator Eugen Wilhelm, a lawyer in the annexed Alsace-Lorraine who used the pseudonym Numa Praetorius and served as the main book reviewer for the WhK's *Jahrbuch*, did specifically praise Hirschfeld's efforts to distinguish Soldatenprostitution from regular prostitution. Because Wilhelm was himself exclusively attracted to soldiers and took steps to find a soldier with whom he could have romantic relationship, he thus looked favourably on Hirschfeld's depiction of long-term contacts between conscripts and their male civilian lovers, who "treated" them (rather than focusing on sordid, one-time trysts in public parks or brothels in which soldiers were paid directly for sex).[58] Nevertheless, Wilhelm, who travelled frequently during the 1890s, including locations where male-male sexual acts were not criminalized, took his colleague to task for inaccurately claiming that this illicit economy only flourished in countries with anti-sodomy laws.[59] In this view, he is also supported by the widely travelled American expatriate and homosexual rights activist Edward Prime-Stevenson, who, writing under the pen name Xavier Mayne, asserted that soldier-prostitution "has become enormously diffused and obvious in Europe, as in the Orient. The common soldier, likewise the soldier of better than humble grade, in almost every country, every military administration and garrison town, exercises largely clandestine prostitution."[60]

Ironically enough, however, Hirschfeld's most vocal critic was none other than Hans Ostwald, the man who originally commissioned and published the sexologist's guidebook as part of his multivolume series. In fact, just two years later, in 1906, Ostwald published his own book on male prostitution in Imperial Berlin, in which he took Hirschfeld to task for what he called "false sentimentality."[61] Rather than downplaying Soldatenprostitution in the chapter on "soldier- and semi-prostitution," Ostwald took a materialist approach to the issue by emphasizing the economic reasons motivating soldiers to sell sexual favours and laying the blame on the army itself: "The military has created one of the ugliest phenomena by pressing the soldier – someone who was making a decent living with his hands or his head – into the lowest of pay scales"

(84). According to Ostwald, the military produced the conditions of male prostitution by impoverishing otherwise self-sufficient men to the point that they needed to seek out alternative sources of revenue.

Thus, in contrast to Hirschfeld's clear discomfort with the term "prostitution," Ostwald's pamphlet kept and even strengthened that label, which he claimed "deserved to be called by this disgusting name" (84). And as a pioneer of the modernist form of collage, Ostwald pointedly and repeatedly used Hirschfeld's own words against him: "When homosexuals and those who support them claim that in regard to soldiers it does not involve a professional or commercial sale [*berufs- und gewerbsmäßige Hingabe*] of their bodies that must be emphatically disputed. And it can be disputed with Dr. Hirschfeld's own words" (84). In fact, much of the short chapter on Soldatenprostitution consists of quotations – some marked as such, others simply lifted but unacknowledged – from *Berlins Drittes Geschlecht* and material published in the WhK's *Jahrbuch für sexuelle Zwischenstufen*. Thus, after quoting at length Hirschfeld's discussion of the various material and immaterial advantages that motivate soldiers to seek contact with civilian homosexuals, Ostwald concluded that it provided incontrovertible evidence of prostitution: "The lack of money, the desire to lead a more comfortable existence, these are the mainsprings of the soldier's interactions with homosexual. That is in fact the essential thing about prostitution: to sell yourself for some kind of advantage. And that is clearly discernible in Soldatenprostitution" (85). For Ostwald, reaping any material advantages from sexual or romantic relationships was per definition prostitution, which is why, in the same chapter, he labelled any relationship between men from two different classes as "semi-prostitution" (*Halbprostitution*).

Yet Ostwald's collage technique did not merely quote and comment on Hirschfeld's text; it also significantly altered various passages in order to emphasize the illicit sexual nature of these military-civilian contacts. For example, instead of replacing Hirschfeld's description of a soldier bar with his own eyewitness version, Ostwald appropriated the sexologist's account but substantially embellished it such that these civilian "gentlemen" could be seen "nearly always casting smitten looks of desire at their burly artilleryman or svelte dragoon, now and then probably laying a hand on the tightly fitting pants" (85). Ostwald's additions to Hirschfeld's text call up a fantasy scenario in which men, whose privileged class background and wealth was marked by their fine clothes, are blatantly (and possessively) leering at "their" manly and attractive soldiers, occasionally touching them lasciviously through their body-hugging uniforms. As a result, Ostwald insisted that "one only needs to enter one of the numerous soldier bars ... and one will be convinced that real prostitution is happening" (85).

In contrast to Hirschfeld's fantasy of public decorum and chaste domesticity, then, Ostwald's tavern scene located the phenomenon of Soldatenprostitution in the public space of the bar. And whereas Hirschfeld's description rendered the sexual contacts between soldiers and civilians invisible to the uninitiated heterosexual visitor, who supposedly would never notice anything amiss, in Ostwald's fantasy scenario they become shockingly and unmistakably obvious. Indeed, the ability of sexually normal people to see the homosexual men's desires allows the scene to stand in for the sexual acts themselves, which Ostwald, like Hirschfeld, never described in detail. Of course, by restoring sexual desire to the phenomenon of Soldatenprostitution, Ostwald could present his bar scene as a more accurate representation of reality. But it is also easy to see all the trimmings of a homophobic fantasy in his tableaux of well-dressed civilians lecherously ogling and caressing "their" soldiers. Like the lecherous Jew in anti-Semitic fantasies, the homosexual here has bought the German soldier for his sinister sexual pleasures, no less an act of robbery because he has paid for it.[62]

However, perhaps the ultimate fantasy that Ostwald offered was one in which his supposedly authentic depiction of Soldatenprostitution supported Hirschfeld's efforts to decriminalize homosexuality:

> Homosexuals and their friends would do themselves the greatest favour if they would simply call things by their real name. Every false sentimentality, every attempt to hush up the facts must call for the sharpest criticism – which is absolutely warranted. Homosexuals should say honestly: Yes – prostitution by soldiers does exist; we are forced to seek illegitimate gratification of our drives because legitimate [satisfaction] is banned and forbidden. Precisely the existence of prostitution by male soldiers is probably most suited to effect a change in the laws and in people's attitudes. (88)

Though once again his words mimic Hirschfeld's, the claim seems misguided at best. Most prominently, there is a distinct disconnect between his earlier acknowledgment of the materialist causes of male prostitution by soldiers (for which the military was to blame) and the political campaign for homosexual rights. In particular, Ostwald's tavern scenario not only attributed sole agency (and thus culpability) entirely to the homosexual civilian but also depicted him as someone who preyed upon masculine but essentially innocent soldiers. Indeed, the very means by which homosexuals were supposed to "shock" the public into decriminalizing homosexuality relied on a scandalous violation of soldiers' sexual innocence.[63]

The false optimism of both Hirschfeld and Ostwald became apparent once the broader public was forced to confront the scope of Soldatenprostitution in the wake of testimony at the first Harden-Moltke trial in October 1907, just one year after Ostwald's pamphlet was published. By all accounts, the revelation was inadvertent. Apparently in response to a question about whether homosexual excesses were a common occurrence among soldiers in the Garde du Corps, Johann Bollhardt, the former soldier called to testify about the homosexual orgies that Lynar had organized (which Harden believed Moltke had attended), stated that such things were "now forbidden."[64] In response to the enormous laughter his comment provoked among those allowed to remain in the courtroom during his sexually explicit testimony, the witness explained that he was referring to the illicit relations between male civilians and soldiers in his former unit, and the uniform regulations meant to prevent them: "I mean, it is now forbidden to go out in white pants and high boots; earlier it was allowed, that was, in a manner of speaking, the signal [*Erkennungszeichen*], and soldiers dressed like this were sexually harassed (*belästigt*) a lot by men."[65]

Because the press, which supplied their own stenographers, removed sexually explicit testimony in the published transcripts of the trial, it is unclear whether Bollhardt provided additional details about such interactions. The social-democratic Magdeburg *Volksstimme* offered a slightly different account of what was said: "I meant that differently: Whenever a soldier used to go out in white pants and high boots, then he would be accosted a lot by men. That was the sign [*Zeichen*]. That is now forbidden by the regiment."[66] In either case, his testimony that the elite Guard unit's stunning dress uniform served as a "signal" or "sign" to homosexuals offered clear public confirmation of a flourishing underground sex market. And the commander's decision to forbid soldiers from donning the uniform for everyday evenings on the town indicated that they were aware of what had been transpiring and what particular uniforms signified to homosexual civilians in the evenings in particular locations. It is likely the case, however, that these uniforms had become a "sign" or "signal" to homosexuals only because conscripts in this unit had a history of donning the stunning dress uniforms for prostitution. In fact, soldiers sometimes solicited from uninterested male civilians, especially in parts of the Tiergarten that were well-known for Soldatenprostitution. In his memoir, for instance, Tresckow recalled that "recently it even happened that Minister [of the Interior] von Bethmann [who became chancellor in 1909], who was by chance taking a walk there, was made such an offer. When he informed me of this indignantly, I had patrols conduct surveillance of the area."⁶⁷

Nevertheless, as Bollhardt indicated, soldiers in dress uniforms also experienced unwanted overtures and even sexual harassment from homosexual civilians. This claim is also corroborated by stories reprinted in the WhK's publications. For instance, in 1893 a drunken man was apparently arrested for making lewd propositions to a military guard in Berlin.⁶⁸ Similarly in 1907, a French abbot, who was propositioning soldiers in a park during a visit to German-annexed Metz, was forcibly taken by one of these soldiers to the latter's nearby guardhouse, where he was handed over to the local police.⁶⁹ And in the wake of the Harden-Moltke trial, such incidents (or their reporting) seemed to increase. Thus, in 1908, the successor to the *Monatsbericht* reported on the arrest of a Frankfurt man who sought to purchase illicit sexual favours from a soldier of the 81st Infantry Regiment on guard duty as well as on the sentencing of a fifty-year-old tailor in Danzig for making immoral requests of a string of artillery soldiers.⁷⁰

In any case, the press reaction to Bollhardt's testimony, like the circumspect coverage of what he actually said, ranged from outrage to silence. For example, because the *Coburger Zeitung* did not actually cover either the testimony about the "orgies" at Lynar's residence or Bollhardt's admission about male prostitution, it never addressed the issue directly. But in "A Serious Afterword to the Moltke-Harden Case," it reproduced an editorial from the "strict Protestant" and conservative *Reichsbote*, which only obliquely addressed the issue of male prostitution by soldiers: "[W]hatever horrific things the Moltke-Harden case has revealed, it is only a symptom, an effect, not a cause. Wherever … venal self-advancement [*feiles Strebertum*], wherever reckless greed and hedonism [*Erwerbs- und Genußsucht*] reign, … that is where the ground has been cleared for vice."⁷¹ For conservative papers, Soldatenprostitution was simply a result of the general decay of morals in a modern, materialistic society. Other papers, such as the high-brow, liberal *Vossische Zeitung*, also never mentioned the issue of prostitution by soldiers directly.

Unsurprisingly, Germany's first tabloid paper, the *BZ am Mittag*, was less circumspect. Even before closing arguments began in the trial, its editor opined:

> The benefit of this court case for the general public rests on moral, social, and political grounds. The revelation of perversities will doubtless call forth a lively discussion of issues related to Paragraph 175, while at the same time giving reason for heightened vigilance vis-à-vis the danger that

young and untainted [*unbelastet*] individuals are prostituting themselves for money or because they are forced to [*durch Zwang*] [...]

It is Harden's achievement that he has put the material for judging our internal conditions in the hands of the public. It falls to public opinion to draw from it the political consequences.[72]

Though unusual in explicitly mentioning soldiers' involvement in male prostitution, the editorial muddied the waters by suggesting that sometimes prostituting soldiers were "forced" to do so. The mention of force is undoubtedly a reference to the sex "orgies" that Major von Lynar organized, discussed in the previous chapter. Though Lynar may have compensated the soldiers who participated in his sex parties (Bollhardt denied receiving any money), most commentators regarded it instead as a situation in which soldiers felt coerced to participate by a superior officer.[73] But from the paper's point of view, both were simply "perversities" whose revelations required a debate about the merits of Paragraph 175. As a publication of the liberal Ullstein House, the *BZ am Mittag* often supported the WhK's efforts to decriminalize same-sex activity among men, though its position often varied. For instance, in the wake of the death of the steel magnate Friedrich Alfred Krupp, likely a suicide, following news reports of his sexual escapades with young Italian men on the island of Capri in 1902, the paper called for the repeal of Paragraph 175.[74] But in response to another scandal just three years later, it urged the Reichstag to proceed cautiously on the issue.[75] It clearly viewed the issue of male prostitution by soldiers as a similar call for caution, for unlike homosexuals, these young men were supposedly "untainted." The word, of course, indexed the long-standing presumption in the sexological community that sexual inversion represented a form of degeneration or pathology.[76] In any case, as the editorial's concluding praise for Harden's efforts, Soldatenprostitution offered liberal papers yet one more reason for demanding a more politically powerful public sphere with the capacity to provide better oversight of the military.

In any case, the *BZ am Mittag* was certainly not wrong in expecting that the revelations of the trial would lead to lively public debate. Along with the sexual abuses of conscripts by homosexual officers, the Reichstag took up the issue of male prostitution by soldiers on 22 November 1907, with representatives from nearly every party taking the opportunity to express their dismay. Most speakers chose to focus on the actions of Lynar and Hohenau (discussed in the previous chapter). And as in the more circumspect editorials, many speakers chose not to mention Soldatenprostitution explicitly, preferring to quote, as Peter Spahn of the Center Party did, Harden's accusation "that whole regiments are contaminated [*verseucht*]."⁷⁷ One important exception, though, was August Bebel, the longtime leader of the Social Democrats. Even after Chancellor Bernhard von Bülow had rejected Spahn's allegations by insisting that "the conditions of the declining Roman Empire do not reign in the German Army," the head of the SPD party zeroed in on the military's hypocrisy and lack of transparency:

> Why did someone [*man*] issue the order in Potsdam that the troops of the Gardes du Corps are no longer permitted to go out in white leather pants and tall boots [*Kanonenstiefel*]? Such an edict could only have come from the regimental commander, and yet the general commander of the Guards appeared at the trial and testified that he did not know anything, all of it was unfamiliar. There is thus at least one regiment that is contaminated and which was forbidden to appear off-duty [*außerdienstlich*] in their usual garb ... It is so bad – you can read it in the press – that the individuals who sell themselves as male prostitutes are not even afraid of the police, but rather the police are afraid of them.⁷⁸

Bebel's sharp attack not only targeted the apparent prevalence of soldiers operating as male prostitutes in the elite Guards but also implied that the commander of the guards, Lieutenant-General Gustav von Kessel, had lied under oath at the Harden-Moltke trial in order to cover up the army's knowledge of Soldatenprostitution. (Because Tresckow had personally discussed with Kessel ways of combatting Soldatenprostitution, the police commissioner was also shocked that the general had unabashedly lied under oath.)⁷⁹

As with the illicit behaviours in Lynar's residence discussed in the previous chapter, caricaturists offered the public various images to concretize what was meant by words like "tainted," "untainted," and "contaminated." For instance, a multicoloured drawing in the 26 November issue of *Der Wahre Jacob* imagined, as its title indicated, the "Nightlife in Potsdam" (Figure 3.1). Prominently visible against the dark night in his white cuirassier uniform, a soldier trolling for customers accosts an older officer walking by in a darker overcoat (suggesting he's from another unit): "Well now, big guy [*Dicker*], do you want to come with me?" By placing the event in Potsdam rather than Berlin, the drawing imagines Soldatenprostitution as something that occurs primarily within the military but outside the hierarchical strictures in which soldiers were compelled to sexually submit to the desires of superiors. Indeed, addressing the officer so informally and casually suggests a brazen reversal of military hierarchies. But the greater threat is signalled in

116 Uniform Fantasies

Figure 3.1. "Nightlife in Potsdam," caricature produced in response to testimony by Johann Bollhardt at the first Harden-Moltke libel trial. From *Der Wahre Jacob*, Nr. 557 (26 November 1907), p. 5615. Universitätsbibliothek Heidelberg.

the feminization of the soldier as a prostitute, symbolized by the small women's purse hanging from his hands, the lipstick he sports, and the demure effeminate pose he strikes, with his knees touching and his hands bashfully clasped in front of his genitals. The image intimates that engaging in prostitution threatened to render all soldiers as effeminate as the civilian homosexuals who chased after them.

But with so many deputies issuing broad accusations against the military and the Prussian Guard units in particular, the Prussian war minister, Karl von Einem, addressed the body immediately after Bebel finished speaking. After denying other unrelated allegations Bebel made in his speech, he turned to the issue of Soldatenprostitution: "Now, gentlemen, I must concede a different point to Deputy Bebel. The evil that Bebel speaks about has admittedly grown significantly in Berlin over the past decades. That's also what Harden was referring to when in his trial he said that whole regiments are contaminated. There may be an exaggeration or two in such claims. But the facts are indeed quite clear that our soldiers resist only with great effort the assaults that scoundrels [*Buben*] from civilian circles are making against them."[80] At one level, Einem's public statement amounted to a surprising concession, since he not only acknowledged the phenomenon publicly but also explicitly concurred with both Bebel and Harden, two men he clearly held in great disdain. Despite some exaggeration on their part, Einem essentially agreed with their assessment that Soldatenprostitution had become a significant problem over the past decades and that its reach had "contaminated" whole regiments.

Yet even as his speech seemed to acknowledge the reality and extent of the problem, the war minister in fact offered his listeners a fantasy scenario by insisting on the "fact" (*Tatsache*) that homosexual civilians were the aggressors and that military personnel could barely defend themselves against them. By designating such sexual advances as an attack, Einem of course absolved soldiers of any responsibility for their involvement, while reconfiguring the army's mission from one of disciplining its wayward soldiers to one of protecting these defenceless victims. Thus, the military's countermeasures – for instance, placing restrictions on wearing the distinctive and erotically charged dress uniforms after dark – was less a sign of the army's effort to reassert control over its soldiers than a "necessary [regulation] in order to protect these people from the attacks perpetrated by perverse members of the civilian population [*vor den Angriffen der pervers veranlagten Teile des Zivilpublikums*]."[81] Moreover, the metaphor of attack desexualized these encounters by recasting them in military metaphors. The solution for Einem, then, was essentially a military one: to implement measures within the army – such as placing restrictions on which uniforms could be worn during soldiers' free time as well as which bars they could patronize – in order to keep its healthy and normal troops safely out of reach of homosexual aggressors in the civilian population.

Though nearly all Reichstag deputies who spoke after Einem praised the war minister's forthright manner in acknowledging the problems, not every member was satisfied with his explanations. For instance, Eduard David, who belonged to the SPD's reformist wing, saw Einem's effort to tar the reputation of civilian homosexuals as an attempt to divert attention from the alleged sexual abuse of soldiers by officers. In addition to the SPD, many homosexuals also seemed to have taken offence at Einem's characterization of homosexual civilians as "scoundrels." Taking a page from Ulrichs's playbook, the anonymous author of *Das perverse Berlin* gave clear expression to his indignation: "There are not any paragraphs in our entire penal code that forbid civilians from cultivating intimate relationships with soldiers that otherwise do not violate the law. Therefore the homosexual who maintains such non-punishable contacts does not have to allow himself to be berated with insults and derogatory words. Not even from a Prussian war minister."[82] Among other criticisms, *Das perverse Berlin* also ridiculed the idea that manly soldiers were barely capable of defending themselves against civilian homosexuals. He noted that while the latter were seen as essentially weak and effeminate, the former were actually armed with daggers, trained to kill, and could easily – and legitimately – have resorted to violence to protect themselves.[83] Indeed, as we have seen, several newspaper articles reprinted in WhK publications show soldiers arresting or even firing on male civilians who made unwelcome sexual propositions to them, especially when they were on duty.

It is not difficult, then, to see the war minister's emphasis on "homosexual aggression" as the kind of fantasy that flew in the face of reality rather than the kind that actually structured it. Nevertheless, I want to suggest that for all its flimsiness, Einem's characterization of these sexual trysts as homosexual "aggression" did accurately represent the military's sense of its powerlessness to check homosexual desire. Moreover, other parts of Einem's speech suggested that sexual propositions from "aggressive" homosexuals not only constituted an assault on soldiers' innocence but also on his own. For example, the war minister prefaced his remarks on Soldatenprostitution by declaring: "I have never read anything about such things; they were foreign to me, and they were disgusting."[84] By claiming not to have any knowledge of homosexual desire – in itself "disgusting" – prior to these revelations, Einem implied that his own sexual innocence, that is, his lack of knowledge of (homo)sexual matters, has been defiled by his need to investigate the matter. This investment in innocence, in a lack of knowledge, also extended to the troops themselves. Rather than receiving training in how to respond to unwanted solicitations from homosexual civilians, or, as the author of *Das perverse Berlin* pointed out, how to use their training in deadly force, the army's relatively recent uniform regulations were essentially paternalistic: in regulating the garment inciting desire, the army sought not only to prevent such advances but also to effectively shield the soldiers from the knowledge of homosexuality required to respond appropriately.

It would seem, then, that for the military leadership and public alike the problem of Soldatenprostitution originated just as much in the *knowledge* of the illicit relations (and the resulting fantasies that arose out of the dearth of details) as in the sexual acts themselves. But it was exactly this insistence on a lack of knowledge that *Das perverse Berlin* sought to reveal as a false account. As the book noted, the war minister's efforts to lay the blame for Soldatenprostitution on homosexual aggression failed to take account of the soldiers' own active participation in the underground economy. After all, civilian men had no authority over the soldiers: "No, Herr von Einem! If homosexuals really do dare to approach soldiers, the former only do so because they know that such advances are not unwelcome to the latter. Of course, there may sometimes be exceptions. But it has also been the case that soldiers who have sought out such connections have also made mistakes – that is, approached civilians who weren't homosexual. Does Herr von Einem know nothing about that? Or that soldiers have also turned out to be blackmailers?"[85] By questioning the war minister's claim of ignorance, *Das perverse Berlin* implied that he was suppressing evidence. But the book's rejoinder also sought to change the terms of debate by making the soldier the primary agent in such transactions: even if homosexuals sometimes took the first steps, it was only because the soldiers had made it clear that they, as a whole, welcomed such advances. Thus, any unwelcome sexual advances initiated by homosexual civilians merely formed the "exception" to the rule, in part because they did *not* conform to the subordinate and deferential code of behaviour expected of civilians.

In the dearth of reliable facts, then, the main pronouncements about Soldatenprostitution before and even after the shocking revelations at the first Harden-Moltke trial offered fantasy scenarios that, while claiming to provide clear examples of what was "really going on," merely obfuscated the issue through scenes and tableaux that supported the authors' political agendas. To the extent that these fantasies were too

120 Uniform Fantasies

patently obvious as such, they provoked revisions and alternative scenarios. Yet despite the conflicts between Hirschfeld and Ostwald (over whether these relations constituted prostitution or how to use them to support the decriminalization of Paragraph 175) or the debate between Einem and the anonymous author of *Das perverse Berlin* (about who primarily initiated these illicit sexual contacts), all nonetheless, explicitly or implicitly, acknowledged that the military uniform had become an erotic fetish object for homosexual civilians. How that came to be and what it reveals about the erotic economy of militarism and the tensions between knowledge and fantasy is the focus of the next section.

In/appropriate Desire: The Queer Fetish for Military Uniforms

Though the war minister's effort to portray German soldiers as innocent victims of homosexual aggression failed to convince either homosexual activists or members of the SPD, he found more common ground in depicting the homosexual desire for men in uniform as a pathological manifestation. After protesting his disgust and lack of familiarity with the topic, Einem explained that he had "been moved to read about this issue in brochures and scientific texts, and from those it is quite clear that the men who are afflicted with this passion search out those men who appear to them to be the strong, the perfect ones in terms of manly strength."[86] As a result, he continued, "porters, coachmen, and draymen are supposed to be special objects of their desire, and one of the most famous experts in this scientific-medical question, Dr. Moll, has written that these people encounter bravery and strength in the soldier, quasi in the uniform, and that is exactly what they are looking for."[87] Einem's public reference to Albert Moll is striking, for it indicates that sexology was being taken seriously as an authoritative field not only by the homosexual vice unit of the Berlin police, whose officers worked closely with both Hirschfeld and Moll, but also by those at the highest levels of German government – at least in this matter. (Though there is no evidence for it in the memoirs of either Tresckow or Einem, it seems probable that Einem was directed to Moll's work by the Berlin police since it is clear that commanders regularly sought out Tresckow's counsel.) Einem, of course, used Moll's sexological research to pathologize homosexuals for their "affliction" more generally, but also for their specific desire for lower-class men – especially soldiers in uniform, who represented the masculine ideal they were searching for.

A multicoloured caricature that appeared on the cover of the 14 November edition of the Viennese-based *Die Muskete* anticipated Einem's words by a few weeks (see Figure 3.2). Entitled "Hero

Uniform Fetishism, Male Prostitution, and German Soldiers 121

Figure 3.2. "Hero Worship," caricature produced in response to testimony by Johann Bollhardt at the first Harden-Moltke libel trial. Cover illustration from *Die Muskete: Humoristische Wochenschrift* (14 November 1907), p. 1. Österreichische Nationalbibliothek Vienna. Call Number: 449976-D.5.1907–1908.

Worship" (*Heldenverehrung*), the image features a physically strapping soldier, dressed in the white uniform and knee-high boots of the Prussian Guard cuirassiers and wearing a helmet with a prominent metal imperial eagle on top, his left hand on his sword hilt. As the manly soldier confidently strides through what looks to be the Tiergarten, he seems to be oblivious to the horde of admiring men – mostly well-dressed civilians with a couple of visible officers – following respectfully behind, straining their necks and eyes to gawk at the incarnation of masculinity. But though, like Einem's words, the image foregrounds the desire of the wealthier homosexuals, who it would seem are driving the prostitution, it stops short of suggesting that military personnel could barely defend themselves against the admiration of homosexuals, for in place of the effeminate soldier-prostitute soliciting men, the artist has emphasized the soldier's muscularity and weaponry as part of the essential attributes that elicit homosexual desire.

The centrality of the cuirassier uniform in the caricature also emphasizes the importance of military dress to the entire economy of Soldatenprostitution, which in Einem's characterization of the sexological literature is reduced to an accident: that which is "quasi" to the homosexual's desire, rather than the key locus, which in the war minister's understanding lies in the body underneath, that is, the bravery and strength it merely represents. In fact, like his avoidance of the terms homosexual or Urning in favour of "these people" or "perverted" civilians, Einem stopped short of specifically naming the pathological condition he was describing – that is, not only same-sex desire, but especially fetishism. Though fetishism joined sadism, masochism, and contrary sexual sensation (as a catch-all for same-sex desire conceived of as gender inversion as well as an incipient form of transgender identity) as one of the four primary pathologies in Krafft-Ebing's diagnostic schema, Foucault has suggested that fetishism "served as the guiding thread for analyzing all the other deviations" of the sexual instinct for "in it one could clearly perceive the way in which the instinct became fastened to an object."[88] Moreover, in the nineteenth century, fetishism assumed increasing importance not only as an analytical category for understanding sex but also as a term of economic analysis as well. The two applications, however, were not as far apart as they might seem, for as Foucault pointed out, the discourse of sexuality was itself "caught between a law of reality (economic necessity being its most abrupt and immediate form) and an economy of pleasure which was always attempting to circumvent that law."[89]

Despite ascribing special importance to fetishism, Foucault's work avoided drawing on sexology, psychoanalysis, or even Marxism to understand how the sexual instinct became fastened to objects, viewing these approaches as either misguided (as in the case of Marxist analyses of sexuality) or as forms of control that his study was criticizing (as in the case of sexology and psychoanalysis).[90] Yet Marxist and psychoanalytic theories of fetishism are useful for thinking about both male prostitution by soldiers and the queer predilection for uniforms that underlay it. Soldatenprostitution, after all, is sexual behaviour that involves economic exchanges. In addition, Marx's approach to commodity fetishism also holds promise for understanding the fetishization of uniforms as a consequence of the army's own practices, which, in turn, derive from the way that capitalism organized social relations more generally in Imperial Germany. Moreover, combining Marx's notion of commodity fetishism with psychological and psychoanalytic approaches not only opens up a new understanding of the queer fascination for uniforms in Imperial Germany, it also suggests a way to read military policy as itself marked by uniform fetishism.

From its origins as a concept, fetishism was conceived as a problem of meaning – of ascertaining the "true" meaning or value of various objects. In its colonialist beginnings, the term designated those objects that another culture treated as valuable but from a Western colonialist's point of view appeared "objectively" worthless.[91] Drawing in part on this colonial legacy, Marx's concept of the commodity fetish inverted the hierarchical positions to the extent that, under capitalism, it is European industrial society that misunderstood the true meaning of objects – in this case, the commodities produced under capitalism – by seeing them as things with their own intrinsic values rather than as products of social labour.[92] Likewise, Binet defined sexual fetishes as the "worship of things that are inappropriate for serving the immediate goals of procreation."[93] In this case, the fetishist ascribed meaning and value to body parts and objects (especially articles of clothing) that were, from the perspective of human procreation, worthless. Though historically distinct and addressing disparate issues, all three conceptions of fetishism (colonial, Marxist, and sexological) presumed that there was an objective truth about the meaning and value of objects that others – "primitive" societies, capitalist subjects, and pathological individuals – failed to know or understand.

But as is the case with ideology, which gives a desirable but distorted view of reality, we can also read fetishism as a problem of fantasy. In the application of the term to sexuality, Binet identified fetishism as a pathology of fantasy and imagination, claiming that fetishists replaced reproductive coitus with fantasy: "They obtain their climax by means of their fantasy. With them, the joys of the imagination accompany the material pleasure, increase it, and provide it with its entire value."[94] Likewise, Marx's account of commodity fetishism theorized that the exchange of commodities in a capitalist system has transformed social reality into something else marked by fantasy. According to Marx, social relations (organized forms of labour) adopt "the fantastic form of a relation between things" that then "appear" to the human brain "as independent beings endowed with life."[95] And he applied the label fetishism to designate this "fantastic form" that "attaches itself to the products of labour, so soon as they are produced as commodities, and which is therefore inseparable from the production of commodities."[96] For Marx, then, the marketplace of commodities established a system of exchange value that obscured both the object's use value and the social value of the human labour that produced it. Because these inanimate objects took on a life of their own in relation to each other, the producers (and consumers) treated them all as fetishistic objects – without realizing it: "[W]henever, by an exchange, we equate as values our different products, by that very act, we also equate, as human labour, the different kinds of labour expended upon them. We are not aware of it, nevertheless we do it."[97] Like ideological fantasies, commodity fetishism works to the extent that people are not aware of this layer of dissimulation, even as it guides their behaviour. As Žižek summarizes, in "the Marxian formula 'they do not know it, but they are doing it': the illusion is not on the side of knowledge, it is already on the side of reality itself, of what the people are doing. What they do not know is that their social reality itself, their activity, is guided by an illusion, by a fetishistic inversion."[98]

Though Marx is talking about economic systems and not sexual desire, his theory offers one important avenue for thinking about uniform fetishism, especially in relation to male prostitution by soldiers. Though officers were required to purchase their uniforms (the army supplied uniforms to conscripts), military dress was not a typical commodity with exchange value for army personnel.[99] Nevertheless, the parade, gala, and dress uniforms were imbued with a fetishistic meaning from the start by their function as markers of social distinction within the social relations that prevailed in Imperial Germany. At the Prussian court, for instance, military officers outranked civilians such that generals came before ministers, including even the chancellor.[100] Meanwhile, the expected civilian deference to the man in uniform was a staple among the anecdotes from this period. For example, the historian Eda Sagarra recalled an incident involving her father when he was visiting a colleague at the University of Berlin. As the two scholars were strolling down one of the busy streets, "they were approached by a young officer with a crimson stripe on the trousers, denoting membership of the General Staff." According to Sagarra, the German professor "stepped down to the roadway as he passed; my father, protected by his ignorance of the language and the custom of the country, walked on." Though Sagarra's father was surprised to find himself being scolded by the insulted officer, he was more taken aback by "the anxiety of the professor [trying] to explain to the young blood that my father was a foreigner and knew no better."[101]

Though civilians were expected to be able to identify different units by their uniforms, military dress of any kind marked its wearer as special. As Lt.-General Albert von Boguslawski explained:

> If one asks us whether we want to concede a special place to the officer in these current conditions, we answer unconditionally with yes, but not because of the individual person, but rather only because of the dignity of the clothes he wears. The Kaiser wears these clothes as well as the entire army from general down to the youngest recruit. The word about the king's coat, as much as it is anathema to all shades of democracy, has its meaning through that fact. If on that account the clothes impose certain obligations on its wearer, then it can also lay claim to being respected by all citizens.[102]

In Boguslawski's account, the king's body – clothed in the military uniform – imbued all uniforms with a special "dignity," bathing its wearer in an aura of superiority vis-à-vis "mere" civilians. As Frevert notes, this "caste spirit" was not confined to the officer corps but also "spilled over into the troops," leading to cases of violence when conscripts "asserted their higher social standing" with working-class men around the same age.[103] In fact, the prestige of the military uniform operated as a form of symbolic compensation for these poorly paid conscripts.[104] In these cases, social relations were expressed (or negotiated) through articles of clothing. Though everyone knew that members of the armed forces were also mere mortals, they and the public behaved as if they possessed an innate superiority merely because of their uniform.

Beyond their larger role in making manifest social relations between military personnel and civilians, military uniforms also exhibited social hierarchies within the armed forces that in turn reflected the structural inequalities of a capitalist society. Most obviously, within each regiment the insignias of rank on the uniform denoted the codified distribution of power stretching from conscript to general. And much like the social relations under capitalism, these ranks also replicated the class structures of society, with membership in the officer corps reserved for sons of the nobility and the educated bourgeoisie, while conscripts and non-commissioned officers were drawn from the petit-bourgeoisie, peasantry, and working classes. And because the officer corps of each unit elected its new members from among the qualified candidates for active or reserve commissions, it also tended to reflect the social habitus of its own officers, in effect reproducing social hierarchies across the various units. Thus, even as late as 1913, the officer corps of particular Guard units were exclusively drawn from the higher nobility – a circumstance that repeatedly led to heated debates in the Reichstag.[105] But even for common soldiers, there was a clear pecking order, with members of the cavalry looking down on foot-soldiers, and Guards believing themselves "better than any other soldiers."[106] As a result, according to Bernhard Neff, the annual enlistments for cavalry units consisted primarily of conscripts who volunteered for the service, even though it required three years instead of two.[107]

Of course, because each company had its own unique uniform, the "definite social relation between men," to borrow Marx's phrasing, was – parallel to commodities like coats (one of Marx's favourite examples) – woven into the uniforms themselves, creating social distinctions not only between military personnel and civilians but also between different units. For example, since by tradition Hohenzollern princes were given honorary commissions as lieutenants in the First Regiment of Foot Guards at the age of ten, this unit's uniforms – with their striking crimson cuffs and trim – conferred enviable cachet.[108] But other units with even flashier uniforms also became coveted commissions. For instance, after ascending to the throne, Wilhelm II's favourite uniform was none other than that of the Garde du Corps, with its white pants, breastplate, and tall riding boots (see the three figures on the left in Figure 0.1). Their only rival for opulence was probably the uniform of the Hussars, which, true to its Hungarian origins as a cavalry unit, sported shorter jackets secured with braided cords, a cap made of seal fur (otter fur for officers), and edged trimming around the pants seat and riding boots.[109] In winter, the Guard Hussars exchanged their cloth jackets for ones made of fur, which during parades in the summer were draped over a shoulder (see the two figures on the right in Figure 0.1). As calvary units, both invariably drew their officers from only the most socially privileged backgrounds, who in essence paid for the honour of wearing ostentatious forms of military dress that confirmed their special social status in their own eyes – as well as in the eyes of others.

As "a fantastic form of a relation between things," military uniforms thus constituted a fetish in Marx's sense to the extent that they embodied and represented these social relations. On this basis, however, they also emerged as fetish objects within a broader erotic economy, which tended to reiterate the same social valuations, that is, the exclusivity of the particular units' officer corps and its pay scale for recruits (with the better-paid guard cavalry units on top and more technical branches on the bottom). For instance, already in *Psychopathia Sexualis*, Krafft-Ebing reported as "well-known fact" that "the female heart has a predominant weakness for military uniforms, whereby the cavalry-man maintains an advantage over the infantry-man."[110] And according to Moll, Einem's source of knowledge for his Reichstag speech, sexologists had also documented "a preference for the military" among homosexuals that also reflected these hierarchies.[111] Krafft-Ebing, for example, offered several case histories of male homosexuals drawn to men in uniform. Case 114, an unmarried merchant in his early thirties, confessed that "above all, I have been attracted for a long time to the robustly healthy and yet delicate bodies [*feinen Körperformen*] of cadets, who with their handsome uniforms and refined natures [*feinen Wesen*] especially excite my desire."[112] To the extent that the German public tended to view cadet academies as "the 'aristocrats' nursery garden'" in which families from lower birth were excluded, this man's individual fetish also reflected broader social hierarchies.[113]

Of course, not every man in military uniform was an actual soldier. According to Hirschfeld, "among the prostitutes in Berlin one can find ... sailors who have never touched a ship ... or soldiers who have never held a gun in their hand," thanks in part to a certain guesthouse "whose owner – a homosexual military tailor – had amassed an entire wardrobe of costumes, above all the uniforms of regiments."[114] Hirschfeld explained: "I learned of this unusual place through an Urning from southern Germany who, thanks to a recommendation from back home, could satisfy his craving for a *Gardekürassier* directly after he arrived [in Berlin] late in the evening. After I expressed my surprise at how quickly he was able to find a cuirassier, he explained that this innkeeper had said that there was nothing easier than making a cavalryman out of an infantryman."[115] While military dress was designed to diminish the individuality of the soldier in favour of the uniformity of all members of a troop, here the exchangeability of the uniform further emphasized the exchangeability of the soldier. For uniform fetishists, the uniqueness of the uniform trumped the individuality of its wearer, furthering the exchangeability of the sexual partner underneath it: a cavalryman was any soldier in a cavalry uniform. Indeed, as Walter Benjamin pointed out, prostitutes combined the function of "seller and sold in one."[116] In the case of Soldatenprostitution, the uniform transformed the soldier into a commodity which he could then – as the seller – exchange for money. This transformation of bodies into an exchangeable ware is, of course, commodity fetishism par excellence. As Marx noted early on in the *Economic and Philosophic Manuscripts of 1844*, "prostitution is only a *specific* expression of the *general* prostitution of the *labourer*."[117]

The interchangeability of soldiers in favour of the distinctness of the uniform points to the role of fantasy not only in the marketplace of commodities but also in the erotic economy of desire. According to Binet, the fetishist experienced a chance association between his beloved and "a secondary and insignificant detail," to which he ascribed an excessive sexual meaning.[118] All subsequent sexologists agreed that the fetish was triggered by, as Krafft-Ebing explained, "some event which determined the association of lustful feeling with the single impression. This event must be sought for in the time of early youth, and, as a rule, occurs in connection with the first awakening of the sexual life."[119] Freud, of course, famously claimed to trace back the initial impression of most male fetishists to a realization that the mother had no penis, which precipitated the boy to cover up that traumatic knowledge (since it implied the possibility of his own castration) with a fascinating substitute – a foot, a shoe. But the psychoanalyst's real contribution to the debate was his formulation of a "divided attitude" in which simultaneous disavowal was combined with affirmation: in his theory, "that women were castrated and that they were not castrated."[120] As Žižek explains, in contrast to "the Marxian formula 'they do not know it, but they are doing it,'" the divided consciousness of the erotic fetish operates according to a different "formula of fetishistic disavowal: 'I know very well, but still …'"[121] That is, to stick with Freud's formulation, the fetishist knows very well that his mother never had a penis (and hence was not castrated), but he fantasizes and acts (through his worship of the foot or the shoe) as if she had had one.

The uniform fetishism of queer men from Ulrichs onward exhibited this divided attitude. As we saw in the introduction, Ulrichs's earliest erotic fantasies revolved around the insuppressible image of a soldier – always nameless and non-descript – climbing through his bedroom window.[122] Coming at the onset of puberty, Ulrichs's fantasy has all the hallmarks of the founding event that, according to Krafft-Ebing, "as a rule, occurs in connection with the first awakening of the sexual life."[123] In addition, there is an awareness of excitement as well as a repression or disavowal of its sexual nature from his consciousness, such that his fantasy never went beyond the initial thought, for as he insisted the scenario was "completely without a goal" and "not in the least directed toward any particular pleasure."[124] Moreover, because Ulrichs claimed that this fantasy was never accompanied by masturbation, it may be the case that it drew additional strength from his suppression of sexual expression, since, as Binet argued, "chastity ... stimulates the erotic fantasy."[125]

Other homosexuals reported similar childhood experiences. For instance, Hirschfeld quoted the recollections of one Urning seeing a military officer for the first time: "In front of the soldiers marches an officer, the first I had ever seen in my life. – He is tall, burly [*kräftig*], with a blond moustache and blue, twinkling eyes. Every movement of his is strength and life and joy – – it seemed to me as if he were the cheery military music that I heard, as if he were the clear, cloudless sky and the pure, delightful autumn air that surrounded me." He continued: "A feeling of enormous, endless joy, of an urge to do or make something [*Taten- und Schaffensfreudigkeit*] and at the same time a horrible, suffocating desire overcomes me such that I involuntarily raise my hands aloft – and then begin to cry – unaware myself why."[126] Though Hirschfeld's informant is reporting on a childhood event, it is striking that he uses the present tense to talk about an instance in his distant past. In dissolving the intervening years, it suggests the event's lasting impression, which lives on as if it remained as fresh and vivid as the first time it happened.

Yet despite the luminous clarity of the image, there is something inexplicable in the event for Hirschfeld's informant, some part of the experience that is inaccessible to his consciousness. Thus, in contrast to Ulrichs's claims that the soldiers were in some sense a patently natural object of desire – "handsome bodies in their prime" – we need to look at what, to some degree, remained disavowed or hidden from the subject's own psyche and that produced the "divided consciousness."[127] One clue comes in Ulrichs's additional explanation for the Urnings' attraction to soldiers: "However, we also find freshness of spirit and, above all, that charming spiritual virginity among soldiers, and truly nowhere else than among them: that dewy innocence of mind and unpretentious self-awareness, a naivete which is still ignorant of urban vanity and coquetry."[128] Thus, even more attractive than their physical appearance was a specific innocence, defined in opposition to sexual experience, sexual knowledge, and self-awareness of their own sexual attractiveness. As Ulrichs explained to his Dioning readers: "If I am not mistaken, you feel exactly the same way as you would in the presence of an innocent, unspoiled country maiden."[129]

This fantasy of sexual innocence, I want to suggest, is the foundation for what is both known and disavowed in the queer uniform fetish. Moreover, this fetishism took two diametrically opposed forms, one based in a fantasy of the power of romantic love and one based in a fantasy of sexual perversion as innocence. Ulrichs laid out this first fantasy in his writings when he theorized that heterosexual soldiers (Dionings, in his nomenclature) might be moved "to grant favours to a petitioning Urning" out of sympathy or a "bond of love," especially if he were "convinced that what the Urning feels for him is nothing but true and heartfelt love," even as he specified that Urnings also needed to compensate soldiers for these favours.[130] The double consciousness here is of course clear: despite the financial incentives for the soldier in the relationship, the homosexual fantasizes that the heterosexual soldier he has fallen in love with might also love him back. This fantasy seems to have been nourished by the difference between soldiers and professional male prostitutes in the account provided by Ulrichs's more knowledgeable informant, who distinguished between "young Dionings with low intentions" and the longer-term relationships the Urnings established with soldiers, where the transactional nature of the relationship was cloaked through a pretence of generosity and gifts: the Urning "whose wallet is emptied to defray the costs of 'an extra pair of pants' or some other luxury item."[131]

This split consciousness is even particularly apparent in the diaries of the otherwise clear-eyed commentator and WhK member, Eugen Wilhelm.[132] According to his biographer, Kevin Dubout, in the late 1880s and early 1890s, Wilhelm began visiting the various soldier brothels that operated near the scattered barracks in Strasbourg. As Dubout explains, such brothels catered to a poorer clientele and were thus dirtier and dingier than more upscale heterosexual bordellos.[133] In reaction to the environs and the transactional nature of the sexual experience, which repelled him, Wilhelm eventually sought out an alternative: visiting the more upscale heterosexual brothels to have the madam (*Puffmutter*) or the female prostitutes themselves help find a suitable soldier. In the fall of 1889, he was apparently introduced to a soldier named "Toni" with whom he promptly fell in love. To support his own romantic fantasies about the relation, Wilhelm never paid for sex directly but instead offered gifts, especially gifts of money. As he wrote "Toni" on 15 January 1890: "If you might need money, just write it to me openly and unashamedly, you know how much I would like to send you a New Year's gift and that you can also accept it from me."[134] Nevertheless, moments of doubt inevitably disrupted this fantasy of romance and mutual love. For instance, after another request for money a few months later, Wilhelm recorded in his diary: "*He asks for money, which initially displeases me*. Might that be the *only* reason why he writes me?" As Dubout notes, "the request for money disenchanted the relationship because it put into question its 'authenticity' and pushed less ideal motives into the foreground."[135]

Though many queer civilians fantasized about finding a long-term lover among the ranks, Soldatenprostitution also elicited a second fantasy that circulated around a quite different conception of sexual innocence in which heterosexual men sometimes engaged in same-sex acts – either for lack of women or out of friendship. While it seems likely that same-sex behaviour did occur in the all-male space of the Imperial German barracks, the only evidence comes from the 1913 autobiography of a working-class author who recalled from his infantry service in Hamburg in the late 1880s that "whenever I walked through the rooms, I often noticed that soldiers were unabashedly flirting [schmeichelten] with each other, sitting on the same footstool, kissing each other like girls in love. No one was offended by the insipid doings [dem faden Treiben]. Why play the moral outraged individual when the military society was itself responsible [schuld] for the unnatural [widernatürich] conditions that drove them to immorality."[136] While, as Frevert rightly points out, Bergg tows the SPD line in blaming the military for this immoral behaviour, it is also important to note that such behaviour was not taken as a sign of homosexual identity, but rather a kind of "insipid" behaviour provoked by the dehumanizing, all-male space of the army.[137] The implication was that such men were not only intrinsically "normal" (there is no sense in Bergg's description that a homosexual identity was even a legitimate possibility) but also *morally innocent* to the extent that they were not responsible for their actions, for the real cause for this perverse behaviour was their forced isolation in single-sex military barracks.

To pursue this second queer uniform fantasy of what I call "perverse innocence," I want to turn to the two scenarios offered by the anonymous author of *Das perverse Berlin*, which he introduces as evidence that soldiers were actively prostituting themselves and not, as the war minister claimed, merely the innocent victims of harassment by homosexual civilians. In the first scenario, a soldier

> in the squadron or company … tells his – mostly younger – comrades that one can earn some easy money in a certain way. Such a promise awakens their curiosity – as well as their desire for money. When did a young man – especially a soldier – ever have too much money! Thus, the silent sin is passed on from year to year. Sometimes the participation in such commerce with homosexuals is weaker, sometimes stronger. That depends only on the influence of the one who seduces his comrades; or on the profits his acts of mediation bring in.[138]

In the second scenario, a young male prostitute actually enlists in the army in order to use the uniform to increase his appeal and his illicit income. His newfound wealth, however, eventually awakens a jealous curiosity in his comrades, which the author of *Das perverse Berlin* imagines as the following: "'Gosh, Hans, where did you get all that money that I see you with? And who bought you the fine new dress uniform?' asks one or the other soldiers who sleep in the same room as Hans ... Next time, Hans takes his curious comrade with him, and since he's a pretty boy – everyone, after all, looks nice in a uniform – within just a short time he has a relationship – or even more than one!"[139] In both of these quite imaginative scenarios, the actively desiring homosexual, who played such a prominent role in the war minister's speech in Parliament, has been removed from the picture entirely and replaced by a knowledgeable peer – either one who infiltrated the military ranks or was already on the inside. Thus, rather than the victim of homosexual advances, it was the soldiers' insatiable appetite for money – can a young man, especially a poor soldier, have too much of it? – that leads them astray.

As an account offered by a homosexual author, these two scenarios tell us less – indeed, probably nothing – about the actual desires and motivations of the soldiers or, for that matter, any libidinal economy within the military itself. Yet they do tell us much about the structure of the anonymous author's desire for soldiers. As Žižek contends, "fantasy does not simply realize a desire in a hallucinatory way: rather ... a fantasy constitutes our desire, provides its co-ordinates; that is, it literally 'teaches us how to desire.'"[140] The first set of coordinates has, of course, already been clear from the start: the soldiers' masculinity and the erotic appeal of the uniform. But it is also apparent that the soldiers' innocence, in particular their sexual innocence, served as another important coordinate of desire. The two scenarios offered by *Das perverse Berlin* in fact preserve the soldiers' innocence since their desire for money, while a desire in its own right, was not a *sexual* desire (and certainly not a desire for sex with another man). By emphasizing the characteristic of prostitution as the soldiers' fundamental motivation, the author of *Das perverse Berlin* bracketed and implicitly dismissed the possibility that any soldiers might also have been seeking sexual satisfaction themselves. Moreover, the second scenario modifies the first in that the soldiers' desire for money turns out to be strangely congruent with the military's own values, for Hans not only uses the uniform to increase his appeal, but in fact funnels at least some of his illicit profits back into the purchase of a new dress uniform.

The next coordinate of desire is related to the previous one: in both fantasy scenarios offered by *Das perverse Berlin*, the desire for money is never a desire that appears alone, within an individual soldier, but instead arises out of his interactions with his fellow soldiers. Yet rather than merely a friendship of convenience, the new shared secret about Soldatenprostitution invariably reinforces their camaraderie, much as the shared secret around the sadistic punishment of Big L. initially strengthened the bonds between the cadets in Wildenbruch's novella (see the discussion in chapter 2). Thus, the scene of Hans's apparent interrogation is the communal setting of the barracks, and the interrogators are the "one or the other soldiers who sleep in the same room," a curious detail that seems to imbue the setting with an additional erotic subtext. But while seduction into prostitution at the hands of an older or more experienced comrade is, of course, a seduction into sex work, the seduction does not itself constitute a sex act. The distinction is critical because it casts the homosexual's desire and participation as fundamentally tangential to the practice of Soldatenprostitution. Here, the two imagined scenarios stage not only the soldiers' (hetero)sexual innocence, but the non-homosexual nature of their bonds with each other as well. Ultimately, the image of the heterosexual soldiers bonding with each other – in this case through their shared secret about how to earn money through prostitution – elicits the homosexual's desire by underwriting their fundamental heterosexuality (confirmed by the stipulation of payment).

These two scenarios suggest the importance of sustaining the core fantasy of the soldiers' innate, unchanging, and incontrovertible heterosexuality against any facts that indicate otherwise. As Ulrichs noted in his chapter on "Soldatenliebe" (Soldier love), "The more feminine the Urning's mind, the more manly the Dioning necessary to love him."[141] For Ulrichs, manliness is equated with a man's inherent and primary attraction to women. Moreover, there are striking similarities between the fantasies of civilians like Ulrichs or the anonymous author of *Das perverse Berlin*, and the fantasies of men – "military chasers," as they are called today – who are exclusively or primarily attracted to uniformed members of the armed forces. As the self-described military chaser Steven Zeeland admits: most men like himself "are at least as eager as conservative gay activists to believe in the existence of true, oh-so-rigid *heterosexuals* whose same-sex experiences *don't really count*. Indeed, it is precisely this sense of difference that drives us on. Without it, there would be no space to chase."[142] The fantasy of such men, then and today, is not to have sex with a *gay* man in the military, but rather to have sex with a straight man in uniform, and thereby have access, even if only momentarily, to a libidinal economy marked in *Das perverse Berlin* as *non-homosexual* male bonding. While this fantasy of having sex with Dionings or heterosexual soldiers may hold a transgressive appeal, the primary allure seems to be a fetishized notion of military camaraderie, since, at least from the vantage point of military chasers today, "the military love of comrades is something that gay life can't offer."[143] Much like Adam and Eve in the Garden of Eden before their expulsion for eating from the tree of knowledge, the sexually innocent and unaware male camaraderie of soldiers is an ideal state of grace from which gay men are excluded on account of their knowledge of their own same-sex sexual desire – a desire that also makes them aware of their fundamental difference from other men.[144]

The fantasy scenarios from *Das perverse Berlin* offer two important insights for this form of uniform fetishism in Imperial Germany. The first is that, for all the attempts – from Ulrichs to this anonymous book – to explain the phenomenon of Soldatenprostitution with the expanding tools of *scientia sexualis*, this will to knowledge – about the motivations of the homosexual – is accompanied by a will *not* to know about the putatively heterosexual soldiers, that is, not to subject them to the "careful" analysis of *scientia sexualis*, not to compel them to confess the secrets of their own desires but instead to presume their innocence even when they engaged in perverse behaviour. Indeed, in place of that knowledge, for instance, *Das perverse Berlin* offers up a fantasy of a pre-lapsarian "Barracks of Eden" in which, like the scene in Franz Bergg's memoirs, soldiers are perversely willing to engage in sexual play with other men, but are essentially innocent because their willingness is not motivated by sexual desire for other men (but rather by boredom or a lack of women). Thus, even as it promises to explain the "truth" of how soldiers came to engage in male prostitution, these scenarios articulate instead the desire of homosexual civilians who pay for sex with "straight" soldiers, that is, men who are merely, in modern parlance, "gay for pay."

The second is that for all its insistence on offering a fundamentally different account, *Das perverse Berlin* ultimately corroborates the war minister's key claim in front of the Reichstag: that manly soldiers are essentially innocent and heterosexual, and that it is exactly this fundamental "truth" that makes them so desirable to homosexuals. Yet the truth that must not be known, that must remain the object of a fundamental misunderstanding (*méconnaissance*, as Foucault puts it), is the pleasure that those on the political side of the army – the army leadership as well as the "state-supporting" segments of the German public – *also* take in the "innocent" masculinity, the "innocent" camaraderie of the rank-and-file soldiers, and the thrilling sight of the military uniform.[145] In fact, it is possible to read Einem's characterization of the men that, according to Moll, homosexuals desire as a self-description of the military's own recruiting practices, for like "the men who are afflicted with this passion," the military also "search[ed] out those men who appear to them to be the strong, the perfect ones in terms of manly strength" from the lower classes.[146] After all, as Frevert notes, "the army's strict standards on fitness ensured that only the largest, strongest, straightest and healthiest men were actually enlisted, and their subsequent physical training enhanced these advantages."[147] Likewise, the army's own uniform fetishism – based in the specialness conferred by military dress on its wearer – also made it possible for most people to, in Einem's words, "encounter bravery and strength in the soldier, quasi in the uniform."

Conclusion

This shared investment in the soldiers' innocence helps explain the public's outrage when the phenomenon of Soldatenprostitution did emerge into the broad light of day. For the brouhaha that greeted the revelations at the first Harden-Moltke trial indexed the public's sense that homosexuals were defiling and stealing (even if buying) the source of their pleasure: the soldiers' essential innocence. Indeed, because most German homosexual fantasies underlying Soldatenprostitution never challenged but instead reinforced the fantasy that all soldiers were incontrovertibly heterosexual and, in terms of homosexuality, sexually innocent, the only solution to the crisis brought about by such knowledge was to expel the homosexual as its putative cause. As police commissioner Tresckow concluded, "In any case, the trials with all their disclosures have damaged the homosexuals' cause more than they helped, since public opinion has quite rightfully been outraged over their brash behaviour."[148] The former military officer and leading anti-Semite Max Liebermann von Sonnenberg was even more explicit in his Reichstag speech. In response to Bebel's renewed call for abolishing the anti-sodomy law, Liebermann asserted: "Gentleman, under one condition, I would also be for striking Paragraph 175 – namely, if another law were created in its place that would punish such lapses with banishment to a colony. This colony would have to be located in the South Seas and cleared of all other inhabitants first."[149] This idea of banishing homosexuals recapitulates the punishment that befell Adam and Eve following their decision to taste the forbidden fruit from the Tree of Knowledge in Eden. But it is all too easy to detect a surplus of sadistic glee in Liebermann's invocation of a more powerful law and a more draconian punishment for same-sex transgressions.

Nevertheless, it should not be surprising that despite its flimsiness, it was Einem's account that ultimately sutured, at least for the "state-supporting" parties and their constituents, the rupture caused by the public's awareness of Soldatenprostitution. This act of sealing up, however, was not secured first and foremost by a "will to knowledge" about homosexuals' desires, as it might initially seem, but rather by a more fundamental "will to nonknowledge" about the military's own desires and those of its civilian supporters. As Liebermann asserted again, though his was by no means a lone voice: "I, at least, must admit that I was as excited as a child at Christmas by the Christmas present that the war minister gave us yesterday. (Bravo calls from the right!) The clear, sharp words of a soldier [*Soldatenworte*] have shooed away [*verscheucht*] like a fresh wind the stench of putrefaction hovering over our people. The power of lies is frighteningly big."[150] Liebermann's claim about the power of lies was, of course, directed against those who "mistakenly" believed that whole regiments were "contaminated" with homosexuality as a result of the revelations about Soldatenprostitution and other matters issuing from the Harden-Moltke trial – and who spoke their outrage in the Reichstag prior to hearing from the war minister. But the sentence more accurately characterizes the power of fantasy to shape and reshape reality, even in the face of facts that, from another point of view, might say otherwise. For the "gift" that the war minister gave was not any new knowledge but rather the occlusion of knowledge, and hence the ability of the discourse of militarism to keep, wrapped up and under wraps, what it "stubbornly" refused to see. The circularity of Liebermann's claim points to the power of the militarist fantasy, since the integrity of the war minister's military words – "the clear, sharp words of a soldier" – vouches for the integrity of the soldiers themselves and excises any need for making the prostituting soldiers an object of scrutiny.

Focusing on the role of fantasy in sexology, in the representations of Soldatenprostitution, and in the political discussions that ensued in newspapers and Parliament not only tells us much about the German soldier's role as an obscure object of desire but also yields some useful theoretical insights for investigating the history of sexuality, especially in cases where historians confront a dearth of reliable information. Foucault may be right to claim that "the will to nonknowledge" is merely another "vagary of the will to truth." After all, the war minister's exposition of the nature of the homosexual's desire, which drew on Moll's sexological "knowledge," offers as a clear example where the will to knowledge operated as a strategy of power. But it seems just as important to see Einem's elucidation of knowledge about homosexual desire as somehow derivative of his efforts to *not know* about his own or the public's desires and pleasures – its own uniform fetishism and investment in the sexual innocence of soldiers. As we have seen, the "divided consciousness" of fetishism is based on a "will to nonknowledge" – that is, fantasy – that also has powerful effects of its own. Moreover, its "stubbornness" suggests that "the will to nonknowledge" is not easily vanquished by knowledge claims, for the formula for this form of fetishistic disavowal is "I know very well, but still …" As a result, Žižek observes, fantasy does not merely obfuscate these ruptures or antagonisms, but derives its force from them: "An ideology really succeeds when even the facts which at first sight contradict it start to function as arguments in its favour."[151] In this case, the uniform fetishism of the war minister and his political supporters testifies to fantasy's tenacity, for the deep pleasure it provides makes it quite resistant to "facts" and rational argument.

Chapter Four

Camping in His Own Private Militarism: Thomas Mann's Queer Art of Failure and the Fantasies of Military Service

In 1900 Thomas Mann found himself conscripted into the German Army as a "one-year volunteer." Since he had been rejected for military service twice before, the Lübeck native was rather surprised and delighted at being found fit for active duty at his third and final appearance before the military review commission. Coming at the start of the new century and just as he turned twenty-five himself, Mann – who would later alter details in his autobiographical writings in order to indicate that his life was guided by an overriding numerical logic – initially viewed his upcoming military service as predestined to be extraordinarily fateful, or as he wrote to a friend, "providential."[1] And as it turned out, the brief experience of military service did, in fact, prove fateful, though not in the way that he had originally envisioned, for he sought and received a medical discharge before three months had passed. It was, for the budding writer, an abject lesson in what Jack Halberstam has called "the queer art of failure."[2] Unfortunately, though, Mann's inability to live up to the disciplinary regime of the military did not, in fact, yield what Halberstam imagines to be the most tantalizing reward that queer failure offers: an "escape [from] the punishing norms that discipline behavior," such as heteronormativity and the standards of masculinity.[3] Rather, Mann's failure as a soldier led him to redouble his efforts to live and write, as he later put it, "like a soldier."

Perhaps because of its brevity, Mann's army stint has not yet attracted the sustained attention of scholars. Yet his failure as a one-year volunteer is interesting for a number of reasons, not least because it made its way into several important literary works, including one written by his brother (explored in the next chapter). More significantly, it did little to curb his persistent fascination with military masculinity, army uniforms, and service to the nation, unleashing a number of elaborate fantasies that continued right up through the First World War (and beyond). In addition to its value for Mann scholars, attending to the variations of these fantasies offers useful avenues for exploring the relationship between military service and same-sex identity in Imperial Germany – especially for homoerotically inclined men like Mann, who kept their distance from the organized queer emancipation movement. In fact, unlike most such men, Mann left a significant archive of these fantasies in the numerous letters, essays, and literary works he wrote during this period.

Mann's subsequent reworking of his military service also presents an interesting case study for re-examining the concept of militarism. Most historians have tended to view the number of conscripts, the length of their service, and their continued participation in veterans' associations and related groups as important evidence for the pervasiveness of military values throughout Imperial Germany, concluding that, as Ute Frevert puts it, "good citizens became distinguished less by their economic or cultural services and more by their ability and readiness to use weapons to defend their country."[4] Yet as Benjamin Ziemann and others have pointed out, this "official militarism" from the top spawned other militarisms from below that either, in the case of far-right groups emanating from the bourgeoisie, directly challenged the political status quo, or, in the case of men from working-class, petit-bourgeois, and peasant backgrounds, "appropriated the prestige of the military for their own purposes and with their own meanings."[5] Though Mann's enlistment was tightly bound up with his class privileges, it would be a mistake to assume that his understanding of military service aligned neatly with "the official façade of Wilhelmine militarism." In fact, Mann's attitude towards military duty was deeply ambivalent, at times dreading it and conniving ways to avoid it entirely, at other times embracing the idea of a year in uniform. Because of their individualistic and idiosyncratic constancy, I designate Mann's rich fantasies about military service in Imperial Germany "his own private militarism."[6]

My investigation into Mann's private militarism is divided into three parts that roughly follow the chronology of his life and literary production. In the first section, I probe the author's initial expectations about military service itself, for they open an important perspective into the individual psyche's complex interactions between the exciting fantasy of donning a colourful uniform and the harsh reality of military training and service. Though Mann later destroyed his diaries from this period, his letters to his childhood friend and confidante Otto Grautoff and the painter Paul Ehrenberg, with whom he had fallen in love around this time, indicate the extent to which his thoughts about military service were suffused with a range of fantasies and fears about his own masculinity, his erotic attraction to men, and his literary ambitions. This section also turns to two autobiographical essays to explore the rhetorical strategies he subsequently employed to "positively" spin his early discharge – and his failure to live up to the military norms for masculinity – for a broader public. Both demonstrate the resourcefulness of "his queer art of failure," which not only attribute his shortcomings as a soldier to the military's faulty standards as well as to an error made by the doctor during his enlistment screening but also transform this and other failures into ironic signs of his success.

Mann's ignoble discharge from the military did little to extinguish his initial interest in soldiering; in fact, it had quite the opposite effect, as he developed in his fiction ever more elaborate fantasies about military uniforms and service. The second section turns to the most famous of his uniform fantasies: the enlistment scene in the *Bekenntnisse des Hochstaplers Felix Krull: Der Memoiren erster Teil* (Confessions of Felix Krull, confidence man: The early years), which he drafted between 1909 and 1910. This chapter – a creative reworking of Mann's three appearances before the military recruitment board – articulates his most concerted effort to "appropriate the prestige of the military" for his own purposes and with his own meanings. At the same time, the novel also offers one of German literature's most sustained interrogations of the concept of fantasy. Just as important, though, as the subject matter of this fictional work, is its literary style, usually viewed as a modern adaption of the picaresque that departs from Mann's legendarily serious tone, which he called "erotic irony."[7] However, less well recognized – by critics and perhaps even by Mann himself – is that *Felix Krull* employs a very different form of irony, one more akin to gay male camp. Already in Mann's day, this aesthetic sensibility was closely associated with the wit of the effeminate aesthete Oscar Wilde, some of whose works Mann seems to have read in German translation.[8] But campy forms of ironic exaggeration and excess were also a prominent tone among the drag queens, fairies, and "aunts" who participated in the thriving queer scenes in Berlin and other parts of Central Europe. Thus, despite Mann's lack of sustained engagement with Wilde's oeuvre and his studious avoidance of German queer scenes, works like *Felix Krull* can expand our understanding of the ways his fiction is bound up with queer cultures of the day.

The final section then turns to Mann's aggressive and unconditional support of Germany in the First World War, especially the various essays that he wrote in the fall of 1914. Though ostensibly a defence of Germany's conduct of the war on behalf of "culture" (*Kultur*), they also offered Mann a new opportunity to extend his fantastical identification with soldiers and further articulate his aesthetics as deeply aligned with German militarism, a project that he undertook in *Betrachtungen eines Unpolitischen* (Reflections of a nonpolitical man), his most tortured and tortuous work. In addition to contextualizing Mann's wartime essays in relation to other German writers, I also connect them back to similar efforts by leaders in the queer emancipation movement to support the war. More significantly, Mann's wartime essays raise questions about the political independence of any individual or group that in the pre-war period sought to appropriate the prestige of the military for their own purposes.

In addition to its relevance for thinking through the concept of militarism, Thomas Mann's case presents a number of advantages to scholars working on this period. First, his hopes and fears about donning an army uniform offer insight into the relationship between military service, the psyche, and discourses about masculinity and male sexuality. And because his conception of his own military service – and military service more generally – was deeply embedded in his fantasy life and imagination, his writings enable us to hone some tools for theorizing the complex relationship between reality, fantasy, and ideology at the level of the individual. Yet for all its idiosyncratic individuality, Mann's own private militarism also has broader relevance, for as Todd Kontje argues, "Mann's efforts to come to terms with his troubled sexuality were symptomatic of a widespread sense of masculine crisis in early twentieth-century Germany."[9] Finally, focusing on Mann raises important methodological questions about sources. While he never wrote a full-fledged autobiography (and his two autobiographical essays include many false statements and ironic exaggerations), the author himself famously proclaimed of his fiction that "all of it is autobiography."[10] Thus, using Mann as a case study can also clarify the value of using literary sources to understand the past, as well as the methodologies required to unpack their historical significance.

The Volunteer Conscript

Universal military service in Germany had been in place for almost a century by the time that Thomas Mann began his brief stint in the army. First introduced in Prussia in 1813 during the Napoleonic Wars, conscription was part of the fundamental reorganization of the army in the wake of its shameful defeat to French forces in 1807. And in the wake of German unification following the Franco-Prussian War in 1870–1, all other German states were forced more or less to adopt the Prussian model of conscription.[11] However, despite the relative rigidity of its system, Prussia also instituted a shorter form of service for its most privileged citizens in 1822.[12] As the name implies, the position of the "one-year volunteer" (*Einjährig-Freiwilliger*) reduced the length of service from three years (two for the infantry after 1893) to just one. In addition to the significantly shorter time spent in active service, the one-year option came with a range of unique privileges, including the right to postpone the start of one's military service for up to three years, the opportunity to choose one's unit and location, the ability to live off-base following the initial training period, and complete exemption from demeaning duties on base, such as cleaning the kitchen, the barracks, or the grounds. One-year volunteers were also allowed to hire their own manservant from within the ranks to clean their uniforms and polish their boots and buttons. In fact, the release time from menial chores of all sorts enabled many one-year volunteers to pursue other interests during their year of active service, such as attending classes at the university.[13]

The largesse of the state, however, came at a steep price. To obtain the qualification certificate for one-year voluntary service, candidates needed to submit proof of good moral standing (*Unbescholtenheitszeugnis*) from either their school or the police, evidence of the requisite academic qualifications, and an affidavit from their father or legal guardian that they had the financial means to purchase their own uniforms, weaponry, lodging, and meals for the entire year.[14] These substantial costs, which ranged from 1,750 to 2,200 marks for the infantry, 2,300 to 2,700 marks for the artillery, and 3,400 to 3,600 marks for the cavalry, significantly exceeded the average yearly income for all men employed in the trades as well as that earned by many educated men.[15] Though Thomas Mann's father had left the family a considerable inheritance upon his death in 1891, coming up with the funds was not as easy as it seemed since the executors denied his request to use some of the estate's capital, leaving his mother to cover expenses from the interest she received.[16] The requisite educational attainment also posed some initial challenges, for Mann was an admittedly terrible student who had been held back three times.[17] Even so, after his widowed mother moved the family to Munich in 1892, Mann remained in Lübeck to finish just enough schooling to automatically qualify academically for the right to serve as a one-year volunteer – and avoid having to take an examination.[18]

Certainly, having young men of means pay for their own military training benefited the state's coffers. But from the army's perspective, the main goal of the one-year voluntary position was to develop the necessary personnel for its reserve officer corps. Meanwhile, the short-term advantages that one-year volunteers enjoyed during their active service were complemented by the long-term benefits of obtaining a commission as a reserve officer, since in a social and political system in which the army held such real and symbolic power, such appointments translated into professional advantages. Yet not every man who qualified as a one-year volunteer was eager to become a reserve officer – or even, for that matter, keen to spend a full year in uniform. Thomas Mann, for example, took the opportunity to put off his military service for three years, explaining to his friend and confidante Otto Grautoff, "I *can* always join earlier, which I will, however, refrain from doing. For now at least I am carefree in this regard."[19] Moreover, in advising his younger friend, who was about to turn twenty and needed to register with the military authorities, Mann came close to committing sedition, announcing: "[I]f one is drafted, one can always behave – I know of one example here – so physically unfit [*untauglich*] that they will send you away."[20] A few months later, as he made plans with his brother Heinrich to spend the next year or more travelling around Italy and elsewhere, Mann announced to Grautoff that "I probably won't see our rightfully much valued fatherland again before 1898; admittedly, unless the army's medical officer takes pity on me, the Moloch of 'militarism' awaits me then. But I do not like spending too much time thinking about it; it crouches like a big-eyed beast, gray and hideous behind the colourful, sweet playfulness of the near future."[21] Thus, for all his efforts to obtain his qualification certificate, Mann's views about his own possible military service were far from enthusiastic.

As it turns out, Mann's hopes for sympathy from his future medical examiner were not entirely unrealistic. According to Frevert, in Imperial Germany only about "one-third of all those eligible as one-yearers went on to perform military service, while most were discharged as physically unfit for service."[22] As might be expected from such a large bureaucracy, the regulations governing such decisions were rather Byzantine, though an understanding of them is helpful for piecing together Mann's enlistment.[23] For instance, all registered candidates in their twentieth year (or, in Mann's case, since he exercised his right to delay, in his twenty-third year) had to report to their local recruiting commission (*Ersatzkommission*), composed of the commander of the reserve militia, the district administrator (*Landrat*), and a military doctor. The latter conducted a preliminary examination to determine whether the potential recruit was physically and mentally fit for service, conditionally fit, currently unfit (*zeitig untauglich*), or permanently unfit. The results were then passed on to the upper recruiting commission (*Oberersatzkommission*), which was led by the region's infantry brigade commander, who made the ultimate determination. While those found permanently unfit were either struck from the rolls or, if possible, assigned to register with the last reserves (*Landsturm*), those deemed fit or conditionally fit were entered into the lottery that was used to determine which of them would be called for military service. Those found unfit at the time of the preliminary examination but not permanently unfit were required to return each of the next two years for another medical examination to see if their physical condition had improved. If on the third examination the candidates' physical condition again fell short of the threshold for fitness, they were assigned to register with the last reserves and removed from the recruitment rolls. All those called up for military service, however, once again underwent a medical screening in their assigned unit, where they might once more be found unfit for service. Those deemed unfit at this stage were remanded back to the upper recruiting office to undergo yet another medical examination whose decision was final.

Though we don't know the exact details of Mann's medical examinations, it seems that he was initially found temporarily unfit when he reported to the recruiting board in 1898 and again in 1899. Only in 1900 did a medical officer clear him for service. By this time, Mann's antipathy towards military service seems to have morphed into anxious enthusiasm. As he reported to Grautoff on 2 September 1900, he visited the barracks of the Royal Bavarian Infantry Lifeguards on the first of the month, where he was impressed enough by their elegant uniforms to mention them explicitly.[24] Nevertheless, because he had been "ordered to return the following day *for an additional examination*" and because he feared the gymnastics component associated with infantry training, he decided to opt for a commission in the artillery.[25] Unfortunately, however, he found himself forced to return to the infantry when the artillery, which was limited to four one-year volunteers per unit, informed him that they had no more openings.[26] Though clearly annoyed by the lack of real options for fulfilling his military service, Mann was even more upset by the possibility of no military service at all, complaining to Grautoff: "[N]ow I'm constantly worried that I will in the end be found unfit for the infantry. Damn this uncertainty about whether I will actually taste the strong, fresh life for which I nourish such a perverse desire!"[27] Fortunately for Mann, days later he could trumpet that "I was *admitted* today into the [Royal Bavarian] Infantry Lifeguards *without* a repeat exam."[28]

As Mann's ironic and off-handed comment about his "perverse desire" for the "strong, fresh life" of the army slyly suggests, his fantasy of military service was deeply connected to his sexuality, especially his homoerotic fantasies about Paul Ehrenberg, a painter he had recently

Figure 4.1. Thomas Mann and Paul Ehrenberg in a field with their bicycles. ETH-Bibliothek Zürich, Thomas-Mann-Archiv / Photographer: Unknown / TMA_0027.

met through friends of his sisters and whom Mann later called the "central affair of my heart."[29] According to Hermann Kurze, Ehrenberg was "nice and sociable, frank and talkative; he must have attracted the solitary and melancholy Thomas Mann onto the side of an active life without long shilly-shallying," which not only included going out to plays, concerts, cafes, and parties, but included what seem to be physically arduous treks by bike.[30] A photograph taken during one of these bike trips (Figure 4.1) coyly captures their relationship, with a moustached Thomas leaning on his bike on the left, his jacket seemingly fastidiously buttoned, and Paul on the right, striking a decidedly masculine open stance, with his left hand confidently perched in his pocket and his coat unbuttoned. Perhaps as a sign of the strictures against physical intimacy between men, the primary connection between the two has been transferred onto the bikes, whose front tires sidle up to one another.

Mann's homoerotic interest in Ehrenberg comes through in the letter he sent him in which he announced his conscription as a one-year volunteer:

> But hear now the prettiest of the stories. At the beginning of this month, in fact on the 6th (the issue requires accuracy), their lordships of the Higher Reserve Commission, to whom I had the honour of presenting myself, classified me as fit for all branches of the army; it follows that on the 1st of October, to the consternation of all enemies of the Fatherland, I shall shoulder a gun ... What do you say to that? As for me, I am (may you believe it or not) in complete agreement with it and assure you that the gleeful [*schadenfrohe*] and mocking [*moquante*] facial expression that you have had since reading the second line of this paragraph, is simply out of place. First of all, I see that the German Army just won't be able to do without me in the long run. But, second, as an arrogant decadent I imagine it extremely exhilarating to be firmly and ruthlessly berated for an entire year, for which I will probably give sufficient cause ...[31]

Though we will delve more deeply into gay camp in the next section, it is worth pointing out here some of the campier elements visible in this letter. First and foremost is the aestheticization of the news of his conscription, which has been turned into not just a story, but the "prettiest" of all those in the letter – itself an ironic way to designate one's induction into the military, the manliest of all male rites of passage in Imperial Germany. The story further extends this campy announcement with its use of exaggerated designations ("their lordships") and excessive detail, such as the convoluted accuracy of the event's dating. (As it turns out, 6 June was Mann's twenty-fifth birthday, and the tone of this letter suggests that the news of his fitness for military service represented a birthday present of sorts.) All these elements, of course, serve to delay – and thus heighten – the dramatic conclusion: "I shall shoulder a gun," which marks a double incongruity: a simple fact that hardly needs such a convoluted build-up, except that it signals a deeper incongruity between Mann's masculinity – which man tells pretty stories with such exaggeration and witty precision? – and the masculinity of soldiers. According to Kristin Mahoney, this kind of "detailing miniscule worlds and tiny events in an excessive and ornate style" is a characteristic of what she calls the "camp modernism" that started to appear in Britain in the decade-and-a-half following Oscar Wilde's 1895 trial and disgrace.[32] He then concluded the story on a lighter note: "In short, you will have to cordially excuse me when upon your return to Munich you run across me at Lula's [Mann's sister's] wedding adventurously costumed as a brutish mercenary who steals the silver, drinks to excess, repeatedly spits on the floor, and overall behaves stylishly like a German foot soldier [*Landsknecht*]." The humour of the conclusion derives from the excess boorishness that someone so effete would supposedly exhibit.

As the letter to Ehrenberg suggests, Mann's antipathy towards military service seems to have diminished in the face of his actual conscription, for he went on to insist that "all joking aside, I am honestly glad, that I wasn't turned away again."[33] More significantly, though, by repeatedly embedding Ehrenberg's imagined response within the letter, Mann seeks not only to control his friend's reception of the news but also to give the impression that his military service is primarily meaningful to the extent that it is imagined to influence Ehrenberg's image of Mann. Thus, at one level, Mann's sudden change of heart about his military service can be read as part of his attempt to woo Ehrenberg. Because, according to Anthony Heilbut, Mann "considered himself unattractive, ineligible for a handsome youth's attention," it seems likely that the certificate of military fitness was an attempt to brandish his own masculine credentials to the object of his affection.[34] Indeed, Mann goes out of his way to paint for Ehrenberg a hypermasculine image of himself in uniform at his sister Lula's wedding – as if that kind of boorish but incontrovertible evidence of promised masculinity would be sufficient to elicit the desires of his friend. Yet even more than his future manliness in uniform, though, it is the letter's irony – displayed in his deft handling of narrative and commanding control over language in the choice diction – that seems designed to seduce. In early 1901 he even considered dedicating one of the chapters in *Buddenbrooks* to Ehrenberg, which, he admitted to Grautoff, was a wish not only "to do something, to sacrifice something, to offer up something to him" but also "to let him see my power, to embarrass him a little by having his name flaunted."[35] If Mann couldn't (yet) be the attractive masculine man worthy of another young man's affections, he could always resort to seducing him through prose.[36]

The flip side of Mann's erotic fantasy of military service was undoubtedly what a year in the army could mean for himself as a *décadent*, one of Mann's key themes in his early writings.[37] Decadence, as Max Nordau understood it, was intimately linked to sickliness and degeneration, seeing "in the life and conduct of the men who write … 'decadent' works … the confluence of two well-defined conditions of disease …, degeneration (degeneracy) and hysteria, of which the minor stages are designated as neurasthenia."[38] Thus, Mann opined to Ehrenberg, military service offered "the only way to drive the nervous idiosyncrasies [*Mätzchen*] out of me; and if I lose a year for my civilian efforts, I am convinced that this year will add ten more to my life." Nevertheless, the prospect of failure also loomed large, for he admitted to the object of his affection that "[o]f course, it is possible that I won't be able to tolerate it and that after a few weeks they will have to let me go again; but I hope for the best."[39] Again, the passage gives voice to Mann's foreboding about his inability to hack the rigours of military life. But what stands out about Mann's view of the military was not only that the upcoming year promised to give him long-lasting physical health but also that it carried the prospect of overcoming what he saw as his constitutional nervousness and other worrisome tics that signalled the possibility of degeneration. Mann's familiarity with the concept was prominently featured in *Buddenbrooks*, whose "striking correspondence with anthropological insights" so impressed one eugenicist that he could not tell whether the author "drew his views from his own methodological research or from pure empiricism."[40]

In addition, Mann's concerns also reflected sexological discourses, especially Krafft-Ebing's *Psychopathia Sexualis*, which viewed same-sex desire explicitly and repeatedly "as a functional sign of degeneration."[41] Hans Wysling contends that Mann "read the works of Krafft-Ebing, among others."[42] Indeed, Anna Katharina Schaffner has recently argued that Mann's depictions of homosexuality in *Buddenbrooks*, again just being completed in this moment, "owe much to Richard von Krafft-Ebing's theories on sexual perversions."[43] But while a few of Krafft-Ebing's case studies depicted highly masculine men who were sexually attracted to other men, *Psychopathia Sexualis* and other works from the period most often portrayed homosexuality as "closely related to artistic inclinations, to hyperesthesia and a weak physical constitution."[44] In fact, Mann's decision to marry in 1905 is not unlike many of the men in Krafft-Ebing's tome who feel obligated to marry "either out of ethical or social considerations."[45] Yet Mann's distance from the queer emancipation movement, especially the WhK (he only signed its petition to repeal Paragraph 175 in 1922), seems at least in part due to its tendency to cleave to the sexological literature's equation of same-sex desire with sexual inversion and effeminacy in men.[46] Even as Mann made use of the more masculine Hellenic tradition in *Death in Venice* (1912), it was not until the war that he began to connect up his work and sexuality with the queer scene's masculinist tradition, primarily through the writings of Hans Blüher. In addition to attending a lecture by Blüher on 11

February 1918, he picked up the second volume of Blüher's *Die Rolle der Erotik in der männlichen Gesellschaft* (The role of eroticism in male society), which led him to decide that all his writing up to that point expressed "my sexual inversion."[47]

Though the evidence for it is scant, Mann apparently did not make a terrible soldier. Viktor Mann later recalled that his elder brother "was a quite proper soldier in his flashy blue dress uniform with the red collar, the silver braiding, the shiny buttons and the black patent-leather sword-belt."[48] It certainly made an impression on their mother who, upon seeing her second-eldest son for the first time in uniform, was, according to Viktor, "visibly moved and also a little proud."[49] There is no record of whether Ehrenberg ever saw Mann in uniform or what impression it made on him if he did. But military service was not just about dressing up in the costume of masculinity. As it turned out, Viktor also reported that he and the family cook once watched his brother at his drill exercises through the base's high iron fence: "After peering around for a while we spotted Tommy in file formation in a recruit detachment, which was practising grips with dummy rifles. He was doing it quite well. The cook expressly confirmed my impression, and she was knowledgeable about all things military because she was going out with a sergeant."[50] Since he was only twelve at the time, the older Viktor clearly felt the need to back his adolescent impressions of his older brother's military prowess with the attestation of a supposedly informed adult.

But as with most wish fulfilments, reality proved nothing like the fantasy. Faced with disillusionment and in recognition of the foolhardiness of his decision, Mann sought a way out. The solution presented itself in the form of a slight injury, an inflamed tendon that swelled his ankle during a parade drill. As he wrote in a letter to his brother Heinrich at the end of November, Mann repeatedly reported sick, "partly because I really was, partly to make them release me."[51] To the younger brother's chagrin, however, his act failed to convince the junior battalion doctor, who saw no significant problem with the injury and sent him back to duty. While Mann deliberately over-exercised the ankle in order to once again land back in the infirmary, connections ultimately proved more efficacious than the injury itself. With the help of his mother, he secured the support of her physician, who was apparently good friends with the battalion's chief medical officer. Though the latter could also not detect any serious injury, Mann recalled years later, he nevertheless ordered the junior battalion doctor to look at a print of Mann's foot on charcoaled paper and "see something that [wasn't] there."[52] In the end, Mann's premonitions about his potential inability to stick it out in the military had come true. Before the start of the new year, he was released from his military obligations and returned to civilian life.

Perhaps predictably, Mann's subsequent pronouncements on his failed military service not only elided the complex interplay between fantasy and experience but also further distorted the record through fanciful and campy falsifications. In "Im Spiegel" (In the mirror), an explicitly ironic self-portrait commissioned in 1907, Mann described his induction into military service in exaggerated – and factually inaccurate – terms: "Tanned, gaunt, and in a rather ragtag condition [*in ziemlich abgerissenem Zustande*] as I returned to Munich, I saw myself finally forced to make use of my certificate for voluntary service."[53] Despite the exaggerations, however, Mann's phrasing captured the combination of compulsion and free will contained in the official designation of "one-year voluntary service" – curiously reduced here to just "voluntary service." In particular, the words "finally forced" (*endlich genötigt*) suggest an overall framework of compulsion within which Mann nevertheless had the room to exercise an option, that is, "to make use" (*Gebrauch machen*) of his certificate. Even more than in word choice, however, Mann's sense of free will shines through in his inventive chronology, which placed the timing of his military service immediately after his extended stay in Italy rather than two-and-a-half years later.

Moreover, the essay also marks one of Mann's first public expressions of his own idiosyncratic version of "the queer art of failure" – one that ironically led to his triumphant success as a writer. Thus, in addition to his poor grades, lack of business acumen and ambition, and bohemian lifestyle, Mann did not shy away from mentioning his early dismissal from the army: "But if anyone hopes to hear that I proved myself to be somehow fitter in the military realm than in these others, he will be disappointed. After just a quarter year, even before Christmas, I was given a simple [*schlicht*] discharge since my feet could not adapt to that ideal and manly gait called the parade march and I was constantly laid low with tendonitis."[54] Within the logic of his essay, he could tout his failure to live up to the masculine ideal of the army, especially since he denigrated it to mere showmanship: superfluous parade marches that hold little practical value for battle and that can only be ironically called "that ideal and manly gait." Nevertheless, he quickly mitigated any lasting impression of his physical inadequacy: "But the body is to a certain extent subordinate to the mind, and if there had been the slightest love for the business in me, I would probably have been able to master [*bezwingen*] the affliction."[55] In this account, Mann's tendonitis was merely a question of mind over matter – and his mind just wasn't in the game. Thus, rather than evincing a lack of masculinity, his failure derived from the insufficiency of the military itself, which just didn't appeal to him, in part because its parading marches were just not masculine enough.

Mann subsequently reversed himself in his autobiographical essay "Lebensabriß" (A sketch of my life), which he wrote in 1930 at the behest of the Swedish Academy upon receiving the Nobel Prize in Literature: "I had 'to serve my year,' which, however, since my declaration of fitness was a psychological mistake, was reduced to three months. Once or twice I was held back because of a narrow chest and a nervous heart, but had now blossomed into youth [*Jugenblüte*] to such an extent that it was able to mislead the on-duty staff doctor about my eligibility."[56] By putting quotation marks around the phrase "serve my year," Mann not only indicated the use of common jargon but also emphasized his own ironic distance to the entire experience: military service was an outside imperative that carried no personal significance. Moreover, by depicting his admission to the military ranks as a "psychological mistake" on the part of the military doctor who certified his fitness, he once again deflected attention from any real physical deficiencies that might have led to his early dismissal.

Ultimately, for all their deliberate inaccuracies and selective omissions, these subsequent autobiographical accounts continue to testify to the voluntary dimensions of Mann's compulsory enlistment. Even as these essays acknowledge the slight physical deficiencies that led to his dismissal, they pale next to the intellectual powers that turn out to be the real reason behind his early discharge: he just didn't want to be there enough to compel his body to submit to the physical demands of army discipline. But it would be inaccurate to conclude from these autobiographical statements that Mann's dismissal had freed him from submitting to the standards of military masculinity, for his fictional writings in the subsequent decade following his discharge evince a continual effort to deal more thoroughly and honestly with both his homoerotic desires and his attraction to militaristic ideals.

The Literary Draft Dodger

If in his autobiographical writings Thomas Mann seemed all too willing to subordinate reality – in the form of dates and details – to a higher narrative structure, his literary works are less removed from his life than the designation of fiction might suggest. Indeed, in drawing on the lives and backgrounds of people he knew (such as the family members and residents of Lübeck who populate *Buddenbrooks*) or in explicitly portraying his homoerotic desires (most especially in *Death in Venice*),

Mann's fiction hewed famously, even scandalously close to "reality."[57] As Kurzke concludes, "Thomas Mann did not believe in making things up."[58] Following Mann's own claim that "all of it is autobiography," Helmut Koopmann points out that he "never put any obstacles in the way of his readers, should they wish to discover in his works their author and his problems: his self, his experiences, and his problematic relationship with the world – and with himself."[59] But even when he changed particular details of his life to fit the narrative arc of the story, Koopmann insists that "the reader recognizes with ease that Thomas Mann is writing about himself, yet pretending to write about other people, events, and objects."[60] Thus, in more thorough ways than in his autobiographical essays Mann used his fiction to interrogate his own life experiences and articulate what they meant, for, as Herbert Lehnert has noted, Mann "needed the fictional orientation in order to come to terms with the world."[61]

In the years between his early discharge from the army and the start of the First World War, Thomas Mann returned several times to the meaning of military service and military uniforms in connection to his own sexuality. For instance, his second novel, *Königliche Hoheit* (Royal highness) features a uniformed monarch as a stand-in for Mann as artist, whose mission to represent – and save – his kingdom includes marrying the daughter of a wealthy American, a stand-in for his wife Katia, herself the daughter of a wealthy Jewish scion of a railroad and coal magnate. This self-conscious and self-consciously heterosexual fairytale based on Mann's personal and professional "success" was, however, a critical flop when it was published in 1909, leading Mann to turn to works that explored his unresolved homosexual longings. While *Death in Venice* is easily the most famous of these, other works deal more directly with Mann's queer relationship to the military. In this section, I want to focus on the most famous of these, *Confessions of Felix Krull, Confidence Man: The Early Years*. Though published in 1954 and usually treated as the author's final work, the novel's first two books, roughly the entire first half, were in fact completed between 1911 and 1913, including its famous scene before the military enlistment board, in which Felix Krull spectacularly "fails" his test of fitness.[62] While this scene can be read as Mann's revision of his own failed enlistment, it also articulates a new fantasy of what military service might have meant for himself.

Late in life, as he began to take up work again on *Felix Krull*, Mann called the book his "homosexual novel."[63] Though Krull is pursued (unsuccessfully) by one homosexual guest at the hotel, the older Lord Kilmarock, and flirts with many other male figures, the designation seems curious for a novel that features its titular hero's romantic and sexual escapades with several female figures, including the family's maid Genovefa and the hotel guest Diane Houpflé. Yet in taking up the challenge posed by Mann's designation, critics have unearthed a wealth of homosexual allusions woven into the text and demonstrated that even the heterosexual sex scenes are rife with what his daughter Erika called "the out-and-out pederastic ('gay') essence" (*das Erz-Päderastische ['Schwule']*) of the sex between Krull and Houpflé.[64] Though my reading builds on this scholarship, I also want to suggest that the novel's queerness fundamentally resides in its style, in particular its affinity with the aesthetics of gay male camp. Though this aesthetic, as Susan Sontag famously noted in her groundbreaking 1964 essay "Notes on Camp," is notoriously difficult to define, it has served a long-term function within gay male communities as a sensibility that affirms a cultural distinctiveness from the heteronormative world, particularly its norms for masculinity.[65] As Richard Dyer explains, "camp is not masculine ... [but rather] a way of being human, witty and vital (for the whole camp stance is full of vitality), without conforming to the drabness and rigidity of the hetero role."[66]

While Oscar Wilde, to whom Sontag dedicated her essay, has served as one of the first and most famous exemplars of this style, camp was also a prominent feature of the distinctly unmasculine queer scenes that were thriving in Germany and Central Europe by the late nineteenth and early twentieth centuries.[67] According to Krafft-Ebing's subjects and informants, for instance, men who participated in such scenes regularly referred to themselves as "aunts" or "sisters."[68] Meanwhile, in *Berlins Drittes Geschlecht*, Hirschfeld offered much more detail about camp practices in the Imperial German capital: private parties that included "harmless fun" in which "Urnings who appeared especially manly" were forced to put on female articles of clothing such as hats and scarves; the famous Urning balls that invariably featured drag performances and for which many men appeared in drag, including some with "impressive [*staatlichen*] moustaches or even full beards," and so-called "stag nights" (*Herrenabende*), which were theatre-like events (*theaterartige Veranstaltungen*) in which "famous literary works were parodied" by having men play serious female roles for humour.[69] Though *Felix Krull* stops short of displaying these explicit forms of gay camp, it does exhibit the four features that Jack Babuscio identifies as particular to gay camp: irony, aestheticism, theatricality, and humour.[70] In addition to the queer erotic parody of Krull's sexual escapades with women, these features are most apparent in the novel's style, with Krull's penchant for ironic self-presentation, elaborately staged ruses, relentlessly aestheticized language rich with linguistic precision and self-consciously, even fussy complexity, and the author's hilariously inventive character names and witty word plays.

Camp is also, as Halberstam points out, a privileged mode of queer failure, for "in true camp fashion, the queer artist works with rather than against failure."[71] In contrast then to *Royal Highness*, his failed novel of heterosexual success, *Felix Krull* could be called a successful novel about queer failure. Written in first-person, the narrative purports to be the memoirs of a con artist confined to a prison cell, perhaps the most tangible sign of his overall failure, which, though, because the novel was never completed, is forever deferred in the narrative. Moreover, *Felix Krull* is also a subversion of the classic (and typically heteronormative) bourgeois stories of success: the *Bildungsroman* and the tradition of literary autobiography. In recounting his evolution from a young, middle-class German boy from a small town in the Rhineland into an international swindler who travels from Paris to Lisbon under the assumed identity of the Marquis de Venosta, Krull offers numerous examples of his talent for deception. Though the first book relates several incidents in which even as a young boy he exploited his powers of imagination to achieve his immoral wishes, his international career as a con artist only takes off after the suicide of his father (following the bankruptcy of his sparkling wine business), when his godfather arranges an unpaid training position for him at the Hotel St. James and Albany in Paris. Within the story's narrative arc, the prospect of military service looms as a threat to Krull's departure from Germany to Paris since, as he reports: "I could not and might not go in search of the wide world until my military affairs [*Militärverhältnis*] had been straightened out."[72] Moreover, since he had not, like Thomas Mann himself, "achieved the privileges of the educated classes," that is, the minimum schooling required to serve as a one-year volunteer, Krull would have to complete at least two years as a "common recruit" should he be found fit for military service – an unacceptable delay for one so eager to experience the world (84).

But if the military represents the potential intrusion of reality into Krull's life of fantasy, finding a way out of having to serve becomes an opportunity for deploying his skills as a fabulist, deceiver, and budding con-man. Near the beginning of the chapter, he tells the reader that "his feelings of anxiety [*Beklemmung*] were transformed into that joyful trepidation [*Beklommenheit*] we feel whenever we are on the point of testing our abilities on a great, even enormous task" (101). The task, of course, is to convince the medical doctor that he was unfit for duty. Lest the reader think that Krull would rely solely on his wits for such a monumental undertaking, he takes great pains to show his disciplined preparations:

conversations with a former conscript residing at his mother's boarding-house, studious reading of various military and medical textbooks, and repeated practise by candlelight in front of a mirror in "nightly solitude" (102). These preparations, of course, metaphorically represent Mann's own disciplined efforts as the author writing the scene. They also, I suggest, seem uncannily similar to the exhaustive preparations that many drag queens undertake in assembling their outfits and developing their affected mannerisms and outsized personas. In fact, though Krull is, like most of Mann's protagonists, another fictional alter-ego of its author, his exuberant performative persona in all its homosexual excess (openly flirting with men and the "out and out pederastic" nature of his sex with women) marks him as fundamentally different from tragic alter-egos like Gustav Aschenbach or constrained ones like Prince Klaus-Heinrich. In this sense, Krull is very much Mann's own drag persona – the kind of person Mann could never be: attractive, confident, and at ease with being queer, including his patent lack of interest in traditional masculine pursuits like soldiering.

To avoid military service, Krull successfully simulates an epileptic fit. But as Klaus Hermsdorf pointed out a while ago, "the artful simulation is actually neither the necessary condition for his triumph nor for the scene's humour ... His deception succeeds because it is built on the productive knowledge of the military system and its psychology."[73] Psychologically, the military's profile included "the bottomless contempt" for all civilians, shared even by those on the lower rungs of the military hierarchy.[74] For instance, Krull recounts entering the barrack's large waiting room, where an uncouth subaltern was making fun of the "notable educational achievements" of the recruits whose names he was calling out: "'Doctor of Philosophy!' he exclaimed and laughed derisively, as if he wanted to say 'We'll drive that out of you, my little friend!'" (105). As a result, the army presumed that many civilians were eager to find a way to avoid their compulsory military service. Mann himself recorded one surprising example in a letter to his brother Heinrich in which he offered details of his short experience in the military for use in *The Loyal Subject*: "Another item for you. In connection with 'squad room,' I just remembered an incident: Someone was actually released as unfit because he announced to the Chief Reserve Commission that he was homosexual."[75] This bold route out of military service was clearly not one that Mann himself ever seemed willing to consider. And it's not one that he allows his protagonist to consider either – though, as we shall see, it does lurk in this scene's camp excess. Much more common, though, were attempts to feign physical infirmities during the medical screening – a route Mann himself had seditiously conveyed in a letter to Grautoff.[76] And, in fact, as Krull waits in the outside dressing room, he overhears one recruit's "clumsy prattle about a bout of pneumonia, which obviously failed to achieve its transparent purpose, since it was cut short by a declaration of his unconditional fitness for service" (109). From Krull's point of view, the recruit's talk of his pulmonary illness was only too easy to read as a ploy for a medical certification of unfitness.

In seeking his medical exemption, Krull sets about the task quite differently – and with more camp artistry. To begin with, his plan for getting a medical discharge reverses the usual scenario that had so clearly failed the recruit ahead of him. In particular, instead of embodying the healthy bourgeois son who clumsily claims to suffer from a debilitating physical condition, he plays a young man so eager to get into the army that he tries to hide an illness that would make him ineligible for duty. In this sense, Krull parodies the macho "ooh-rah" masculinity that might see the military as its natural habitus – here played to excess, and hence a sign of mental illness rather than health. The deception also relies on the military examiner's condescension towards civilians, as well as on his professional arrogance as a doctor – a profession that, as Foucault's work has often pointed out, was accustomed to wielding its superior medical knowledge over others. In this case, the novel is also a queer parody of the sexological and other medical-scientific efforts to diagnose and explain illnesses like "sexual inversion."

Central to Krull's strategy is his theorization of fantasy's power to alter the perception of reality. As the fictional autobiography of a conman, *Felix Krull* constitutes a deep interrogation – and even celebration – of the power and pleasure of fantasy as the foundation of art more generally, and fictional storytelling in particular. Early on, for instance, the protagonist exclaims to his readers "what a glorious gift imagination (*Phantasie*) is, and what satisfactions it affords!" (17). Indeed, presumably like the real author of the novel, Krull insists that "the sole condition under which I am capable of living is the independence [*Ungebundenheit*] of the intellect [*Geist*] and imagination [*Phantasie*]" (42). But if Krull's mode of being requires freedom of imagination, the freedom to indulge in fantasy, his success in deceiving others is based on wrapping the fantasy he is weaving around a kernel of truth, for the illusions that form the basis of a successful con is "that which ... has not yet entered wholly into the realm of the actual" (44). In other words, for a fantasy to succeed in convincing others, it must be *probable* – something that could (but had not yet) become "actual."

Krull's con scheme in front of the military recruiting board relies on a number of partial and potential truths. First, there is his performance of an epileptic fit, which is based on his study of a medical textbook. He also supplies many truthful answers to the questions that the medical examiner puts to him: he does plan to become a waiter; his mother is running a boarding-house, though not one as large as he claims; his father did manufacture sparkling wine, did imbibe alcohol, and did commit suicide. The doctor, of course, eventually interprets the latter as evidence for Felix's unfitness. As he explains to the review board following Krull's simulated seizure, "My examination shows that there is obviously a hereditary taint from his alcoholic father, who, after his business failure, ended his life by suicide" (123). Such a sentences seems a direct parody of Krafft-Ebing's *Psychopathia Sexualis*, which, abounding with confident aetiologies, such as this one in Case 126, admittedly seems to parody itself through its own excessive enumeration of hereditary taint: "Ilma S., aged twenty-nine; single, merchant's daughter; of a family having bad nervous taint. Father was a drinker and died by suicide, as also did the patient's brother and sister. A sister suffered with convulsive hysteria. Mother's father shot himself while insane. Mother was sickly, and paralyzed after apoplexy."[77] But ironically, the most accurate statement of fact is the very first exclamation Krull utters upon entering the examination room: "I am entirely fit for service" (111). In this case, however, the usurpation of the doctor's authority provokes the arrogant man to eventually reach the opposite conclusion, in part because the enthusiasm it expresses for compulsory military service raises his concern about the protagonist's mental state.

But while Krull does in fact simulate an epileptic seizure of epic proportions, the budding conman's deceit – like the author of creative fiction – is also thoroughly linguistic. Though ordered to refrain from all personal commentary, Krull proceeds to overwhelm the exasperated medical examiner with a torrent of words. For instance, instead of answering questions with a simple yes or no, the protagonist's responses repeatedly address the lowly medical examiner with increasingly elaborate military and civilian medical titles above the man's rank: surgeon-general (*Herr Generalarzt*), military surgeon (*Herr Militärarzt*), chief physician (*Herr Chefarzt*), commanding officer of the military hospital (*Herr Lazarettkommandant*), physician-major (*Herr Stabsphysikus*), battalion physician (*Herr Bataillonsmedikus*), and war surgeon (*Herr Kriegsarzt*). As a parody of the German – and military – passion for professional titles, it is reminiscent of the habit in German homosexual scenes of referring to fellow Urnings with feminine names and titles, which ranged from feminizing men's names – Paul became Paula – to adopting elaborate aristocratic names like "Wally von Trauten, Berta von Brunneck," to conferring or appropriating female titles of nobility like countess, marquise, duchess, princess, queen, and empress.[78] (Beyond the titles Krull uses in this scene, Mann's camp comes out in the panoply of exaggerated aristocratic titles he invents throughout the novel.) Of course, within this scene, their inconsistency is designed to raise the doctor's suspicions about Felix's mental derangement and incapacity. Yet their exaggerated inaccuracy in fact correctly captures the doctor's inflated perception of his superiority as a medical authority and military officer. Thus, after one attempt to correct the hapless recruit's misappellations, the doctor gives up. Krull's (and Mann's) strategy can be summed up in Philip Core's dictum, apparently taken from a 1922 essay by Jean Cocteau, that "camp is the lie that tells the truth."[79]

Krull's excessive and flowery speech also raises the doctor's suspicions. For example, in response to the simple question of whether he has had any serious illnesses, the protagonist attests that "to the best of my knowledge I am entirely healthy and have always been so, if I may pass over certain insignificant fluctuations in my state of health" (113). In contrast to the previous recruit's hapless attempt to emphasize his previous pulmonary illness, Krull pretends to hide his – a move that can only make a doctor suspicious. According to Hermsdorf, in comparison with the clipped speech of the military doctor, Krull's stylized language is, like the title "doctor of philosophy," the very hallmark of his civilian disposition and is designed to "reinforce in the military doctor the impression of having before him his ridiculous enemy, the personified civilian, the bourgeois decadent."[80] Yet it is important to note that its overly ornate precision far exceeds the register of most forms of bourgeois civilian speech – the sober discourse of business and politics, the abstraction of academic texts – and as such marks out Krull as a very particular decadent: the homosexual devoted to linguistic surface and appearance over reality, albeit surfaces and appearances that reveal some truth about the reality underneath.[81] In fact, his speech seems to channel Wilde's own campy formulations, enshrined in one of the aphorisms that Sontag's "Notes on Camp" quotes: "[I]n matters of great importance, the vital element is not sincerity, but style."[82]

Moreover, in contrast to the fellow civilian who announced his homosexuality during one of Mann's appearances before the military recruiting board, Krull's queerness is embedded in the campy hiddenness that calls attention to itself. According to Core, camp exaggerations express a "desire to conceal something and to reveal it at the same time," much like its role vis-à-vis the pre-Stonewall closet, where camp humour marked its purveyor's homosexuality without ever naming it explicitly.[83] In particular, the protagonist's overly precise speech reinforces the doctor's dawning awareness that it might likely be a symptom of some hidden medical condition. In any case, the doctor informs Krull, "Your manner of speech is marked by a distinct lack of restraint, which frankly struck me some time ago. What is actually the matter with you? [*Was ist eigentlich mit Ihnen?*]" (113). Thus intrigued, the doctor sets about trying to extract the necessary information from the talkative but supposedly self-ignorant man standing in front of him. The knowing glances that he repeatedly casts to the other assembled men in the room with every nugget of evidence he uncovers, such as the father's profession and suicide, suggests that he thinks he is leading the investigation. In a way, Krull's epileptic seizure is only the belated physical confirmation of the lack of military fitness that he has already demonstrated through his unrestrained and campy language.

It is tempting to read the scene as Mann's literary revenge on the military. In "A Sketch of My Life," Mann blamed his certificate of fitness on his medical examiner's "psychological mistake," that is, his mistaken impression that Mann's body was physically healthy enough for military service.[84] Here the psychological mistake is again made by the military doctor, for he is the one now duped by Mann's protagonist. *Felix Krull* also seems to reverse the mind-body duality with which Mann later sought to prevent a reading of his early medical discharge as a sign of physical inadequacy and lack of masculinity. Whereas in "Im Spiegel" he insisted that "the body is to a certain extent subordinate to the mind, and if there had been the slightest love for the business in me, I would probably have been able to master [*bezwingen*] the affliction," here Krull harnesses the power of the mind to subordinate his body such that he could convincingly mimic an epileptic seizure.[85] Thus, Mann portrays his protagonist's achievement as the same kind of masculine mastery over his body that is required by the military – but in this case, being used against the institution of privileged heterosexual masculinity. Core seems to grasp this truth in one of his own cryptic adages that open his essay: "CAMP is essential to military discipline."[86]

More intriguingly still, the scene reverses Mann's earlier equation of military service with health, that is, when he wrote to Ehrenberg that he viewed military service as "the only way to drive the nervous idiosyncrasies [*Mätzchen*] out of me."[87] Of course, Krull expands those "nervous idiosyncrasies" into the performance of a full-blown epileptic fit. In response to the eager recruit's plea to overlook his epileptic seizure and allow him to serve, the arrogantly blind military examiner informs him more than once that "the military is no sanatorium" (*Heilanstalt*) (123, 124). Of course, the joke is that Krull is not really sick and in need of a cure (and, it would seem in hindsight, neither did Mann, who became an important author following the publication of

Buddenbrooks, the novel he had been toiling over during the years of his own medical examinations for military service). Thus, as a spectacular reversal of Mann's early discharge and his personal humiliation at his masculine insufficiency, Krull's deception is a queer one that emerges out of Mann's own mastery of camp aesthetics. As a humorous reversal of Mann's earlier failure, the scene resonates with camp's ultimate function as what Dyer calls "a form of self-defense," explaining that "the fact that gay men could so sharply and brightly make fun of themselves meant that the real awfulness of their situation could be kept at bay – they need not take things too seriously, need not let it get them down."[88] In this case, both the queer figure and its author can have the last laugh at the expense of the representatives of the institution that claims to best exemplify heterosexual masculinity.

Ultimately, the protagonist's success in evading his military obligations seems to suggest that Mann has completely reversed his stance on the army in favour of the freedom of imagination provided by the civilian life of a writer. Yet despite Krull's success in avoiding military duty, and thus having to share Mann's fate, the novel is far from articulating a critique of military service or the ideology of German militarism behind it. Indeed, as Mann protested in a 1918 letter to Paul Amann, the military examination scene's "offensiveness is admittedly only superficial, and at bottom [Krull] is a militarist, like all my heroes."[89] The observation is not merely an apologetic defence of the scandalous portrayal of German military officer as incompetent (something that could only appear unseemly in a time of war), but is in fact a point of view grounded quite clearly in the novel itself. Thus, when the triumphant if rather exhausted protagonist returns to the dressing room, the non-commissioned officer on duty has this to say: "[I]t's a shame for you, Krull, or whatever your name is! You're a proper fellow, you would have amounted to something in the army. One can see right away whether a man is going to get anywhere with us. It's a shame about you; you have what it takes at first sight, you would certainly have made a fine soldier. Who knows if you mightn't have made sergeant major if you'd signed on after your required service!" (125). Unlike the overconfident doctor who was tricked by Krull's performance, this simple soldier sees through the conman's charade. But rather than viewing the protagonist's desire to avoid military service as proof of an incorrigible civilian constitution (like the title of doctor of philosophy that he had earlier derided), the NCO recognizes it as grounded in the same discipline and self-mastery required of any soldier.

The soldier's words lead the draft dodger to imagine, much like Mann before him, "how splendidly, naturally and convincingly the military uniform would have become me, what a satisfying effect my figure would have made in it, for however long I would have worn it" (125). Nevertheless, Krull recognizes that the daily life of the army lacks "the one pre- and fundamental condition of freedom" (126), which he claims is necessary for his life. Still, the NCO's attestation of his military suitability pleases Krull, who draws the key distinction between living *like* a soldier (*soldatisch*) versus living *as* a soldier (*als Soldat*): "Even if I thence lived like a soldier, it would have been a foolish misconception, if I had therefore believed I should live as a soldier" (126). He concludes: "[I]t may be said that to live like a soldier, but not as a soldier; figuratively but not literally, to be allowed to live allegorically, spells true freedom" (126). Thus, *Felix Krull* rewrites the antagonism between art and army into parallel but separate spheres. Rather than being too effeminate for the military, and thus incompatible with the army's expectations for masculinity, Mann implies that army life is simply too rigid to be compatible with this new hero – or, for that matter, the creative writer whose calling requires the same kind of heroic self-discipline as the conman and the soldier. The implication is that Mann, as the author of *Felix Krull* and now a renowned writer, no longer needed to don a uniform or endure the physical hardship of drill to exhibit his male self.

It is clear that the scene's equation between Krull's discipline as a producer of convincing illusions and the discipline required of the German soldier is an example of Mann's use of allegory and symbolic irony. According to Harvey Goldman, Mann's characters "are forced to dwell in two realms: they are both realistic and elaborately allegorical, very human and tools that constantly reflect on contemporary debates in Mann's world."[90] Though, as Goldman concedes, "this makes for very rich novelistic work," it can also lead such work astray, resulting in "endings that are false to the novels' stories and characters and betray the novel's logic."[91] This kind of unintended queer art of failure was the fate of Mann's second novel, *Royal Highness* (*Königliche Hoheit*). As Izenberg notes, "However much Mann later argued that the novel's allegorical style was a developmental step to his later work, it was and is a failure, not so much because it is a Ruritanian fairy tale with little relevance to anyone except a self-identified prince, but because it is tonally unpersuasive."[92] In particular, Mann's portrayal of the prince's marriage with the wealthy American heiress as an austere or severe happiness ("ein strenges Glück") rings hollow as an actual account of romance (let alone a fairytale one), even as it clearly matched Mann's own understanding of his 1905 marriage to Katia Pringsheim.[93]

In the case of *Felix Krull*, however, the matter is even more complicated. On the one hand, the novel is, among many things, an allegory about writing and reading fiction and the role played by fantasy and imagination in that process. According to Michael Beddow, this structure encompasses a persistent doubling, including "the techniques of writing which Felix employs; the techniques of writing employed [by the author] to create the figure of Felix; the implied responses of the 'fictitious' reader (to whom Felix addresses himself); and the implied responses of the 'real' reader (who recognises Felix as a fictitious creation)."[94] For Beddow, the novel's brilliance lies in "the delight in fiction *as* fiction," which offers "an exhilarating sense of freedom: freedom from the absolute dominion of facticity, granted by the imagination."[95] However, to the extent that *Felix Krull* leaves reality behind in pursuit of its allegorical dimension, the novel breaks with its protagonist's (and hence the novel's) own fundamental observation: that for fantasy to be effective, it must still have a connection to reality, even if that lies only in its *potential* to become reality. Thus, the novel's palpable lack of what Lacanians call the Real – the sense of a reality below and behind the web of the linguistic signs and social conventions that structures our everyday reality – can, as a whole, make for exhausting reading. Even fans of camp have pointed out that one of the "drawbacks" of this gay aesthetic is that "[i]t tends to lead to an attitude that you can't take anything seriously," because "everything has to be turned into a witticism or a joke."[96]

But the other complication resulting from the novel's allegorical celebration of fantasy is exactly the "exhilarating sense of freedom" it promises. As we saw, Krull's existence "like a soldier" is in principle quite compatible with the military, a fact certified by the unnamed NCO who attests to the draft dodger's potential to make it far as a conscript. But though the hero rejects the army life because it symbolized a space of "unfreedom," it also implies that the fabulist – whether Felix or the author who created him – has achieved that freedom. Of course, the full allegorical significance of Felix Krull's memoirs is that he is writing them from his prison cell. Thus, at some point in his fictitious life, there was a collision between his fantasies and the reality in which he spun them. Likewise, the limits of Mann's fantasy of the soldier-author who can produce freely outside the discourse of German militarism becomes apparent as soon as war – itself a monstrous form of the Real – overtakes the continent in 1914.

A Writer Goes to War

In the final weeks running up to the First World War, Mann privately voiced dread about the pending conflagration as well as tentative optimism that war might still be averted. For instance, on 30 July 1914, two days after Austria had declared war on Serbia, he wrote to his brother

Heinrich: "I must say that I feel shocked and ashamed by the awful pressure of reality. Up until today I was optimistic and disbelieving – we (*man*) are too civilized (*civilen Gemütes*) to think that the monstrous is possible. I also tend to believe that people (*man*) will push the thing only to a certain point. But who knows what insanity can seize Europe when it gets carried away."[97] Much like the looming compulsory military service for Krull as well as the young Mann, the prospect of war represents "the awful pressure of reality" that imperils everyday life, either by destroying its tentative foundations or by revealing it to be merely an illusion. In labelling war as "the monstrous" (*das Ungeheuerliche*), his very terminology here is strikingly similar to the Lacanian conceptualization of the Real as a monstrosity, a horror that lurks beneath the façade of civilization. As Žižek notes in reference to the two world wars, "[t]he ultimate and defining moment of the twentieth century was the direct experience of the Real as opposed to everyday social reality – the Real in its extreme violence as the price to be paid for peeling off the deceptive layers of reality."[98]

But while Mann here feared war as an "insanity that can seize Europe," just a week later, on 7 August, his position had already shifted. Though he still viewed war as a "disaster" (*Heimsuchung*) that would likely leave him financially "ruined," he now informed his brother that his own personal fate was miniscule in the face of "the radical upheavals [*Umwälzungen*], namely the spiritual [*seelische*] ones, that such events will necessarily bring in the end! Doesn't one have to be thankful for the completely unexpected, to be allowed to experience such great things?"[99] In addition, Mann admitted to feeling "an enormous curiosity" as well as "the deepest sympathy for this hated, fateful and mysterious Germany that, even if it has not deemed 'civilization' as the highest good, is in any case getting ready to crush the most depraved police state of the world," by which he likely meant France.[100] In place of the horror, which Mann believed would bring about his financial ruin, he now expressed a thankfulness for the opportunity to experience the spiritual transformation that war promised "to bring in the end." Mann's change of perspective represents what Žižek calls "the passion for the Real" – this hope that a war involving all the European empires would make it possible to escape the superficial trappings of what Lacan has labelled the Symbolic – the realm of words, symbols, and civilization that Mann had just celebrated in *Felix Krull*.[101] And Mann's curiosity – his fascination with the Real – was also accompanied by a growing sympathy with Germany. In Mann's eyes, Germany's preparations to crush France as an exponent of a corrupt and artificial civilization put it on the right side – of the Real as well as of history and sympathy.

Within days of the start of fighting on 12 August 1914, Mann's sympathy for Germany developed into a full-blown effort to defend his homeland's war effort against the harsh words of its critics inside and outside the country – perhaps most especially his brother, who castigated Wilhelm II's decision to go to war and predicted the country's eventual failure and resulting doom.[102] Thomas Mann's effort began with "Gedanken im Kriege" (Thoughts in war), an essay that he started drafting in August and that was published in November in *Die neue Rundschau*, the leading German literary journal of the day.[103] It was followed by the shorter "Gute Feldpost" (Good military mail), drafted in September or October, and then *Friedrich und die Große Koalition* (Frederick the Great and the grand coalition), a longer and particularly notorious defence of Germany's war effort that he wrote between September and December.[104] Following these inflammatory essays, he spent much of the rest of the war writing *Betrachtungen eines Unpolitischen* (Reflections of a nonpolitical man), a monumental apologia in which he sought to account for his wartime support of Germany within the context of his entire oeuvre.[105] This tome also amounted to a literary fratricide in which he savagely attacked his brother's valorization of the political and democratic writer. In fact, the book was as much a declaration of war on Heinrich as it was a book about the First World War.[106]

It is perhaps not surprising that Mann rose to defend his country in its first major war in his lifetime, especially since he was certainly not alone among German writers.[107] As Wolfgang Mommsen explains, nearly all academics and writers – historians, philosophers, social scientists, and writers – in Germany viewed it as "their national duty to counter the Allied criticism, particularly from Britain, of the illegitimacy of Germany's war policy, which allegedly or in actuality was driven by a naked striving for power and lacked any moral justification."[108] While the fifty-one-year-old Richard Demel actually enlisted, nearly all of the established German-language poets and authors – Stefan George, Gerhart Hauptmann, Hermann Hesse, Hugo von Hofmannsthal, and Rainer Maria Rilke – wrote odes to the war.[109] Moreover, Julius Bab, writing in the *Literarisches Echo* on 1 October 1914, claimed that 50,000 war poems were being written each day, mostly by newcomers.[110] Thus, Mann could rightfully attest in "Gedanken im Kriege" "how the hearts of poets were immediately set ablaze, now that war had come [*als jetzt Krieg wurde*]!"[111]

The queer emancipation movement also enlisted in these efforts to support and justify the war effort. By April 1915, the WhK's newsletter reported that half of its membership was serving in some capacity in the military.[112] Likewise, Adolf Brand, the editor of masculinist journal

Der Eigene (The special one), spent two years in the army, during which the Community of the Special (*Gemeinschaft der Eigenen*) ceased meeting.[113] Even the socialist Magnus Hirschfeld participated in the early effort to justify Germany's entry and conduct in the war. In a 1914 pamphlet entitled "Warum hassen uns die Völker? Eine kriegspsychologische Betrachtung" (Why do nations hate us? A consideration of the psychological aspects of war), the sexologist sought to provide a social-scientific analysis of anti-German sentiment throughout the world, for which he blamed Britain.[114] Hirschfeld's essay is chock full of the jargon of social psychology – mass psychology, induced affect, state of fear, hallucination, the unconscious, fatalism, fanaticism – which he uses to portray the world's anti-German hatred as an irrational mental state. And though Imperial Germany's treatment of homosexuals is not explicitly invoked to justify its belligerent pursuit of victory, this prideful defence by the country's most prominent crusader for queer tolerance represents an early full-blown example of what Jasbir Puar calls homonationalism.[115]

Yet in contrast to Hirschfeld's tone, which laments the war as itself the result of an irrational psychology that can only breed additional irrational states (in the enemy), Mann's enthusiasm for the war is of a completely different calibre – more aggressive, more fantastical, and, I want to suggest, even more homosexual. Indeed, the ruthlessness of his rhetorical attacks on Germany's enemies, in particular France, and his unconditional defence of Germany's execution of the war, including its invasion of neutral Belgium, remain shocking. Beddow, for instance, laments "his colossal conformity, his wholesale and exuberant acceptance of official propaganda, his willful blindness to historical, political, social and indeed moral considerations which someone of his proven perceptiveness should have had neither difficulty in seeing nor qualms about expressing."[116] Moreover, his efforts to defend Germany against the chorus of international intellectuals led him, as Goldman puts it, "to a gross submissiveness to the least admirable aspects of German culture and politics," including proud support of Germany's authoritarian state and, in his celebration of Frederick the Great, its history of ruthlessly obtaining whatever it wanted through military means.[117] In fact, as Kontje points out, "at its most disturbing," *Reflections of a Nonpolitical Man* "embraces elements of conservative thought that would soon inform the National Socialist movement."[118]

For our purposes, however, what is most conspicuous about Mann's writings during this time is not only his unbridled support of Prussian-German militarism but also the fantastical nature of that support. Fantasy, of course, is a central response to the Real. As Nick Mansfield explains, the Real "is not a place where our truth offers us deliverance and comfort. The Real remains a site of horror. This is why we can only engage with it by way of fantasy."[119] Mann, of course, never experienced the carnage of the war directly. As Kurzke reminds us, his "customary life – work at his desk, theater, concerts, reading tours, vacations in Bad Tölz – continues during the war, reduced by frequent illness and in the last year also affected by scarcity of foodstuffs."[120] Thus, the fantasy that he constructed in response to the war was very different from that of Ernst Jünger in the trenches, who, as Žižek reads him, "was already celebrating face-to-face combat as the authentic intersubjective encounter."[121] Instead, the fantasy that Mann constructed in response to the Real of war was the fantasy of escaping the deadlock of his own subjectivity. As Kurzke helpfully summarizes:

> (1) The war liberated him from disorientation and gave his life sense and a goal again. (2) The war liberated him from a creative crisis. (3) The war gave him permission for open fraternal hate. (4) The war offered chances to satisfy his ambition for greatness and to become a national poet. (5) The war allowed him to show himself as a "man," in defiance of those who had made him contemptible as a sissy, house-mouse, and fine gilt-edged soul. (6) In a subtle way the war even seemed to offer solutions for the conflict between intellect and life, between the world of his father and the world of his mother, between marriage and homoeroticism, between the dream of power and rank on the one hand and the dream of love and union on the other – and not only solutions but intoxicating syntheses![122]

Thus, "the radical changes [*Umwälzungen*], namely the spiritual [*seelische*] ones," that Mann detected in the onset of war, were, in his case, the promise of his own spiritual transformation and the resolution of all conflicts in the Symbolic realm – between his homoerotic feelings and his heterosexual marriage, between the military masculinity of the *Tat* (act) and the civilian masculinity of the word, between Heinrich's literary ethos and his own – that would all be made possible by war's unveiling of the Real.

But rather than representing a fundamental break with the past, Mann's fantastical engagement with the Real of the First World War came in the form of a redoubling of his symbolic-allegorical approach to the world, albeit with some new coordinates. One of these new coordinates was Germany itself, which in Mann's eyes represented an aggrieved victim of a conspiracy between France, England, and Russia. In "Gedanken im Kriege," for instance, Mann writes: "We had never believed in war; our political insight had never extended to recognizing the necessity of the European catastrophe. As moral beings, though – yes, as such we had seen the disaster coming, or what is more, had even longed for it in some kind of way; had felt in our deepest hearts that the world, our world, just couldn't go on anymore." Nevertheless, he continued, "Of course we knew this world of peace and the garrulous civilized mode of behaviour – better, excruciatingly much better than the men whose awful and impersonal mission it was to unleash the fire: we were capable of suffering more deeply with our nerves, with our soul than they were."[123] Though Mann at this point still viewed the war as a catastrophe, that catastrophe had now become a necessary one thanks to the spiritual deadlocks that had made it impossible for the pre-war world to continue the way it had been.

This sense that the previous way of life was exhausted was already a theme in some of Mann's pre-1914 works, notably *Death in Venice*, which related the tragic story of a highly respected and self-disciplined writer who loses all self-dignity in his pursuit of a prepubescent boy in the cholera-ridden city. Goldman asserts that "Mann's pre–World War I works thus tell a story of the exhaustion of strength that can no longer be squeezed out of the ascetic self alone, making necessary the search for other sources of power."[124] But perhaps most important about Mann's rhetoric in "Gedanken im Kriege" is that his ascetic individuality has now been replaced by a collective "we." Certainly, Mann saw expressions of common purpose in both the official proclamations – Wilhelm II's speech on 1 August that "I no longer recognize parties or religious confessions; today we are all German brothers and only German brothers" – and in the enthusiasms of fellow members of the bourgeoisie (though not, as we know now, many in the working class).[125] Yet Beddow is also right when he concludes that "for Thomas Mann, patriotic enthusiasm did not bring a release from psychological self-absorption and disabling introspection, but rather the monstrous projection of those private concerns on to world affairs. He did not 'forget himself' in his devotion to the national cause: rather, he reinterpreted the national cause so that it became a generalization of his own personal pre-occupations."[126] As a result, Goldman points out, "everywhere Mann defends Germany he is implicitly defending himself."[127]

Though Mann identified with his homeland, he also repeatedly identified it – and thus himself – with the historical and proto-gay figure of Frederick the Great (r. 1740–86). As Mann wrote in "Gedanken im Kriege," "Germany is today Frederick the Great."[128] To be sure, the Prussian king served as an attractive and handy historical allegory for Germany in the First World War. Because the Prussian monarch faced a coalition of Austria, France, Russia, Saxony, and Sweden in the Seven

Years' War, it was easy for Mann to insist that "it is his fight that we are pursuing to its end, that we have to pursue once again. The coalition has changed a little, but it is his Europe, the Europe allied in hate, that cannot tolerate us, that even now does not want to tolerate him, the king."[129] Though Mann was living in Bavaria and hailed from Hanseatic Lübeck, which was absorbed into Prussia as a result of the 1864 war against Denmark and the 1866 war against its former ally Austria, his glorification of Frederick the Great viewed all of Germany history through a Prussian lens. But just as importantly, Frederick was also the homosexual on the throne – and at the head of the army. In "Frederick the Great and the Grand Coalition," Mann portrays the young crown prince as a stereotypical modern homosexual – "thoroughly unmilitaristic ... civilian, lax, even feminine" – much as Mann himself appeared – to himself and to his enemies, on whom the prominence of homoerotic, even homosexual, themes in his work was not lost.[130] (In the five years or so before the start of the First World War, Mann carried on public feuds with two fierce critics, Alfred Kerr and Theodor Lessing, who both made it known that they found Mann's masculinity to be, at best, questionable – the latter referred to him as "Tommy, the little woman" [*Tomi, das Weibchen*].)[131] Izenberg thus finds that "an autobiographical undertone is unmistakable in Mann's descriptions and analyses of Frederick ... Frederick was unmistakably Mann's hero."[132] In addition to his "homosexuality" and misogyny, Frederick also served as a model "of the naturally weak individual who persists despite exhaustion," which is, for Mann, "the paradigm for the nation and the self."[133] To the extent that the First World War resurrected the homosexual Prussian king as its model, it also made it possible for homosexuals (and homosexual writers) like Mann to imagine themselves as enlisted in – and vitally important to – the German war effort.

In point of fact, there is a pervasive continuity between his pre-war and wartime writing in his effort to portray the creative writer as a soldier. In "Gedanken im Kriege," for instance, Mann suggested that war and art are "deeply connected" through more than just "allegorical aspects" (*gleichnishafte Beziehungen*).[134] After professing that "it always seemed to me that it is not the worst artist who recognizes himself in the image of the soldier," Mann offered an exhaustive list of their shared values:

> That victorious warrior principle of today: organization – it is of course the first principle, the essence of art. The mutually reinforcing operations of enthusiasm and order; system; the strategic creation of foundations, continuous construction and pushing onwards with "lines of

communication"; soundness, precision, prudence, bravery, steadfastness in the face of trials and defeats, in battle with the tenacious resistance of the material; contempt for all that which is called "security" in civilian life ("security" is the favorite concept and loudest demand of the citizen), the habituation to a dangerous, tense, attentive life; ruthlessness against oneself, moral radicality, devotion to the most extreme, martyrdom [*Blutzeugenschaft*], complete deployment of all the forces [*Grundkräfte*] of the body and soul, without which it appears ridiculous to undertake anything; finally, as an expression of discipline and honor, a sense for the decorative and the sparkling [*das Schmucke, das Glänzende*]: All this is actually military and artistic at the same time. With apt justice has one called war an art form.[135]

Mann's effort to make war and art interrelated enterprises pursued in parallel domains extended and deepened, of course, the allegory he invoked in *Felix Krull*. But it also seemed to stand in obtuse relationship to the realities of war that most soldiers were experiencing on the front lines at the time and in the trenches shortly thereafter. Likewise, his portrayal of the writer as one habituated "to a dangerous" life, ruthless against himself, deploying "all the forces of body and soul" for the cause of art can only appear at best insensitive vis-à-vis those men who were actually dying on the fields and in the trenches, where they also faced intense stress and privation.

Nevertheless, Mann persisted not only in using the war to try to resolve his personal and professional roadblocks but also in aggrandizing his own contributions as a writer on behalf of Germany's war effort. In "Gute Feldpost," for instance, Mann attributed an important role to writers and thinkers in the conflict: "But war, like all life, has always needed the intellect [*Geist*]."[136] The essay concludes: "I know full well [*Ich weiß wohl*], would know it even without a note of greeting and confirmation from *there* [the front], that my thinking and writing were and are not without connections to the events. My little work, mortal and only half-good, as might be the case – if there is in its allegories some trace of what is coarsely called 'German militarism,' then it has honour and reality, then it has the reality of its honour and its spirit."[137] Though Mann seemed to coyly diminish the value of his work as potentially only "half-good," the very self-abnegating move was at the same time a self-aggrandizing one since that work has been refashioned as an expression of the spirit of German militarism. For rather than being quashed and rendered superfluous by the exigencies of war, writing had become, at least in his eyes, even more important. As Mann asserted against the few German intellectuals critical of the war (especially his brother), "the mind [*Geist*] you handwringers, was '*never closer*' to life right now."[138]

Perhaps most surprising in "Gute Feldpost" was Mann's attempt to rework his own unfitness for military duty into a sign of service: "What is artistic freedom and artistic fate? – To live in allegory. – Name an example! – Here is one: to live like a soldier, but not as a soldier. – But there is no honour in that; for honour has only one reality. – Really? The great Kant, however, was a cripple who would not even have been fit for garrison duty, and he was the first moralist of German soldierdom [*Soldatentum*]."[139] What is striking about this paragraph is not merely the direct quotation from *Felix Krull* (as then not yet published) but also its structure as a conversation between Mann and an unidentified sceptic (either his brother's voice or his own internal doubts). Here, Mann sought to defend his own strategic military value as an apologist for German soldiers in the manner of Kant: a moral voice on behalf of obedience, soldiering, and war. Thus, though Mann was consigned to live allegorically (already a burden as he experienced it), he was willing to serve as an intellectual soldier. That the great ironic author was not being ironic here is reinforced by his continual address to those intellectuals who, like his brother, resisted following his example: "You who are too smart to devote yourself and mockingly look on at those who do – make whatever you want out of what I am telling you, laugh at me coarsely or with a sneer because I am simple [*genügsam*], sentimental or vain enough to be happy about it – I defy you, it's all the same to me."[140] Perhaps the most enduring effect of the war was the resulting self-seriousness of his prose, which lost all traces of campiness.

It is perhaps no surprise, then, that he introduced his magnum opus of the war, *Confessions of a Nonpolitical Man*, as itself a form of military service. Though, as he informed readers in the preface, he originally thought he had "discharged his duty to the day and the hour" when he wrote his early war essays, especially the longer "Frederick the Great and the Grand Coalition," he soon realized that his attempt to return to his pre-war writing projects, including, especially *The Magic Mountain*, "proved to be an error," much like the "psychological mistakes" made during Krull's and his own repeated appearances before the military recruiting board: "I was, like hundreds of thousands of others who were taken from their paths by the war, 'drafted,' estranged, and held for long years from my true calling and occupation."[141] The military allegory continues: "It was not the state and the army that 'drafted' me, but the times themselves: to more than two years of military service of the mind – for which I was, by birth and by skill, finally just as little suited spiritually as was many a companion in misfortune physically for real duty on the front or at home, and from which I, not exactly in the most even frame of mind, a war casualty, as I should probably say, return today to my deserted worktable."[142] While others were off fighting on the front, Mann was brazen enough to portray his multi-year writing effort as a "military service of the mind." Perhaps most shocking, though, is his appropriation of the phrase "war casualty" (*Kriegsbeschädigter*), a designation that, as one of his biographers notes, "every member of the army of arm- and leg-amputees, of the victims of blindness and poison gas had to perceive as a mockery [of their sacrifice]."[143]

Nevertheless, unlike the texts written in the early days of the war, this opening paragraph is infused with the irony for which Mann is aptly famous. Though he frames his entire project in military language, some of the terms are enclosed in quotation marks, signalling an awareness that they are not entirely accurate for one who was, in fact, not drafted by the army, but rather spent the entire war at his desk in the comfort of one of his two homes. Moreover, other grandiose claims – such as his claim to be "a war casualty, as I should probably say" – are parenthetically qualified. In fact, by acknowledging that he is "not exactly in the most even frame of mind," he provides good reason for readers to be suspicious of his own judgment in the matter. (Of course, his grandiose claim of being a "war casualty" seems to prove that he is *not* "in the most even frame of mind.") Most importantly, by admitting that he was not up to the task of being a soldierly writer, that he is now mentally damaged from his effort, Mann seems to indicate that he is starting to disconnect the "soldierly" discipline of the writer from the actual soldier. It may have been tactless, but it was a beginning.[144]

Conclusion

In light of Mann's obtuse resistance to knowing the facts surrounding the war, his ruthless embrace of Germany's most belligerent qualities, and his bottomless narcissism, which peaked in astounding feats of self-aggrandizing and dense pages of solipsistic prose, it is easy to agree with Todd Kontje's understated assessment that "getting to know Mann better has not necessarily made him more likable."[145] Nevertheless, the vagaries of Mann's twenty-year fantasy of military service remain revealing on many levels. Perhaps the most obvious revelation is the persistence of the fantasy of military service, which seemed to first arise as Mann was finally deemed "fit" and which survived his actual failure as a soldier in 1900. For an impressively self-disciplined writer who struggled with his prose, the allegory of soldier-author proved irresistible in the heady atmosphere of militarism in Wilhelmine

Germany. Thus, even when acknowledging his early medical discharge in his autobiographical writings, Mann took pains to portray his physical inadequacy as a personal mental resistance to the army's most controversial and least warlike attribute, the parade step, implying he could have remained a soldier if his heart had been in it. In his literary writings in the decade or so afterwards, Mann translated his own sense of masculine inadequacy and separateness from the period's manly ideal – the soldier – into its own form of artistic soldiering: as he put it in *Felix Krull*, "to live like a soldier, but not as a soldier; figuratively but not literally," which for Krull and Mann alike "spell[ed] true freedom." Thus, rather than resolving the gap between fantasy and reality in favour of reality, Mann proved adept at modifying his fantasy. Because he equated fantasy and literature with freedom, he could imagine he had developed an inner resistance to *actual* military thinking and values even as he continued to understand his own lifestyle and literary process as a form of self-discipline that rivalled that of actual soldiers.

This insular and solipsistic form of German militarism – what I have been calling Mann's own private militarism – does not testify to a penetration of military values into bourgeois society from above, as the internalization of official doctrine. Instead, Mann's fantasy of military service largely arose in response to the exigencies of civilian life, in particular his sense of his own inadequacy and lack of desirability as a man who was fundamentally attracted to other men (and adolescent boys). As we saw, Mann's response to his impending induction into the military in 1900 was significantly shaped by his same-sex desires and sense of self. The result was two contradictory fantasies: on the one hand, Mann hoped that a year of military service might cure his homosexuality and effeminacy; but on the other, military service was also part of his homoerotic flirtation with Paul Ehrenberg, since he imagined that his newfound masculinity as a soldier might secure him the latter's affection. Admittedly, the military's promise of masculine credentials was itself an unintended by-product of Germany's system of conscription, for the extension of military service to all men as an essentially moral duty of citizenship transformed the admission to military service and its certificate of fitness into the standard of masculinity against which all men had to measure themselves. That a writer of Mann's talent should turn to military service rather than *Bildung* as an allegory for orienting himself testifies to the growing efficacy of the soldier's hegemonic masculinity in Germany at this time.

Finally, and most importantly, whatever ironic distance Mann professed from actual military service and the politics of German militarism, about which he seemed especially ignorant, the outbreak of war revealed this inner distance to be a ruse that only functioned in times of peace. Mann's "nonpolitical" capitulation to Germany's declaration of war thus raises doubts about Benjamin Ziemann's larger claim that soldiers, veterans, and others in Imperial Germany largely escaped the ideological hold of German militarism. Though there is no doubt that Ziemann is right to point to a "plurality of 'militarisms'" that "did not conform with the official façade of Wilhelmine militarism," this difference – so flexible in times of peace – did not necessarily provide any room to manoeuvre once war had been declared.[146] After all, as Žižek's work makes clear, an individual's or social group's internal distance from the state's dicta may be "the central formal feature of ideology" itself.[147] Though it would take Germany's immanent defeat before sailors, soldiers, and civilians alike could rise up against their masters in uniform to declare an end to the war – and the end to the autocratic rule of a uniformed monarch – one of the few who seemed to see through the fantasies and self-deceptions of German nationalists like Mann was his older brother Heinrich, whose critique is the focus of the next chapter.

Chapter Five

Perversions of Fantasy: Parody and the Left-Liberal Critique of German Militarism in Heinrich Mann's *The Loyal Subject*

Though Thomas Mann's fantasmatic identification with German soldiers during the First World War represented an extreme form of queer military politics, it is important not to lose sight of the fundamental misalignment between military politics and sexual politics in Imperial Germany. As we have seen, the military leadership remained explicitly hostile to queer emancipation, especially when the behaviour of both civilian "military chasers" and closeted officers threatened to tarnish the army's public reputation. Just as significant, though, the military politics of the Scientific-Humanitarian Committee (WhK), let alone those of the masculinists, diverged significantly from the military politics of most of its non-queer supporters, which hailed from socialist and left-liberal parties. As we have seen, these parties not only constituted the Reichstag's most strident critics of Prussian military policies and practices (among other aspects of the Imperial German status quo), but were just as likely to make use of sexual concepts like homosexuality and sadism as a weapon against the military leadership.

These discrepancies were, in fact, in full view during the first discussion of the WhK's petition on the floor of the Reichstag on 31 May 1905, which, as Magnus Hirschfeld recognized, represented "an important stage in our movement," marking "the first time that a public session in the Reichstag, perhaps even in any Parliament, discussed the weal and woe of homosexuals."[1] During the debate, which Hirschfeld reproduced in the pages of the *Jahrbuch*, Dr. Johann Thaler of the Catholic Center Party followed the logic of the morality movement in arguing that "homosexuality shatters the foundation of the state, it shatters marriage and family, it initiates a decline in the population or at least the lowering of population growth; it weakens therefore the power of the state."[2] Thaler also made it clear that the legalization of same-sex activity would have dire consequences for Germany's military readiness, since the power of the state "rests on its numerical superiority [*Übergewicht*] over other states."³ This moral and political opposition to queer emancipation rested, of course, on a universalizing conception of same-sex desire, which presumed that homosexuality could be acquired and spread through seduction and/or a lack of moral fortitude. Legalizing same-sex behaviour would supposedly encourage this kind of behaviour, leading to the moral decay of society and a perilous decrease in the number of marriages, families, and future soldiers. Thus, in addition to viewing homosexuality as a sinful vice (*Laster*), these groups saw its widespread indulgence as a danger to state and society.⁴

Meanwhile, the SPD's Friedrich Thiele hewed closely to the WhK's claim that same-sex desire was not "something sick, but rather only a natural deviation from the typical pattern."⁵ In response to arguments that same-sex acts "would undermine the health and the battle-readiness [*Wehrhaftigkeit*] of the German people," he espoused one of the SPD's long-standing arguments that the greater danger to the population's military readiness lay in the unequal distribution of material resources in Imperial Germany, such as "the interminable misery of living conditions [*Wohnungselend*] in the big cities, the terrible diet caused by the insufficient compensation of workers, [and] the many additional sanitary deficiencies [*santitäre Mißstände*] in large and small communities."⁶ The petition was also supported by Georg Gothein of the Freeminded Union. Though he did not address homosexuality's impact on Germany's military readiness directly, it was implied in his efforts to counter accusations that homosexuality harmed the state: "Certainly, if everyone were so constituted [*veranlagt*], then the state would die out; but here it only involves a relatively small contingent of the population, and one could just as easily see a threat to the state in excessive gambling, drinking, in libertinism in other areas."⁷ Like most supporters of the WhK petition, Gothein held a minoritizing view on same-sex identity, in which only a small number of people were actually homosexual. Moreover, his references to other widespread social dangers suggested that if opponents of decriminalizing consensual male-male sex acts were serious about the health of state and society, they should be focusing on these other, patently more important moral problems. Finally, rather than conceding military masculinity to the opponents of queer emancipation, he strongly implied that supporters of the petition evinced much more of the qualities one seeks in a soldier: "[W]hoever decides to sign such a petition needs a sizeable portion of courage in order to show himself ready for all the false insinuations and speculations that unfortunately are spoken in such a situation."⁸ Gothein's distinction between the courage of one's convictions and conformity to social dictates and conventions was in fact a central tenet of the long-standing left-liberal critique of many controversial aspects of German military policy, such as the expectations that officers resolve insults to their honour by issuing challenges to duel.[9]

Yet the period's most famous, influential, and enduring left-liberal critique of German militarism and the citizenry's "anticipatory obedience" came in in a novel by Thomas Mann's older brother Heinrich.[10] *Der Untertan* (*The Loyal Subject*) tells the story of Diederich Heßling, a man who betrays the liberal-humanistic principles of his bourgeois background through a phantasmatic over-identification with the German emperor Wilhelm II and his authoritarian and militaristic values. Most of the action takes place in the 1890s, shortly after Wilhelm II's accession to the throne, when a new kind of national chauvinism began to shape public discourse and displace more liberal tones in the bourgeoisie.[11] Besides a few pages devoted to the protagonist's childhood and family life at the very beginning of the novel, the first two chapters are set in Berlin, where he attends university, has a brief love affair with the daughter of his father's business associate, joins a duelling fraternity through which he gets introduced to far-right politics, and serves briefly in the army before obtaining an early discharge. The four subsequent chapters are set back in Heßling's provincial hometown, the fictive Netzig, where he ruthlessly "delivers" Netzig politically to the Kaiser by provoking a lèse-majesté trial and making deals with the two traditional "political enemies" of the bourgeoisie: on the one hand, the Prussian nobility, represented by the president of the government board (*Regierungspräsident*) Otto von Wulckow, and, on the other, the working-class Social Democrats, represented by his own machinist, Napoleon Fischer. In addition to providing an inversion of the *Bildungsroman* by depicting its hero's regression into a subservient and defective subject (rather than his development into a mature, fully formed, and autonomous individual), the novel provides a panorama of Wilhelminian society through its setting in urban Berlin and small-town Netzig. Because of the extensive research Mann conducted for the novel and its scathing depiction of Imperial Germany, it is easy to understand why the book eventually became a litmus test and proxy in the famous and long-running "Kaiserreich debate" among historians of this period.[12]

Completed just weeks before the start of the First World War, the novel can perhaps be considered the final literary work of Imperial Germany – as well as the period's most relentless left-liberal critique of military masculinity. Though its serialization was prematurely interrupted by the outbreak of war, its publication in book form in December 1918 made it into an overnight sensation, significantly overshadowing

Thomas Mann's *Reflections of an Unpolitical Man*.[13] Indeed, if Thomas's *Reflections* offered a ruthless one-sided settling of accounts with his brother, with whom he publicly feuded over their different stances in the war, it is also possible to read *The Loyal Subject* in part as Heinrich's critical portrait of his younger brother. As Helmut Koopmann has amply demonstrated, the two brothers primarily carried out an extended dialogue with one another through their fiction and essays.[14] But though *The Loyal Subject* does not appear in Koopmann's study, I follow him in seeing their literary dialogue mirrored in one of the few images depicting the two together (Figure 5.1).[15] Like in *Reflections*, which offers a solipsistic critique of Heinrich, in this double portrait, taken in 1900, Thomas sits facing his older brother but chooses to gaze out to the viewer – or inward – rather than respond directly to the person standing next to him. Meanwhile, a standing Heinrich looks down on his younger sibling (perhaps not just literally but also figuratively), while offering the camera only a profile of his face. Like this double portrait, *The Loyal Subject* demonstrates this knowing glance, and I suggest it serves as the basis for Heinrich's cryptic statement about Thomas's wartime jingoism in his 1917 letter to him: "The opposition of your spirit [*Geist*] I knew from before, and if your extreme position in the war has astonished you, for me it was foreseeable."[16] (To be sure, the novel was also a self-critique. Early in his career, Heinrich had championed startlingly reactionary ideas as an editor of the *völkisch* and anti-Semitic journal *Das Zwanzigste Jahrhundert* [The twentieth century], for which he also contributed numerous polemical pieces.)[17]

But I also want to use *The Loyal Subject* and Heinrich Mann's position in the fraternal feud with his brother as a way to interrogate the underlying fantasies of masculinity and male sexuality in the left-liberal critique of German militarism. Because Heinrich was not only aware of his brother's homoerotic desires but, like Thomas, also familiar with the sexological discourse of the era, I proceed by reading the representation of Diederich Heßling's character in dialogue with sexology's discourses on the various sexual perversions related to effeminacy as they emerged over the late nineteenth and early twentieth centuries: homosexuality conceived as sexual inversion (beginning in the 1860s with Karl Heinrich Ulrichs's works); masochism, a concept introduced by Richard von Krafft-Ebing in 1890; and transvestism, a term coined by Hirschfeld in 1910. In contrast to Thomas Mann's efforts to deploy irony in order to reconcile his "unmanly" identity with German military values, *The Loyal Subject* depicts these "pathological" forms of effeminacy as the cause of its anti-hero's illiberalism – and his failure to achieve the period's bourgeois ideal of the autonomous male subject. Most significantly, the

178　Uniform Fantasies

Figure 5.1. Heinrich Mann (standing) and Thomas Mann (seated). Munich around 1900. ETH-Bibliothek Zürich, Thomas-Mann-Archiv / Photo: Atelier Elvira / TMA_0017.

novel reverses the value of fantasy that Thomas Mann laid out in *Felix Krull*. Whereas fantasy – as imagination – supposedly guaranteed Felix Krull's artistic freedom (and by extension its author's as well), fantasy – as a pathological disavowal of reality – structures Diederich Heßling's subservience to Wilhelm II and the militaristic spirit of his age.

The Loyal Subject is without doubt a brilliant satire. Yet for all its insight into the psychopathology of the bourgeois militarist, the novel's use of parody ultimately undermines its own critical ethos. Though literary theory has offered multiple and conflicting definitions of parody, I follow Simon Dentith in understanding it as "any cultural practice which provides a relatively polemical allusive imitation of another cultural production or practice."[18] Not only does Mann's novel parody the cultural practices and discourses of right-wing bourgeois militarism, but it presents its anti-hero as a parody of Wilhelm II, especially in his most self-aggrandizing male poses. But though *The Loyal Subject*'s parody exhibits a queer energy in its satiric send-up of the era's displays of aggressive masculinity, it nonetheless falls short of achieving the function that Judith Butler identified in explicitly queer forms of parody – in particular, gay male drag – in *Gender Trouble*: the capacity to reveal all gender enactments as "an imitation without an original."[19] In fact, Mann's novel, which can be read profitably through psychoanalytic theory, reminds us that parody, even in the service of left-liberal critiques of the political status quo, can have conservative agendas in other areas, such as in gender and sexual politics. In this case, the parodic representation of Diederich Heßling's erotic inclinations and gender performances veers into a queerphobic construct that tells us more about liberal fantasies about militarism and authoritarianism than about those political phenomena themselves. More damaging still, *The Loyal Subject* uses Heßling's fantasies as objects of ridicule in order to shame a figure whose sense of identity is in fact, like Thomas Mann's own, already painfully disfigured by the shame of his own gender inadequacy. As a result, although the novel sets out to criticize military masculinity as a perverse expression of an innate effeminacy, it suggests instead that gender discipline in Imperial Germany's civil society might actually have been more severe and punitive than in the military itself.

Psychopathia Homosexualis

Because Diederich Heßling has an affair with one woman before marrying another, it's perhaps odd to contend that the discourse on sexual inversion has any relevance for understanding his character as pathologically effeminate. Yet his heterosexual love interests evince a puzzling lack of desire for women compared with his often explicit infatuations with male figures in the novel. Moreover, the novel depicts his attraction to Guste Daimling, who becomes his wife, as rooted in her rather lasciviously queer flirtation with him during their first encounter as adults. For this depiction of lacklustre or perverse heterosexuality, Heinrich Mann's brother, Thomas, may have served as an inspiration and model. No doubt, the conceptualization of Heßling as someone with unconscious homosexual desires also derived from the picture of General Kuno von Moltke that emerged at the Harden-Moltke Trial in 1907 (discussed in chapter 1), which occurred around the time that Mann drafted a ten-page plan for the novel in his notebook.[20] Moltke, as we saw, was the first man publicly outed as a homosexual without any evidence that he had ever engaged in sexual behaviour with another man.

But before we pursue the depiction of Heßling's effeminacy as sexual inversion, it is perhaps best to start at the beginning. In fact, the novel announces the theme of the protagonist's effeminacy in its very first sentence: "Diederich Heßling was a weak [*weiches*] child, who best liked to dream, was frightened of everything, and suffered frequently from earaches" (9). This opening is characteristic for Mann's prose style throughout the novel, which, as Theo Buck notes, excels at representing complex ideas in extremely dense and efficient sentences.[21] In this case, the opening gambit specifies three forms of weakness, which are the very antithesis of ideal masculinity: one is physiological (his earaches), suggesting not only some congenital problems with his health, but a physiological defectiveness on the inside. (It also slyly establishes the protagonist's connection to his hero, Wilhelm II, who suffered from otitis.)[22] Meanwhile, the other two forms of weakness denote psychological deficits: a fear of everything (reality) that is offset by a pleasure in daydreaming and fantasy, which seems to promise an escape from reality. The text illustrates the child's fear of reality through his attachment to the familiar, enclosed spaces of the warm and cosy parlour in winter and the "narrow garden" in summer (9), where his imagination runs wild: "Whenever Diederich looked up from his storybook, his beloved book of fairy tales, he became frightened. A toad – half-as-big as himself! – had clearly been sitting next to him on the bench! Or there at the wall was a gnome sticking half out of the ground and squinting at him!" (9). Though young Diederich is afraid of reality, the novel makes clear that the perception of danger is in fact a result of his overactive imagination, which infuses reality with fantastical figures that, in turn, make the world – even the enclosed garden – seem so dangerous.

The effeminacy of his overactive imagination is underlined by its close association with his mother, who, the narrator explains, "nourished him with fairy tales" and "imparted her fear" of rational and technological modernity, such as "the new, bustling streets and the horse-drawn tram that went through them" (11). Mann scholars have tended to view Frau Heßling as a victim of the period's patriarchal oppression of women, a reading reinforced by Diederich Heßling's own subsequent tendency to "project his aggression" onto her.[23] But as Ariana Martin convincingly argues, Frau Heßling's methods of raising her son are, in the terms of the novel, partially responsible for his emotional underdevelopment, since she inculcates in him a "diffuse sentimentality" that impedes his social, psychological, and mental maturity.[24] Indeed, both figures relished "twilight hours overflowing with sentiment. On festive occasions, they jointly extracted the last drop of emotion by singing, piano-playing and telling fairy tales" (11). In particular, her own inconsistent and highly emotional treatment of her son seems to inhibit his ability to develop any meaningful relationship with others, especially women, for her relationship to her son swings between emotional extremes: "She prayed with the child 'from the heart' rather than according to set phrases, which gave her flushed cheeks. She also beat him, but hand over foot and consumed with vindictiveness" (11). In response, he essentially treats her the same, for "he exploited her tender hours; but he never felt any respect for his mother" (11). As a result, rather than representing the young boy's first love object, as Heinrich Mann's own mother apparently did, she is merely an object with limited value.[25]

Though Diederich Heßling has a heterosexual affair before marrying Guste Daimling, *The Loyal Subject* repeatedly exploits his fundamental "likeness" (*Ähnlichkeit*) to his mother to raise questions about the reliability and strength of the protagonist's presumed heterosexuality and to indicate instead an underlying and even more powerful sexual inversion. As we have seen, same-sex desire constituted the most important nineteenth-century sexological discourse on effeminacy. Following the lead set by Karl Heinrich Ulrichs and Carl Westphal before him, who both viewed same-sex desire as a form of gender inversion, Krafft-Ebing systematically defined different degrees of acquired and congenital "contrary sexual sensation" based on the extent to which men exhibited feminine traits or reported identifying with heterosexual women vis-à-vis their male partners. Moreover, Krafft-Ebing stressed that the "determining factor" for diagnosing homosexuality "*is the demonstration of perverse feeling for the same sex; not the proof of sexual acts with the same sex.*"[26]

Like with Krafft-Ebing's cases of "acquired homosexuality," where same-sex desire emerges after earlier heterosexual experiences, Heßling's homoerotic desires originate after he experiences an initial attraction to Agnes Göppel, the daughter of one of his father's business associates whom Heßling first meets on the fourth Sunday after his arrival in Berlin. According to Martin, Agnes represents the *femme fragile* that served as Mann's ideal of femininity in his literary works from the 1890s.[27] Her sudden presence while Heßling is talking with her father "embarrasses" (*peinlich berührt*) him and causes him to feel clammy (*feucht*) with the discomfort occasioned by this first-time experience of erotic attraction (18). But while the intensity of that desire often leads to an impulsive "rush of chivalry" (22), his feelings for her also invariably remind him of his own innate and embarrassing weakness. Thus, after he secretly buys her a ticket to the concert she wanted to see, "he moved through the crush [of the Berlin streets] feeling softer and softer [*immer weicher*] and happier and happier" (24). This sense of weakness is reinforced by his interactions with Göppel's lodger, an engineering student from Mecklenburg named Mahlmann who sees Heßling as a rival and repeatedly threatens and humiliates him. But rather than direct his grievances against Mahlmann, the protagonist takes them out on Agnes. Thus, he harboured "still more resentment [*Groll*] against Agnes than against Mahlmann. For Mahlmann called for admiration whenever he ran after someone in the middle of the night to punch in his top hat – even as Diederich in no way misrecognized the warning that such an action carried for himself" (26).

Although Agnes gives off clear signals that she prefers Heßling over Mahlmann (27), the protagonist is repeatedly turned off by her feminine softness. For instance, after she drops her purse and then picks it up herself, "she thanked him anyway, quite softly [*weich*] and almost ashamed – which annoyed Diederich. 'Coquettish women are something ghastly [*Gräßliches*],' he thought" (19). Then after he once applies a bandage to a finger she cut, he reacts to his own powerful desires by denigrating her: "The air suddenly became so hot and thick [*schwül*], he thought: 'If only I [*man*] didn't have to always touch her skin! She is disgustingly soft [*weich*]'" (20). After Mahlmann arrives and monopolizes her attention, Heßling has time to discover that "she was actually not pretty": "She had a flattened nose that was too small, and freckles were plainly visible on its narrow bridge. Her light brown eyes were too close together, and they blinked when she looked at anyone. Her lips were too thin, as indeed was her whole face. 'If she did not have that mass of reddish-brown hair over her forehead and that white complexion …' He noted, too, with satisfaction that the nail of the [bleeding] finger he had licked was not quite clean" (20).[28] Thus, even as he still acknowledges his attraction to specific areas of her body – in particular, her auburn hair and her pale skin – Heßling is otherwise pleased to see that she is less than perfect, and even deficient in her hygiene.

Scared off by Mahlmann's threats, Heißling next encounters Agnes three years later after his politicization in the duelling fraternity and immediately following his first encounter with his hero and model, Wilhelm II. In contrast to many early interpretations, which contend that Heßling's relationship to Agnes holds the promise of saving him from his fate as a "loyal subject," Martin argues persuasively that his love for Agnes is "simply pretend romantic love, and this romantic theatre proves to be a ham comedy."[29] While she interprets the relationship as Mann's rejection of his own youthful infatuation with the figure of the *femme fragile*, it is also important to see it as evidence of Heßling's surprising lack of authentic heterosexual desire. Thus, when Agnes first makes the moves on him back in his apartment, Heßling is "terribly shocked" (*furchtbar erschrocken*) and he initially responds according to a script of romantic behaviour: "He pressed his mouth into her hair, rather deeply, because he felt he was obligated to" (68) – even though her hair was, in his estimation, the feature that attracted him the most. Moreover, his relationship to her merely echoes the sentimentality that marked the childhood hours he shared with his mother. Thus, after dropping her off at her home, he returns to his apartment, where he writes her a letter claiming that "he had also waited for her these last three years, but that he had not had any hope because she was too beautiful for him, too fine and too good; … that she was a saint, and now that she had deigned to descend to him, he lay prostrate at her feet" (72). Of course, the next morning he found his words "an embarrassing exaggeration" and shelved the letter in his desk drawer (72). While Heßling's letter to Agnes demonstrates his attempt to respond to her fantasy about him, it does not hold up to the light of day the next morning and the much more powerful fantasies about masculinity that drive his life.

However, the authenticity of desire that is absent from his relationship with Agnes is, in fact, much more present in his relations with men. But if Mahlmann's threatening form of masculinity commands Heßling's begrudging admiration, then its positive form, in his eyes, is represented by the law student Wiebel, his mentor in the duelling fraternity he is pressured into joining during his second year at the University of Berlin. Though Wiebel's elegant "English fabrics," "refined manners," and "quiet, arrogant feudal voice" (35) initially make Heßling aware of his own inferiority, the novel also emphasizes the powerful erotic attraction his patron exerts over him:

> Diederich succumbed each time to the thrill [*Schauer*] of so much aristocratic refinement [*Vornehmheit*]. Everything about Wiebel seemed to him exquisite [*erlesen*]: that the reddish beard hair grew far above his lips and that his long, curved fingernails curved under rather than, as in Diederich's case, upward; the strong manly scent that emanated from Wiebel, even his protruding ears which increased the effect of his part, and his cat-like eyes which were embedded in his thick-set temples. If [Heßling] had had a tail, he would have gratefully wagged it. His heart expanded with happy admiration. If his wishes had ventured so high, he would also have loved to have such a red neck and sweat all the time. (35–6)[30]

The law student Wiebel represents the educated middle-class student (*Bildungsbürger*) in his negative Prussian form, that is, as an imitation of the aristocracy. Of course, Heßling's desire to be like Wiebel – here presented as a wish bordering on the impertinent – presages his subsequent fantasmatic identification with Wilhelm II, when Heßling not only parrots the emperor's most ridiculous and shocking statements but also uncannily formulates phrases that the Kaiser pronounces only later. As Eve Sedgwick has argued, such identification became a trope of homosexuality: "The (relatively new) emphasis on the 'homo,' on the dimension of sameness, built into modern understandings of relations of sexual desire within a given gender, has had a sustained and active power ... to show how close may be the slippage or even the melding between identification and desire."[31] Meanwhile, the reference to Heßling's desire to "wag" as "if he had had a tail" is part of the novel's repeated association of his behaviour with a dog who is entirely attuned to the whims of his master. It also shrewdly alludes to the homoerotic adulation of Wilhelm II by Kuno von Moltke and other members of the Eulenburg circle, and enshrined in the words that Moltke supposedly said while holding the handkerchief that Eulenburg left behind after one of his visits: "Meine Seele, mein Alterchen, mein einziger Dachs!" (literally: my soul, my little old one, my only dachshund).[32] In fact, this phrase was taken up in a 1907 caricature (Figure 5.2) that appeared in a special issue devoted to the Harden-Moltke trial in the liberal, Berlin-based satirical magazine *Lustige Blätter*, featuring a romantic encounter between a pig – a reference to homosexuality as a *Schweinerei* (swinish business) – and a dachshund prominently wagging his tale.

But what is so remarkable about this passage is the extent of Heßling's libidinal infatuation with Wiebel himself. While he soberly assesses

Parody and Critique in Heinrich Mann's *The Loyal Subject* 185

Figure 5.2. "Tête-à-tête," caricature produced in response to testimony by Lily von Elbe at the first Harden-Moltke libel trial. *Lustige Blätter: schönstes buntes Witzblatt Deutschlands* (5 November 1907), p. 5. Österreichische Nationalbibliothek Vienna. Call Number: 457621-D.

Agnes's looks, whose erotic pull is reduced to her auburn hair and delicate pallor (and diminished by her freckles, thin lips, and dirty fingernails), Heßling is captivated by Wiebel's most patently unappetizing traits: his unnatural downward-curving fingernails, the reddish hair that grows far above his lips, his protruding ears that exaggerate the part in his hair, and his profuse sweating and repellant body odours. Of course, that Heßling should be mesmerized by what would disgust most readers makes the passage funny. But while such traits are unattractive in reality, Heßling's powerful imagination imbues them with allure. Indeed, their negative connotations only serve to demonstrate the strength of his erotic attraction to Wiebel, in contrast to his anaemic interest in Agnes.

In addition, he is also drawn to Wiebel's association with Prussian nobility and military service, which is, in turn, reinforced by the latter's repeated references to his cousin, a von Klappke, who he claims is serving with the Second Grenadier Guards regiment Kaiser Franz Joseph (36). The mention of Klappke offers another occasion for Heßling to fantasize about Wiebel: "Diederich tried to imagine a Wiebel in the uniform of a Guards officer; but so much distinction [*Vornehmheit*] could simply not be dreamed up [*nicht auszudenken*]" (36–7). Here Heßling's power of imagination hits its apparent limit in picturing his idol decked out in the uniform of an exclusive Guards regiment known for having the tallest and physically strongest men.[33] While the impression is that a uniformed Wiebel represented the kind of manly perfection that surpassed the protagonist's powers of imagination, the erotic undercurrent of his infatuation with his mentor also suggests that Wiebel's full militarization might also come too close to representing Heßling's sexual desire. The implication is that such a literal image would not only exceed the sanctioned homoerotic economy of the all-male space of the fraternity but also force the protagonist to confront the existence of his unconscious desires.

Even after he has returned home to Netzig following the completion of his studies and his unceremonious abandonment of Agnes after she sleeps with him, Heßling continues to be attracted to men in uniform. Thus, after attending an afternoon tea at the home of the Regierungspräsident von Wulckow, at which he sees his sister Emmi flirt with a certain Lieutenant von Brietzen, a colonel passes Heßling and his sisters in the street: "Diederich stared after him for a long time. 'I know,' he said, 'one shouldn't turn around; but that is simply the finest [*Höchste*], it simply draws you to it'" (340). Heßling's attraction to a man in uniform is so strong that it overrules his public manners. The impression is that the libidinal energies on display in Emmi's flirtation with Brietzen have brought his own to the forefront.

Nevertheless, unlike the majority of Krafft-Ebing's homosexual patients, Heßling is largely unconscious of his homoerotic attractions and hence neither acts on them nor sees them as problems requiring solutions, whether that be the cure that many patients sought or the kind of social validation of their desires that others called for (and that the queer emancipation movement hoped to deliver). In their unconsciousness, in fact, they resemble much more closely Hirschfeld's diagnosis of Kuno von Moltke, another effeminate homosexual who harboured a long-time devotion to Wilhelm II and Prince Philip Eulenburg. As in his relationship to Agnes, Heßling's attractions towards other men exist largely in his fantasy life. Moreover, in their existence chiefly as fantasies, they also mirror Thomas Mann's sexuality, who seems to have preferred to live out his attractions to men solely within his fantasies and writing while refraining from acting on them or even naming them as homosexual, let alone as evidence of his sexual identity (at least until he reads Hans Blüher's work during the First World War). But in contrast to Heßling's articulation of his love for Agnes – the letter he never sends her is merely a script with "grand words" that he derides the next day as "unmanly and discomfiting" (*unmännlich und unbequem*) (72) – these "male fantasies" serve to orient his desires. As Lacanian psychoanalysis explains, fantasy is not the expression of one's own authentic desire, but rather tells us what we desire: "The original question of desire is not directly 'What do I want?' but 'What do others want from me? What do they see in me? What am I to others?'"[34] In this sense, Heßling's more authentic fantasies stage his attempt to fill the void at the centre of his own subjectivity and achieve some kind of stable social and psychological identity as a man. The man he desires, and whose desires he seeks to fulfil – Wiebel here and Wilhelm II more generally – is also the man he fantasizes he can become.

Yet if Krafft-Ebing assumes homosexuality can be acquired even after amorous experiences or erotic thoughts involving members of the "opposite" sex, Heinrich Mann's novel suggests that Diederich Heßling – like the author's brother, Thomas Mann himself – may represent a case of what might be called *acquired heterosexuality*. In Thomas Mann's case, his pursuit of Katja Pringsheim seemed not only to be a flight from the impossible and unhappy desire for Paul Ehrenberg but also an expression of his underlying homosexual orientation. As his biographers point out, Katja was rather a tomboy with boyish looks. Anthony Heilbut reports that she "had a masculine directness, a disdain for sentimentality, and a riotous sense of humor, ... combin[ing] a boyish appearance with an intelligence not conventionally female."[35] Moreover, like Thomas Mann's frequent inclusion of brother and sister twins into his prose as instances of erotic and aesthetic desires, he seems to have been a little smitten with her twin brother Karl.[36]

A similar process seems to be at work in Heßling's initial flirtation with Guste Daimchen, whom he first encounters on the train back to Netzig after he has callously dismissed Herr Göppel's entreaties to marry Agnes after he slept with her. Like Thomas's wife, Guste appears to have been a tomboy of sorts, for Heßling recollects that she "always climbed over the garden wall" to visit the Heßling home (103). Moreover, in contrast to the *femme fragile* and the "disgustingly elegant" women that Heßling chased away from the train compartment after he rudely took off his shoes and put his stockinged feet on the seat next to them, Guste is almost masculine in her in departure from the feminine norm. Not only does she not protest the protagonist's poor manners, but she also proceeds to pull a sausage from her bag, which she eats, rather unladylike, with her hands while throwing him a smile. The move not only "disarms" him but attracts him as well. In sizing her up he notes, "the chubby, rosy face with the fleshy mouth and the small, insolently flat nose; the blond hair, nice, smooth and proper, the neck, which was young and fat, and, in her half-gloves, fingers, which held the sausage and which themselves resembled rosy little sausages" (102–3). Thus, in contrast to Agnes, who was thin, pale, and a little sickly, Guste's unladylike manners and physique are a far cry from the *femme fragile*. In her healthy and fleshy girth, she more closely resembles Heßling himself – as well as his dead friend, "fat Delitzsch," another Neuteutonian with whom he felt a particularly special connection. Meanwhile, the sausage and her sausage-like fingers, which come last in Heßling's appraisal and thus stand out to him as her most alluring attributes, imbue her with rather obvious phallic attributes. Indeed, her lewd consumption of the sausage while casting sly smiles calls to mind an obscene come-on for an illicit homosexual tryst. (In fact, the emphasis on her flat nose, her fat neck, and her sausage-like fingers holding a sausage also resonate strongly with Figure 5.2, the caricature of the pig, with Heßling as the dachshund.)

As it turns out, the protagonist is most taken with her ability to pair casual and confident lewdness with severe self-defence. When Heßling goes to grab her by the waist, she immediately deals him a slap in the face. "She gave a full-throated laugh and winked at him lewdly [*unzüchtig*] with her small eyes. 'You can have a piece of sausage, but nothing else.' Without wanting to, he compared her way of defending herself with Agnes' helplessness, and said to himself: 'One can confidently marry someone like this'" (103). Though Agnes's fragility initially elicited feelings of chivalry from Heßling, it eventually represented a dangerous lure that too often elicited the soft core underlying his manly veneer. After he had abandoned her following their weekend away, she had been too meek to do more than stand silently under his apartment window in the pouring rain and send her equally helpless father to try to persuade Heßling to marry her. In contrast, though Guste rebuffs his unchivalrous advances with a harsh slap, Heßling is nevertheless drawn to her ability to stand up to him and even punish him. To explore this dimension of Heßling's sexuality and its significance for his male identity, we need to turn to the subject of masochism, which through Guste's lack of ideal femininity is linked to Heßling's unconscious sexual inversion.

Psychopathia Masochismus

Like Heßling's homoerotic effeminacy, which can be traced back to his earliest interactions with his mother, the origins of Heßling's masochistic tendencies are also situated in his childhood development, this time in relation to his father. Identified in the novel only as Herr Heßling, the father represents the traditional masculinity of the previous generation, particularly in its association with Prussian militarism. In addition to fighting in the wars of German unification under Wilhelm I, Herr Heßling's physical appearance – with the "weather-beaten face of a non-commissioned officer" (*Unteroffizier*) and "his silvery Kaiser beard" – is reminiscent of the first emperor of unified Germany and the grandfather of Wilhelm II. Despite the father's fear-inducing power, "one is supposed to love him" and "Diederich did love him" (9). This love, in turn, is based in the father's symbolic authority to punish Diederich's misdeeds: "Whenever [he] had pilfered food between meals [*naschen*] or had lied, he moved around the office desk smacking his lips and cringing shyly like a dog until Herr Heßling noticed something amiss and took the rod from the wall" (9).[37]

If the young Diederich loves his father because of the latter's power to punish his misdeeds, this is because he feels an inner sense of guilt that is, in turn, constituted by his similarity to his mother. The feminine origin of his guilt is illustrated through a signature event that occurs when, as a child, he allows his father's female employees to steal buttons (*Knöpfe*) from the cloth rags they are processing as raw material for the paper factory in exchange for getting some for himself. After young Diederich exchanges his stash for candies, his crime comes to light. In addition to the crime's connection to the female employees, Herr Heßling traces it back to his wife's influence. As we learn from the narrator, who ventriloquizes the elder Heßling's thoughts, the father "completely disagreed with the mawkish [*gefühlsselig*] ways of his wife. She ruined the child for life. Moreover, he caught her telling lies exactly like little Diedel. No wonder, since she read novels! And the chores that he had given her were not even done by Saturday evening. She gossiped with the maid-servant instead of getting to work [*sich rühren*]" (10–11). According to the omniscient narrator, Herr Heßling "didn't even know that his wife also snuck food between meals, just like a child ... If she had dared to go into the workshop, she too would have stolen buttons" (11). From the perspective of Diederich's father (as well as the narrator), the young boy and his mother were essentially similar – and feminine – in their penchant for lying, stealing, and snacking between meals. Meanwhile, from Diederich's point of view "her similarity to himself" led him to go "through life with too much of a bad conscience, which could not be justified before God" (11). Diederich's "bad conscience" resides in his awareness of his similarity to his mother, and thus his innate effeminacy. Of course, his view of himself represents an internalization of his father's derogatory view of his mother, since, according to Žižek, "the symbolic space acts like a yardstick" against which individuals measure themselves.[38]

In addition to shaping his negative self-image as defectively effeminate, Diederich Heßling's exaggerated respect and love for his father (and other authority figures) and his lack of respect for his mother inevitably exert a powerful influence on his sexuality in the form of masochism. This impulse, which mimics the punishments exacted by his father, initially appears when he is playing with his school friends. Though the young Diederich derives enjoyment from meting out punishments, both real and imaginary, he in fact prefers to be on the receiving end: "For he only felt safe and sure of his ground when he himself was getting the beating. He hardly withstood the malady [*Übel*]. At the most, he *requested* of his pals: 'Just don't beat me on the back, that's not healthy'" (14, emphasis in original). While the practice of requesting beatings from friends smacks of masochistic play with homoerotic associations, the word choice of "Übel" connotes a sexual habit akin to masturbation – the great childhood "scourge" and, in Krafft-Ebing's aetiology, one of the key causes of sexual inversion.[39]

It is thus no surprise that towards the very end of the novel, Heßling's marriage to Guste spontaneously transforms into a clear case of masochism. While the two are alone in the drawing room where he reads aloud from the *Lokal-Anzeiger*, supposedly the only newspaper that Wilhelm II ever read, Guste (whose name slyly points to Wilhelm II's wife, Auguste Viktoria of Schleswig-Holstein) suddenly becomes bored, narrows her eyes, and starts pestering him with her knees: "He wanted to express yet one more nationalist thought, but Guste said with an uncharacteristically severe voice: 'Nonsense' [*Quatsch*]; Diederich, however, far from punishing this infringement [*Übergriff*], blinked at her, as if he expected more" (445). When he makes the first move by trying to embrace her, she reprises her role in the train compartment by suddenly delivering "a powerful slap on the face" (445). Instead of reasserting his patriarchal authority, Heßling "stands up and ducks, panting, behind a curtain" only to re-emerge with fear and "dark longing" in his eyes. Feeling confident, Guste rises and starts hissing commands like "On your knees, you miserable slave [*Schklafe*]!" and "Now worship my glorious form [*herrliche Gestalt*]!" (446). After making him lie on his back and walking all over his belly, she informs him, "I am your mistress and you are my subject [*Untertan*]" (446). She then orders him to "Get up and march!" to the bedroom, commanding him to "Enjoy it!" (*Freu dich*) (446) as she begins to call him indecent (*wenigst anständigen*) names from behind.

By calling him an "Untertan" in this scene, Guste literally names Diederich Heßling's primary role in life, which in this case takes the form of an erotic subjection to his wife. Heinrich Mann was, of course, familiar with Leopold von Sacher-Masoch's work, which he deeply admired. Indeed, in 1906 and 1907, when he had just begun working on *Der Untertan*, Mann had been in contact with the Sacher-Masoch's widow and his publisher in Vienna about acquiring the rights to his unpublished and out-of-print novellas and reissuing them with a forward by himself.[40] But even if he did highly respect Sacher-Masoch's oeuvre, it seems much more likely that his understanding of masochism as a sexual perversion derived from Krafft-Ebing's *Psychopathia Sexualis*, which he had read in 1891. Back then he wrote to his friend Ludwig Ewers that he was suffering from "a morbid [*krankhaft*] sensuality" that worried even himself: "Krafft-Ebing, whose 'Psychopathia Sexualis' I recently read, indeed says that lust [*Begierde*] grows in the degree of frequency with which the sexual object changes. But with me it is reversed. I have found a horizontal girl that embodies to a great extent the ideal that my senses must have created of the feminine form: This voluptuous [*üppig*] slenderness drives [*reizen*] me to excess."[41] In her study of Mann's early prose as evidence of his engagement with the natural sciences of his day, Helga Winter concludes that "even with all the critical distance that the young Heinrich Mann shows towards the work of Krafft-Ebing, those impulses that make their way into Mann's thought can hardly be overestimated," especially, she notes, for his understanding of the concepts of sadism and masochism.[42]

Though Gilles Deleuze reads the severe punishments in Sacher-Masoch's works as a ritual to "obliterate" the father's "role and his likeness [in the son] in order to generate the new man," a view that might resonate with Mann's difficult relationship with his own father, Krafft-Ebing's approach to the gendered dimensions of sexuality rests on a traditional conception of men as active and aggressive sexual partners and women as passive ones.[43] As a result, masochism – which the Viennese sexologist defined as "the unlimited subjection to the will of a person of the opposite sex" – and sadism – defined as "the unlimited mastery of this person" – necessarily appear in *Psychopathia Sexualis* as extreme versions of male and female attributes: "While sadism may be looked upon as a pathological intensification of the masculine sexual character in its psychical peculiarities, masochism rather represents a pathological degeneration of the distinctive psychical peculiarities of woman."[44] Thus, according to Krafft-Ebing, "it cannot be doubted that the masochist considers himself in a passive, feminine *rôle* towards his mistress and that his sexual gratification is governed by the success his illusion experiences in the complete subjection to the will of his consort. The pleasurable feeling, call it lust, resulting from this act differs per se in no wise from the feeling which woman derives from the sexual act."[45] While Deleuze's conception of masochism may be relevant for understanding Mann the author, it is Krafft-Ebing's version that largely guides the representation of the scene of domination and submission between Heßling and his wife.

Moreover, Heßling's masochistic subordination to Guste also reinforces his homoerotic effeminacy since, according to Krafft-Ebing, "the masochistic element is so frequently found in homosexual men."[46] In particular, his masochistic relationships with Guste is consistent with his submissiveness towards higher-ranked men, especially in his initial encounter with the Kaiser, which concludes the first chapter. In this scene, which takes place in February 1892 when there were several days of protests by unemployed workers demanding jobs and bread, Wilhelm II led his troops ceremoniously through the protesters down Unter den Linden to the Tiergarten, Berlin's large central park, which police had cordoned off. In his enthusiasm for the Kaiser and his martial performance, Heßling successfully eludes the security forces and makes his way into the park, where he comes face-to-face with Wilhelm II atop his steed. The Kaiser, suspecting an anarchist assassin, "glared [*anblitzen*] down at him from his horse, piercing him. Diederich tore the hat from his head, his mouth agape, but no scream came out. Coming to a sudden stop, he slipped and landed with a thud, legs in the air, in a pool of dirty water. The Kaiser laughed ... turned to his escorts, slapped his thighs, and laughed. The guy was a monarchist, a loyal subject [*ein treuer Untertan*]!" (64).

The similarities between this scene and Heßling's subsequent masochistic scenario with his wife are striking. Whereas in that scene, Guste stands above her husband, in this scene the Kaiser on his steed sits high above his subject on the ground. In both cases, they wield their power over their "subject" in the same way, by glaring (*anblitzen*). As if hypnotized, Heßling's subordination in each scene is marked by his speechlessness: here the inability to scream, despite his gaping mouth; there, his stunned silence, blank stare and heavy breathing as she yells "nonsense," slaps his face, and, after walking on his belly, asks him if he's had enough. And in both scenes Heßling winds up on his back. If with Guste he assumes the submissive position of a dog, who shows its underbelly to its mistress, here his tumble into a puddle of mud provides an even stronger image of Heßling's abasement. Thus, if the husband role-plays an Untertan in his scene with Guste, here he is the literal (because political) embodiment of the term, which historically designated those who were "subject" to state authority, and in particular, to monarchical rule.[47]

But it is not only the symmetry between the scenes that supports a reading of Heßling's subjection to the Kaiser as masochism, for the protagonist himself imbues the Kaiser's appearance on the streets of Berlin with libidinal power. Watching the emperor and his troops march down Unter den Linden, Heßling is swept away: "The power that rides over [*hingehen*] us and whose hooves we kiss! Which rides over hunger, defiance and scorn! Against which we can do nothing because we all love it! ... We are but an atom of it, a disappearing molecule of something it has spit out ... We live in it, we share in it, we are merciless against those who are located far away from it, and we triumph, even when it smashes us to pieces: for thus does it justify our love!" (63–4). The repetition of the word love indicates the extent to which this form of politics is eroticized. Indeed, the parade scene stages his hallucinatory pleasure at being trampled by the Kaiser's horses, whose hooves he imagines kissing as they ride over him, even at the risk of his being crushed to bits. In Lacanian psychoanalysis, this passion at the risk of one's own life is what distinguishes jouissance as unbearable enjoyment from mere pleasure.[48] In the case of masochism, though, the punishment does not merely signify the risk but the locus of passion as well. The scene being staged here in Heßling's fantasy is the *aphanisis* or self-obliteration of the subject as he imagines moving close to what Žižek calls "the phantasmatic kernel," the void around which subjectivity circulates.[49]

Masochism, in fact, serves an important psychological function in Heßling's political subservience. By making it a voluntary act that one eagerly submits to rather than something imposed from the outside or from above, the subject – in this case, Heßling himself – can avoid the destructive and humiliating violence of its forced actualization in social reality. Indeed, whenever Heßling perceives that he is not in control of his own submission but rather forced to submit, he rebels like a bourgeois liberal subject who expects to be treated respectfully. For example, when he is called to the office of the Regierungspräsident Otto von Wulckow, the latter initially ignores him and treats him with less respect than his dog, which is allowed to enter the office first and which snarls at the guest "with bared teeth" (330). Here, Heßling's status is lower than a dog's. But in this case he internally resists the imposed humiliation: "'Nasty brute,' Diederich thought – and suddenly it boiled up in him ... 'Who am I that I have to put up with this. My lowest machinist would not allow me to treat him this way. I have a doctorate. I am a city commissioner! This ignorant lout [*ungebildeter Flegel*] needs me more than I need him'" (330). It is significant that at this moment of rebellion against the representative of the traditional Prussian elite, Heßling thinks of his bourgeois credentials – his educational achievements and his patrician involvement in municipal politics. Of course, the lesson learned is short-lived. When reading the *Lokal-Anzeiger* later, Heßling "is filled with deep satisfaction by the Kaiser's dachshunds, which don't need to pay attention to the long trains of the women's dresses at court. The plan took shape in him to wholly grant this same freedom to his Männe at their next soiree" (445). It is telling that his dog's name (Männe) sounds like a diminutive form of the German word for man (*Mann*).

But the voluntary desire for self-obliteration is not Heßling's only psychic response to the humiliating capacity of power. More significant is the way his masochism enables him to avoid taking responsibility for his own enjoyment (jouissance) by making it the fulfilment of another's desire and pleasure, in particular the one figure who represents the Law. As Žižek explains, "[T]he pervert's aim is to establish, not to undermine, the Law."[50] Here it is important to note the way psychoanalysis conceives of the Law. In *Totem and Taboo*, Freud speculates that the (paternal) law is never neutral, but originated in a crime: the murder of the primal father.[51] Similarly, Lacanian psychoanalysis postulates that the Law is inherently split into the Name-of-the-Father (the Symbolic and the written rules of the legal order) and "the obscene underworld of unwritten rules" that is disavowed but absolutely necessary for the very functioning of the legal order.[52] Masochistic perversion responds directly to this split in the Law by turning the obscene underside of the law into the Law itself: "In the 'normal' state of things, the symbolic Law prevents access to the (incestuous) object, and thus creates the desire for it; in perversion, *it is the object itself* (say, the Dominatrix in masochism) *which makes the law.*"[53] The novel emphasizes this dimension when Heßling's tumble in the mud delights his master: "The Kaiser laughed ... turned to his escorts, slapped his thighs, and laughed" (64). Likewise, in the masochistic "sex scene" between Heßling and his wife, he does not have to take responsibility for his own desires, since his sexual pleasure is commanded by Guste (*Freu dich!*) and symbolized by his sudden inability to talk.

Yet it would be a mistake to see Heßling's masochism as a reversal of the patriarchal nature of his marriage. The text maintains that even after this scene, Guste "was conscious upon entering a room that the right of way was owed to the husband" and that at the dinner table "it was her business [*Sache*] to see from the furrows on his brow whether one should leave him undisturbed or shoo away his worries with chatter" (442). Yet even in exercising his patriarchal powers, Heßling avoids taking responsibility for his own pleasure by transforming his wife's submissiveness into a means of ensuring Wilhelm II's gratification. The rules of the house, for example, are largely those of the Kaiser: "Next to the coffee pot on the red-checkered table cloth, with the imperial eagle and imperial crown in the checkers, lay the Bible, and Guste was required [*war gehalten*] to read aloud from it every morning. On Sundays they went to church. When Guste bridled against going, Diederich said earnestly, 'It is desired [*erwünscht*] at the top'" (442). The tablecloth, with its embroidered imperial symbols, emphasizes that the presence of the Bible in their home is primarily a consequence of Wilhelm II's religiosity. And in attributing their church-going habits to the Kaiser's wishes, Heßling acts as the masochistic pervert who "pretends to speak from the position of knowledge (about the other's desire) which enables him to serve the other."[54] Yet even as Wilhelm II, who insisted that he received his mandate to rule from God, orders the ritual devotion to God, Heßling in fact reverses the traditional symbolic hierarchy by replacing God with the Kaiser as the big Other "who watches over me from beyond, and over all real individuals."[55] Thus, Heßling forces the family to go to church not to please God but to please the Kaiser who desires it.

In fact, the primacy of pleasing the Kaiser initially disrupts Heßling's sexual relations with his wife. For example, at the brunch following his wedding ceremony, he is awarded an "Order of the Prussian Crown, Fourth-Class" from the Kaiser through Wulckow's shady agent, a first-lieutenant who had arrived that morning to execute the purchase of the paper factory as part of a complicated real estate deal meant to enrich Wulckow and his relations. The honour, which elicited in the groom "a bliss that he could scarcely bear," exceeds his happiness at getting married (360). Moreover, both the medal and the Kaiser are present during the newlyweds' first connubial act on their honeymoon in the overnight train to Zurich: "'Before we get down to business [*zur Sache schreiten*],' [Heßling] said in a clipped manner [*abgehackt*], 'let us remember His Majesty, our most gracious Kaiser. For the business has a higher purpose, that we do His Majesty credit and deliver brave soldiers.' 'Oh!' went Guste, who was carried away into a higher glory by the gleaming item on his breast. 'Is – that – you – Diederich?'" (361). Heßling's channelling of the Kaiser in this scene constitutes one of the hilarious fantasmatic encounters between Wilhelm II and his loyal subject that dramatically mark the conclusion of each chapter, in this case, the fifth one. Because of his fantasmatic identification with Wilhelm II, Guste is left to wonder whether she is actually about to have sex with her husband or the Kaiser himself. But what is important here is the way that the loyal subject reconceives the first and most intimate act of his married life as a form of "business" to be undertaken on behalf of the Kaiser and his need for future soldiers. He is thus like certain homosexuals in *Psychopathia Sexualis*, who "are relatively potent, in so far that in marital intercourse they incite their imagination, and, instead of thinking of their wives, they call up the image of some loved male person. But for them coitus is a great sacrifice, and no pleasure."[56] Thus, Heßling's invocation of the Kaiser imbues the heterosexual scene with homosexual energy.

The Kaiser also remains a psychic presence on Diederich and Guste's honeymoon, further underlining the homoerotic nature of Heßling's masochism. While in Zurich, the newly married husband reads in the newspaper that Wilhelm II is conducting a state visit in Rome, and he immediately breaks off their stay in Switzerland to head to the Eternal City and act as the Kaiser's personal bodyguard. Though his enthusiasm sparks Guste to imagine throwing her veil and the roses from her hat at Wilhelm II's feet, Heßling fantasizes aloud about the Kaiser taking a liking to Guste: "'And when he sees you and you make an impression on him?' Diederich asked and smiled feverishly. Guste's bosom began to heave, and she lowered her lids. Diederich, who panted, ripped himself free of this terrible tension. 'My male honour [*Mannesehre*] is holy, which I herewith declare. But in this case …'" (364). Heßling's panting, of course, presages his response to the later scene of masochism in their living room. And though a wife's affair with another man constituted one of the most serious insults to a man's honour, he not only imagines giving the Kaiser permission to sleep with his wife, but clearly derives libidinal pleasure from the very idea, for the image of fulfilling Wilhelm II's desire (through his bride) leaves him panting. The Kaiser thus serves in the groom's erotic fantasy as a third party, much like the Greek (and his other doubles) do in Sacher-Masoch's fiction.[57]

Psychopathia Transvestitis

In addition to masochism and sexual inversion, *The Loyal Subject* also associates its protagonist's militarism with an incipient notion of transvestism, seen as another pathological manifestation of effeminacy in individuals assigned male at birth.[58] Because same-sex desire was originally conceived in terms of sexual inversion, Carl Westphal – and Krafft-Ebing after him – viewed habitually cross-dressing individuals as representing another degree of sexual inversion, even in the absence of same-sex desires. Though Magnus Hirschfeld also developed his model of homosexual identity as a form of gender inversion, the Berlin sexologist was also the first to recognize the existence of transgender subjectivities as separate from homosexuality, assigning it the name transvestism. Despite its frequent contradictions, logical problems and abrupt conclusions, *Die Transvestiten* (The transvestites), which Hirschfeld published in 1910, attempted to offer a systematic explanation of cross-dressing as, in the words of the book's subtitle, an "erotic drive."[59] The book begins with seventeen medical case studies (all but one of whom was assigned male at birth), followed by a series of analytical chapters designed to distinguish the phenomenon of cross-dressing from other sexual anomalies such as homosexuality or masochism. The second half consists of another set of chapters on various historical and ethnographical issues associated with transvestism, such as the role of cross-dressing in the theatre and in criminal acts. Yet as Hirschfeld knew too well from his many homosexual interlocutors and his own attendance at the regular balls held in Berlin, many homosexuals also occasionally or even regularly cross-dressed. Thus, in order to distinguish transvestites from homosexuals, he insisted that the two groups had fundamentally different sexual orientations. While homosexuals were attracted to others of the same gender, Hirschfeld argued that the sexuality of transvestites revolved around clothing. Moreover, he emphasized that most of his case studies were living in conventional heterosexual marriages and expressed anathema towards being viewed as homosexuals. (Nevertheless, as Darryl Hill notes, Hirschfeld ignored that many did harbour desires that exceeded that heterosexuality and a few even fantasized about having sex with men.)[60]

In order to represent the "trans" in transvestism, Hirschfeld's theory required both stable gender binarisms and explicit gender differences in clothing. According to the study's author, transvestites experienced a discrepancy between their "physical" sex (assigned at birth) and what might be called their internal gender identity. In this case, donning the clothes of the opposite sex contradicted the "physical" sex (assigned at birth) but corresponded to and expressed an "inner" or psychological gender identity. His theory also required distinguishing erotic transvestism from mere theatre. In the chapter on drag performances, for instance, he insisted that male actors who cross-dressed did so as part of their profession; transvestism counted only if they wore women's clothes off the stage, too. Indeed, he found it significant that none of his case-study subjects ever appeared on stage, which supposedly indicated that "these persons, consciously or unconsciously, feel that the wearing of women's apparel is an erotic activity and, therefore, feel an understandable shyness and hesitation about opening themselves to the eye of the public."[61] For Hirschfeld, not just deviant but nearly all erotic activity was marked by shyness or shame and was opposed to public exhibition.

Admittedly, *The Loyal Subject* depicts Heßling's desire to wear uniforms as explicitly theatrical and part of a broader thematization of theatricality (*Schein* as opposed to *Sein*) that runs through the entire novel. Like his beloved Kaiser, Heßling has a penchant for spectacle and theatre, which he invariably mistakes for reality.[62] Thus, as Kaiser leads his troops through the protesting crowds in the novel's first chapter, Heßling and his fellow Untertans mistake the theatricality for reality. After an old veteran tells the protagonist to pay attention, for "one day children will read about it in their school books" (61), Heßling absurdly trumpets that "this is just as good as the Battle of Sedan!" (63), during which German forces defeated the French Army and took Napoleon III prisoner. While Heßling and the others misrecognize or conflate the Kaiser's actions with actual incidents of enduring historical impact, a young artist in the crowd recognizes it as mere show: "theater, and not even good" (62). Meanwhile, Heßling's own everyday existence is reduced to a theatrical imitation of Wilhelm II, particularly his speech and his tendency to "glare." Thus, in response to the cynical artist, "Diederich looked at him and tried to glare [*blitzen*] like the Kaiser" (62). Though this parody of Wilhelm misses the mark by failing to change the actor's opinion, more than quality is at issue in the novel's critique of Heßling's theatricality. For unlike professional actors, Heßling, the Kaiser, and the other targets of the novel's satire repeatedly mistake their own performance for reality. (Conversely, Heßling is also incapable of recognizing theatre as anything but a mimetic representation of reality. For example, when attending professional theatre, he interprets the libretto literally, comparing the figures in *Lohengrin* to figures from his life: "But the Heerrufer made him wistful, for he resembled, to a hair, his former fellow student fat Delitzsch in all his former beer candour [*Bierehrlichkeit*]. As a result he looked more closely at the faces of the vassals [*Mannen*] and found Neuteutonians everywhere" [347].)

Despite Hirschfeld's effort to distinguish cross-dressing (as a private, erotic activity) from drag (as a form of theatre), Mann's novel portrays Heßling's appearance in uniforms as *both* a drag show and an unconscious form of erotic cross-dressing, whereby the standard of what counts as cross-dressing is measured not against an individual's physical gender (assigned at birth) but instead their psychological gender (regardless of whether the individual identifies with it). In particular, rather than offering an authentic expression of his physical and psychological masculinity, uniforms serve to hide his effeminate nature. For example, while wearing the official uniform of the Neuteutonian fraternity in public, Heßling muses through the text's interior monologue:

> Diederich was not guided by pride or personal considerations, but solely by his lofty idea of the honor of his corps. He himself was a mere individual, and therefore nothing; whatever rights, whatever dignity and importance he enjoyed, were conferred upon him by the corps. He was indebted to it for his physical advantages: his broad white face, his paunch which inspired the freshmen with respect, and the privilege of appearing on festive occasions in top boots and wearing a cap and sash – the pleasure of the uniform! Of course, he still had to give way to a lieutenant, since the fraternity to which he belonged was clearly the higher one; but at least he could interact fearlessly with a streetcar conductor without the danger of being yelled at by him. His manliness was threateningly inscribed on his face in the slashes which split his chin and cut through his cheeks all the way into his close-cropped hair. What satisfaction to show them daily and freely to every- and anyone. (39)

The passage emphasizes a couple of important contradictions between Heßling's pleasure in wearing his uniform and his underlying effeminacy. First, his paunch suggests a lack of masculinity since body fat is associated not only with the female body but also the lazy way it is procured, wich connects Heßling's body back to his mother who pilfered food between meals, shirking her work responsibilities to gossip with the servant. Second, because the uniform does not so much express his fearless masculinity as protect him from the dangers of other men, including the fear of being yelled at by a lowly, uniformed municipal employee, it also falls short of the honourable masculinity he seeks to portray, for it is merely a prop for managing his unmasculine fear. Finally, his Neuteutonian masquerade even extends to the duelling scar on his face, the result of the sword duel (*Mensur*) that served as an initiation ritual in the fraternity.[63] Though an inscription of the masculine "uniform" on his body, the scar here connotes mere surface, since its function is purely for display. It is a costume like all the rest – a part of his drag impersonation of masculinity.

Yet despite the theatricality of uniform-wearing, the interplay between gendered clothing, pleasure, and shame also marks Heßling's behaviour as a case of transvestism in Hirschfeld's sense. For instance, in the sexologist's interpretation of his case studies, a sense of shame in the pleasure they took in wearing women's clothes signalled their erotic investment in cross-dressing. According to Hirschfeld, this sense of shame accounted for why they never appeared on stage in drag shows. Conversely, Heßling seems to derive pleasure from exhibiting his masculine clothes, making him appear shameless. Yet while shamelessness might indicate an absence of shame, it is not an absence of the *category* of shame, whose presence is signalled in Heßling's apparent disregard for modesty. To label persons or actions "shameless" is to claim that they have surpassed the boundaries of social or moral decorum that normally dictate appropriate behaviour. What makes Heßling shameless is the public exhibition of his pleasure, which like erotic acts should remain hidden. But while Hirschfeld's case studies derive pleasure from donning the clothes that correspond to their inner gender identity, thus moulding their physical bodies to match their psychological needs, Heßling's uniform exhibits his pleasure in disguising his physical and psychological effeminacy – and his failure to embody an autonomous and socially confident male identity, which is the source of his shame.

Heßling's "shameless" techniques to deny his underlying "shameful" effeminacy no longer help him, however, when he enters the army for his required one-year service. There are two incidents that mark the protagonist's short military career as a failure to achieve real masculinity or even maintain his gender masquerade. The first occurs during the medical screening of all new recruits, when he is forced to stand naked. Without his second-rate fraternity uniform, Heßling's beer belly no longer contributes to his masculine authority but rather reverts to a sign of his fundamental effeminacy. When the army doctor stands in front of him, the former gives the belly a mocking (*höhnisch*) look that provokes laughter from the entire assemblage of men and leaves the protagonist with no option other than to lower shamefully his glance to his belly. In response to Heßling's flabby appearance, the doctor promises that military service will make a man out of him: "We'll soon massage the fat off you. Just four weeks of training and I guarantee you that you'll look like a real Christian" (48). The reference to Christianity signals that not all men at this time had access to hegemonic masculinity through military service in Germany. In fact, the medical examination scene emphasizes all of those excluded from military service on the basis of their degenerate and defective bodies: the physically defective man who cannot hear properly, the "dirty" Jew with the name Levysohn, and the actor who, after passing the physical exam, announces that he is a homosexual. All three, of course, symbolize some aspect of Heßling himself: his childhood ear troubles, his lack of true Christian belief, and his unconscious homoeroticism.[64]

There are two ways to read the actor's public declaration of his homosexuality in *The Loyal Subject* – a scene that Heinrich in fact borrowed –

and further embellished – from his brother Thomas's own physical exam (see the previous chapter).[65] On the one hand, the actor might be a homosexual who performed a role of manliness such that he could pass the physical exam, whereupon he then decides to reveal the "truth" of his homosexuality.[66] The public revelation makes the doctor turn red with embarrassment at the exposure of his inability to recognize the signs of effeminacy and keep such men out of the army. On the other hand, by making him an actor, the novel also suggests that the actor is not a homosexual hiding his "true" effeminacy through an act, but a (heterosexual) actor merely performing a homosexual role: "One of the men, an actor with an expression of indifference on his face, turned around, presented himself to the staff doctor once again and said in a loud voice, carefully enunciating each word: 'I would like to add that I am homosexual'" (48). Actors, by profession, perform theatrical roles that have little bearing on their personal identity or disposition, something that Heßling is incapable of understanding. By publicly naming himself a homosexual – with the careful articulation of an actor on stage – the actor implies that he was in fact manly enough to get into the army, but a good enough actor to "declaim" an identity that offered a ticket out of having to serve for one or more years. As the expression of indifference on his face indicates, he is rather unmoved by his military certificate of fitness, since his sense of manliness does not derive from membership in a self-consciously manly institution. Moreover, his loud announcement also signals his autonomy from the opinions of the other men in the room, especially the authority figure of the doctor. But regardless of whether the actor is a homosexual or is merely performing one, he builds an important contrast to Heßling (and Thomas Mann, as well), who both find their own effeminacy all too real and all too shameful.[67] Heßling's vehement public expression of indignation over the actor's "shameless action" (*schamloses Verfahren*), however, confirms his similarity to him as well as his perception that the act of self-revelation involves shame, something Heßling is desperately attempting to avoid. It also indicates that the acting skills of the novel's protagonist are inferior to those of the actor since unlike someone who controls his performance, Heßling is someone whose body gives him away. "Theater, and not even good," we might conclude.

Indeed, Heßling's ability to perform masculinity reaches its limit in the military uniform. Though the doctor promises to make a man out of him, the protagonist is, of course, unable to meet the real physical demands placed upon his lazy and effeminate body in the army, for the physical challenges of military performance differ significantly from the patently non-physical activities – drinking beer! – that characterized life in the fraternity. Consequently, in contrast to his love of the fraternity uniform, the authentic uniform only brings pain: "The uniform, which in any case was cut too closely in order to ensure a tight, upright fit, became an instrument of martyrdom after the meal. What did it matter that the captain appeared unspeakably daring and warlike as he sat on his horse giving commands when one, running and panting, felt the soup sloshing about undigested in the stomach. The objective enthusiasm which Diederich was prepared to feel had to retreat behind his personal distress" (51). Heßling's uniform problems stem from the gendered correspondence that must inhere between the uniform and the body that wears it. Instead of facilitating an empty performance of masculinity (the kind of performance that he sees the captain providing) or even a performance of masculinity that Heßling imagines could reconfigure his fat and feminized body as masculine (the fraternity uniform), the military uniform serves as one of the mechanisms for training the masculine body: the replacement of fat with the disciplined male form.

Yet Heßling's ultimate failure to become a disciplined soldier comes in the form of a foot injury he believes he suffers while marching through the military training exercises (51) – an element that, again, is borrowed directly from Thomas Mann's biography.[68] Though *The Loyal Subject* makes it clear that there is no real injury, the protagonist at times seems to be unable to distinguish reality from hoax, underlining his cowardly avoidance of the rigours of army life as well as suggesting that his foot injury is hysterical in nature – and thus yet another symptom of his similarity to women like his mother. Moreover, as an unreal and invisible injury, Heßling's foot problem resembles the (inner) ear problems mentioned in the novel's first sentence, once again emphasizing his defective body as insufficiently strong, disciplined, and healthy – that is, insufficiently masculine. Ultimately, his success in using his fake foot injury to obtain an early medical discharge from the army keeps him from achieving the masculinity (and the reconfiguration of his body to fit the uniform) promised by the army doctor at the exam.

By making military service and military dress the stable symbols of masculinity, the novel exposes Heßling's gender masquerade through its failure. Yet the use of parody and "military drag" to criticize the protagonist raises ethical and practical-political questions about the novel's social commentary. By ridiculing Heßling for not meeting the military's definition of masculinity, *The Loyal Subject* undermines its own potential for social critique, for the novel's use of the trope of transvestism inevitably relies on a natural correspondence between masculinity and the military uniform. By depicting Heßling's failure to meet the masculine standards of the military uniform, *The Loyal Subject* paradoxically adopts the soldier as the real embodiment of masculinity – the same standard that Heßling uses and that the novel seemingly seeks to criticize as a form of theatre and false self-presentation.

That military uniforms did not, however, serve as reliable signs of masculinity can be gleaned, paradoxically, from Hirschfeld's attempt to use them to illustrate the transvestism of women. Because no other occupation, the sexologist mused, "has been considered so much a male privilege as that of the soldier and warrior," historical stories of women who donned military uniforms represented the most extreme and visible proof of female-to-male transvestism in a work that included only one individual assigned female at birth.[69] At the same time, however, because colourful, ostentatious, and heavily ornamented forms of dress were associated almost exclusively with fashion, Hirschfeld acknowledged that "people [*man*] occasionally meet with the view that the colorful and sparkling, decorated, pressed [*das Geputzte und Gezierte*] and ironed soldier's uniform is more worthy of a vain woman than a serious man."[70] The indefinite pronoun "man" leaves open the question of who is making these assertions and how widespread they might be. Based on his own account of the links between visibility and femininity, however, it might just as well signal Hirschfeld's own nagging afterthoughts following his discussion of women soldiers, for his choice of words to discuss military uniforms are variations on the ones he uses to discuss women's clothes – though here such concepts as *geputzt* are attributes of the uniform whereas in his discussion of women's apparel they are qualities of the women's psychic constitution, their inner drive (*Putztrieb*) or obsession (*Putzsucht*) to dress up in fancy clothes.

Though the sexologist attempted to circumvent a possible link between military uniforms and femininity by observing that male animals often have brighter colours than their female mates and that in primitive societies the warrior-husband "far outshines the woman in painting and tattooing, in feather ornamentation and other decoration," such arguments did not confront the reigning conclusion that ornamentation in modernity had become identified with femininity.[71] The paradox that results from Hirschfeld's use of uniforms to represent masculinity – that is, that uniforms might ultimately be more feminine than masculine – suggests that civilian bourgeois culture also at times required the visibility of military masculinity for its own gendered organization of culture, even as it could not ensure that the uniform's gendered meaning remained stable within bourgeois culture's system of gender.

Conclusion

Despite its stunning success as a runaway bestseller following Germany's defeat in the First World War, *The Loyal Subject* remains one of the most controversial pieces in the entire German literary canon.[72] The controversy began even before its publication in full. On one side, were nationalist and conservative authors like Thomas Mann, who, without explicitly naming the novel, dismissed *The Loyal Subject* as a "caricature without any basis in reality [*Zerrbild ohne Wirklichkeitsgrund*]."[73] For the younger brother, Heinrich's novel "descended" (*herabsteigen*) into "a social-critical expressionism without impression, responsibility and conscience, which depicts businessmen who don't exist, workers who don't exist, social 'conditions' that at best might have existed in England around 1850, and which brewed out of such ingredients its agitation-loving murder stories."[74] As he concluded, "[S]uch a social satire would be nonsense (*Unfug*), and if it deserved a more noble name, a more noble one than that of an international libel and a national slander, it would be this: ruthless aestheticism."[75]

In contrast, critics on the left quickly and enthusiastically welcomed the novel as *the* prescient literary portrait of the age. For instance, Kurt Wolff, who became Heinrich Mann's publisher in 1916, penned an enthusiastic letter to his business manager after the latter had sent him the manuscript. Writing in 1916 from the Balkans, where he was stationed as a first lieutenant in the XIth Army Division during the war, Wolf concluded:

> *Der Untertan*: I just finished reading the text of the book and am bowled over [*hingerissen*]. Here is the beginning of a specification [*Fixierung*] of German conditions that has been completely missing for us – at least since Fontane. Suddenly, here is a work, grand and unique, which, fully developed, could be for German history and literature what Balzac's work was for the First, Zola's for the Second Empire. And for our time it is much more: this book, written 2 years before the war, is – in another sense – for us a priori what for the French is a posteriori a *Débacle*. The Germany of the first years of Wilhelm II's reign, seen as a condition that had to provoke the war of 1914.[76]

By this time, Heinrich Mann himself had also come to the same conclusion. In 1915, two years before his conciliatory letter to Thomas, he penned in his notebook a letter of apology to his novel's "hero": As an author, he began, "he knew more about him than anyone, but not that he would take it so far [...] The author never believed that his hero [*Held*] would experience the ultimate consequence of his existence, the war against Europe."⁷⁷ By 1929, when a new edition was reissued, Mann envisioned that *The Loyal Subject* might continue to offer "a warning example" that could "enlighten a new generation" – that "one can be a complete 'Untertan' even in a republic."⁷⁸ Subsequent critics have gone so far as to claim that the novel "anticipated fascist practices with amazing clarity."⁷⁹ It is thus not surprising that the left-liberal critique of fascism, particularly the efforts of the Frankfurt School, developed a theoretical approach that in many ways mirrored Heinrich Mann's novel.

But rather than an objective account of the gendered and libidinal nature of its protagonist's behaviour, the novel tells us much more about the set of fantasies structuring the left-liberal critique of militarism and, eventually, fascism. For instance, in his devastating assessment of Theodor Adorno's *The Authoritarian Personality*, which he calls "probably the most deeply flawed work of prominence in political psychology," John Levi Martin highlights the authors' problematic "confirmation bias" that led them to "construct a typology that would 'get at' phenomena they believed they *knew* to take place, leading to an asymmetric interpretive strategy that was invisible to the authors."⁸⁰ Meanwhile, Thomas Mann was perhaps the first to point out that *The Loyal Subject* is actually an inversion of its author's fantasy of France: "Good Lord, what civilization's literary man makes out of France, republican France whose reality is apparent to the sober [*nicht betört*] gaze in literature and life!"⁸¹ Though the younger brother in turn painted the Third Republic in the direst terms as a moral swamp of anarchy, he nevertheless correctly identified the fantastical nature of Heinrich Mann's image of France: "For him, France is not a reality, but rather an idea! Very good! But he measures German reality against this idea!"⁸²

Similarly, Heinrich Mann and the authors of *The Authoritarian Personality* shared an ideological and queerphobic investment in the heterosexual male subject of liberalism.⁸³ For the authors of *The Authoritarian Personality*, this meant that fascists and proto-fascists "were said to possess a 'pseudo-masculinity.'"⁸⁴ Meanwhile, in the forward to the 1929 edition of *The Loyal Subject*, Mann called upon his readers to protect themselves from the political dangers of authoritarianism by remaining masculine: "We will still have to learn to be more responsible. We will have to pay attention to our security and our dignity [*Würde*], to our manly pride."⁸⁵ More troubling, of course, is the underlying queer- and transphobia in the left-liberal critique of militarism and fascism. Randall Halle, for instance, has convincingly shown that Wilhelm Reich,

Erich Fromm, and Theodor Adorno repeatedly identified fascism with unconscious homosexuality: "[N]o sexual act signified the homosexual – at least no homosexual act. The individual who submitted to fascist authority was homosexual because of his character."[86] In Mann's case, the homophobic view of Heßling's unconscious homoerotic desires also contradicted his own support for the German homosexual emancipation movement.[87]

Moreover, Mann never demonstrated much sympathetic understanding for his younger brother's homoerotic longings.[88] For instance, in an 1890 letter to their mutual friend Ludwig Ewers, who in their youth often served as a go-between for the two brothers, he offered this advice for his "poor brother Tomy [sic]," then just fifteen years old: "Just let him come into the age where he is no longer being watched [unbewacht] – and is sufficiently well off to express his puberty. A hearty sleep cure with a passionate, not all too used up [angefressen] girl – that will cure him. Don't tell him that, though. Ironize the story; that helps."[89] The older brother also expressed disdain for Thomas's adolescent homoerotic poetry, cattily informing Ewers: "In reading his latest poems (which I enclose) I never lost the distressing [peinlich] feeling that in a similar way only Platen, the knight of the holy ass, has given me. This mushy, sweetly sentimental 'friendship' poesy ... If *that* is *real* feeling (sad enough, if this is the case!) – I decline the fruit, don't even touch the cheese, but rather sneak away."[90] In Heinrich's eyes, even Thomas's published novels were still marred by his homoerotic nature. In the notebook draft of his lengthy response to Thomas's attack on Heinrich's novel *Die Jagd nach Liebe*, the older brother offered this frank assessment of the younger one's work: "Up to now you have only elaborately portrayed a single woman for her own sake (and not for the sake of an idea, as in Tristan): Toni Buddenbrook."[91] And yet even she was insufficiently drawn, for "all sexual energy is cleanly cut out."[92] For Heinrich, the contrast between the two could be summed up by this one point: "You [are] a writer in whose books exclusively the men (which can be reduced to one) are interesting; in my case, you are dealing with someone who his whole life long has considered nothing more important than the woman."[93]

Most troubling of all, though, are the ethical implications of *The Loyal Subject*'s narrative techniques, which satirize Heßling through his fantasies. Rather than merely portraying the protagonist's motives, the narrative ensures his rehumiliation in the reader's eyes by exposing his inner desires and fantasies about masculinity to public ridicule. While such a narrative strategy might illuminate Heßling's motivations, this technique (and the laughing-knowing reader it intends) disavows an awareness that nobody's public image or self-esteem would likely survive the persistent revelation of his or her interior, subconscious wishes. If, as Freud claims, men's fantasies always revolve around ambition (when they don't revolve around sex), it seems far more likely that readers share more similarities with the protagonist than we would care to admit.[94] Thus, it might be worth considering whether such fantasies can account for behaviour as completely as Heinrich Mann's novel seems to suggest. In fact, rather than targeting Heßling's effeminacy, it might make more sense to put the blame on the unrealizable masculine ideals – not just militaristic ones about bravery and honour but also bourgeois ones about autonomy and independence – that drive the protagonist to perform masculinity so excessively. By using the shaming genre of satire to expose his attempt to hide his shameful effeminacy, *The Loyal Subject* undercuts its own critique of (militaristic) social institutions by putting the burden once again on Heßling, abjecting him (as insufficiently autonomous) instead of criticizing the institutions and mechanisms of shaming and disciplining, including bourgeois society's own expectations and values.

Ultimately, then, *The Loyal Subject*'s strategy of shaming suggests several potential paradoxes about the relationship between bourgeois culture and military culture. First, the narrative's relentless harshness towards its protagonist reveals that the modes of social discipline attributed to the army might actually be less distinct from the ideals of *Bildung* and male interaction in bourgeois society itself. Certainly, the novel's use of Heßling's failure in the military to underline his failure to achieve masculine autonomy attests to the coherence between German bourgeois culture's standard of masculinity after 1870 and the military's own rather than any fundamental difference between the two. Second, *The Loyal Subject*'s intensification of Diederich's shame through his failure to achieve bourgeois autonomy in the narrative – that is, the narrative's adoption of the same standards of masculinity against which Heßling fails in the plot (his failure to stand up to Mahlmann, for instance) – suggests that for at least some individuals, bourgeois expectations about gender performance may in fact have been more severe than the expectations of the army and other kinds of demonstrably masculine organizations, such as fraternities.

Epilogue: The War on Fantasy

Arriving in the German capital in January 1913, merely one and a half years before the start of the First World War, the American painter Marsden Hartley proved once again W.E.B. Du Bois's 1893 observation that "it is the omnipresent soldiery of Berlin that first catches the American visitor's attention."[1] Writing to his niece just days into his two-week visit, Hartley gushed that "Berlin is a charming city and very gay with the handsome officers and soldiers."[2] But while Du Bois focused on the political and social dynamics surrounding the military uniforms, Hartley's eye fastened exclusively on the men who wore them, snidely contrasting their "fine extravagance of physical splendour" with the "sickliness" of the French men he had met during his year in Paris.[3] Indeed, frustrated by the French capital's insular and uninviting art scene, the American painter spent much of his time there with "a small German coterie" around the sculptor Arnold Rönnebeck and his visiting cousin Karl von Freyburg, whom Hartley described as "a most charming and excellent young German officer."[4] Thus, shortly after departing Berlin, he immediately began hatching plans, as he wrote to his friend, mentor, and business manager Alfred Stieglitz to "go to Germany as soon as I can make arrangements – to live and work there for a time."[5] Yet in opting to relocate to Berlin, Hartley was seeking out not only a more conducive and appreciate creative environment than what he found in the stuffy French capital but also the erotic possibilities that beckoned in Germany's largest city, which was conveniently located near Potsdam, where Freyburg was stationed as a lieutenant in the exclusive Prussian Fourth Guards.

In the two decades between Du Bois's Berlin residency and Hartley's arrival, the Prussian Army's impact on public life in the city had remained largely unchanged. Like Du Bois, who witnessed that "all Prussia rushes pell-mell to see the ever-passing regiment," Hartley used a postcard of a military procession featuring "Our Kaiser and our Crown Prince" to inform Gertrude Stein, whom he had grown close to in Paris, that "this is one of the daily happenings here in Germany. It is a genius that celebrates itself remarkably – it stimulates my early fondness for the pageant."[6] In fact, Hartley was treated to some of the last glorious military pageantries of the era, arriving just in time for the week-long celebration of the marriage between Wilhelm II's only daughter, Victoria Luisa, and Ernst August III of Hanover, which in May 1913 brought together for one last time royalty from across Europe, including the King and Queen of England, the Czar, and other Crown heads of state. The following month Hartley enthusiastically watched as the city also played host to the 25th Crown Jubilee of Kaiser Wilhelm II's ascension to the Prussian and Imperial thrones, an event marked by equally lavish parades, floats, and military processions.

But while Berlin's military pomp remained much the same as it was during Du Bois's sojourn, Hartley encountered a much more visible, organized, and self-confident queer culture than Du Bois might have noticed in 1893. The German capital and its abutting cities were the epicentre of the country's queer emancipation movement, with both the Scientific-Humanitarian Committee (WhK), founded by Magnus Hirschfeld and a few others in 1897, and Adolf Brand's Community of the Special (GdE) meeting, publishing, and agitating for legal change. In particular, the WhK mounted extensive public education operations and undertook original medical and social-scientific research into queer identities and desires. Though the organization never came close to convincing the Reichstag to strike Paragraph 175 from the criminal code, its effectiveness in making same-sex desire a topic of educated conversation and public debate ignited fierce opposition from vocal morality groups (as well as hostility from masculinists in the GdE over its promulgation of same-sex desire as a congenital form of gender inversion). Alongside the vibrant political movement, Berlin also hosted numerous queer bars, cafes, and elaborate balls, all safely operating thanks to the Berlin police department's policy of toleration. If Hirschfeld reported the existence of eighteen to twenty exclusively queer establishments in 1904, he claimed to know of thirty-eight by 1913.[7]

Though ostensibly separate, Germany's military and queer worlds were, as we have seen, never far apart, for the Prussian-German military was integrally caught up in queer scenes and politics from the start. In fact, a number of threads repeatedly stitched these two realms together. Perhaps most fundamentally, soldiers' physical training and body-hugging uniforms transformed them early on into fetishistic objects of same-sex desire. While this attraction figured prominently in

Ulrichs's own influential efforts to develop a non-pathological theory of queer identity in the 1860s, soldiers' miserable pay also made them sexually available to bourgeois Urnings like Ulrichs such that, by the 1890s, a bustling underground economy of Soldatenprostitution emerged in municipalities with large contingents of troops. Though these forms of queer life focused on recruits or non-commissioned officers, higher-ranked personnel also featured prominently in propaganda by and for the WhK, which until 1907 deployed closeted homosexual officers driven to suicide as ideal victims in a melodramatic campaign to win public support. Finally, as the embodiment of an increasingly unstable hegemonic ideal of masculinity, military personnel and their uniforms also offered German writers avenues for ironically appropriating this ideal (as in the case of Thomas Mann) or, conversely, satirizing the enthusiasm for martial self-presentation as an effeminate, masochistic, and transvestite pathology (in the case of his brother Heinrich).

The army leadership was generally a weak and ill-prepared opponent against the onslaught of sexual discourse. For instance, despite consulting with the police, blacklisting bars, and issuing new regulations about dress uniforms, army commanders seemed unable to thwart their recruits from engaging in male prostitution. And though military courts, at least outside of Bavaria, were generally empowered to prevent the public from learning about crimes committed by officers, this policy of administrative secrecy often had the opposite effect, serving instead, as Georg Simmel has pointed out, "to heighten by phantasy" what is secret and unknown.[8] Since, as Foucault explained, sexuality operated "as *the* secret," the army's critics were also able to reinterpret its efforts to hide instances of physical mistreatment or abuse of authority as evidence of sadism, especially when actual sexual acts were involved and became public.[9] Likewise, the scientific discourse on homosexuality convinced a court of law – and large swaths of the public – that Lt.-General Kuno von Moltke, the commandant of Berlin and one of the Kaiser's closest friends, was an effeminate homosexual hiding underneath the masculine veneer of his military uniform. These volatile and interrelated scandals served to redouble the military's efforts to consolidate the uniform's association with heterosexual masculinity. Yet even as such scandals wielded a normative bourgeois sexual discourse to discipline wayward army officers, including aristocratic ones, the process of narrowing martial masculinities further eroticized uniform personnel in ways that could not be so easily controlled.

Though these tensions came to a spectacular explosion in the first Harden-Moltke trial in 1907, the shock waves reverberated beyond the scandal's sputtering denouement in 1909. Because of Hirschfeld's ill-fated involvement in Harden's homophobic campaign against General Kuno von Moltke and other high-ranking members of the Kaiser's entourage, many members left the WhK in droves, and its funding dried up. And not only was the WhK's campaign to strike Paragraph 175 from the criminal code dead in the water but it also had to contend with proposed revisions to strengthen the repressive law. Nevertheless, after recovering from a vicious smear campaign against his reputation, Hirschfeld resumed his political and scientific activities, producing his important study of cross-dressing in 1910 as well as his monumental compendium on homosexuality in 1913.[10] Moreover, the trial had done much to publicize not only Hirschfeld's understanding of same-sex desire and identity as a kind of congenital inversion of the sexual instinct but also those of his rivals, like Benedict Friedlaender and Hans Blüher, who theorized a more masculinist and social constructionist understanding of same-sex desire derived from Ancient Greek models or rooted in the anthropological notion of the *Männerbund* (exclusively male associations).[11]

While Du Bois's 1893 essay demonstrated an early awareness of the deep connection between Prussian-German militarism and sexuality, Hartley lived out that erotic fascination with uniformed personnel and thematized it in his work. Like Thomas Mann, the American painter was deeply ambivalent about his desire for men, referring to it even late in life as "that subject."[12] He also seems to have shared the German writer's disdain for effeminate homosexuals along with his struggle to live up to the masculine ideals he admired.[13] Both men, of course, used their creativity as an outlet for their repressed – or in Hartley's case, not always so repressed – desires. But while Mann's literary works were apt to be more open and explicit about his homoerotic longings than he seemed to be in his own life as a married man and father of six, the fount of Hartley's distinctly abstract art was, as Bruce Robertson notes, "the erotic character of 'objects,' the fetishistic power of things rare, beautiful or common."[14]

This fetishistic celebration of the German military and its uniforms is apparent in one of his first major works completed in Berlin. According to Hartley, his 1913 oil painting, *The Warriors*, sought to capture the spiritual essence of the parade he witnessed during the celebration of the royal wedding:

> The morning came for the entry through the Brandenburg Tor of the Hohenzollen [sic] princess and her duke to be – the Pariser Platz was packed jammed to the stoops and windows with those huge cuirassiers of the Kaiser's special guards – all in white – white leather breeches skin

tight – high plain enamel boots – those gleaming blinding medieval breast plates of silver and brass – making the eye go black when the sun glanced like a spear as the bodies moved. There were the inspiring helmets with the imperial eagle and the white manes hanging down – there was six-foot of youth under all this garniture – everyone on a horse – and every horse white – that is how I got it – and it went into an abstract picture of soldiers riding into the sun, a fact to take place not so longer after – for all of these went out into the sun and never came back.[15]

Though we shall return to the impact of the First World War on Imperial Germany's uniform fantasies, it is worth dwelling first on Hartley's fetishistic attention to the details within this larger scene: the overwhelming number of soldiers that filled the square, the repeated references to their physical size, each "huge" and "six-foot of youth," the notation of their uniform specifics down to the body-hugging white leather pants, a colour reinforced by the uniformly white horses they rode on, and the gleaming breastplates capable of sending a spear of blinding light directly into the eye of the beholder. As Hartley's description reveals, "the whole scene was fairly bursting with organized energy and the tension was terrific and somehow most voluptuous in the feeling of power – a sexual immensity even in it – when passion rises to the full and something must happen to quiet it."[16]

If the syntax of this last sentence, with its additive and building impressions, reproduces Hartley's feeling of an almost unbearable passion in search of release, then *The Warriors* replicates visually the scene's organized energy, terrific tension, and voluptuous power (Figure E.1). In the centre foreground, encased in a series of round or vertically oblong and dome-like half circles, are four mounted figures. The bottom three, portrayed in profile, show white-uniformed soldiers on horses marching in step on whitish clouds atop of a deeply red orb that partially juts up from below the bottom edge of the frame. Above these is a similar horseman, seen from behind. Each of the riders is encased in his own halo, an effect seemingly produced by watching these figures against the shining sun. This foreground tableaux is positioned on top of a sea of mounted cuirassiers riding away from the viewer in the background, dissected by larger, fainter orbs of light. To be sure, the painting exhibited Hartley's development as an artist, combining, as Barbara Haskell has noted, "the pictorial energy of the Blaue Reiter Expressionists with the tightly knit, collage format of the Cubists" into "a remarkable synthesis of the expressive with the structured."[17] But its symmetries and hieratic arrangement also gave the work, as Jonathan Weinberg observes, "the quality of an altarpiece for a militaristic cult."[18] Though the abstract

Figure E.1. *The Warriors*, oil painting by Marsden Hartley, 1913. Minneapolis, MN, The Regis Collection. Photo: akg-images.

nature of the figures and their placement disrupts any appreciation of the body-hugging nature of the white leather breeches that so appealed to Hartley, the emphasis on primary colours – reds, yellows, and their mélange into various shades of orange – imbues the military iconography with an erotic and kinetic vitality throughout.

Though Weinberg reads the painting's title as "a reminder that the pageant is a celebration of potential aggression," I see *The Warriors* as indicative of the much larger and more fundamental *méconnaissance* at the heart of all the uniform fantasies circulating in Imperial Germany, including its queer ones: the occlusion of war and violence behind the enticing façade of colourful uniforms and highly choreographed parades. After all, while German unification emerged out of a sequence of three wars engineered by Otto von Bismarck, the Second Empire's forty-three years of existence were largely peaceful – with the exception of three far-away colonial wars, each of which was carried out with horrific violence and devastating atrocities.[19] In the public's mind – and likely in the minds of many soldiers and officers – the actual brutality of war was reduced to a figment of the glorious past, which doubled as a brazenly unrealistic dream of romantic heroism to be achieved in a future conflagration.[20] Even as a few thinkers and writers warned that industrialized warfare would look far different and more horrific than battles of the past, these voices had difficulty piercing the music of military marches and the cheers of celebrating crowds – or were harassed and sometimes censored when they did.[21]

The power of these military spectacles – enshrined in Hartley's painting – cannot be overestimated. While their erotic nature illustrates Foucault's contention that sexuality emerged as a dense transfer point for all forms of power, Žižek's conception of fantasy offers a way to see the underlying presence of violence, destruction, and war as an inherent part of this libidinal fascination with military uniforms and the powerful physical bodies underneath. For fantasy draws its power – and holds our fascination – through the presence of the Real (a designation that includes the murderous and self-destructive impulses of the death drive) that it seems to hide from consciousness. As Ute Frevert argues, soldiers fundamentally differed from civilians through their training to kill, noting that this special skill "was precisely what gave [the parading troops] that unique aura, an equal mix of fear and awe."[22] And this difference was visibly marked by the military uniform, which also included the requisite dagger or sword. Meanwhile, the effect of hundreds or thousands of nearly identical men marching past in uniform conveyed "a primeval power, tamed by discipline" that offered civilian attendees a sublime experience (*erhabene Gefühle*). The thrill was so great that, according to Frevert, recollections of those attending these parades found their way into nearly every "memoir by contemporaries of the Wilhelminian era, whatever their gender or class."[23] And, as we saw in Hartley's written recollections, the sublime and ineffable majesty of the marching uniformed soldiers found expression in the text's own strain against the limitations imposed by grammar, just as it appears visually in *The Warriors* in the background formation of riding soldiers that spill over the borders of the canvas.

Marches, of course, are spectacles that celebrate the destructively sublime power of the Real only obliquely; war, with its explosive violence of killing, maiming, and dying, puts soldiers and civilian victims –

as well as, in a different way, their loved ones – into an all too direct encounter with the obliterating dimension of the death drive. War, as the saying goes, changes everything – including fantasies. Though the First World War eventually toppled Germany's monarchical system and ushered in the Weimar Republic, its most immediate victims were the various uniform fantasies explored in this book. Gone were the diverse and colourful parade uniforms, replaced by the field gray outfits that had been introduced in 1910 but restricted to manoeuvres. Gone too were the countless "handsome officers and soldiers" whose "fine extravagance of physical splendour" had so delighted Hartley's eye. Those who left for battle included Rönnebeck, now Hartley's best friend, and Freyburg, in whom the American artist was in love and whom he had seen often in Potsdam and Berlin.

Despite his celebration of German militarism in *The Warriors*, Hartley, who, like Thomas Mann, had never had any interest in politics, was aghast at the prospect of a full European war, telling Stieglitz on 30 July 1914, "I cannot see how Europe can willingly plunge itself into a war – especially when it is so directly concerned with two nations. It doesn't seem policy – but here it is."[24] The American was particularly worried about his German friends: "A small issue is that I do not like to see my best friends going to battle – Rönnebeck, Lieut. Von Freyburg – and one or two others I know. All are hoping for peace naturally as war is sure to be devastation – minor or major."[25] Though Hartley's emphasis on "small" and "minor" seem to be a defence mechanism against the overwhelming dimensions of the war, the outbreak of fighting only heighted the artist's incredulity and despair:

> [T]hat which is truly heartrending is to see Germany's marvelous youth going off to a horrible death – this has been the dreadful vision – seeing these thousands simply walk out of homes leaving wives and children and all – never to [come?] – and going with a real extasy for war is the only modern religious extasy – the only means of displaying the old time martyrdom – one shall not forget these handsome smiling faces going by – waving hands throwing kisses and shouting *auf Wiedersehen*. Now many are silent and will remain so forever – and many are coming back broken wickedly. All this in our modern day!![26]

Like his panegyric recollection of the military spectacle he sought to capture in *The Warriors*, Hartley's sentences, which heap impression upon impression without much order, suggest the impossibility of capturing his "dreadful vision" in words.

216 Uniform Fantasies

Figure E.2. Postcard photograph of Karl von Freyburg on horseback, around 1913. Photograph by Oscar Streich, Berlin-Charlottenburg. Beinecke Rare Book and Manuscript Library. YCAL MSS 578. Marsden Hartley collection.

As if the artist had seen into the future, a wounded Rönnebeck returned to Berlin to recuperate while Freyburg died on the battlefield in October 1914. The news turned Hartley's dread into despair. In a letter to Stieglitz, he confided: "You know what an intense thing friendship always was and is for me – and can appreciate therefore the acute pain of this experience … These last days have for me become a little too painful – in the knowledge of the loss of my friend who was in all respects one among a thousand – so fit in every possible sense to survive a long life – and grace society with his charming personality and this is but one instance among countless."[27] Very little is known about Freyburg, who as the son of an established family of Prussian officers seems to have been brought up in the kingdom's main cadet school just outside of Berlin before he obtained a commission in the Fourth Guard Foot Regiment.[28] In addition to spending time with Hartley and Rönnebeck in Berlin, where he would have had occasional guard duty at the Neue Wache, Freyburg likely received a steady number of visits from Hartley in Potsdam.[29] Among Hartley's personal effects at the time of his death was a photograph of a German officer on horseback, which may be of Freyburg, who mentioned enclosing one in a letter to Hartley at the latter's request (Figure E.2).[30] Nevertheless, because of the dearth of reliable information, the nature of the relationship between the American painter and the Prussian lieutenant remains unclear. Thomas Weißbrich suggests that their relationship may have amounted to "more than a platonic friendship."[31] Though Dieter Scholz detects a heartfelt and even erotic dimension in the extant correspondence, he concludes that the "thoroughly formal" tone of the letters indicates that the relationship probably never became sexual.[32] Jonathan Weinberg, meanwhile, points out that Hartley, like many of his middle-class contemporaries, preferred to have casual or anonymous sex with lower-class men in cities, believing that "the quality of male friendships may be undermined by sex."[33]

Though Freyburg's death initially interrupted Hartley's ability to create – he confessed to Stieglitz in March 1915 that "for many weeks I could not do anything or write anything" – it eventually resulted in a series of paintings that are not only counted among the American's best works but also represented some of the most modern paintings of the day.[34] Though twelve works make up the War Motifs series, the first and most famous is undoubtedly the oil painting *Portrait of a German Officer* from 1914 (Figure E.3), Hartley's largest work to date.[35] With the initials KvF in the bottom left, the canvas seems discreetly intended as a portrait of Karl von Freyburg. Indeed, based on a letter that Rönnebeck wrote to the collector Duncan Phillips after Hartley's death, scholars have reconstructed numerous associations that point to his dead friend, including a black-and-white chequered chess board. Most prominent, however, is the collage of military paraphernalia: the flags of the Prussian Cavalry and the German Army (the latter upside down); an officer's helmet with a horsehair parade brush; a Prussian officer's sash, portepee (sword-knot), cockades, collars, braids, and epaulettes (one bearing the number twenty-four, the age at which Freyburg was killed); and, at the top, the band for the iron cross, which the lieutenant was awarded shortly before he fell.[36] Painted on a sombre black background, the funereal image harkens back to the tradition of *Gedenkbilder* (memento-mori tableaux) of fallen soldiers whose absence is signified only by the weapons and other objects they left behind on the battlefield.[37]

Despite the clear context for this painting, Patricia McDonnell rightly cautions that "Hartley's German paintings resist single readings."[38] As she notes elsewhere, "these works are many things at once – a memorial to von Freyburg, and an elegiac tribute to the masses of war dead, a major synthesis of modernism's pictorial vocabulary, a heavily coded expression of Hartley's life in Berlin's vibrant homosexual culture and the role of the German military in that culture, a sophisticated reprise

218   Uniform Fantasies

Figure E.3. *Portrait of a German Officer*, oil painting by Marsden Hartley, 1914. New York, Metropolitan Museum of Art. Photo: akg-images.

of transcendentalist and Jamesian philosophies Hartley admired, and an outpouring of the artist's internal and subjective response to his own situation in Berlin as the world waged war."[39] As a psychological expression of Hartley's tortured relationship to his own sexuality, the paintings can also be read as "his habitual presentation of desire in a context that included death."[40] In this case, as Weinberg somewhat later points out, "it was war and death that finally gave Hartley the opportunity to represent his love for Freyburg."[41] Before August 1914, Hartley barely mentioned Freyburg in his letters to Stieglitz, but once Freyburg was dead, he repeatedly wrote of his adoration for the officer, at times, even forgetting that he had already informed Stieglitz that Freyburg had been killed."[42]

For our purposes, though, the paintings also marked the death-strewn end of the exuberant and queer "uniform fantasies" of Imperial Germany. In contrast to the efforts of the WhK and its supporters to link the tragic death of an officer to the cause of queer emancipation, Hartley's War Motif collages of military detritus amounts only to a discreet, highly coded visual language "to both hide and reveal a homosexual content to different audiences," for, as McDonnell notes, only "those who knew the artist was gay might have also understood that the young German officer memorialized likely had had a special love relationship with the artist."[43] And rather than a self-confident, even orgiastic celebration of fetishistic longing and desire for soldiers in their colourful, body-hugging dress, *Portrait of a German Officer* depicted a fragmented uniform laid out in the shape of a headless body. Gone is the vitally alive and irresistibly attractive soldier or officer who exerted his allure over queer men from Ulrichs to Hartley, and in its place there is only an elegiac, "flattened out ... surface, the patterns of flags and medals, as if the torso within had disappeared, leaving only the uniform" in broken pieces.[44]

Perhaps fittingly, the end of Hartley's erotic fetishization of the German military uniform occurred in a dream that he recorded in a letter he addressed to Freyburg, part of his unpublished collection, *Letters Never Sent*: "A singular white light arose out of the mangled heap of coils, up my entire right side – left facing myself as a spectator – growing brighter and whiter to the point of striking incandescence, and then there appeared in the whiteness of the illumination a full length image of yourself clad in full uniform but the uniform, purged of all military significance, was white."[45] Though Weinberg asks parenthetically "how one would know it was a full uniform if it was so purged" of military insignia, the point, it seems to me, is that the colourful uniforms – which had ceased to exist anyway – no longer exerted the same powerful erotic charge.[46]

At the same time that it extinguished the erotic "uniform fantasies" of the Second Empire, the First World War transformed other queer fantasies about the military and incited new ones. As we have seen, the outbreak of hostilities enabled Thomas Mann – and countless others, queer and not – to indulge in patriotic and heroic fantasies about war, Germany's military mission, and their own contributions to the war effort far from the actual frontlines. Meanwhile, other queer men donned uniforms themselves. Hirschfeld touted that 50 per cent of the WhK's members and many thousands of other German homosexuals had enlisted who were "ready to sacrifice their life for the fatherland." For Hirschfeld and his collaborators on *The Sexual History of the World War*, this enthusiastic support for the war effort was a "strange phenomenon" (*merkwürdige Erscheinung*), not only because most male homosexuals were, according to his theories, effeminate and ill-suited to the exigencies of combat but also because many had suffered from "the constant threat of Paragraph 175 and the social condemnation [*Achtung*] of same-sex love in Germany."[47] And yet at the front, many queer soldiers experienced a radically different and strangely more accepting world than they knew in Imperial Germany. On the one hand, as Jason Crouthammel reports, military authorities were reluctant to prosecute homosexuals unless coercion was involved, believing that "such investigations would damage the prevailing masculine idea" of the military.[48] On the other hand, the front changed the way men interacted with one another. In particular, the traumatic experiences of trench warfare forced many heterosexual men to re-evaluate their masculine ideals and find emotional support from comrades, allowing many to experience or accept erotically charged relationships among men, including explicitly sexual ones. Indeed, Thomas Kühne contends that comradeship was an ambiguous and multivalent concept that not only propagated "combat cohesion and fighting power," but also "served as a synonym for male friendship, even male love, of homoeroticism and tenderness."[49]

Two primary queer political fantasies emerged out of these wartime experiences. First, many homosexual veterans saw their wartime service as a path to full citizenship and social acceptance. They returned to civilian life with a newfound confidence in creating the vibrant and more visible queer scenes that the 1918 German Revolution and the republic's new constitution made possible. Though many queer men and women adopted pacifist stances, they also took up a more combative politics that, as Crouthammel points out, to some extent refashioned the homosexual emancipation movement "as a militant fighting force surrounded by enemies."[50] Though the queer emancipation movement radically expanded during this time into a mass movement, it was not able to achieve its long-standing goal of decriminalizing sexual acts between men without significant compromises.[51] Nevertheless, this new queer politics in a more forceful key was also accompanied by a move away from Hirschfeld's gender inversion theories. Instead, leaders and writers embraced a self-consciously masculine politics that, while distancing themselves from the misogyny and anti-Semitism of the masculinists, nevertheless tended to castigate effeminate men as degenerates who were holding back the movement.[52]

But, second, not all queer veterans of the war embraced the liberal politics of the Weimar Republic. Thus, a second political fantasy took hold that was rooted in the masculinist politics of the *Männerbund* (male society). In the aftermath of defeat, many male-loving veterans participated in the Freikorps units, which were involved in skirmishes against Bolsheviks on the eastern frontier, putting down revolutionary uprisings in Berlin, Munich, and elsewhere, or attempting their own coups. Certainly the most famous of these was Ernst Röhm, Hitler's closest associate and the leader of the SA (*Sturmabteilung*), the paramilitary wing of the Nazi Party. Because of the many injuries he had suffered during the war, Röhm had impeccable masculine credentials that enabled him to be rather open about his same-sex desires, despite the Nazi Party's official condemnation of homosexuality as a form of degeneration. As a result, according to Andrew Wackerfuss, over the course of the 1920s, "homosexuality in SA ranks became a prominent feature that both attracted and repelled adherents of the Nazi movement."[53]

Meanwhile, though the Social Democrats (SPD) had officially championed the decriminalization of sexual acts between men, it also had a history of using homosexual smear campaigns against its enemies, including the steel magnate Friedrich Alfred Krupp in 1902 and the Prussian nobility and army leadership during the Eulenburg Affair in 1907–9. In 1932, just as Hitler was running against Paul von Hindenburg for the office of president, the SPD orchestrated a front-page campaign to out Röhm as a homosexual by publishing indiscreet letters he had written.[54] As a result, the left began to conflate fascism and male homosexuality such that, as Andrew Hewitt has noted, homosexuality became "an allegory of fascism."[55] Yet Röhm was able to weather the crisis within the Nazi Party (thanks to Hitler's steadfast support). Moreover, the scandal seems to have done little damage to the Nazi's electoral support because of what Laurie Marhoefer has called "the Weimar settlement on sexual politics," in which sexual freedom was granted to previously excluded groups, like homosexuals, but only at the expense of others, in particular male and female prostitutes. Thus, "a conservative or liberal voter who was attracted to the NSDAP and read about the scandal ... had a narrative ready at hand that would help him or her to ignore Röhm's sexuality when he or she voted."[56]

Nevertheless, both queer fantasies – that queer men and women could achieve full inclusion in the Weimar Republic or that National Socialism would tolerate male homosexual behaviour as an integral part of the

Männerbund – were extinguished in June 1934 during the Night of the Long Knives, when Hitler and Himmler's SS moved against Röhm and the leadership of the SA, including his homosexual lieutenant, Edmund Heines. Though, in fact, these actions were taken in order to quash the unruly elements in the SA that were plaguing Hitler's efforts to govern and maintain popular support, the Nazis publicly justified the purge as a "storm of purification" to "cleanse" the SA of "degenerate elements."[57] Consequently, the operation served, according to Wackerfuss, "as the final settlement of homosexuality's troubled place in the SA and the Nazi movement."[58] In fact, the Night of the Long Knives merely extended to Nazi Party members and SA men the repressive policies the Nazis had begun applying to civilian homosexuals shortly after taking power: shutting down queer establishments and publications, ransacking Hirschfeld's institute, raiding Adolf Brand's house and confiscating his materials, and ramping up the prosecution of men under Paragraph 175, which they further strengthened in 1935.[59] Moreover, in contrast to the German Army's mixed prosecution of same-sex behaviour in the First World War, the Wehrmacht seems to have continued to prosecute instances of homosexuality among all ranks rather severely during the Second World War, even into the final months when defeat was all but certain.[60] The Nazi persecution of homosexuals, however, did little to disrupt leftist equations of fascism with homosexuality either during or after the Third Reich. And ironically, that very murderous homophobic and anti-Semitic history also seems to have imbued Nazi uniforms and regalia with a disturbing erotic appeal within some American, British, and Scandinavian pornography and sadomasochistic role-playing (both gay and straight) as the very erotization of what is most taboo.[61]

Though urban queer scenes seem to have returned fairly quickly in post-war Germany, the aggressive effort to return to "normality" proved hostile to queer activism. The Nazi amendment to Paragraph 175 remained on the books and, as Dagmar Herzog has shown, Christian churches, which had long opposed the queer emancipation movement in Germany, were effective in linking the Holocaust and other crimes to Nazi sexual immorality while presenting Christian "sexual propriety as the cure for the nation's larger moral crisis."[62] Only in the 1960s, when a new generation of German liberals and leftists mistakenly assumed that "the Third Reich had been at its core sex-hostile and that the Holocaust was the perverted product of sexual repression," would there be widespread support for decriminalizing sex between men.[63] After West Germany legalized consensual sexual acts between men in 1969, there was an immediate expansion of gay scenes and politics in the country.[64] Meanwhile, though East Germany repealed its criminalization of sex between men one year earlier in 1968, its pronatalist policies and lack of a queer scene or movement did little to change the fortunes of gay men who, as Josie McLellan explains, still "faced sometimes insurmountable difficulties in meeting potential partners, finding suitable living space, building a social life, and coming out to family and friends."[65]

Yet in spite of their legal reforms, both German states sought to isolate their post-war militaries from homosexual men, an easy task as long as sexual acts between men remained illegal. Nevertheless, even following the decriminalization of such acts in 1968 in the GDR, homosexual men were, according to Tom Smith, still "considered unsuitable for military careers and were routinely dismissed." He notes that even after homosexuality was given legal parity with heterosexuality in 1988, the East German National People's Army (*Nationale Volksarmee*) "issued secret guidelines on surreptitiously circumnavigating the law to continue dismissing homosexuals from full-time military careers."[66] Meanwhile, in the late 1960s, the Ministry of Defence was actively involved in the West German government's plans to decriminalize sexual acts between men. Though it formally proposed a separate subclause that would have excluded the *Bundeswehr* from the decriminalization of homosexuality, that approach was rejected in favour of fixing the age of consent for same-sex behaviour higher than for consensual sex between men and women, and explicitly criminalizing sex between men between the ages of eighteen and twenty-one.[67] This law, which was immediately denounced as "Lex Bundeswehr" in left-liberal circles, was amended in 1973 to set the age of consent for male-male sexual activity at eighteen. Yet even as homosexuality did not make men unfit for military service as a conscript, the Bundeswehr prohibited sex between soldiers as part of its code of conduct. It also continued to dismiss officers whose same-sex identity (outside of any sexual acts) became known.[68] But while gay rights activists castigated the military for its discrimination against gay men, the queer emancipation movement that formed in West Germany no longer sought to tie its fortunes to the prestige of the military – a testament to the army's diminished cachet in post-war West Germany.

But if queer politics has diverged from military politics in post-unified Germany, the same cannot be said for other countries with strong military traditions and vigorous queer activist movements. Thus, many of the issues explored in *Uniform Fantasies* have appeared today (or in the recent past) in various headlines and slogans, such as "gays in the military" and the outing of officers, uniform fetishism and the gay subculture of "military chasers," or debates about whether men in uniform are more masculine or more insecure about their identity. While the debates and developments in Imperial Germany can help defamiliarize these contemporary debates and open up new critical perspectives, the military politics of the first queer emancipation movement also helps us to see the risks of such a reliance on military service for queer rights – for both queer individuals and others. As we saw with Moltke's trial and the queer movement in the Weimar period, the militarization of queerness tends to favour self-consciously masculine or butch identities at the expense of other queer and non-queer modes of being. Moreover, as other military dimensions of the Eulenburg Affair demonstrate, homosexuals can quickly become convenient scapegoats for the public scandals that ensnare them. More dangerously still, queer support for the First World War (and later the Nazi movement) channelled legitimate claims for full citizenship for queer individuals into what Jasbir Puar has called "homonationalism," in which queer social inclusion (or the promise of it) seems only attainable at the expense of others, whether internal "enemies" (Jews, male prostitutes, and effeminate men) or external enemies outside the borders.

In addition to these insights, I also hope that many of the methodologies employed in this study will prove useful for scholars working on other eras and other settings. My effort to integrate psychoanalytic tools of analysis into a Foucauldian framework points towards new ways of doing the history of sexuality, one that not only follows the operations of sexual discourse from the medical clinic and literary text to the army barracks and panegyric war essays but also helps to uncover the unconscious motivations that drove these discursivities. Indeed, with their messy circuits of power and underlying antagonisms, these discourses and realities on the ground gave rise to a rich variety of personal and social fantasies that themselves became factors in the actions of institutions and individuals alike. While the resulting portrait of this culture lacks the precise abstractions of Hartley's German paintings, I hope it has conveyed some of the same colourful and dynamic vitality.

Notes

Preface

1. W.E.B. Du Bois, "The Present Condition of German Politics," *Central European History* 31, no. 3 (1998): 171. The manuscript was never published in Du Bois's lifetime. See Kenneth Barkin, "W.E.B. Du Bois and the Kaiserreich," *Central European History* 31, no. 3 (1998): 166–9.
2. He describes his experiences in more detail in W.E.B. Du Bois, "Interview of W.E.B. Du Bois by William Ingersoll, May 24, 1960," in *The Reminiscences of William Edward Burghardt du Bois, 1963*, ed. William T. Ingersoll (Alexandria, VA: Alexander Street Press, 2003), 111–19.
3. On Du Bois's Germanophilia, see Kenneth Barkin, "W.E.B. Du Bois' Love Affair with Imperial Germany," *German Studies Review* 28, no. 2 (2005): 285–302.
4. Du Bois, "German Politics," 171, 172.
5. Du Bois, "German Politics," 172.
6. Du Bois, "German Politics," 172.
7. Robert Beachy, *Gay Berlin: Birthplace of a Modern Identity* (New York: Alfred A. Knopf, 2014), 47. See also Jens Dobler, *Zwischen Duldungspolitik und Verbrechensbekämpfung: Homosexuellenverfolgung durch die Berliner Polizei von 1848 bis 1933*, Schriftenreihe der Deutschen Gesellschaft für Polizeigeschichte e.V. (Frankfurt: Verlag für Polizeiwissenschaft, 2008).
8. In addition to Beachy's *Gay Berlin*, recent overviews in English include Marti M. Lybeck, *Desiring Emancipation: New Women and Homosexuality in Germany, 1890–1933* (Albany, NY: SUNY P, 2014); Robert Deam Tobin, *Peripheral Desires: The German Discovery of Sex* (Philadelphia: U of Pennsylvania P, 2015); Clayton John Whisnant, *Queer Identities and Politics in Germany: A History, 1880–1945* (New York: Harrington Park Press, 2016).
9. See, for example, Hubert Kennedy, *Karl Heinrich Ulrichs: Pioneer of the Modern Gay Movement* (San Francisco: Peremptory Publications, 2002); Ralf

Dose, *Magnus Hirschfeld: The Origins of the Gay Liberation Movement*, trans. Edward H. Willis (New York: Monthly Review, 2014); Manfred Herzer, *Magnus Hirschfeld und seine Zeit* (Oldenbourg: De Guyter, 2017).

10 See, for example, George L. Mosse, *Nationalism and Sexuality: Middle-Class Morality and Sexual Norms in Modern Europe* (Madison: U of Wisconsin P, 1985); Gert Hekma, Harry Oosterhuis, and James D. Steakley, eds., *Gay Men and the Sexual History of the Political Left* (New York: The Haworth Press, 1995); Lybeck, *Desiring Emancipation*.

11 See, for example, James D. Steakley, *The Homosexual Emancipation Movement in Germany*, Reprints ed. (Salem, NH: Ayer, 1993).

12 See, for example, Harry Oosterhuis, *Stepchildren of Nature: Krafft-Ebing, Psychiatry, and the Making of Sexual Identity* (Chicago: U Chicago P, 2000); Ralph M. Leck, *Vita Sexualis: Karl Ulrichs and the Origins of Sexual Science* (Urban: U of Illinois P, 2016).

13 See, for example, Scott Spector, *Violent Sensations: Sex, Crime, and Utopia in Vienna and Berlin, 1860–1914* (Chicago: U of Chicago P, 2016); Dobler, *Zwischen Duldungspolitik und Verbrechensbekämpfung*.

14 See, for example, Edward Ross Dickinson, *Sex, Freedom, and Power in Imperial Germany, 1890–1914* (Cambridge: Cambridge UP, 2014); Martin Lücke, *Männlichkeit in Unordnung: Homosexualität und männliche Prostitution in Kaiser und Weimarer Republik* (Frankfurt: Campus, 2008).

15 See, for example, Heike Bauer, *The Hirschfeld Archives: Violence, Death, and Modern Queer Culture* (Philadelphia: Temple UP, 2017); Laurie Marhoefer, "Was the Homosexual Made White? Race, Empire, and Analogy in Gay and Trans Thought in Twentieth-Century Germany," *Gender & History* 31, no. 1 (2019): 91–114; Daniel J. Walther, "Racializing Sex: Same-Sex Relations, German Colonial Authority, and *Deutschtum*," *Journal of the History of Sexuality* 17, no. 1 (2008): 11–24; Heike I. Schmidt, "Colonial Intimacy: The Rechenberg Scandal and Homosexuality in East Africa," *Journal of the History of Sexuality* 17, no. 1 (2008): 25–59.

16 See, for example, Norman Domeier, *The Eulenburg Affair: A Cultural History of Politics in the German Empire* (Rochester, NY: Camden House, 2015); James D. Steakley, "Iconography of a Scandal: Political Cartoons and the Eulenburg Affair," *Studies in Visual Communication* 9, no. 2 (1983): 20–51; James D. Steakley, *Die Freunde des Kaisers: Die Eulenburg-Affäre im Spiegel zeitgenössischer Karikaturen*, trans. Jost Hermand (Hamburg: MännerschwarmSkript, 2004).

17 The concept of hegemonic masculinity was developed in R.W. Connell, *Masculinities*, 2nd ed. (Berkeley: U of California P, 2005).

18 Klaus Theweleit, *Male Fantasies*, vol. 1, *Women, Floods, Bodies, History*, trans. Stephen Conway in collaboration with Erica Carter and Chris Turner (Minneapolis: U of Minnesota P, 1987); Klaus Theweleit, *Male Fantasies*, vol. 2,

Male Bodies: Psychoanalyzing the White Terror, trans. Erica Carter, Chris Turner, and Stephen Conway (Minneapolis: U of Minnesota P, 1989).
19 Jessica Benjamin and Anson Rabinbach, Foreword to Theweleit, *Male Fantasies*, vol. 2, *Male Bodies*, xiii.
20 See the helpful discussion in Dagmar Herzog, *Sex after Fascism: Memory and Morality in Twentieth-Century Germany* (Princeton, NJ: Princeton UP, 2005), 240–6.
21 Michel Foucault, *The History of Sexuality, Volume I: An Introduction*, trans. Robert Hurley (New York: Vintage Books, 1978), 11.
22 See Lybeck, *Desiring Emancipation*, 84–5; Kirsten Leng, *Sexual Politics and Feminist Science: Women Sexologists in Germany, 1900–1933* (Ithaca, NY: Cornell UP and Cornell University Library, 2018), 115–20.
23 Georg Simmel, "Der Militarismus und die Stellung der Frauen," in *Aufsätze und Abhandlungen, 1894 bis 1900*, ed. Heinz-Jürgen Dahme and David P. Frisby (Frankfurt/Main: Suhrkamp, 1992), 49. All translations are my own unless otherwise noted.
24 For a brief overview of the feminist implications of Nightingale's nursing activities during the Crimean War (1853–6), see the introductory essay by Michael D. Calabria and Janet A. Macrae in Florence Nightingale, *Suggestions for Thought*, ed. Michael D. Calabria and Janet A. Macrae (Philadelphia: U of Pennsylvania P, 1994), ix–xl, esp. xviii–xxi. On Bertha von Suttner's feminist politics, see Brigitte Hamann, *Bertha von Suttner: A Life for Peace*, trans. Ann Dubsky (Syracuse: Syracuse UP, 1996), esp. chap. 13. On Frieda von Bülow, see Lora Wildenthal, *German Women for Empire, 1884–1945* (Durham, NC: Duke UP, 2001). On German women's subsequent equation of their activities during the First World War with military service, see Adrienne Thomas, *Die Katrin wird Soldat: Ein Roman aus Elsaß-Lothringen* (Berlin: Im Propyläen-Verlag, 1930); Marie-Elisabeth Lüders, *Das unbekannte Heer: Frauen kämpfen fur Deutschland, 1914–1918* (Berlin: E.S. Mittler & Sohn, 1936).
25 See, for example, Jason Crouthamel, *An Intimate History of the Front: Masculinity, Sexuality, and German Soldiers in the First World War* (New York: Palgrave Macmillan, 2014); Laurie Marhoefer, *Sex and the Weimar Republic: German Homosexual Emancipation and the Rise of the Nazis* (Toronto: U of Toronto P, 2015).
26 Volker R. Berghahn, "The German Empire, 1871–1914: Reflections on the Direction of Recent Research," *Central European History* 35, no. 1 (2002): 76.
27 Geoff Eley, Jennifer L. Jenkins, and Tracie Matysik, "Introduction: German Modernities and the Contest of Futures," in *German Modernities From Wilhelm to Weimar: A Contest of Futures*, ed. Geoff Eley, Jennifer L. Jenkins, and Tracie Matysik (London: Bloomsbury, 2016), 3.

28 David Halperin, *How to Do the History of Homosexuality* (Chicago: U of Chicago P, 2002), 15; Laura Doan, *Disturbing Practices: History, Sexuality, and Women's Experience of Modern War* (Chicago: U of Chicago P, 2013), 61.
29 Doan, *Disturbing Practices*, 90.
30 In 1928 Du Bois "dismissed forthwith" Augustus Granville Dill, his most loyal "disciple and student, then my co-helper and successor to part of my work," from his posts at the NAACP after the latter had been arrested for, as Du Bois subsequently called it, "molesting men in public places." In his autobiography, he insisted "I had before that time no conception of homosexuality. I had never understood the tragedy of an Oscar Wilde." Perhaps as a result, Du Bois claims to have "spent heavy days regretting my act." See W.E.B. Du Bois, *The Autobiography of W.E.B. Dubois: A Soliloquy on Viewing My Life from the Last Decade of Its First Century* (New York: International, 1968), 272. Meanwhile, he also inveighed against the queerness of the Harlem Renaissance, especially the leading role played by Alain Locke. According to Du Bois's biographer, "Alain Locke's brand of homosexuality, circumspect yet evident, was a factor in Du Bois's distaste for the man." David Levering Lewis, *W.E.B. Du Bois – Biography of a Race, 1868–1919* (New York: H. Holt, 1993), 162. Locke, like Du Bois before him, also attended Harvard and also spent a year studying at the University of Berlin in 1911, which inaugurated his own love affair with the country. Locke, for example, returned to Germany twice before the First World War, and nearly annually from 1919 to 1935, most likely because of its lively and welcoming queer scene. See Kenneth Barkin, "W.E.B. Du Bois and the German *Alltag*, 1892–1894," *The Journal of African American History* 96, no. 1 (2011): 9.
31 Seth Clark Silberman, "'Youse Awful Queer, Chappie': Reading Black Queer Vernacular in Black Literatures of the Americas, 1903–1967" (PhD diss., U of Maryland, 2005), 234.
32 Meyer Weinberg, ed., *The World of W.E.B. Du Bois: A Quotation Sourcebook* (Westport, CT: Greenwood, 1992), 208. The statement appears in *Russia and America: An Interpretation* (1950), an unpublished manuscript in the W.E.B. Du Bois Papers at the University of Massachusetts, Amherst. Du Bois's claim, of course, has remained controversial, especially for US scholars. See Barkin, "Du Bois' Love Affair with Imperial Germany," 286–7. On the nature of his non-university experiences in Germany, including romantic and sexual ones with women, see Du Bois, *The Autobiography of W.E.B. Dubois*, 270; Barkin, "W.E.B. Du Bois and the German *Alltag*, 1892–1894," 1–13.

Introduction

1 For background on Ulrichs, see Kennedy, *Karl Heinrich Ulrichs*; Beachy, *Gay Berlin*, 3–41.

2 Karl Heinrich Ulrichs, *Memnon*, ed. Hubert Kennedy, 12 vols., vol. 7, *Forschungen über das Rätsel der mannmännlichen Liebe* (Berlin: Verlag rosa Winkel, 1994), 54. For my rendering of Ulrichs's words into English, I consulted Karl Heinrich Ulrichs, *The Riddle of "Man-Manly" Love: The Pioneering Work on Male Homosexuality*, trans. Michael A Lombardi-Nash, 2 vols., vol. 2 (Buffalo, NY: Prometheus Books, 1994), 377.
3 Ulrichs, *Memnon*, vol. 7, 54.
4 Ulrichs, *Memnon*, vol. 7, 55.
5 Ulrichs, *Memnon*, vol. 7, 55.
6 Ulrichs, *Memnon*, vol. 7, 55.
7 By this time, Ulrichs had already had several love affairs with soldiers as evidenced by poems he wrote to them: Andreas F, a Hussar, in 1851, and Heinrich von St., a member of the Garde du corps, in 1855. See Kennedy, *Karl Heinrich Ulrichs*, 27, 37.
8 Karl Heinrich Ulrichs, *Ara spei*, ed. Hubert Kennedy, 12 vols., vol. 5, *Forschungen über das Rätsel der mannmännlichen Liebe* (Berlin: Verlag rosa Winkel, 1994), 71. The courtship rituals are described on 79–80.
9 Ulrichs, *Ara spei*, vol. 5, 79, 81.
10 On the advantages of using the word "scene" in place of "subculture," see Whisnant, *Queer Identities and Politics in Germany*, 11.
11 Du Bois, "German Politics," 171–2 (discussed in the preface of this volume).
12 On the history and origin of the term, see Volker Berghahn, *Militarism. The History of an International Debate, 1861–1979* (New York: St. Martin's, 1982); Werner Conze, Michael Geyer, and Reinhard Strumpf, "Militarismus," in *Geschichtliche Grundbegriffe: Historisches Lexikon zur politisch-sozialen Sprache in Deutschland*, ed. Otto Brunner, Werner Conze, and Reinhart Koselleck (Stuttgart: Klett-Cotta, 1978), 1–47. For a useful summary of militarism in Imperial Germany, see Roger Chickering, "Militarism and Radical Nationalism," in *Imperial Germany, 1871–1918*, ed. James Retallack (Oxford: Oxford UP, 2008), 196–218.
13 Particularists in the southern German states, especially Catholics, resented Prussian dominance and articulated some of the first important critiques of militarism inside Germany. See Conze, Geyer, and Strumpf, "Militarismus," 26–9. Similarly, the Social Democratic Party (SPD) articulated another important critique of militarism as part of capitalism. Moreover, the SPD was officially opposed to a standing army, arguing instead for replacing it with a militia (*Miliz*) along the model of Switzerland. Nevertheless, its critiques of Prussian military policy in the Reichstag were often inconsistent. See Nicholas Stargardt, *The German Idea of Militarism: Radical and Socialist Critics, 1866–1914* (Cambridge: Cambridge UP, 1994); Bernhard Neff, "*Wir wollen keine Paradetruppe, wir wollen eine*

Kriegstruppe …":Die reformorientierte Militärkritik der SPD unter Wilhelm II. 1890–1913 (Cologne: SH-Verlag, 2004).
14 Stig Förster, *Der doppelte Militarismus: Die deutsche Heeresrüstungspolitik zwischen Status-Quo-Sicherung und Aggression 1890–1913* (Stuttgart: Franz Steiner Verlag, 1985).
15 Benjamin Ziemann, "Militarism," in *The Ashgate Research Companion to Imperial Germany*, ed. Matthew Jefferies (New York: Routledge, 2015), 375.
16 *Verfassung des Deutschen Reichs. Gegeben Berlin, den 16. April 1871. Text-Ausgabe mit Ergänzungen, Anmerkungen und Sachregister*, ed. Ludwig von Rönne, 3rd expanded ed. (Berlin: J. Guttentag, 1878), 116.
17 For an overview of German uniforms, see Georg Ortenburg and Ingo Prömper, *Preussisch-Deutsche Uniformen von 1640–1918* (Munich: Orbis Verlag, 1991). For a comparison of German uniforms with other armies of the period, see Herbert Knötel, Jr. and Herbert Sieg, *Uniforms of the World: A Compendium of Army, Navy, and Air Force Uniforms, 1700–1937*, trans. Ronald G. Ball (New York: Charles Scribner's Sons, 1980).
18 Dagmar Herzog, *Sexuality in Europe: A Twentieth-Century History*, New Approaches to European History (Cambridge: Cambridge UP, 2011), 30. Edward Ross Dickinson likens the debates to "a Hollywood saloon brawl that starts at one table and expands out into chaos." See his *Sex, Freedom, and Power*, 304.
19 Foucault, *The History of Sexuality, Vol. I*, 43.
20 Foucault, *The History of Sexuality, Vol. I*, 103.
21 Beachy, *Gay Berlin*, xiv.
22 See Edward Ross Dickinson and Richard F. Wetzell, "The Historiography of Sexuality in Modern Germany," *German History* 23, no. 3 (2005): 291–305; Franz X. Eder, "The Politics of Discourse," *Contemporary European History* 22, no. 2 (2013): 283–8; Edward Ross Dickinson, "Complexity, Contingency, and Coherence in the History of Sexuality in Modern Germany: Some Theoretical and Interpretive Reflections," *Central European History* 49 (2016): 93–116.
23 On Foucault's foundational role, see Kadji Amin, "Genealogies of Queer Theory," in *The Cambridge Companion to Queer Studies*, ed. Siobhan B. Somerville (Cambridge: U of Cambridge P, 2020), 20–1.
24 Eve Kosofsky Sedgwick, *Epistemology of the Closet* (Berkeley: U of California P, 1990).
25 Halperin, *How to Do the History of Homosexuality*, 109.
26 Judith Butler, *The Psychic Life of Power: Theories in Subjection* (Stanford: Stanford UP, 1997), 86–7.
27 Foucault, *The History of Sexuality, Vol. I*, 55. On this point, see Jeffrey Schneider, "Soliciting Fantasies: Knowing and Not-Knowing About Male Prostitution by Soldiers in Imperial Germany," in *After the History*

of Sexuality: German Interventions, ed. Dagmar Herzog, Helmut Puff, and Scott Spector (New York: Berghahn Books, 2012), 126–7, 135–6.
28 Foucault, *The History of Sexuality, Vol. I*, 73.
29 Judith Butler, *Gender Trouble: Feminism and the Subversion of Identity* (New York: Routledge, 1990), 136.
30 Lyndal Roper, "Beyond Discourse Theory," *Women's History Review* 19, no. 2 (2010): 314.
31 Joan Wallach Scott, *The Fantasy of Feminist History* (Durham, NC: Duke UP, 2011), 5.
32 Joan W. Scott, "The Incommensurability of Psychoanalysis and History," *History and Theory* 51, no. 1 (2012): 82–3. For a discussion of critical history, see Doan, *Disturbing Practices*, 38–9, 80–93.
33 See Amin, "Genealogies of Queer Theory," 21.
34 See Lee Edelman, *No Future: Queer Theory and the Death Drive* (Durham, NC: Duke UP, 2004); Lauren Berlant and Lee Edelman, *Sex, or the Unbearable* (Durham, NC: Duke UP, 2014).
35 Edelman, *No Future*, 7.
36 Edelman, *No Future*, 17.
37 See Robyn Wiegman and Elizabeth A. Wilson, "Introduction: Antinormativity's Queer Conventions," *differences* 26, no. 1 (2015): 11–12.
38 Elizabeth Freeman, *Time Binds: Queer Temporalities, Queer Histories* (Durham, NC: Duke UP, 2010), xxi.
39 Freeman, *Time Binds*, xxi.
40 As a prolific author, Žižek has developed and refined his thoughts in a number of books. See *The Sublime Object of Ideology* (London: Verso, 1989); *For They Know Not What They Do: Enjoyment as a Political Factor*, 2nd ed. (London: Verso, 2008); *The Parallax View* (Cambridge, MA: MIT, 2006).
41 Amin, "Genealogies of Queer Theory," 25.
42 Charles Shephardson, "History and the Real: Foucault with Lacan," *Postmodern Culture* 5, no. 2 (1995).
43 See, for instance, *Soldaten-Bilderbuch für die deutsche Jugend* ([Berlin?]: n.p., [1900?]).
44 Paul Hildebrandt, *Das Spielzeug im Leben des Kindes* (Berlin: G. Söhlke, 1904), 284–5. On the production and marketing of toy soldiers in Germany at this time, see Bryan Ganaway, "Consuming Masculinity: Toys and Boys in Wilhelmine Germany," *Edinburgh German Yearbook* 2 (2008): 101–2.
45 Hildebrandt, *Das Spielzeug*, 282.
46 Dr. Grävell, "Die Uniform als Erzieher," *Pädagogisches Archiv: Monatsschrift für Erziehung und Unterricht* 46, no. 12 (1904): 738.
47 Thomas Nipperdey, *Deutsche Geschichte 1866–1918: Arbeitswelt und Bürgergeist*, vol. 1 (Munich: C.H. Beck, 1993), 133. See also John Harvey, *Men in Black* (Chicago: U of Chicago P, 1995), 9–39; Anne Hollander, *Sex and Suits* (New York: Knopf, 1994), 79f.

48 Alexander Rose, "Clearing the Fog of War," *MHQ: Quarterly Journal of Military History* 24, no. 4 (2012): 42–7.
49 For an overview of this debate, see Neff, *"Wir wollen keine Paradetruppe ..."*
50 Several richly illustrated books on German uniforms were marketed to the general reading public. See, for instance, G. Krickel and G. Lange, *Das Deutsche Reichsheer in seiner neuesten Bekleidung und Ausrüstung* (Marzoll: Eikon-Verlag. Faksimile-Nachdruck, 1977 [1888/90]).
51 Sharon Marcus, "Reflections on Victorian Fashion Plates," *differences* 14, no. 3 (2005): 24. See also Heidi Brevik-Zender, "Interstitial Narratives: Rethinking Feminine Spaces of Modernity in Nineteenth-Century French Fashion Plates," *Nineteenth-Century Contexts* 36, no. 2 (2014): 110.
52 Elisa Glick, *Materializing Queer Desire: Oscar Wilde to Andy Warhol* (Albany, NY: SUNY P, 2009), 7. See also Alison Matthews David, "Decorated Men: Fashioning the French Soldier, 1852–1914," *Fashion Theory* 7, no. 1 (2003): 3–38; Jennifer Craik, *Uniforms Exposed: From Conformity to Transgression*, ed. Joanne B. Eicher, Dress, Body, Culture (Oxford: Berg Publishers, 2005).
53 Robert von Zedlitz-Trützschler, *Twelve Years at the Imperial German Court*, trans. Alfred Kalisch (New York: George H. Doran, 1924), 6.
54 Zedlitz-Trützschler, *Twelve Years*, 7.
55 Elizabeth Otto, "Real Men Wear Uniforms: Photomontage, Postcards, and Military Visual Culture in Early Twentieth-Century Germany," *Contemporaneity* 2, no. 1 (2012): 26.
56 Alfred Vagts, *A History of Militarism: Civilian and Military* (New York: Free Press, 1967), 32 (emphasis in original). According to Volker Berghahn, Vagts, who served as an officer in the German Army in the First World War, offered "one of the fullest and most important attempts to come to terms with the problem of militarism." Berghahn, *Militarism*, 41.
57 Kerstin Flintrop, "Die Disziplinierung des männlichen Körpers – Uniformen im historischen Vergleich von Schnittführung und Verarbeitung," in *Nach Rang und Stand*, ed. Stadt Krefeld (Krefeld: Deutsches Textilmuseum, 2002), 29–31.
58 Because uniforms required straight lines, many military personnel had to don corsets. See Ernst-Friedrich Suhr, "Deutschland vor dem ersten Weltkrieg – Bilder aus einer Gesellschaft," in *Das Menschenschlachthaus: Bilder vom kommenden Krieg*, Sammlung Alter Kinderbücher (Munich: Weismann Verlag, 1980). Meanwhile, according to an American eyewitness, "nearly all the Austrian officers and many of the Viennese policemen wear corsets, and you can see the corsets displayed in the men's furnishings windows." Mary Ethel McAuley, *Germany in War Time: What an American Girl Saw and Heard* (Chicago: The Open Court, 1917), 209.
59 Colin McDowell, *The Man of Fashion: Peacock Males and Perfect Gentlemen* (London: Thames and Hudson, 1997), 79.

60 From the report of the State Attorney's Office of the Superior Court in Hildesheim to the Justice Ministry in Hanover on 1 December 1854, quoted in full in Kennedy, *Karl Heinrich Ulrichs*, 31–3, here 31.
61 Kennedy, *Karl Heinrich Ulrichs*, 32. As Isabel Hull notes, even as southern and western German states adopted the Napoleonic Code, which decriminalized same-sex behaviour between men and other moral crimes, these often returned through the regulations that civil society demanded as "necessary for the maintenance and reproduction" of itself. See Isabel V. Hull, *Sexuality, State and Civil Society in Germany, 1700–1815* (Ithaca, NY: Cornell UP, 1996), 408.
62 Kennedy, *Karl Heinrich Ulrichs*, 87.
63 For the text of the criminal code, see Friedrich Oppenhoff, ed., *Strafgesetzbuch für das Deutsche Reich, mit Commentar*, 12th expanded ed., ed. Theodor Oppenhoff (Berlin: Georg Reimer, 1891), 422. On the German term and its translation into English, see Robert Deam Tobin, "Sexology in the Southwest: Law, Medicine, and Sexuality in Germany and Its Colonies," in *A Global History of Sexual Science, 1880–1960*, ed. Veronika Fuechtner, Douglas E. Haynes, and Ryan M. Jones (Berkeley, CA: U of California P, 2017), 145–6.
64 Ellen Crowell, "Queer," *Victorian Literature and Culture* 46, no. 3–4 (2018): 816–20.
65 Siobhan B. Somerville, Introduction to *The Cambridge Companion to Queer Studies*, ed. Siobhan B. Somerville (Cambridge: U of Cambridge P, 2020), 2.
66 For a thorough discussion of Ulrichs's role in developing modern approaches to same-sex desire and identity, see Leck, *Vita Sexualis*.
67 See Karl Maria Kertbeny, *Schriften zur Homosexualitätsforschung*, ed. Manfred Herzer, vol. 22, Bibliothek rosa Winkel (Berlin: Verlag rosa Winkel, 2000). On Kertbeny, see Spector, *Violent Sensations*, 94–9.
68 See Carl Westphal, "Die conträre Sexualempfindung, Symptom eines neuropathischen (psychopathischen) Zustandes," *Archiv für Psychiatrie und Nervenkrankheit* 2 (1870); Richard von Krafft-Ebing, *Psychopathia Sexualis, mit besonderer Berücksichtigung der conträren Sexualempfindung: Eine klinische-forensische Studie*, 7th enlarged and revised ed. (Stuttgart: Ferdinand Enke, 1892); Albert Moll, *Die konträre Sexualempfindung*, 3rd ed. (Berlin: Fischers Medicinische Buchhandlung, 1899).
69 Magnus Hirschfeld, "What People Should Know about the Third Sex," in *Berlin's Third Sex*, trans. James J. Conway (Berlin: Rixdorf Editions, 2017), 101–26.
70 Sedgwick, *Epistemology of the Closet*, 85.
71 Elisarion von Kupffer, *Lieblingminne und Freundesliebe in der Weltliteratur: Eine Sammlung mit einer ethisch-politischen Einleitung* (Leipzig: Max Spohr, 1899).

72 See, for example, Sigmund Freud, *Three Essays on the Theory of Sexuality* (1905), in *The Standard Edition of the Complete Psychological Works of Sigmund Freud*, ed. and trans. James Strachey, vol. 7 (London: Hogarth, 1953), 123–246.
73 See Beachy, *Gay Berlin*, xi.
74 Sedgwick, *Epistemology of the Closet*, 45 (emphasis in original).
75 Immanuel Kant, "An Answer to the Question: What Is Enlightenment?," trans. David L. Colclasure, Jeremy Waldon, Michael W. Doyle, and Allen W. Wood, in *Toward Perpetual Peace and Other Writings on Politics, Peace, and History*, ed. Pauline Kleingeld (New Haven, CT: Yale UP, 2006), 17, 18 (emphasis in original).
76 Hull, *Sexuality, State and Civil Society*, 410.
77 See Leng, *Sexual Politics and Feminist Science*.
78 The New Woman served as the discursive identification of those female-identified individuals challenging the strictures of the sex-gender system. Lybeck, *Desiring Emancipation*, 2.
79 As Robert Deam Tobin points out, "the concept of Jewishness became an important model for those thinking about same-sex desire." Tobin, *Peripheral Desires*, 83. On the alliances between parts of the women's movement and the queer emancipation movement, see Leng, *Sexual Politics and Feminist Science*, 115–51; Lybeck, *Desiring Emancipation*, 83–116; Tracie Matysik, *Reforming the Moral Subject: Ethics and Sexuality in Central Europe, 1890–1930* (Ithaca, NY: Cornell UP, 2008), 166–72.
80 Karl Heinrich Ulrichs, *The Riddle of "Man-Manly" Love: The Pioneering Work on Male Homosexuality*, trans. Michael A Lombardi-Nash, 2 vols., vol. 1 (Buffalo, NY: Prometheus Books, 1994), 109.
81 Ulrichs, *The Riddle of "Man-Manly" Love*, vol. 1, 107–8.
82 Reproduced in Kennedy, *Karl Heinrich Ulrichs*, 107–9.
83 For a thorough and finely nuanced summary of his effort to address the Congress, see Kennedy, *Karl Heinrich Ulrichs*, 132–41; Beachy, *Gay Berlin*, 3–6.
84 On the factors that led to retaining the law, see Beachy, *Gay Berlin*, 33–9.
85 On the Scientific-Humanitarian Committee and Hirschfeld's leadership, see Dose, *Magnus Hirschfeld*; Beachy, *Gay Berlin*, 85–119; Herzer, *Magnus Hirschfeld und seine Zeit*.
86 On Hirschfeld's deletions of particular passages, which Ferdinand Karsch, an early collaborator in the WhK, criticized as a castration, see Kennedy, *Karl Heinrich Ulrichs*, 96, 98, 100, 102, 152, 209, 211, 242.
87 I thank one of my anonymous readers for pointing out to me the link between Du Bois's approach to the paradox of German politics and the paradoxical nature of the queer emancipation movement's deep and wide-ranging investment in the military.

88 Jasbir Puar, *Terrorist Assemblages: Homonationalism in Queer Times*. Next Wave: New Directions in Women's Studies, ed. Inderpal Grewal, Caren Kaplan, and Robyn Wiegman, 10th anniversary ed. (Durham, NC: Duke UP, 2017).

89 Bauer, *The Hirschfeld Archives*; Marhoefer, "Was the Homosexual Made White?," 91–114.

90 The Institute was ransacked by Nazi students on 6 May 1933, with many of its holdings incinerated at the infamous book-burning on 10 May. See Dose, *Magnus Hirschfeld*, 65–6, 94–5. Nearly all of the Prussian military archives in Potsdam were destroyed by Allied bombs on 14 April 1945. See Holger H. Herwig, "An Introduction to Military Archives in West Germany," *Military Affairs* 36, no. 4 (1972): 121–4.

91 Foucault, *The History of Sexuality, Vol. I*, 11.

92 The scholarship on the Eulenburg Affair is now quite extensive. For a brief overview, see Steakley, "Iconography of a Scandal." For more thorough discussions in English, see Isabel V. Hull, *The Entourage of Kaiser Wilhelm II., 1888–1918* (Cambridge: Cambridge UP, 1982); Domeier, *The Eulenburg Affair*.

93 On Wilhelm II's system of "personal rule," see Hull, *Entourage*, 83–97; John C.G. Röhl, *Wilhelm II: The Kaiser's Personal Monarchy, 1888–1900* (Cambridge: Cambridge UP, 2004), esp. 873–9. For a very different view, see Christopher M. Clark, *Kaiser Wilhelm II* (Harlow, England: Longman, 2000), 80–6.

94 In a set of articles in the fall of 1906, Harden made claims that only Eulenburg and few others would understand. See "Praeludium," *Die Zukunft* 57 (17 November 1906), 251–66; "Dies irae," *Die Zukunft* 57 (24 November 1906), 287–302. Eulenburg used an intermediary to immediately negotiate a truce by promising to retire from politics and by relocating with his family temporarily to Switzerland. It was only when he returned to Berlin in January 1907 to accept his investiture into the Order of the Black Eagle that Harden, sensing a breach in the contract, formulated his accusations more explicitly. See "Roulette," *Die Zukunft* 59 (27 April 1907), 117–30; "Nur ein paar Worte," *Die Zukunft* 59 (15 June 1907), 367–74; "Die Freunde," *Die Zukunft* 59 (22 June 1907), 405–25.

95 Bernhard Bülow, *Memoirs of Prince von Bülow*, trans. Geoffrey Dunlop and F. A. Voigt, vol. 4 (Boston: Little, Brown, and Company, 1932), 123. Bülow read a wide range of novels in French and English as well as German, including some of the bestsellers of *Trivialliteratur*, though he noted that the latter works "are not made to serve as a compass for the sometimes stormy passage upon the world's great stream. Theodor Fontane and Maria von Ebner-Eschenbach serve this purpose better" (123).

96 Sarah Kay, *Žižek: A Critical Introduction*, Key Contemporary Thinkers (Cambridge: Polity, 2003), 69.
97 For a detailed discussion, see in particular the first chapter in Dominick LaCapra, *History, Literature, Critical Theory* (Ithaca, NY: Cornell UP, 2013), 12–30.
98 Martin J. Wiener, "Treating 'Historical' Sources as Literary Texts: Literary Historicism and Modern British History," *Journal of Modern History* 70, no. 3 (1998): 620.
99 The debate about Imperial Germany's modernity remains strong. See Geoff Eley, Jennifer L. Jenkins, and Tracie Matysik, eds., *German Modernities from Wilhelm to Weimar: A Contest of Futures* (London: Bloomsbury, 2016).

1. Outing Officers: Queer Activism, Melodrama, and the Harden-Moltke Trial

1 Dose, *Magnus Hirschfeld*, 42.
2 Sedgwick, *Epistemology of the Closet*, 68.
3 Peter Brooks, *The Melodramatic Imagination: Balzac, Henry James, Melodrama, and the Mode of Excess*, 2nd ed. (New Haven, CT: Yale UP, 1995), viii.
4 See David Mayer, "Encountering Melodrama," in *The Cambridge Companion to Victorian and Edwardian Theater*, ed. Kerry Powell (Cambridge: Cambridge UP, 2004), 149.
5 Brooks, *The Melodramatic Imagination*, xvii.
6 Rohan McWilliam, "Melodrama and the Historians," *Radical History Review* 78 (2000): 60.
7 See Peter Brooks, "Psychoanalysis and Melodrama," in *The Cambridge Companion to English Melodrama*, ed. Carolyn Williams (Cambridge: Cambridge UP, 2018), 277–88.
8 See Angus McLaren, *The Trials of Masculinity: Policing Sexual Boundaries, 1870–1930* (Chicago: U of Chicago P, 1997), esp. 37–8; James M. Donovan, "Culture and the Courts in France: The *Plaidoirie Sentimentale* in the Nineteenth and Early Twentieth Centuries," *Law and History Review* 35, no. 3 (2017): 789–828.
9 The queer fascination with suicide was quite pervasive. See Samuel Clowes Huneke, "Death Wish: Suicide and Stereotype in the Gay Discourses of Imperial and Weimar Germany," *New German Critique* 46, no. 1 (2019): 127–66.
10 McWilliam, "Melodrama and the Historians," 70.
11 Benedict Friedlaender, "Schadet die soziale Freigabe des homosexuellen Verkehrs der kriegerischen Tüchtigkeit der Rasse? Ein vorläufiger Hinweis," *Jahrbuch für sexuelle Zwischenstufen* 7 (1905), 463–70.
12 Benedict Friedlaender, "Aus der Denkschrift für die Freunde und Fondzeichner des Wissenschaftlich-Humanitären Komitees im Namen

der Sezession des Wissenschaftlich-Humanitären Komitees," in *Die Liebe Platons im Lichte der modernen Biologie* (Treptow/Berlin: Bernhard Zack, 1909), 203.

13 Hirschfeld, for instance, never publicly came out as a homosexual since this sexual identity would have undermined his scientific authority on the topic. See Dose, *Magnus Hirschfeld*, 29. Others, such as Eugen Wilhelm – an early member of the WhK advisory committee (*Obmännerkollegium*), the group's foremost legal expert, and the long-standing book review editor for the *Jahrbuch für sexuelle Zwischenstufen* (*JfsZ*), the WhK's scholarly journal – used the pseudonym Numa Praetorius even after the discovery of his homosexuality forced him to resign his appointment as a judge in Prussian Strasbourg. See Kevin Dubout, *Der Richter und sein Tagebuch: Eugen Wilhelm als Elsässer und homosexueller Aktivist im Deutschen Kaiserreich* (Frankfurt: Campus, 2018), esp. 252–324.

14 Magnus Hirschfeld, *Von einst bis jetzt: Geschichte einer homosexuellen Bewegung 1897–1922*, ed. Manfred Herzer and James D. Steakley (Berlin: Verlag Rosa Winkel, 1986), 54. The book is a collection of recollections published from 1922 to 1923 in *Die Freundschaft*, a leading popular magazine for homosexuals in the Weimar Republic. Though Dubout raises understandable doubts about the reliability of Hirschfeld's belated recollections, one important indication for Bülow's attendance is a cryptic claim in Hirschfeld's annual report for 1905–6, in which he boasted that one of the first financial supporters of the organization was "a member of the von Bülow family" – an effort to tout the early patronage of someone related to Bernhard von Bülow, Germany's chancellor at the time. See Dubout, *Der Richter und sein Tagebuch*, 252n2; Magnus Hirschfeld, "Jahresbericht 1905–1906," *Jahrbuch für sexuelle Zwischenstufen* 8 (1906): 891.

15 Hirschfeld, *Von einst bis jetzt*, 54.

16 Magnus Hirschfeld, "Petition an die gesetzgebenden Körperschaften des deutschen Reiches," *Jahrbuch für sexuelle Zwischenstufen* 1 (1899), 239–80. The petition called for the repeal of Paragraph 175 of the penal code.

17 Its first four honourary signatures represented medicine (Richard von Krafft-Ebing), law (Franz von Liszt), the arts (Ernst von Wildenbruch), and politics (August Bebel).

18 "I. Komiteeangelegenheiten," *Monatsbericht des Wissenschaftlich-humanitären Komitees* 6, no. 10 (1 October 1907), 190.

19 "Abrechnung (pro 1904)," *Jahrbuch für sexuelle Zwischenstufen* 7 (1905): 1075; "Abrechnung (pro 1905)," *Jahrbuch für sexuelle Zwischenstufen* 8 (1906): 933.

20 Though we don't have a list of the signatures of the secessionist manifesto, there were enough questions about whether the Moll who signed the

document might have been the Berlin neurologist Albert Moll (by this time Hirschfeld's nemesis in sexological circles), that the steering committee felt obligated to clarify that the signature belonged to the retired lieutenant. Magnus Hirschfeld et al., "Zur Richtigstellung," *Monatsbericht des Wissenschaftlich-humanitären Komitees* 6, no. 4 (1 April 1907), 62. A larger excerpt of Friedlaender's text is available in his "Denkschrift." Despite the marked anti-feminism of the secessionist program, Moll was a member of the short-lived Demokratische Vereinigung (Democratic Union), whose party platform called for the "realization of legal equality for all classes, confessions, nationalities, parties, and both genders." Quoted in Elisabeth Altmann-Gottheiner, "Die deutschen politischen Parteien und ihre Stellung zur Frauenfrage," *Zeitschrift für Politik* 3 (1910): 596.
21 Moll was elected to the city council of Wilmersdorf, then an independent municipality abutting Berlin. See "Aus Berliner Vororten. [Die Auflösung der bürgerlichn Demokratie.]," *Kommunale Praxis: Wochenschrift für Kommunalpolitik und Gemeindesozialismus,* 26 October, 1912, 1335.
22 Magnus Hirschfeld, "Jahresbericht 1902/3," *Jahrbuch für sexuelle Zwischenstufen* 5 (1903): 1298–9. Prince Georg also wrote and published dramas under the pseudonym Georg Conrad and was one of the first to recognize and promote the talents of Ernst von Wildenbruch. Hirschfeld, "Jahresbericht 1902/3," 1303.
23 Hirschfeld, "Jahresbericht 1902/3," 1300, 1302.
24 "Komitee-Mitteilungen," *Vierteljahresberichte des Wissenschaftlich-humanitäres Komitees* 1, no. 4 (July 1910): 441–2.
25 Hirschfeld, *Von einst bis jetzt*, 149.
26 Hirschfeld, *Von einst bis jetzt*, 149.
27 Hirschfeld, *Von einst bis jetzt*, 150.
28 Dose, *Magnus Hirschfeld*, 68.
29 Heinrich Schurtz, *Altersklassen und Männerbünde: Eine Darstellung der Grundformen der Gesellschaft* (Berlin: Georg Reimer, 1902). See also Andrew Hewitt, *Political Inversions: Homosexuality, Fascism, and the Modernist Imaginary* (Stanford, CA: Stanford UP, 1996), 79–129.
30 Kupffer, *Lieblingminne und Freundesliebe*.
31 Kupffer, *Lieblingminne und Freundesliebe*, 12. My translation of Tüchtigkeit draws on Isabel Hull's, who notes: "What I have translated as 'efficiency' (*Tüchtigkeit*) is more accurately rendered as experienced, energetic activity." Isabel V. Hull, *Absolute Destruction: Military Culture and the Practices of War in Imperial Germany* (Ithaca, NY: Cornell UP, 2005), 143–4.
32 Kupffer, *Lieblingminne und Freundesliebe*, 12.
33 Friedlaender, "Schadet … ?"
34 Friedlaender, "Schadet … ?," 466–7.
35 Friedlaender, "Schadet … ?," 469.

36 Friedlaender, "Schadet ... ?," 469–70.
37 Konrad Linke, "Ich hatt' einen Kameraden – ," *Der Eigene*, June 1905. Reprinted in Konrad Linke, "Ich hatt' einen Kameraden – ," in *Der Eigene: Ein Blatt für männliche Kultur: Ein Querschnitt durch die erste Homosexuellenzeitschrift der Welt*, ed. Joachim S. Hohmann (Frankfurt/Berlin: Foerster, 1981), 155–8. The story won the praise of Numa Praetorius (Eugen Wilhelm), one of Friedlaender's most vociferous critics within the WhK, who called it "an elegantly inspired novelette." See Dr. jur. Numa Praetorius (Eugen Wilhelm), "Die Bibliographie der Homosexualität," *Jahrbuch für sexuelle Zwischenstufen* 9 (1908): 587.
38 On the career of Friedrich Silcher's 1825 song (set to an 1809 poem by Ludwig Uhland), see Uli Otto and Eginhard König, *"Ich hatt' einen Kameraden ...": Militär und Kriege in historisch-politischen Liedern in den Jahren von 1740 bis 1914* (Regensburg: ConBrio, 1999).
39 Linke, "Ich hatt' einen Kameraden – ," 155.
40 See Carlotta Sorba, "Melodrama in Post-revolutionary Europe: The Genealogy and Diffusion of a 'Popular' Theatrical Genre and Experience, 1780–1830," in *Leisure Cultures in Urban Europe, c.1700–1870: A Transnational Perspective*, ed. Peter Borsay and Jan Hein Furnée (Manchester: Manchester UP, 2016), 49–71.
41 Linke, "Ich hatt' einen Kameraden – ," 155.
42 Linke, "Ich hatt' einen Kameraden – ," 156.
43 Linda Williams, "Melodrama Revised," in *Refiguring American Film Genres: History and Theory*, ed. Nick Browne (Berkeley, CA: U of California P, 1998), 54.
44 Linke, "Ich hatt' einen Kameraden – ," 156.
45 Linke, "Ich hatt' einen Kameraden – ," 157.
46 Linke, "Ich hatt' einen Kameraden – ," 157.
47 Williams, "Melodrama Revised," 66–7.
48 Linke, "Ich hatt' einen Kameraden – ," 158.
49 Linke, "Ich hatt' einen Kameraden – ," 158.
50 Freud suggests that this voyeuristic position is a typical marker for fantasies. Sigmund Freud, "'A Child is Being Beaten': A Contribution to the Study of the Origins of Sexual Perversions (1919)," in *The Standard Edition of the Complete Psychological Works of Sigmund Freud*, ed. and trans. James Strachey, vol. 17 (London: Hogarth, 1955), 175–204.
51 Linke, "Ich hatt' einen Kameraden – ," 156–7.
52 Georg Merzbach, "Homosexualität und Beruf," *Jahrbuch für sexuelle Zwischenstufen* 4 (1902): 190.
53 Merzbach, "Homosexualität und Beruf," 190–1.
54 Merzbach, "Homosexualität und Beruf," 191–2.
55 Merzbach, "Homosexualität und Beruf," 193.

240   Notes to pages 38–42

56 Merzbach, "Homosexualität und Beruf," 193.
57 For the figure of 100, see Magnus Hirschfeld, "Ursachen und Wesen des Uranismus," *Jahrbuch für sexuelle Zwischenstufen* 5 (1903): 4. Subsequently republished as a monograph: Magnus Hirschfeld, *Der urnische Mensch* (Leipzig: Max Spohr, 1903).
58 Hirschfeld, "Ursachen und Wesen des Uranismus," 72.
59 Hirschfeld, "Ursachen und Wesen des Uranismus," 72 (emphasis in original).
60 Hirschfeld, "Ursachen und Wesen des Uranismus," 72.
61 Hirschfeld, "Ursachen und Wesen des Uranismus," 73.
62 Hirschfeld, "Ursachen und Wesen des Uranismus," 82.
63 Hirschfeld, "Ursachen und Wesen des Uranismus," 81.
64 Hirschfeld, "Ursachen und Wesen des Uranismus," 80.
65 Hirschfeld, "Ursachen und Wesen des Uranismus," 86.
66 "[Item 29]," *Monatsbericht des Wissenschaftlich-humanitären Komitees*, no. 9 (1 September 1905), 17.
67 "[Item 28]," *Monatsbericht des Wissenschaftlich-humanitären Komitees* 4, no. 10 (1 October 1905), 13–14.
68 Augustin Zarzosa has argued that melodrama is a "response" to suffering: "The realm of melodrama is not a world inhabited by things whose essence threatens to escape us; it is a world in which ideas inflict suffering and, consequently, the epistemological quest is not for an idea that might reveal the essence of things, but for one that might obliterate suffering." "Melodrama and the Modes of the World," *Discourse* 32, no. 2 (2010): 242–3.
69 Magnus Hirschfeld, *Sappho und Sokrates: Wie erklärt sich die Liebe der Männer und Frauen zu Personen des eigenen Geschlechts?* 2nd ed. (Leipzig: Max Spohr, 1902).
70 Hirschfeld, *Sappho und Sokrates*, 3–4.
71 As Hirschfeld recalled in 1928, "I gave up the study of philology and literature for biology and medicine for practical reasons only. My true inclination had always been, and still is, to spend my life in the society of journalists, writers, poets and artists." But though he opted for medicine, he in fact never entirely left literature behind, claiming: "The natural sciences have always left aside the most important aspect of life, which is love. It has been left to the artists and writer. And I decided to make this theme the mainspring of my medical research." Quoted in Charlotte Wolff, *Magnus Hirschfeld: A Portrait of a Pioneer in Sexology* (London: Quartet Books, 1986), 27.
72 Hirschfeld, *Sappho und Sokrates*, 4.
73 Émile Zola, *The Ladies' Paradise* (London: Vizetelly, 1886), 333.

74 Franz Reddi, *Der fremde Gott: Ein Familiendrama in einem Aufzug* (Leipzig: Max Spohr, 1907). Subsequent passages are cited in the text. The play was recently reissued as part of a compilation of other homosexual plays in Manfred Herzer, ed., *Jasminblüthe: Schwule deutschsprachige Theaterstücke um 1900* (Hamburg: Männerschwarm Verlag, 2018). Reddi wrote literary pieces for a variety of Austrian newspapers. An earlier play, *Valet*, was apparently staged in his hometown of Graz in 1902. See the entry for him on the website of the Franz-Nabl-Institute für Literaturforschung, accessed 30 January 2023, https://franz-nabl-institut.uni-graz.at/de/bestaende/vor-und-nachlaesse/bestandsuebersicht/reddi-franz/.

75 Thomas Elsaesser, "Tales of Sound and Fury: Observations on the Family Melodrama," in *Imitations of Life: A Reader on Film & Television Melodrama*, ed. Marcia Landy (Detroit: Wayne State UP, 1991), 79.

76 Manfred Herzer contends that the play was designed as "a critical illustration of Magnus Hirschfeld's *Zwischenstufenlehre* [theory of sexual intermediaries]." Herzer, *Jasminblüthe*, 11. In addition, the characters' reference to the suicide of a young man (Brachfeld) on his honeymoon seems to allude to Hirschfeld's patient.

77 On eugenic thinking in Germany, see Paul Weindling, *Health, Race and German Politics between National Unification and Nazism, 1870–1945* (Cambridge: Cambridge UP, 1989).

78 Herzer, *Jasminblüthe*, 12. Ewers, who was involved in both the WhK and in Adolf Brand's masculinist circle, the *Gemeinschaft der Eigenen* (the community of the special), became a bestselling author and screenplay writer, who joined the Nazi Party in 1931 but fell out of favour by 1934, when his works were banned.

79 Albert Eulenburg, "Zur Einführung (Introduction to Hanns Heinz Ewers's 1905 drama *Enterbt*)," in *Jasminblüte: Schwule deutschsprachige Theaterstücke um 1900*, ed. Manfred Herzer (Hamburg: Männerschwarm, 2018), 126.

80 Williams, "Melodrama Revised," 62.

81 "Prozeß v. Moltke-Harden," *Vossische Zeitung*, 23 October 1907, evening edition, 2.

82 Peter Rosegger, "Im Gerichtssaal (1906)," in *Abenddämmerung: Rückblicke auf den Schauplatz des Lebens* (Leipzig: L. Staackmann, 1919), 229–30.

83 Domeier, *The Eulenburg Affair*, 71.

84 "Prozeß v. Moltke-Harden," *Vossische Zeitung*, 23 October 1907, evening edition, 2.

85 Heinrich Ilgenstein, "Mein System: Bekenntnisse von Maximilian Harden mit verbindendem Text von Heinrich Ilgenstein," *Das Blaubuch*, 31 October 1907, 1329. The quote stems from Harden's denunciation of the Social Democratic Party's 1902 campaign to "out" the armaments industrialist Friedrich Alfred Krupp, who died shortly thereafter (possibly from suicide).

86 As Domeier notes, the German public had never before been granted such access to the intimate goings-on in the bedroom of the Wilhelminian elite. Domeier, *The Eulenburg Affair*, 96.
87 McLaren, *The Trials of Masculinity*, 37–8.
88 Brooks, *The Melodramatic Imagination*, 31.
89 Karsten Hecht argues that the grounds by which the state prosecutor declined to take on Moltke's case are unconvincing. See "Die Harden-Prozesse: Strafverfahren, Öffentlichkeit und Politik im Kaiserreich" (PhD diss., University of Munich, 1997), 60. Others have speculated that the decision to decline was politically motivated and came from Bülow. See Peter Winzen, *Das Ende der Kaiserherrlichkeit: Die Skandalprozesse um die homosexuellen Berater Wilhelms II. 1907–1909* (Cologne: Böhlau, 2010), 56–65; Martin Kohlrausch, *Der Monarch im Skandal: Die Logik der Massenmedien und die Transformation der wilhelminischen Monarchie*, Elitenwandel in der Moderne, ed. Heinz Reif (Berlin: Akademie Verlag, 2005), 186–91.
90 Ann Goldberg, *Honor, Politics, and the Law in Imperial Germany, 1871–1914*, New Studies in European History (Cambridge: Cambridge UP, 2010), 30.
91 Goldberg, *Honor, Politics, and the Law*, 35.
92 In addition to the novice judge named Dr. Kern, the panel that heard the case included two jurors, Friedrich Schieggas, a dairyman, and Emil Neubauer, a master butcher. In conservative circles, having such commoners adjudicate the honour of a Prussian officer and nobleman was itself viewed as an affront to Moltke's honour.
93 Harden eventually heard from others about possible dalliances and parties Moltke had thrown. See Peter Winzen, *Freundesliebe am Hof Kaiser Wilhelms II* (Norderstedt: Books on Demand, 2010), 113.
94 The marriage itself was imbued with political significance because the Kaiser had attended the marriage ceremony and was, in fact, one of the official witnesses. Domeier, *The Eulenburg Affair*, 95.
95 See McLaren, *The Trials of Masculinity*, 95–6.
96 Hugo Friedlaender, "Der Beleidigungsprozeß des Berliner Stadtkommandanten Generalleutnant z.D. Graf Kuno von Moltke gegen den Herausgeber der 'Zukunft' Maximilian Harden," in *Interessante Kriminal-Prozesse*, ed. Hugo Friedlaender (Berlin: Hermann Barsdorf, 1919; rept., vol. 51 of Digitale Bibliothek, CD-ROM), 3991 (pages cited hereafter in the text). Friedlaender's transcript omits the question posed by Justice Kern, which, however, was printed as part of the transcript published in "Prozeß v. Moltke-Harden," *Vossische Zeitung*, 2 October 1907, morning edition, 19.
97 Hecht, "Die Harden-Prozesse," 107.

98 William Harbutt Dawson, a contemporary British author of several books about Imperial Germany, described Christmas as "a festival dear beyond all others to Germans, Protestant and Catholics alike … Throughout Germany [Christmas Eve] is a universal stay-at-home evening. Every family virtually closes its door to the whole world after the sun has set, and the remaining hours of the day are spent in the seclusion of the domestic circle." *Germany and the Germans*, 2 vols., vol. 1 (New York: D. Appleton & Company, 1894), 369–70. On the importance of Christmas in Germany at this time, see also Joe Perry, *Christmas in Germany: A Cultural History* (Chapel Hill: U of North Carolina P, 2010).

99 I borrow the translations of the nicknames from Steakley, "Iconography of a Scandal," 28. The original German words literally mean: my soul, my little old one, my only dachshund. Friedlaender omits Elbe's first sentence, which can be found in the transcript reproduced in the *Vossische Zeitung*: "Prozeß v. Moltke-Harden," *Vossische Zeitung*, 24 October 1907, morning edition, 19.

100 Brooks, *The Melodramatic Imagination*, 44.

101 Brooks, *The Melodramatic Imagination*, 26.

102 According to Hirschfeld, Dr. Kern posed to him the question: "If the sworn testimony of Frau von Elbe, as the court believes, is based on the truth, would you then consider Count Moltke a homosexual?" In Magnus Hirschfeld, *Sexualpsychologie und Volkspsychologie: Eine epikritische Studie zum Harden-Prozess* (Leipzig: Georg H. Wigand, 1908), 8. This question does not appear in various transcripts of the trial. Because Prussian courts did not keep their own stenographers, newspapers sent their own stenographers and produced their own transcripts of major trials. At many points, they merely summarized discussions rather than providing verbatim accounts. For a legal critique of the trial's two forensic reports, see Hecht, "Die Harden-Prozesse," 134–5.

103 "Prozeß v. Moltke-Harden," *Vossische Zeitung*, 23 October 1907, evening edition, 3. Words to similar effect appear in "Der Beleidigungsprozeß Moltke gegen Harden," 4051.

104 From 1907 to 1909, Hirschfeld and Freud – in their mutual search for supporters against the hostile attacks from Moll and others in the scientific-medical community – began to work together, with Hirschfeld visiting Freud for the first time in the spring of 1908, and Freud making donations to the WhK. Because of the foundational differences in methodologies and the conceptualization of homosexuality, the collaboration was rather short-lived. See Herzer, *Magnus Hirschfeld und seine Zeit*, 144–53; Volkmar Sigusch, "The Sexologist Albert Moll – between Sigmund Freud and Magnus Hirschfeld," *Medical History* 56, no. 2 (2012): 98. For a thorough treatment of struggle between Hirschfeld and

psychoanalysis for "clinical authority," see Katie Sutton, *Sex between Body and Mind: Psychoanalysis and Sexology in the German-speaking World, 1890s-1930* (Ann Arbor: U of Michigan P, 2019).
105 Brooks, "Psychoanalysis and Melodrama," 179.
106 Halperin, *How to Do the History of Homosexuality*, 117–21.
107 Foucault, *The History of Sexuality, Vol. I*, 43.
108 Spector, *Violent Sensations*, 145. See also Frank Bösch, *Öffentliche Geheimnisse: Skandale, Politik und Medien in Deutschland und Großbritannien, 1880–1914* (Munich: R. Oldenbourg, 2009), 43. In fact, the Harden-Moltke-Eulenburg trials were responsible for introducing the concept of homosexuality into popular usage in France. See Didier Eribon, "Michel Foucault's Histories of Sexuality," *GLQ* 7, no. 1 (2001): 53.
109 Based on letters written by the longtime WhK member Günther Graf von der Schulenburg, Winzen believes that Hirschfeld may also have been feeding Harden information about the Liebenberg group behind the scenes, just as he apparently also helped the SPD newspaper *Vorwärts* with its exposé of Krupp. See Peter Winzen, "Der erste politische Homosexualitätsskandal im Kaiserreich: Friedrich Alfred Krupp (1854–1902)," *Archiv für Kulturgeschichte* 93, no. 2 (2011): 428–9.
110 Hirschfeld's affidavit, which relied exclusively on Elbe's testimony, did not follow recommendations for forensic testimony laid out by Albert Moll, his nemesis in sexological circles, such as a complete medical examination of the individual (which, admittedly, may not have been possible in this case). See Albert Moll, *Sexuelle Perversionen, Geisteskrankheit und Zurechnungsfähigkeit* (Berlin: Leonhard Simion Nf, 1906), 21–2. More importantly, Moll also warned forensic doctors to resist the urge to state their opinions with too much confidence and certainty. See Albert Moll, *Ärztliche Ethik: Die pflichten des Arztes in allen Beziehungen seiner Thätigkeit* (Stuttgart: Ferdinand Enke, 1909), 464. For a biting critique of Hirschfeld's testimony, see Dr. H. Handtke, "Sachverständigenrappel," *Der Deutsche* 7, no. 7 (10 November 1907): 193–8.
111 Hirschfeld, "Jahresbericht 1905–1906," 1320. See also Steakley, *The Homosexual Emancipation Movement in Germany*, 32–3; Manfred Herzer, *Magnus Hirschfeld: Leben und Werk eines jüdischen, schwulen und sozialistischen Sexologen* (Frankfurt/Main: Campus Verlag, 1992), 70–2.
112 This, as it turns out, was not the case with Hohenau. Because of rumours about his homosexuality, General Gustav von Kessel had sought out the head of the police department vice detail, Hans von Tresckow, to see if they could be verified. Though Tresckow told Kessel that he had no incontrovertible evidence, the police commissioner had himself earlier warned Hohenau to keep a lower profile. Hans von Tresckow, *Von*

Fürsten und anderen Sterblichen: Erinnerungen eines Kriminalkommissars (Berlin: F. Fontane & Co., 1922), 119.
113 Brooks, *The Melodramatic Imagination*, 41.
114 Camill Schaible, *Standes- und Berufspflichten des deutschen Offizierkorps: Für angehende und jüngere Offiziere des stehenden Heeres und des Beurlaubtenstandes*, 3rd revised ed. (Berlin: R. Eisenschmidt, 1896), 51.
115 McLaren, *The Trials of Masculinity*, 55–6.
116 Spector notes a similar move in other trials from this period. See Spector, *Violent Sensations*, 158–65.
117 Sedgwick, *Epistemology of the Closet*, 70.
118 Because this move stemmed from the state's displeasure with the outcome, Hecht deems this an abuse of state power. Nevertheless, as Hecht acknowledges, most commentators believed that taking over a *Privatklage* was well within the state prosecutor's legal power, especially after the publicity surrounding the first trial did in fact damage the reputation of the state. See Hecht, "Die Harden-Prozesse," 192–3.
119 After Eulenburg swore under oath in both the second Harden-Moltke trial as well as Bülow's criminal libel trial against Adolf Brand that he had never committed sexual acts with a man, Harden arranged a trial in Bavaria in which two men testified to the contrary. After a short delay, Prussian authorities arrested the former diplomat, who was then tried for perjury. Because of real or feigned illness, however, the trial, which began in July 1908, was never completed before his death in 1921. But his fall from grace was permanent.
120 Olaf Jessen, *Die Moltkes: Biographie einer Familie* (Munich: C.H. Beck, 2010), 301.
121 The letter has apparently gone missing. See Hull, *Entourage*, 139.
122 "Das Urteil im Prozeß Moltke-Harden," *Vossische Zeitung*, 29 October 1907, evening edition, 1.
123 Hirschfeld reported in December that in front of his door fliers were distributed for an anti-Semitic lecture with the title "Dr. Hirschfeld, a public danger – Jews are our undoing!" "Zur Klärung," *Monatsbericht des wissenschaftlich-humanitäres Komitees* 6, no. 12 (1 December 1907), 232.
124 Hirschfeld, *Sexualpsychologie und Volkspsychologie*, 6–7.
125 *Stenographische Berichte. XII. Legislaturperiode. I. Session*, vol. 229 (1908), 1916.
126 *Stenographische Berichte. XII. Legislaturperiode. I. Session*, vol. 229 (1908), 1916.
127 Hirschfeld, *Sexualpsychologie und Volkspsychologie*, 26.
128 Hirschfeld, *Sexualpsychologie und Volkspsychologie*, 26 (emphasis in original).
129 Using the prosecution of three officers between 20 November and 20 December 1907, as indicative of the army's overall campaign against

homosexuals, one "legal contributor" to the journal that replaced the *Monatsbericht* "calculated out" that Paragraph 175 produced more "casualties" than the 1165 officers who fell in battle during the Franco-Prussian War. The tactical shift from melodrama to dubious statistics was hardly likely to be any more effective. "Materialien," *Zeitschrift für Sexualwissenschaft* 1 (January 1908): 61n*.
130 Hirschfeld, "Zur Klärung," 229.
131 Magnus Hirschfeld, "Einleitung und Situations-Bericht," *Vierteljahresberichte des Wissenschaftlich-humanitäres Komitees* 1, no. 1 (October 1909): 3. The scandal led to a proposed revision to Paragraph 175, which would have increased punishments and extended prohibitions against lesbian sex acts. Because these revisions were never enacted, Dickinson concludes that "the crisis was relatively short-lived." Dickinson, *Sex, Freedom, and Power*, 172. Yet even though financial contributions to the WhK started to increase by 1910, the organization never regained the membership and momentum it had attained in October 1907. See Herzer, *Magnus Hirschfeld und seine Zeit*, 180–2.
132 *Stenographische Berichte. XII. Legislaturperiode. I. Session*, vol. 229 (1908), 1916.
133 Hirschfeld, *Sexualpsychologie und Volkspsychologie*, 11.
134 Hirschfeld, *Sexualpsychologie und Volkspsychologie*, 12.

2. Disciplinary Abuses: From Military Secrecy to Sadism in the Army

1 Edward Field, "A Lesson from History," *United Service: A Monthly Review of Military and Naval Affairs* 7 (1892): 353.
2 Hartmut Wiedner, "Soldatenmißhandlungen im Wilhelminischen Kaiserreich (1890–1914)," *Archiv für Sozialgeschichte* 22 (1982): 162. France was the first military to ban corporal punishment during the French Revolution. In Imperial Germany, some forms of corporal punishment were allowed in penal and work units as well as during wartime. Other major armies continued to resort to the lash, at least for certain crimes, until much later: 1861 in the US, 1863 in Russia, and 1881 in Britain. See John Keep, "Justice for the Troops: A Comparative Study of Nicholas I's Russia and France under Louis-Philippe," *Cahiers du Monde russe et soviétique* 28, no. 1 (1987): 44; George Breckenridge Davis, *A Treatise on the Military Law of the United States*, 2nd ed. (New York: John Wiley & Sons, 1908), 407; Aurele J. Violette, "Judicial Reforms in the Russian Navy during the 'Era of Great Reforms': The Reform Act of 1867 and the Abolition of Corporal Punishment," *The Slavonic and East European Review* 56, no. 4 (1978): 598; Peter Burroughs, "Crime and Punishment in the British Army, 1815–1870," *The English Historical Review* 100, no. 396 (1985): 564.

3 Rudolf Krafft, *Kasernen-Elend: Offene Kritik der Verhältnisse unserer Unteroffiziere und Soldaten* (Stuttgart: Verlag von Robert Lutz, 1895), 11. While Krafft condemns this absolute obedience, German military leaders did acknowledge this ideal openly. For instance, the author of an article on education and instruction in the professional journal devoted to military studies conceded that a soldier "is forced for the time to submit unconditionally to the will of another by relinquishing every thought; it is, in a manner of speaking, a mechanical habit of obedience appropriately called 'Kadavergehorsam,' and which in a military training [*Erziehung*] can never be dispensed with." "Ausbildung und Erziehung: Eine psychologische Studie (Part I)," *Militär-Wochenblatt* 78, no. 65 (1893): 1694.

4 The term *Kadavergehorsam* originated in reference to the submission originally expected of Jesuits. On the origin of this word, see "Kadavergehorsam," in *Digitales Wörterbuch der Deutschen Sprache*, ed. Alexander Geyken (Berlin: Berlin-Brandenburgische Akademie der Wissenschaften), accessed 15 December 2022, http://www.dwds.de/?qu=Kadavergehorsam. This work draws on Wolfgang Pfeifer, *Etymologisches Wörterbuch des Deutschen*, 2nd ed. (Berlin: Akademie-Verlag, 1993), http://www.dwds.de/.

5 See Dennis E. Showalter, "Army and Society in Imperial Germany: The Pains of Modernization," *Journal of Contemporary History* 18, no. 4 (1983): 601; Wiedner, "Soldatenmißhandlungen," 159.

6 *Stenographische Berichte. VIII. Legislaturperiode. I. Session 1890/91*, vol. 3 (1891), 2039.

7 *Stenographische Berichte. VIII. Legislaturperiode. I. Session 1890/91*, vol. 3 (1891), 2039. Meyers's conversational encyclopedia insisted that these perceptions of Fehmic courts were based "on exaggeration." *Meyers Konversations-Lexikon*, 4th ed., vol. 6 (Leipzig: Verlag des Bibliographischen Instituts, 1890), 125.

8 Max Weber, *Economy and Society: An Outline of Interpretive Sociology*, ed. Guenther Roth and Claus Wittich, trans. Ephraim Fishoff et al., vol. 2 (Berkeley: U of California P, 1978), 992–3.

9 See Gordon A. Craig, *The Politics of the Prussian Army, 1640–1945* (Oxford: Oxford UP, 1955), 219–32; Förster, *Der doppelte Militarismus*, 18.

10 *Stenographische Berichte. VIII. Legislaturperiode. I. Session 1890/92*, vol. 6 (1892), 4235.

11 Cited in Craig, *The Politics of the Prussian Army*, 247.

12 Weber, *Economy and Society*, vol. 2, 952 (emphasis in original). See Lisa Blank, "Two Schools for Secrecy: Defining Secrecy from the Works of Max Weber, Georg Simmel, Edward Shils and Sissela Bok," in *Government Secrecy: Classic and Contemporary Readings*, ed. Susan L. Maret and Jan Goldman (Westport, CT: Libraries Unlimited, 2009), 65.

13 Georg Simmel, "The Sociology of Secrecy and of Secret Societies," *The American Journal of Sociology* 11, no. 4 (1906): 441–98. The first German-language version appeared two years later as Georg Simmel, "Das Geheimnis und die geheime Gesellschaft," in *Soziologie: Untersuchungen über die Formen der Vergesellschaftung* (Leipzig: Duncker & Humblot, 1908), 337–402.
14 Simmel, "Sociology of Secrecy," 465.
15 Foucault, *The History of Sexuality, Vol. I*, 57.
16 Foucault, *The History of Sexuality, Vol. I*, 57.
17 Foucault, *The History of Sexuality, Vol. I*, 35 (emphasis in original).
18 Foucault, *The History of Sexuality, Vol. I*, 57.
19 Two recent exceptions to this trend are Hans Rudolf Wahl, *Die Religion des deutschen Nationalismus: Eine mentalitätsgeschichtliche Studie zur Literatur des Kaiserreichs: Felix Dahn, Ernst von Wildenbruch, Walter Flex* (Heidelberg: C. Winter, 2002); and Torsten Leutert, *Ernst von Wildenbruchs historische Dramen* (Frankfurt/Main: Peter Lang, 2004). Neither work, however, addresses Wildenbruch's prose.
20 Ernst von Wildenbruch, "Das edle Blut," *Deutsche Rundschau* 73 (1892): 1–20; Ernst von Wildenbruch, *Das edle Blut*, 24th ed. (Berlin: Freund & Jeckel, 1896). The Grote'sche Verlagsbuchhandlung reprinted *Das edle Blut* regularly in an illustrated edition, most likely for boys: Ernst von Wildenbruch, *Das edle Blut: Eine Erzählung. Neue Ausgabe mit Zeichnungen von Carl Röhling*, 75th ed. (Berlin: Grote Verlag, 1905); Ernst von Wildenbruch, *Das edle Blut: Eine Erzählung. Mit Zeichnungen von H. Skarbina*, 239th–240th eds. (Berlin: Grote Verlag, 1969).
21 By the early 1900s, there were many competing editions of the story as a graded German reader for US students. See, for instance, Ernst von Wildenbruch, *Das edle Blut*, With Introduction, Notes, Vocabularly, and Exercises, ed. Ashley K. Hardy (New York: Henry Holt and Company, 1906); Ernst von Wildenbruch, *Das edle Blut*, With Introduction, Notes, Exercises and Vocabulary, ed. Lee M. Hollander (New York: F.S. Crofts, 1927). Though W.C. Decker complained in 1933 about the continued popularity of Wildenbruch on American syllabi, William I. Schreiber greeted yet another American version of *Das edle Blut* in 1944 as "long overdue." W.C. Decker, "What Shall We Read?," *German Quarterly* 6, no. 1 (1933), 28–38; William I. Schreiber, "[Review of *Das edle Blut*]," *The Modern Language Journal* 29, no. 6 (1945), 558.
22 Ernst von Wildenbruch, *Das edle Blut*, 24th ed., 1. For convenience sake, I will cite from the excellent English translation with subsequent page numbers given in the text: Ernst von Wildenbruch, "Noble Blood," in *The German Classics of the Nineteenth and Twentieth Centuries: Masterpieces of German Literature Translated into English*, ed. Kuno Francke and William Howard, trans. Muriel Almon, vol. 17 (Albany, NY: J.B. Lyon, 1913), 125.

23 Martin Swales, *The German Novelle* (Princeton, NJ: Princeton UP, 1977), 39.
24 Simmel, "Sociology of Secrecy," 462.
25 Since the military leadership viewed contact with civilians as "a threat to the development of soldiers much as might a disease to a newborn," these cadet schools relied on architecture to isolate cadets from the rest of society. John Moncure, *Forging the King's Sword: Military Education between Tradition and Modernization: The Case of the Royal Prussian Cadet Corps, 1871–1918* (New York: Peter Lang, 1993), 104.
26 See the entry for "Koppel" in the *Digitales Wörterbuch der Deutschen Sprache*, accessed 15 December 2022, https://www.dwds.de/wb/Koppel; and *Oxford English Dictionary*, 12th ed., s.v. "copulate."
27 On the "King's Cadets," see Moncure, *Forging the King's Sword*, 90–3.
28 According to Hirschfeld, Wildenbruch was initially approached by Prince Georg of Prussia, a member of the extended royal family and a homosexual supporter of Hirschfeld's Scientific-Humanitarian Committee. Hirschfeld, *Von einst bis jetzt*, 94.
29 In memoirs by graduates of Prussia's military academies, many "recalled with horror" brutal punishments and "orgies of torture." See Moncure, *Forging the King's Sword*, 204.
30 Slavoj Žižek, *How to Read Lacan*, ed. Simon Critchley, How to Read (New York: W.W. Norton, 2006), 79.
31 Moncure, *Forging the King's Sword*, 110.
32 Simmel, "Sociology of Secrecy," 482.
33 Simmel, "Sociology of Secrecy," 472.
34 Slavoj Žižek, *The Plague of Fantasies* (London: Verso, 1997), 22. Though Simmel distinguishes between lying – as an act of commission – and secrecy – as an act of omission – the distinction seems less important than the common nature of deception, and the fact that the cadets share in their knowledge of it.
35 Simmel, "Sociology of Secrecy," 465.
36 Simmel, "Sociology of Secrecy," 466.
37 Simmel, "Sociology of Secrecy," 465–6.
38 Simmel, "Sociology of Secrecy," 461.
39 See Wilhelm Deist, "Die Armee in Staat und Gesellschaft, 1890–1914," in *Militär, Staat und Gesellschaft: Studien zur preußisch-deutschen Militärgeschichte* (Munich: R. Oldenbourg, 1991), 29.
40 Žižek, *How to Read Lacan*, 105–6.
41 The terminology of "severe, persistent and pervasive" is currently used today to define harassment. See "Sexual Harassment Guidance 1997," Department of Education, Office of Civil Rights, 1997, accessed 20 July 2022, https://www2.ed.gov/about/offices/list/ocr/docs/sexhar01.html.

42 Werner Salomon, "Ein Geheimbefehl Herzog Georgs von Sachsen vom Juni 1891 zur Frage der Soldatenmißhandlungen," *Militärgeschichte* 16, no. 5 (1977): 586–7.
43 *Stenographische Berichte. VIII. Legislaturperiode. II. Session 1892/93*, vol. 3 (1893), 2031.
44 *Stenographische Berichte. VIII. Legislaturperiode. II. Session 1892/93*, vol. 3 (1893), 2038.
45 Simmel, "Sociology of Secrecy," 463.
46 See "Strafgerichts-Ordnung," *Bundes-Gesetzblatt des Norddeutschen Bundes*, no. 12 (1867): 229–82.
47 *Stenographische Berichte. VIII. Legislaturperiode. I. Session 1890/92*, vol. 6 (1892), 4259.
48 See Craig, *The Politics of the Prussian Army*, 246–51.
49 See Helge Berndt, "Zur Reform der Militärstrafgerichtsordnung 1898. Die Haltung der Partein im Reichstag," *MGM* 14, no. 2 (1973): 24–26.
50 *Stenographische Berichte. VIII. Legislaturperiode. I. Session 1890/92*, vol. 6 (1892), 4221.
51 See Berndt, "Zur Reform der Militärstrafgerichtsordnung 1898," 14.
52 Berndt, "Zur Reform der Militärstrafgerichtsordnung 1898," 25.
53 Salomon, "Ein Geheimbefehl Herzog Georgs," 587–8.
54 Otto Ernst Schmidt, "Soldaten oder Menschen? Ein Wort über militärische Erziehung und Soldatenmißhandlung," in *Buch der Hoffnung: Neue Folge der gesammelten Essays aus Literatur, Pädagogik und öffentlichem Leben* (Hamburg: Verlag von Conrad Kloß, 1896), 179.
55 Wiedner, "Soldatenmißhandlungen," 184.
56 Richard von Krafft-Ebing, *Neue Forschungen auf dem Gebiet der Psychopathia Sexualis: Eine medicinisch-psychologische Studie* (Stuttgart: Verlag von Ferdinand Enke, 1890).
57 Oosterhuis, *Stepchildren of Nature*, 152.
58 Albrecht Eulenburg, *Sadismus und Masochismus*, ed. Dr. L. Loewenfeld and Dr. Hans Kurella, vol. 19, Grenzfragen des Nerven- und Seelenlebens: Einzeldarstellungen für Gebildete aller Stände im Vereine mit hervorragenden Fachmännern des In- und Auslandes (Wiesbaden: J.F. Bergmann, 1902); Iwan Bloch, *Beiträge zur Aetiologie der Psychopathia sexualis*, vol. 2 (Dresden: H.R. Dohrn, 1903), 23–118; Freud, *Three Essays on the Theory of Sexuality*, 157–60.
59 Krafft-Ebing, *Neue Forschungen*, 1.
60 Krafft-Ebing, *Psychopathia Sexualis*, 7th ed. (1892), 61.
61 Eulenburg, *Sadimus und Masochismus*, 3.
62 Eulenburg, *Sadimus und Masochismus*, 9 (emphasis in original).
63 Eulenburg, *Sadimus und Masochismus*, 9.
64 Foucault, *The History of Sexuality, Vol. I*, 35 (emphasis in original).

65 Other examples include P. Näcke, "Forensisch-psychiatrisch-psychologische Randglossen zum Prozesse Dippold, insbesondere über Sadismus," *Archiv für Kriminalanthropologie und Kriminalistik* 13, no. 4 (1903), 350–72; D.K. Korell, *Pädagogische Irrwege oder Sadismus* (Berlin: Hugo Bermühler Verlag, 1904).

66 Hans Rau, *Der Sadismus in der Armee* (Berlin: Hugo Bermühler Verlag, 1904). Subsequent page numbers from *Der Sadismus* are cited in the text. See also Hans Rau, *Wollust und Schmerz: Eine psychologische Studie* (Oranienburg: Orania-Verlag, 1904); Hans Rau, *Die Grausamkeit mit besonderer Bezugnahme auf sexuelle Faktoren*, 3rd ed. (Berlin: Hermann Barsdorf Verlag, 1913 [1903]); Hans Rau, *Der Geschlechtstrieb und seine Verirrungen. Ein Beitrag zur Seelenkunde* (Berlin: Hugo Steinitz, 1903).

67 *Monatsbericht des Wissenschaftlich-humanitären Komitees* 5, no. 7 (1 July 1906): 159.

68 See, for example, Hans Rau, *Liebesfreiheit! Urninge und Tribaden: Ein Aufruf an das Volk* (Oranienburg: Orania-Verlag, 1903); Hans Rau, *Franz Grillparzer und sein Liebesleben* (Berlin: Barsdorf, 1904); A. Sper, *Lustmörder der Neuzeit* (Berlin: Berliner Zeitschriften-Vertrieb, 1904); A. Sper, *Capri und die Homosexuellen* (Oranienburg: Orania-Verlag, 1903).

69 Leo Berg, "Grausamkeit," in *Aus der Zeit. – Gegen die Zeit: Gesammelte Essays* (Berlin: Hüpeden & Merzyn, 1905), 398–9.

70 See, for example, Dr. Georg Back, *Sexuelle Verirrungen des Menschen und der Natur*, 2nd and 3rd eds. (Berlin: Standard-Verlag, 1910), 329–30.

71 Ernst Keller, "Soldatenmisshandlungen," *Sozialistische Monatshefte* 14, no. 2 (1905): 138.

72 *Stenographische Berichte. XI. Legislaturperiode. II. Session 1905/1906*, vol. 3 (1906), 2446.

73 *Stenographische Berichte. XI. Legislaturperiode. II. Session 1905/1906*, vol. 3 (1906), 2446.

74 Gilles Deleuze, *Coldness and Cruelty* (New York: Zone, 1991), 76.

75 Gayle S. Rubin, "Thinking Sex: Notes for a Radical Theory of the Politics of Sexuality," in *The Lesbian and Gay Studies Reader*, ed. Henry Abelove, Michèle Aina Barale, and David M. Halperin (New York: Routledge, 1993), 11.

76 Compiled from the *Monatsberichte des Wissenschaftlich-humanitären Komitees*, 1905–7. For the text of the criminal code, see Oppenhoff, *Strafgesetzbuch für das Deutsche Reich*, 422.

77 *Militär-Strafgesetzbuch vom 20. Juni 1872. Verordnung über die Disziplinar-Strafordnung für das deutsche Heer vom 31. Oktober 1872. Vorschriften über den Dienstweg und die Behandlung von Beschwerden der MilitärPersonen des Heeres und der Marine, sowie der Civilbeamten der Militär- und Marine-Verwaltung vom 6. März 1873. Kriegs-Artikel für das Heer vom 31. Oktober*

1872. Amtliche Ausgabe (Berlin: Ernst Siegfried Mittler und Sohn, 1883), 26–9.
78 *Monatsbericht des Wissenschaftlich-humanitären Komitees* 4, no. 12 (1 December 1905): 11.
79 *Monatsbericht des Wissenschaftlich-humanitären Komitees* 5, no. 3 (1 March 1906): 69.
80 There was a great deal of confusion in this period about which sexual acts between men constituted a violation of Paragraph 175. Generally, mutual masturbation was held to be legal (if morally wrong), while oral and anal sex were deemed crimes. See Jörg Hutter, "Die Entstehung des § 175 im Strafgesetzbuch und die Geburt der deutschen Sexualwissenschaft," in *Männerliebe im alten Deutschland: Sozialgeschichtliche Abhandlungen*, ed. Rüdiger Lautmann and Angela Taeger (Berlin: Rosa Winkel, 1992), 217; Tobin, "Sexology in the Southwest," 145–6.
81 Friedlaender, "Der Beleidigungsprozeß Moltke gegen Harden," 4014.
82 "Ein politischer Sensationsprozeß," *Volksstimme*, 26 October 1907, 2.
83 *Stenographische Berichte. XII. Legislaturperiode. I. Session*, vol. 229 (1908), 1875.
84 *Stenographische Berichte. XII. Legislaturperiode. I. Session*, vol. 229 (1908), 1875.
85 *Stenographische Berichte. XII. Legislaturperiode. I. Session*, vol. 229 (1908), 1875.
86 Königlich Preußischen Kriegsministerium, ed., *Kompendium über Militärrecht* (Berlin: Ernst Siegfried Mittler und Sohn, 1900), 209.
87 *Stenographische Berichte. XII. Legislaturperiode. I. Session*, vol. 229 (1908), 1913.
88 *Stenographische Berichte. XII. Legislaturperiode. I. Session*, vol. 229 (1908), 1914.
89 Simmel, "Sociology of Secrecy," 465.
90 Steakley, *Die Freunde des Kaisers: Die Eulenburg-Affäre im Spiegel zeitgenössischer Karikaturen*, 12–13.
91 Ursula E. Koch, "Politische Bildzensur in Deutschland bis 1914," *Jahrbuch für Kommunikationsgeschichte* 16 (2014): 141. As Koch notes, because of the wide distribution of these satirical magazines in cafes, libraries, barbershops, and even military officers' clubs, their readership extended far beyond their print runs.
92 Koch, "Politische Bildzensur in Deutschland bis 1914," 137; Ann Taylor Allen, *Satire and Society in Wilhelmine Germany: Kladderadatsch and Simplicissimus, 1890–1914* (Lexington: UP of Kentucky 2014), 3.
93 "Ein politischer Sensationsprozeß," *Volksstimme*, 26 October 1907, 2.
94 The *New York Times* focused on Hohenau more than Lynar, since he was higher in military rank and nobility and had a close relationship with the Kaiser. See "Von Hohenau Trial Opens: Editor Harden, Suffering from Appendicitis, Unable to be Present," *New York Times*, 23 January 1908, 7; "Von Hohenau Acquitted: Court of Honor Finds Him Guiltless – Lynar Sentenced to Jail," *New York Times*, 23 January 1908, 3.

95 "Prozeß Lynar-Hohenau," *Freiburger Zeitung*, 24 January 1908, Morning edition, 2.
96 "Prozess Lynar und Hohenau," *Volksstimme*, 23 January 1908, 3.
97 "Prozess Hohenau-Lynar," *Volksstimme*, 24 January 1908, 8.
98 "Hohenau freigesprochen, Lynar verurteilt," *Volksstimme*, 25 January 1908, 2.
99 *Stenographische Berichte. XII. Legislaturperiode. I. Session*, vol. 230 (1908), 2894.
100 Resolution Nr. 614 in *Stenographische Berichte. XII. Legislaturperiode. I. Session*, vol. 245 (1908), 3638.
101 *Stenographische Berichte*, vol. 230 (1908), 2846.
102 *Stenographische Berichte*, vol. 230 (1908), 2872.
103 *Stenographische Berichte*, vol. 230 (1908), 2895.
104 *Stenographische Berichte*, vol. 230 (1908), 2908.
105 *Stenographische Berichte*, vol. 230 (1908), 2892.

3. The Obscure Object of Desire: Uniform Fetishism, Male Prostitution, and German Soldiers

1 See Ulrichs, *The Riddle of "Man-Manly" Love*, vol. 1, 224.
2 Ulrichs, *The Riddle of "Man-Manly" Love*, vol. 1, 230, 225.
3 Ulrichs, *The Riddle of "Man-Manly" Love*, vol. 1, 241.
4 Ulrichs, *The Riddle of "Man-Manly" Love*, vol. 1, 133–4, 192. As a result of revolutionary unrest in Frankfurt in 1833, Prussia, Austria, and Bavaria had stationed troops there to protect the Bundestag, which met in the city. See Henning Roet, "Frankfurt als Garnisonstadt zwischen 1866 und 1914: Mit besonderem Blick auf die Kriegervereine der Stadt," in *Garnisonstädte im 19. und 20. Jahrhundert*, ed. Robert Bohn and Michael Epkenhans (Bielefeld: Verlag für Regionalgeschichte, 2015), 109–18.
5 Ulrichs, *The Riddle of "Man-Manly" Love*, vol. 1, 210.
6 Between 1871 and 1914, the number of Imperial German garrisons grew from 347 to 450. Robert Bohn and Michael Epkenhans, eds., *Garnisonstädte im 19. und 20. Jahrhundert*, vol. 16, IZRG-Schriftenreihe (Bielefeld: Verlag für Regionalgeschichte, 2015), 7. For a directory of such garrisons, see *Verzeichnis der Garnisonorte der Deutschen Armee und der Kaiserlichen Marine mit Angabe der Truppenteile, Kommandobehörden usw. sowie der Ortsklassen für sämtliche Garnisonorte* (n.p.: n.p., 1910), http://reservistenkrugsammler.de/Garnisonsorte.php.
7 See *Bericht über die Gemeinde-Verwaltung der Stadt Berlin in den Jahren 1861–1876*, vol. 1 (Berlin: In Kommission bei Julius Sittenfeld, 1879), 50; *Bericht über die Gemeinde-Verwaltung der Stadt Berlin in den Jahren 1877–1881*, vol. 1 (Berlin: In Kommission bei Julius Sittenfeld, 1883), 93; *Bericht über die Gemeinde-Verwaltung der Stadt Berlin in den Jahren 1901–1905*, vol. 1 (Berlin: Carl Heymanns Verlag, 1907), 215.

8 Peter Fritzsche, *Reading Berlin 1900* (Cambridge, MA: Harvard UP, 1996), 7.
9 The Hobrecht Plan was commissioned to deal with the city's urban development beyond its eighteenth-century walls, which were taken down in the late 1860s to make room for additional growth. See Claus Bernet, "The 'Hobrecht Plan' (1862) and Berlin's Urban Structure," *Urban History* 31, no. 3 (2004): 400–19.
10 Beachy, *Gay Berlin*, 47. See also Magnus Hirschfeld, *Berlins Drittes Geschlecht*, ed. Manfred Herzer (Berlin: Verlag Rosa Winkel, 1991), 65–114; Andreas Sternweiler, "Leben in der Unterdrückung," in *Goodbye to Berlin? 100 Jahre Schwulenbewegung. Eine Ausstellung*, ed. Schwules Museum and Berlin Akademie der Künste (Berlin: Verlag Rosa Winkel, 1997), 71.
11 Das Königliche Statistische Landesamt, ed., *Statistisches Jahrbuch für den Preußischen Staat* (Berlin: Verlag des Königlichen Statistischen Amtes, 1906), 3.
12 *Berlin Bericht, 1861–1876*, vol. 1, 50; Das Königliche Statistische Landesamt, ed., *Statistisches Jahrbuch für den Preußischen Staat* (Berlin: Verlag des Königlichen Statistischen Amtes, 1910), 3.
13 See the list provided in Kriegsministerium and Geheime Kriegs-Kanzlei, eds., *Rangliste der Königlich Preußischen Armee und des XIII. (Königlich Württembergischen) Armeekorps für 1911* (Berlin: Ernst Siegried Mittler und Sohn, 1911), 47–52.
14 Hirschfeld, *Berlins Drittes Geschlecht*, 96–7. English translation from Magnus Hirschfeld, *Berlin's Third Sex*, trans. James J. Conway (Berlin: Rixdorf Editions, 2017), 61.
15 Jens Dobler, personal communication with author, 2008. On the lack of information about homosexuality in the extant military archives, see Ute Frevert, *A Nation in Barracks: Conscription, Military Service and Civil Society in Modern Germany*, trans. Andrew Boreham and Daniel Brückenhaus (New York: Berg, 2004), 177. On homosexuality in the Berlin police archives, see Dobler, *Zwischen Duldungspolitik und Verbrechensbekämpfung*; Lücke, *Männlichkeit in Unordnung*, 38.
16 Tresckow, *Von Fürsten und anderen Sterblichen*.
17 On the Christian morality movement, see the first section in Dickinson, *Sex, Freedom, and Power*, 13–133.
18 Annette F. Timm and Joshua A. Sandborn, *Gender, Sex and the Shaping of Modern Europe: A History from the French Revolution to the Present Day*, 2nd ed. (London: Bloomsbury, 2016), 7.
19 Herzog, *Sexuality in Europe*, 7.
20 Ulrichs, *The Riddle of "Man-Manly" Love*, vol. 1, 210.
21 Ulrichs, *The Riddle of "Man-Manly" Love*, vol. 1, 286.
22 Rather than killing his primary blackmailer, Hasse had merely injured him. All three blackmailers were subsequently apprehended and prosecuted,

while Hasse was eventually deemed to have not acted voluntarily ("Ausschließung seiner freien Willenbestimmung") and released. See the brief discussion of the case in Friedlaender, "Der Beleidigungsprozeß Moltke gegen Harden," 9–10. For a fuller discussion of the case with reprints of newspaper articles and Reichstag debates, see Hirschfeld, "Jahresbericht 1905–1906," 952–1037.

23 See, for example, "Zeitungsmitteilungen," *Jahrbuch für sexuelle Zwischenstufen* 2 (1900): 457–8.
24 See Frevert, *A Nation in Barracks*, 191–3.
25 See Neff, "Wir wollen keine Paradetruppe …," 201.
26 Anonymous, *Das perverse Berlin: Kulturkritische Gänge* (Berlin: Eckstein, 1908), 94–5.
27 "Besoldung," in *Militär-Lexikon: Handwörterbuch der Militärwissenschaften*, ed. Hermann Frobenius (Berlin: Martin Oldenbourg, 1901), 83.
28 See Frank B. Tipton, *A History of Modern Germany Since 1815* (Berkeley: U of California P, 2003), 187.
29 Frevert, *A Nation in Barracks*, 178. To make ends meet, soldiers relied on shipments of food from home. As one working-class memoirist recalled of his field exercises during his military service, "whoever didn't get his care packages [*Speckpakete*] from home" and was forced to make do with only his allotment of regulation bread, "felt a truly ravenous hunger." Franz Rehbein, *Das Leben eines Landarbeiters*, ed. Paul Göhre (Jena: Eugen Diederichs, 1911), 180.
30 "Bericht der 1. Kommission über den Entwurf eines Besoldungsgesetztes. (Aktenstück Nr. 1615)," in *Verhandlungen des Reichstags. Stenographische Berichte. XII. Legislaturperiode. I. Session*, vol. 257 (1909), 9877.
31 Frevert, *A Nation in Barracks*, 178.
32 Tresckow, *Von Fürsten und anderen Sterblichen*, 123.
33 Tresckow, *Von Fürsten und anderen Sterblichen*, 185.
34 Tresckow, *Von Fürsten und anderen Sterblichen*, 181.
35 Tresckow, *Von Fürsten und anderen Sterblichen*, 182.
36 "Zeitungsmitteilungen," 448 (see n. 23).
37 See Dubout, *Der Richter und sein Tagebuch*, 113.
38 Tresckow, *Von Fürsten und anderen Sterblichen*, 185.
39 Ulrichs, *The Riddle of "Man-Manly" Love*, vol. 1, 247.
40 In fact, Hirschfeld reissued Ulrichs's pamphlets with some radical excisions, especially passages that mentioned anal penetration. Kennedy, *Karl Heinrich Ulrichs*, 152. On the respectability politics of the German homosexual emancipation movement, see Mosse, *Nationalism and Sexuality*, 23–47.
41 On the significance of Ostwald's series, see especially Peter Fritzsche, "Vagabond in the Fugitive City: Hans Ostwald, Imperial Berlin and the

Grossstadt-Dokumente," *Journal of Contemporary History* 29, no. 3 (1994): 385–402; Spector, *Violent Sensations*, 26–30.
42 Philippi, "Berlins drittes Geschlecht von Magnus Hirschfeld (Review)," *Monatshefte für praktische Dermatologie* 40, no. 4 (15 February 1905): 296.
43 Hirschfeld, *Berlins Drittes Geschlecht*, 97–8 (my translation). The term *Hingabe* derives from the verb *hingeben*, which was used euphemistically to refer to having intimate relations with a man. See the entry for "hingeben," in *Digitales Wörterbuch der Deutschen Sprache*, ed. Alexander Geyken (Berlin: Berlin-Brandenburgische Akademie der Wissenschaften), accessed 28 December 2022, https://www.dwds.de/wb/hingeben#d-1-4.
44 Hirschfeld, *Berlins Drittes Geschlecht*, 98 (my translation).
45 Hirschfeld, *Berlins Drittes Geschlecht*, 98. English translation from Hirschfeld, *Berlin's Third Sex*, 62.
46 Case 123, a businessman, explained that "real men, in close-fitting uniform, make the deepest impression on me; and if I have an opportunity to embrace and kiss such a ravishing fellow, ejaculation takes place at once, – a weakness which I attribute to my frequent masturbation." Richard von Krafft-Ebing, *Psychopathia Sexualis, with Especial Reference to Contrary Sexual Instinct: A Medio-Legal Study*, trans. Charles Gilbert Chaddock, MD, 7th enlarged and revised ed. (Philadelphia: F.A. Davis, 1894), 296.
47 Hirschfeld, *Berlins Drittes Geschlecht*, 90. English translation from Hirschfeld, *Berlin's Third Sex*, 58.
48 Hirschfeld, *Berlins Drittes Geschlecht*, 92 (my translation).
49 Hirschfeld, *Berlins Drittes Geschlecht*, 92. English translation from Hirschfeld, *Berlin's Third Sex*, 55–6.
50 Ulrichs, *The Riddle of "Man-Manly" Love*, vol. 1, 134 (my emphasis).
51 Hirschfeld, *Berlins Drittes Geschlecht*, 92–3 (my translation).
52 Hirschfeld's confidence in the value of this fictive scenario can be seen in his repeated use of it in his subsequent writings on male prostitution and Soldatenprostitution. See Magnus Hirschfeld, "Einiges über die Ursachen und Erscheinungsformen der männlichen (nicht erpresserischen) Prostitution," *Archiv für Kriminalanthropologie und Kriminalistik* 52 (1913): 360–1; Magnus Hirschfeld, *The Homosexuality of Men and Women*, trans. Michael A Lombardi-Nash (Amherst, NY: Prometheus, 2000), 837–8.
53 Hirschfeld, *Berlins Drittes Geschlecht*, 94–6.
54 Lisa Duggan, "The New Homonormativity: The Sexual Politics of Neoliberalism," in *Materializing Democracy: Toward a Revitalized Cultural Politics*, ed. Russ Castronovo and Dana D. Nelson (Durham, NC: Duke UP, 2002), 190.
55 Duggan, "The New Homonormativity: The Sexual Politics of Neoliberalism," 189.
56 Puar, *Terrorist Assemblages: Homonationalism in Queer Times*, xx, xxii (emphasis in original).

57 Dr. Hans von Liebig, "Die Grossstadtdokumente (Review)," *Die Umschau: Übersicht über die Forschritte und Bewegungen auf dem Gesamtgebiet der Wissenschaft, Technik, Literatur und Kunst* 11, no. 47 (16 November 1907): 936. The praise for its lack of piquancy comes from a report on a positive review in the *Monatsschrift für Darmkrankheiten und sexuelle Hygiene*, quoted in: "[Item 6]," *Monatsbericht des Wissenschaftlich-humanitären Komitees* 5, no. 3 (1 March 1906): 56. The final statement is from HB, "Großstadt-Dokumente," *Allgemeines Literaturblatt* 15, no. 17 (15 September 1906): 516.
58 See Dubout, *Der Richter und sein Tagebuch*, 114–18.
59 See Dr. jur. Numa Praetorius (Eugen Wilhelm), "'Hirschfeld, Dr. Magnus. Berlins Drittes Geschlecht' (Review)," *Jahrbuch für sexuelle Zwischenstufen* 7 (1905): 720. On Wilhelm's travels, see Dubout, *Der Richter und sein Tagebuch*, 178.
60 Xavier Mayne, *The Intersexes: A History of Similisexualism as a Problem in Social Life* (Naples: Privately Printed, 1908), 212.
61 Hans Ostwald, *Männliche Prostitution im kaiserlichen Berlin* (Berlin: Janssen-Verlag, 1991 [1906]), 88. Subsequent page numbers from *Männliche Prostitution* are citedin the text. All translations are my own.
62 Though associated with Nazi anti-Semitism, fantasies about the "lecherous Jew" were already a staple of anti-Semitic discourse in Imperial Germany, where they often circulated with anti-feminist discourse. For instance, agitation against the hiring of German women in low-level office jobs often invoked lurid fantasies of sexual assaults by Jewish business owners. See Ute Planert, "Weibliche 'Schmutzkonkurrenz' und männliche Ehre: Geschlechterbilder als Machtfaktor im deutschnationalen Handlungsgehilfenverband 1893–1918," *Internationale Wissenschaftliche Korrespondenz zur Geschichte der Deutschen Arbeiterbewegung* 34, no. 3 (1998): 450. See also Panikos Panayi, *Ethnic Minorities in Nineteenth and Twentieth Century Germany: Jews, Gypsies, Poles, Turks and Others* (London: Taylor & Francis Group, 2000), 88. For an analysis of the structural role of fantasy in anti-Semitism more generally, see Žižek, *The Sublime Object of Ideology*, 47–9, 124–8.
63 Ostwald, likely at Hirschfeld's invitation, was later elected to serve as a member of the WhK's large advisory committee (*Obmänner-Kollegium*) "Komitee-Mitteilungen," *Vierteljahresberichte* 1, no. 4 (1910): 441–2. Nevertheless, Hirschfeld continued to dispute his erstwhile editor's interpretation of Soldatenprostitution. In 1913, after repeating his own fictional scenario of domestic bliss, he concluded that "[t]o speak of prostitution in this case, a designation which, for example, H. Ostwald actively supports in his book, *Männliche Prostitution*, seems unjustified." Hirschfeld, *The Homosexuality of Men and Women*, 838. See also Hirschfeld, "Ursachen und Erscheinungsformen der männlichen Prostitution," 361.

64 Friedlaender, "Der Beleidigungsprozeß Moltke gegen Harden," 4014.
65 Friedlaender, "Der Beleidigungsprozeß Moltke gegen Harden," 4014.
66 "Ein politischer Sensationsprozeß," *Volksstimme*, 26 October 1907, 2.
67 Tresckow, *Von Fürsten und anderen Sterblichen*, 185.
68 "Zeitungsausschnitte," *Jahrbuch für sexuelle Zwischenstufen* 3 (1901): 552–3.
69 "[VII. Verurteilungen und Verhaftungen aus § 175. Item 8]," *Monatsbericht des wissenschaftlich-humanitäres Komitees* 6, no. 10 (1 October 1907): 203.
70 "Materialien," *Zeitschrift für Sexualwissenschaft* 1 (1908), 313, 318.
71 "Ein ernstes Nachwort zum Prozeß Moltke-Harde," *Coburger Zeitung*, 2 November 1907, 1.
72 "Der Prozeß Harden-Moltke. Das Opfer der Tafelrunde," *BZ am Mittag*, 26 October 1907, 1.
73 Bollhardt's denial appears in "Ein politischer Sensationsprozeß," *Volksstimme*, 26 October 1907, 2.
74 See Bösch, *Öffentliche Geheimnisse*, 106.
75 See Bösch, *Öffentliche Geheimnisse*, 106, 118.
76 See, for example, Moll, *Die konträre Sexualempfindung*, 434, 433.
77 *Stenographische Berichte. XII. Legislaturperiode. I. Session*, vol. 229 (1908), 1875.
78 *Stenographische Berichte. XII. Legislaturperiode. I. Session*, vol. 229 (1908), 1909.
79 Tresckow, *Von Fürsten und anderen Sterblichen*, 185–6.
80 *Stenographische Berichte. XII. Legislaturperiode. I. Session*, vol. 229 (1908), 1913.
81 *Stenographische Berichte. XII. Legislaturperiode. I. Session*, vol. 229 (1908), 1913.
82 Anonymous, *Das perverse Berlin*, 103.
83 As Frevert explains, the sabre that all soldiers were required to wear "was there to be used, and indeed, under certain circumstances, was actually required to be used," as when a soldier was physically assaulted. Frevert, *A Nation in Barracks*, 181.
84 *Stenographische Berichte. XII. Legislaturperiode. I. Session*, vol. 229 (1908), 1913.
85 Anonymous, *Das perverse Berlin*, 105.
86 *Stenographische Berichte. XII. Legislaturperiode. I. Session*, vol. 229 (1908), 1913.
87 *Stenographische Berichte. XII. Legislaturperiode. I. Session*, vol. 229 (1908), 1913.
88 Foucault, *The History of Sexuality, Vol. I*, 154.
89 Foucault, *The History of Sexuality, Vol. I*, 154.
90 Though Foucault never discussed Marx's writings directly in *The History of Sexuality*, he took issue with contemporary Marxist interpretations of sexuality, which, according to him, sought to derive the social repression of sexuality from capitalist logics: "[I]f sex is so rigorously repressed, this is because it is incompatible with a general and intensive work imperative." For Foucault, of course, "the essential thing is not this economic factor, but rather the existence in our era of a discourse" about sex, particularly the value of talking about it as if it were repressed. Foucault, *The History of Sexuality, Vol. I*, 6–7.

91 See William Pietz, "Problem of the Fetish, I," *Res: Anthropology and Aesthetics*, no. 9 (1985): 5–17.
92 Karl Marx, "The Fetishism of Commodities and the Secret Thereof," in *The Marx-Engels Reader*, ed. Robert C. Tucker (New York: W.W. Norton, 1978), 319–29. On Marx's concepts of the commodity and commodity fetishism, see David Harvey, *A Companion to Marx's Capital* (London: Verso, 2010), 15–47.
93 Alfred Binet, "Der Fetischismus in der Liebe," in *Fetischismus: Grundlagentexte vom 18. Jahrhundert bis in die Gegenwart*, ed. Johannes Endres (Frankfurt/Main: Suhrkamp, 2017), 226.
94 Binet, "Der Fetischismus in der Liebe," 234.
95 Marx, "The Fetishism of Commodities," 321.
96 Marx, "The Fetishism of Commodities," 321.
97 Marx, "The Fetishism of Commodities," 322.
98 Žižek, *The Sublime Object of Ideology*, 32.
99 Because conscripts' uniforms were rarely new but instead passed down from previous recruits, they – especially the everyday uniforms for use inside the barracks compound – were usually a disappointment. As one former soldier recalled about getting his uniform: "Heavens, what a wardrobe! The pants with the patched riding leather could almost stand on its own, it was so stiff, one patch sat on top of the other. The coats appeared to be better, but even some of them must have weathered many a storm; the lining was ripped in many places and the trimming was threadbare." Rehbein, *Das Leben eines Landarbeiters*, 162.
100 Isabel V. Hull, "Der kaiserliche Hof als Herrschaftsinstrument," in *Der letzte Kaiser: Wilhelm II. im Exil*, ed. Hans Wilderotter and Klaus-D. Pohl (Gütersloh/Munich: Bertelsmann Lexikon, 1991), 22. To compensate, most chancellors were given an honorary military rank. As one anonymous author noted about Imperial Germany's fourth chancellor: "Prince Bülow, who has absolutely nothing military about him, had to become a general in the Hussars in order to compete with the [military] toadies [*Schranzen*]." von einem Schwarzseher, *Unser Kaiser und Sein Volk! Deutsche Sorgen*, 6th ed. (Freiburg: Paul Waetzel, 1906), 107.
101 Eda Sagarra, *A Social History of Germany, 1648–1914* (New York: Holmes & Meier, 1977), 242. The passage is also cited in Berghahn, "The German Empire: Reflections," 80.
102 Albert von Boguslawski, *Der Ehrbegriff des Offizierstandes: Ein kurzes Wort zur Aufklärung* (Berlin: Schall und Grund, 1897), 13.
103 Frevert, *A Nation in Barracks*, 154.
104 Frevert, *A Nation in Barracks*, 181–2.
105 See Neff, "*Wir wollen keine Paradetruppe …,*" 180–200.
106 Frevert, *A Nation in Barracks*, 186.

260 Notes to pages 126–9

107 Neff, "*Wir wollen keine Paradetruppe …*," 180.
108 On the commissioning of royals in the unit, see Ex-Emperor of Germany Wilhelm II, *My Early Life* (London: Methuen, 1926), 31–2; John C.G. Röhl, *Young Wilhelm: The Kaiser's Early Life, 1859–1888* (Cambridge: Cambridge UP, 1998), 367. Most male members of the Prussian royal family began their military careers in this unit before eventually rotating through different units as part of their education.
109 Ortenburg and Prömper, *Preussisch-Deutsche Uniformen von 1640–1918*, 91–8.
110 Richard von Krafft-Ebing, *Psychopathia Sexualis, mit besonderer Berücksichtigung der conträren Sexualempfindung: Eine klinische-forensische Studie*, 10th enlarged and revised ed. (Stuttgart: Ferdinand Enke, 1898), 21. On this popular cliché, see Jakob Vogel, "Stramme Gardisten, temperamentvolle Tirailleurs und anmutige Damen: Geschlechterbilder im deutschen und französischen Kult der 'Nation in Waffen,'" in *Militär und Gesellschaft im 19. und 20. Jahrhundert*, ed. Ute Frevert (Stuttgart: Klett Cotta, 1997), 256.
111 Moll, *Die konträre Sexualempfindung*, 267.
112 Krafft-Ebing, *Psychopathia Sexualis*, 7th ed. (1892), 267.
113 Frevert, *A Nation in Barracks*, 155.
114 Hirschfeld, "Ursachen und Erscheinungsformen der männlichen Prostitution," 348.
115 Hirschfeld, "Ursachen und Erscheinungsformen der männlichen Prostitution," 348.
116 Walter Benjamin, *The Arcades Project*, trans. Howard Eiland and Kevin McLaughlin (Cambridge, MA: The Belknap Press of Harvard UP, 1999), 10.
117 Karl Marx, "Economic and Philosophic Manuscripts of 1844," in *The Marx-Engels Reader*, ed. Robert C. Tucker (New York: W.W. Norton, 1978), 82n87 (emphasis in original).
118 Binet, "Der Fetischismus in der Liebe," 234.
119 Richard von Krafft-Ebing, *Psychopathia Sexualis: With Especial Reference to the Antipathic Sexual Instinct*, trans. Franklin S. Klaf, 12th ed. (New York: Arcade, 1998), 145.
120 Sigmund Freud, "Fetishism (1928)," in *The Standard Edition of the Complete Psychological Works of Sigmund Freud*, ed. and trans. J. Strachey, vol. 21 (London: Hogarth Press, 1953), 156.
121 Žižek, *The Sublime Object of Ideology*, 18.
122 Ulrichs, *Memnon*, vol. 7, 54.
123 Krafft-Ebing, *Psychopathia Sexualis*, 12th ed. (1998), 145.
124 Ulrichs, *Memnon*, vol. 7, 55.
125 Binet, "Der Fetischismus in der Liebe," 234.
126 Hirschfeld, *Der urnische Mensch*, 59.
127 Ulrichs, *The Riddle of "Man-Manly" Love*, vol. 1, 242.

128 Ulrichs, *The Riddle of "Man-Manly" Love*, vol. 1, 242.
129 Ulrichs, *The Riddle of "Man-Manly" Love*, vol. 1, 242.
130 Ulrichs, *The Riddle of "Man-Manly" Love*, vol. 1, 230, 225.
131 Ulrichs, *The Riddle of "Man-Manly" Love*, vol. 1, 210.
132 The diaries, which encompass fifty-five numbered volumes, were primarily written in Wilhelm's native language (French) with some phrases in Greek and German. They remain in the private hands of his descendants and have not been published. Dubout, *Der Richter und sein Tagebuch*, 42–3. I thus rely on passages that he transcribed, which he then translated into German, and which I then have translated into English.
133 Dubout, *Der Richter und sein Tagebuch*, 113.
134 Dubout, *Der Richter und sein Tagebuch*, 119.
135 Dubout, *Der Richter und sein Tagebuch*, 119 (emphasis in original).
136 Franz Bergg, *Ein Proletarierleben*, ed. Nikolaus Welter (Frankfurt/Main: Neuer Frankfurter Verlag, 1913), 148–9.
137 Frevert, *A Nation in Barracks*, 177.
138 Anonymous, *Das perverse Berlin*, 106.
139 Anonymous, *Das perverse Berlin*, 108.
140 Slavoj Žižek, *The Plague of Fantasies*, 7.
141 Ulrichs, *The Riddle of "Man-Manly" Love*, vol. 1, 243.
142 Steven Zeeland, *Military Trade* (New York: Harrington Park, 1999), 12 (emphasis in original).
143 Zeeland, *Military Trade*, 1.
144 On the early theological fantasies about sex in the Garden of Eden, see Žižek, *The Plague of Fantasies*, 15.
145 On *méconnaissance*, see Foucault, *The History of Sexuality, Vol. I*, 56.
146 *Stenographische Berichte. XII. Legislaturperiode. I. Session*, vol. 229 (1908), 1913.
147 Frevert, *A Nation in Barracks*, 159.
148 Tresckow, *Von Fürsten und anderen Sterblichen*, 163.
149 *Stenographische Berichte. XII. Legislaturperiode. I. Session*, vol. 229 (1908), 1945.
150 With the exception of the SPD, nearly all speakers expressed their appreciation for the war minister's "detailed, clear, and unadorned words," as Prince Hermann von Hatzfeld, a leader of the Free Conservatives, formulated. Even Otto Wiemer from the Freeminded Party, who admitted not being satisfied with Einem's explanation of the army's hands-off approach to Lynar and Hohenau, decided that "the Reichstag can, I think, be thankful, first because the war minister spoke openly and frankly, and because he declared that these excesses and lapses must be condemned in the sharpest words and that they shall be swept clean with an iron broom." See *Stenographische Berichte. XII. Legislaturperiode. I. Session*, vol. 229 (1908), 1920 and 1932–3.
151 Žižek, *The Sublime Object of Ideology*, 49.

4. Camping in His Own Private Militarism: Thomas Mann's Queer Art of Failure and the Fantasies of Military Service

1 On Mann's predilection for numerology, see Anthony Heilbut, *Thomas Mann: Eros and Literature* (Berkeley: U of California P, 1995), 3.
2 Jack Halberstam, *The Queer Art of Failure* (Durham, NC: Duke UP, 2011).
3 Halberstam, *The Queer Art of Failure*, 3.
4 Frevert, *A Nation in Barracks*, 221. See also Thomas Rohkrämer, "Heroes and Would-Be Heroes: Veterans' and Reservists' Associations in Imperial Germany," in *Anticipating Total War: The German and American Experiences, 1871–1914*, ed. Manfred F. Boemeke, Roger Chickering, and Stig Förster (Washington, DC, and Cambridge: German Historical Institute and Cambridge UP, 1999), 189–215.
5 Ziemann, "Militarism," 375. See also Chickering, "Militarism and Radical Nationalism."
6 The phrase is a pun on the title of Eric Santner's Žižekian-inspired study of Daniel Paul Schreber's schizophrenia, which itself puns on Gus Van Sant's movie, whose title is borrowed from the B-52 song, "My Own Private Idaho." See Eric L. Santner, *My Own Private Germany: Daniel Paul Schreber's Secret History of Modernity* (Princeton, NJ: Princeton UP, 1996); Gus Van Sant, dir., *My Own Private Idaho* (New Line Cinema, 1991); Fred Schneider et al., "Private Idaho," in *Wild Planet* (Warner Bros. Records, 1980).
7 Thomas Mann, *Betrachtungen eines Unpolitischen*, ed. Hermann Kurzke, vol. 13.1, Große kommentierte Frankfurter Ausgabe. Werke, Briefe, Tagebücher (Frankfurt: S. Fischer, 2012), 618. On this concept, see Tobin, *Peripheral Desires*, 185–6.
8 Ernest Schonfield, for example, notes that Mann read *The Picture of Dorian Gray* between 1901 and 1905. Ernest Schonfield, *Art and Its Uses in Thomas Mann's "Felix Krull"* (London: Modern Humanities Research Association, 2008), 62n103. See also James Wilper, "Wilde and the Model of Homosexuality in Mann's *Tod in Venedig*," *CLCWeb: Comparative Literature and Culture* 15, no. 4 (2013), https://doi.org/10.7771/1481-4374.2305.
9 Todd Kontje, *Thomas Mann's World: Empire, Race, and the Jewish Question* (Ann Arbor: U of Michigan P, 2011), 78.
10 Cited in Helmut Koopmann, "Thomas Mann's 'Autobiographical' Stories," in *A Companion to the Works of Thomas Mann*, ed. Herbert Lehnert and Eva Wessell (Rochester, NY: Camden House, 2004), 147.
11 Article 57 in the constitution dictated that "every male German is liable to military service and in the discharge of this duty no substitute shall be accepted." Edwin H. Zeydel, ed., *Constitutions of the German Empire and German States* (Washington, DC: Government Printing Office, 1919), 22.

12 Lothar Mertens, "Das Privileg des Einjährig-Freiwilligen Militärdienstes im Kaiserreich und seine gesellschaftliche Bedeutung," *Militargeschichtliche Mitteilungen* 39, no. 1 (1986): 61.
13 Moritz Exner, *Der Weg zum Einjährig-Freiwilligen und zum Offizier des Beurlaubtenstandes in Armee und Marine*, 2nd ed. (Leipzig: Verlagsbuchhandlung von J.J. Weber, 1897), 28, 43.
14 Exner, *Der Weg zum Einjährig-Freiwilligen*, 19.
15 See Mertens, "Das Privileg des Einjährig-Freiwilligen," 61–2.
16 Klaus Harpprecht, *Thomas Mann: Eine Biographie*, vol. 1 (Reinbek bei Hamburg: Rowohlt Taschenbuch, 1995), 54; Thomas Mann, *Briefe an Otto Grautoff 1894–1901 und Ida Boy-Ed 1903–1928*, ed. Peter de Mendelssohn (Frankfurt/Main: S. Fischer, 1975), 103.
17 Harpprecht, *Thomas Mann: Eine Biographie*, vol. 1, 39.
18 Harpprecht, *Thomas Mann: Eine Biographie*, vol. 1, 59.
19 Mann, *Briefe an Otto Grautoff*, 67 (emphasis in original).
20 Mann, *Briefe an Otto Grautoff*, 67.
21 Mann, *Briefe an Otto Grautoff*, 75.
22 Frevert, *A Nation in Barracks*, 159.
23 An exhaustive compendium of the laws and regulations governing conscription can be found in Robert Hue de Grais, *Heer und Kriegsflotte*, vol. 1, *Allgemeine Bestimmungen* (Berlin: Julius Springer, 1904). A helpful summary can be found in the entry for Ersatzwesen (recruitment system) in *Meyers Konversations-Lexikon*, vol. 5 (Leipzig: Verlag des Bibliographischen Instituts, 1888), 818–19.
24 Mann, *Briefe an Otto Grautoff*, 114.
25 Mann, *Briefe an Otto Grautoff*, 114 (emphasis in original).
26 Exner, *Der Weg zum Einjährig-Freiwilligen*, 27.
27 Mann, *Briefe an Otto Grautoff*, 117.
28 Mann, *Briefe an Otto Grautoff*, 122 (emphasis in original).
29 In a diary entry on 6 May 1934. See Hermann Kurzke, *Thomas Mann: Life as a Work of Art*, trans. Leslie Willson (Princeton: Princeton UP, 2002), 122–37.
30 Kurzke, *Thomas Mann: Life as a Work of Art*, 125.
31 Thomas Mann, *Briefe, 1948–1955 und Nachlese*, ed. Erika Mann, vol. 3 (Frankfurt/Main: S. Fischer, 1965), 423–4. A slightly different and more eloquent – but less literal – translation of the letter can be found in Thomas Mann, *Letters of Thomas Mann*, ed. Richard Winston and Clara Winston, trans. Richard Winston and Clara Winston (New York: Alfred A. Knopf, 1971), 13–16.
32 Kristin Mahoney, "Camp Modernism and Decadence," in *Decadence: A Literary History*, ed. Alex Murray (Cambridge: Cambridge UP, 2020), 342.
33 Mann, *Briefe, 1948–1955 und Nachlese*, vol. 3, 424.
34 Heilbut, *Thomas Mann*, 52.

35 Mann, *Briefe an Otto Grautoff*, 135–6.
36 Heilbut, *Thomas Mann*, 52.
37 See Naomi Ritter, "*Death in Venice* and the Tradition of European Decadence," in *Approaches to Teaching Mann's Death in Venice and Other Short Fiction*, ed. Jeffrey B. Berlin, Approaches to Teaching World Literature, vol. 43 (New York: Modern Language Association of America, 1992), 86–92.
38 Max Nordau, *Degeneration*, translated from the second edition of the German work (New York: D. Appleton and Company, 1895), 15. On Nordau's impact, see Spector, *Violent Sensations*, 46–50.
39 Mann, *Briefe, 1948–1955 und Nachlese*, vol. 3, 424.
40 Eberhard Kraus, "Anthropologisches aus der Romanliteratur," *Politisch-anthropologische Revue: Monatsschrift für das soziale und geistige Leben der Völker* 2, no. 1 (1903): 82.
41 Krafft-Ebing, *Psychopathia Sexualis*, 7th ed. (1894), 187.
42 Hans Wysling, "Thomas Mann als Tagebuchschreiber (1987)," in *Ausgewählte Aufsätze, 1963–1996*, ed. Thomas Sprecher and Cornelia Bernini, Thomas Mann Studien (Frankfurt/Main: Vittorio Klostermann, 1996), 407.
43 Anna Katharina Schaffner, "Richard von Krafft-Ebing's *Psychopathia Sexualis* and Thomas Mann's *Buddenbrooks*: Exchanges between Scientific and Imaginary Accounts of Sexual Deviance," *Modern Language Review* 106 (2011): 487. As Gerald N. Izenberg points out, though, "by the end of the 1880s, it was not necessary to have actually read Krafft-Ebing to 'know' that homosexuality was effeminate." Gerald N. Izenberg, *Modernism and Masculinity: Mann, Wedekind, Kandinsky through World War I* (Chicago: U of Chicago P, 2000), 101.
44 Schaffner, "Richard von Krafft-Ebing's *Psychopathia Sexualis* and Thomas Mann's *Buddenbrooks*," 487.
45 Krafft-Ebing, *Psychopathia Sexualis*, 7th ed. (1894), 256.
46 Kurzke, *Thomas Mann: Life as a Work of Art*, 354.
47 See Heilbut, *Thomas Mann*, 313.
48 Viktor Mann, *Wir waren fünf: Bildnis der Familie Mann*, 3rd ed. (Konstanz: Südverlag Konstanz, 1973), 126.
49 Mann, *Wir waren fünf*, 127.
50 Mann, *Wir waren fünf*, 126.
51 Thomas Mann and Heinrich Mann, *Briefwechsel 1900–1945*, ed. Hans Wysling (Frankfurt/Main: Fischer, 1984), 62. English translation from Thomas Mann, *Letters of Heinrich and Thomas Mann, 1900–1949*, ed. Hans Wysling, trans. Don Renau, Richard Winston, and Clara Winston (Berkeley: U of California P, 1998), 40.

52 Thomas and Heinrich Mann, *Briefwechsel*, 161. Englisch translation from Mann, *Letters of Heinrich and Thomas Mann, 1900–1949*, 115.
53 Thomas Mann, "Im Spiegel," in *Essays*, vol. 1, *Frühlingssturm 1893–1918*, ed. Hermann Kurzke and Stephan Stachorski (Frankfurt/Main: S. Fischer, 1994), 99.
54 Mann, "Im Spiegel," 99.
55 Mann, "Im Spiegel," 99.
56 Thomas Mann, "Lebensabriss," in *Essays*, vol. 3, *Ein Apell an die Vernunft 1926–1933*, ed. Stephan Stachorski and Hermann Kurzke (Frankfurt/Main: S. Fischer, 1994), 191.
57 See Robert Deam Tobin, "The Life and Work of Thomas Mann: A Gay Perspective," in *Death in Venice by Thomas Mann*, ed. Naomi Ritter (Boston: Bedford/St. Martin's, 1998), 225–44.
58 Kurzke, *Thomas Mann: Life as a Work of Art*, 8.
59 Koopmann, "Thomas Mann's 'Autobiographical' Stories," 147.
60 Koopmann, "Thomas Mann's 'Autobiographical' Stories," 148.
61 Herbert H. Lehnert, "Fictional Orientations in Thomas Mann's Biography," *PMLA* 88, no. 5 (1973): 1152.
62 See Hans Wysling, "Archivalisches Gewühle: Zur Entstehungsgeschichte der Bekenntnisse des Hochstaplers Felix Krull," in *Quellenkritische Studien zum Werk Thomas Manns*, ed. Paul Scherrer and Hans Wysling (Bern: Francke, 1967), 234–54.
63 He makes this claim in a diary entry from 25 November 1950. See Andrew J. Webber, "Mann's Man's World: Gender and Sexuality," in *The Cambridge Companion to Thomas Mann* (Cambridge: Cambridge UP, 2002), 81.
64 For a summary of these readings, see Schonfield, *Art and Its Uses*, 34–40. Erika's remarks are quoted on page 38.
65 Sontag revised the essay, originally published in *The Partisan Review* in 1964, two years later. See Susan Sontag, "Notes on Camp," in *Essays of the 1960s & 1970s*, ed. David Rieff (New York: Library of America, 2013 [1966]), 275–92. Many gay critics subsequently lambasted the essay for "removing, or at least minimizing, the connotations of homosexuality" and thereby "kill[ing] off the binding referent of Camp – the Homosexual." Moe Meyer, "Introduction: Reclaiming the Discourse of Camp," in *The Politics and Poetics of Camp*, ed. Moe Meyer (New York: Routledge, 1994), 7. For a critical appraisal that places her essay within her own queer closet (as well as her Jewish identity), see Ann Pellegrini, "After Sontag: Future Notes on Camp," in *Companion to Lesbian, Gay, Bisexual, Transgender, and Queer Studies*, ed. George E. Haggerty and Molly McGarry (Hoboken, NJ: John Wiley & Sons, 2007), 168–93.
66 Richard Dyer, "It's Being so Camp as Keeps Us Going," in *Camp: Queer Aesthetics and the Performing Subject: A Reader*, ed. Fabio Cleto (Edinburgh: Edinburgh UP, 1999), 110–11.

67 On Wilde's formative role, see Gregory W. Bredbeck, "Narcissus in the Wilde: Textual Cathexis and the Historical Origins of Queer Camp," in *The Politics and Poetics of Camp*, ed. Moe Meyer (New York: Routledge, 1994), 51–74; Moe Meyer, "Under the Sign of Wilde: An Archeology of Posing," in *The Politics and Poetics of Camp*, ed. Moe Meyer (New York: Routledge, 1994), 75–109.
68 Krafft-Ebing, *Psychopathia Sexualis*, 12th ed. (1998), 197–8, 252.
69 Hirschfeld, *Berlins Drittes Geschlecht*, 52, 104–6, 111.
70 Jack Babuscio, "The Cinema of Camp (AKA Camp and the Gay Sensibility)," in *Camp: Queer Aesthetics and the Performing Subject: A Reader*, ed. Fabio Cleto (Edinburgh: Edinburgh UP, 1999), 117–35.
71 Halberstam, *The Queer Art of Failure*, 96.
72 Thomas Mann, *Bekenntnisse des Hochstaplers Felix Krull: Der Memoiren erster Teil*, ed. Thomas Sprecher, Monica Bussmann, and Eckhard Heftrich, vol. 12, Große kommentierte Frankfurter Ausgabe. Werke, Briefe, Tagebücher (Frankfurt: S. Fischer, 2012), 75. Subsequent page numbers from *Bekenntnisse* are cited in the text.
73 Klaus Hermsdorf, "Die Geburt eines Schelmen: Zu Thomas Manns Krull-Fragment von 1911," *Weimarer Beiträge: Zeitschrift für Literaturwissenschaft, Ästhetik und Kulturwissenschaften* (1965): 113.
74 Hermsdorf, "Die Geburt eines Schelmen," 114.
75 Thomas and Heinrich Mann, *Briefwechsel*, 162. Englisch translation from Mann, *Letters of Heinrich and Thomas Mann, 1900–1949*, 115.
76 Mann, *Briefe an Otto Grautoff*, 67.
77 Krafft-Ebing, *Psychopathia Sexualis*, 12th ed. (1998), 193.
78 Hirschfeld, *Berlins Drittes Geschlecht*, 82–3.
79 Philip Core, "From *Camp: The Lie That Tells the Truth*," in *Camp: Queer Aesthetics and the Performing Subject: A Reader*, ed. Fabio Cleto (Edinburgh: Edinburgh UP, 1999), 81.
80 Hermsdorf, "Die Geburt eines Schelmen," 114.
81 See Babuscio, "The Cinema of Camp," 120–1.
82 Sontag, "Camp," 270.
83 Core, "From *Camp: The Lie That Tells the Truth*," 81.
84 Mann, "Lebensabriss," 191.
85 Mann, "Im Spiegel," 99.
86 Core, "From *Camp: The Lie That Tells the Truth*," 80.
87 Mann, *Briefe, 1948–1955 und Nachlese*, vol. 3, 424.
88 Dyer, "It's Being so Camp," 110.
89 Cited in Wysling, "Archivalisches Gewuhle: Zur Entstehungsgeschichte der Bekenntnisse des Hochstaplers Felix Krull," 244.
90 Harvey Goldman, *Politics, Death and the Devil: Self and Power in Max Weber and Thomas Mann* (Berkeley: U of California P, 1992), 23.

91 Goldman, *Politics, Death and the Devil*, 23.
92 Izenberg, *Modernism and Masculinity*, 138. Ruritania was the fictional, German-speaking kingdom located somewhere in Central Europe in Anthony Hope's wildly successful 1894 novel *The Prisoner of Zenda*. Ruritanian has come to mean any small fictional place for indulging in a "lingering fascination with royalty, and with royal romance in particular." Nicholas Daly, *Ruritania: A Cultural History, from* The Prisoner of Zenda *to* The Princess Diaries (Oxford: Oxford UP, 2020), 10.
93 In announcing his engagement to his brother Heinrich, for instance, Mann referred to his "bliss" as "something serious, difficult, and severe as life itself – and perhaps what I *mean* is life itself. I didn't 'conquer' it and it didn't 'happen' to me – I have *submitted* myself to it: out of a kind of feeling of duty, a kind of morality, an inborn imperative." Thomas and Heinrich Mann, *Briefwechsel*, 101. English translation from Mann, *Letters of Heinrich and Thomas Mann, 1900–1949*, 68 (emphasis in original). The impression is that after his failure as a one-year volunteer in the army, Mann has become a "volunteer" conscript with a lifelong commission as a soldier in the heterosexual order of marriage.
94 Michael Beddow, "Fiction and Meaning in Thomas Mann's *Felix Krull*," *Journal of European Studies* 10 (1980): 80.
95 Beddow, "Fiction and Meaning in Thomas Mann's *Felix Krull*," 87 (emphasis in original).
96 Dyer, "It's Being so Camp," 111.
97 Thomas and Heinrich Mann, *Briefwechsel*, 169 (my translation).
98 Slavoj Žižek, *Welcome to the Desert of the Real* (London: Verso, 2002), 5–6.
99 Thomas and Heinrich Mann, *Briefwechsel*, 170 (my translation).
100 Thomas and Heinrich Mann, *Briefwechsel*, 170 (my translation).
101 Žižek, *Welcome to the Desert of the Real*, 5.
102 According to an account passed down from Heinrich's first wife, Mimi, to Golo Mann, Thomas Mann's second son, Heinrich told his brother, "You know, don't you, that Germany will lose the war, that its ruling classes will bear the primary blame, that it will necessarily lead to the fall of the monarchy." See Ronald Hayman, *Thomas Mann: A Biography* (New York: Scribner, 1995), 281.
103 Thomas Mann, "Gedanken im Kriege," in *Essays II*, ed. Hermann Kurzke et al., vol 15.1, Große kommentierte Frankfurter Ausgabe. Werke, Briefe, Tagebücher (Frankfurt: S. Fischer, 2012), 27–46. On the origin of the essay, see Hermann Kurzke et al., eds., *Thomas Mann. Essays II, 1914–1926. Kommentar*, vol. 15.2, Große kommentierte Frankfurter Ausgabe. Werke, Briefe, Tagebücher (Frankfurt: S. Fischer, 2012), 9.
104 Mann, "Gute Feldpost"; Mann, "Friedrich und die Große Koalition: Ein Abriss für den Tag und die Stunde," in *Essays II*, ed. Hermann Kurzke

et al., vol 15.1, Große kommentierte Frankfurter Ausgabe. Werke, Briefe, Tagebücher (Frankfurt: S. Fischer, 2012), 47–50, 55–122. On the origin of the essays, see Kurzke et al., *Thomas Mann. Essays II, 1914–1926. Kommentar*, vol. 15.2, 21, 29.
105 Mann, *Betrachtungen eines Unpolitischen*, vol. 13.1.
106 Their political disagreements over German culture, politics, and the First World War led to a formal break in their relationship that lasted from 1914 until 1922. Kontje observes that the *Reflections* "radiates hatred for his brother Heinrich and often seems to have been written with barely contained rage." Kontje, *Thomas Mann's World*, 65.
107 See Günter Häntzschel, "Literatur und Krieg: Aspekte der Diskussion aus der Zeitschrift 'Das literarische Echo,'" in *Kultur und Krieg: Die Rolle der Intellektuellen, Künstler und Schriftsteller im Ersten Weltkrieg*, ed. Wolfgang J. Mommsen and Elisabeth Müller-Luckner (Munich: R. Oldenbourg Verlag, 1996), 209.
108 Wolfgang J. Mommsen, "Einleitung: Die deutschen kulturellen Eliten im Ersten Weltkrieg," in *Kultur und Krieg: Die Rolle der Intellektuellen, Künstler und Schriftsteller im Ersten Weltkrieg*, ed. Wolfgang J. Mommsen and Elisabeth Müller-Luckner (Munich: R. Oldenbourg Verlag, 1996), 2.
109 See Andreas Schumann, "'Der Künstler an die Krieger': Zur Kriegsliteratur kanonisierter Autoren," in *Kultur und Krieg: Die Rolle der Intellektuellen, Künstler und Schriftsteller im Ersten Weltkrieg*, ed. Wolfgang J. Mommsen and Elisabeth Müller-Luckner (Munich: R. Oldenbourg Verlag, 1996), 221–33.
110 Schumann, "'Der Künstler an die Krieger,'" 221.
111 Mann, "Gedanken im Kriege," 30.
112 Whisnant, *Queer Identities and Politics in Germany*, 79.
113 Whisnant, *Queer Identities and Politics in Germany*, 187.
114 Magnus Hirschfeld, *Warum hassen uns die Völker? Eine kriegspsychologische Betrachtung* (Bonn: A. Marcus & E. Webers Verlag, 1914), 7, 10.
115 Puar, *Terrorist Assemblages: Homonationalism in Queer Times*.
116 Michael Beddow, "Thoughts Back in Season? Thomas Mann's First World War Essays and the Problem of German Identity," *Publications of the English Goethe Society* 64 (1996): 18.
117 Goldman, *Politics, Death and the Devil*, 99.
118 Kontje, *Thomas Mann's World*, 65.
119 Nick Mansfield, *Theorizing War: From Hobbes to Badiou* (Basingstoke, England: Palgrave Macmillan, 2008), 159.
120 Kurzke, *Thomas Mann: Life as a Work of Art*, 216.
121 Žižek, *Welcome to the Desert of the Real*, 6.
122 Kurzke, *Thomas Mann: Life as a Work of Art*, 217–18.
123 Mann, "Gedanken im Kriege," 31.

124 Goldman, *Politics, Death and the Devil*, 20. See also the masterful reading of the novel's homoerotic themes in Tobin, *Peripheral Desires*, 185–210.
125 See Jeffrey Verhey, *The Spirit of 1914: Militarism, Myth and Mobilization in Germany* (New York: Cambridge UP, 2000); Christoph Nonn, "Oh What a Lovely War? German Common People and the First World War," *German History* 18 (2000): 97–111.
126 Beddow, "Thomas Mann's First World War Essays," 8.
127 Goldman, *Politics, Death and the Devil*, 93.
128 Mann, "Gedanken im Kriege," 33.
129 Mann, "Gedanken im Kriege," 33–4.
130 Mann, "Friedrich und die große Koalition," 56.
131 See Kurzke, *Thomas Mann: Life as a Work of Art*, 208.
132 Izenberg, *Modernism and Masculinity*, 146–7.
133 Goldman, *Politics, Death and the Devil*, 98.
134 Mann, "Gedanken im Kriege," 29.
135 Mann, "Gedanken im Kriege," 29–30.
136 Mann, "Gute Feldpost," 47.
137 Mann, "Gute Feldpost," 50 (emphasis in original).
138 Mann, "Gute Feldpost," 50 (emphasis in original).
139 Mann, "Gute Feldpost," 48.
140 Mann, "Gute Feldpost," 49.
141 Thomas Mann, *Reflections of a Nonpolitical Man*, trans. Walter D. Morris (New York: Frederick Ungar, 1983), 1.
142 Mann, *Reflections of a Nonpolitical Man*, 1.
143 Harpprecht attributes the rhetoric to Mann's "characteristic lack of tact." *Thomas Mann: Eine Biographie*, vol. 1, 428.
144 Critics have recognized the inherent difference between *Reflections* and his earlier works. Since, as John Seery explains, the book took more than two years to write, its tone and positions fluctuated, moving from "one-sided tirades" that defend Germany's authoritarianism to a deconstruction of his earlier essays. John Evan Seery, "Political Irony and World War: A Rereading of Thomas Mann's Betrachtungen," *Soundings: An Interdisciplinary Journal* 73, no. 1 (1990): 7. Kontje, too, notes that "in the course of writing the *Reflections*, another, less belligerent aspect of Mann's thought began to emerge." Kontje, *Thomas Mann's World*, 81.
145 Kontje, *Thomas Mann's World*, 1.
146 Ziemann, "Militarism," 375.
147 Fabio Vighi and Heiko Feldner, *Žižek: Beyond Foucault* (Basingstoke England: Palgrave Macmillan, 2007), 32.

5. Perversions of Fantasy: Parody and the Left-Liberal Critique of German Militarism in Heinrich Mann's *The Loyal Subject*

1 Magnus Hirschfeld, "Jahresbericht 1904–1905," *Jahrbuch für sexuelle Zwischenstufen* 7 (1905): 1037.
2 Hirschfeld, "Jahresbericht 1904–1905," 1013.
3 Hirschfeld, "Jahresbericht 1904–1905," 1013.
4 Gayle Rubin has pointed out that these moralistic rejections of same-sex behaviour exhibit a number of deceptive casuistries, including "the fallacy of misplaced scale," "the domino theory of sexual peril," and "the lack of a concept of benign sexual variation." Rubin, "Thinking Sex," 11.
5 Hirschfeld, "Jahresbericht 1904–1905," 981.
6 Hirschfeld, "Jahresbericht 1904–1905," 988.
7 Hirschfeld, "Jahresbericht 1904–1905," 1021.
8 Hirschfeld, "Jahresbericht 1904–1905," 1019.
9 See Georg von Below, *Das Duell in Deutschland: Geschichte und Gegenwart* (Kassel: Max Brunnemann, 1896), 71. Though the secondary literature on honour and duelling in Imperial Germany is extensive, historians have remained as divided as the combatants they study. See Jeffrey Schneider, "Dueling and the Fantasmatic Specter of Male Honour in Imperial Germany: The Kaiser's Will and Theodor Fontane's *Effi Briest*," *Literature and History* 31, no. 1 (2022): 26.
10 Heinrich Mann, *Der Untertan* (Frankfurt/Main: S. Fischer, 2000). This edition follows the same pagination as Heinrich Mann, *Der Untertan*, ed. Peter-Paul Schneider, Gesammelte Werke in Einzelbänden (Frankfurt/Main: S. Fischer, 1995). Subsequent page numbers from this edition of *Der Untertan* are cited in the text. All translations are mine, unless otherwise indicated.
11 See Thomas Nipperdey, "War die Wilhelminische Gesellschaft eine Untertanen-Gesellschaft?," in *Nachdenken über die deutsche Geschichte: Essays* (Munich: C.H. Beck, 1986), 4–5.
12 See, for example, Hans-Ulrich Wehler, *The German Empire 1871–1918*, trans. Kim Traynor (Leamington Spa: Berg, 1985), 87–8; Nipperdey, "War die Wilhelminische Gesellschaft eine Untertanen-Gesellschaft?," 6. For an overview, see Reinhard Alter, "Heinrich Mann's Untertan – Prüfstein für die 'Kaiserreich-Debatte'?," *Geschichte und Gesellschaft* 17, no. 3 (1991): 370–89. On Mann's research, see Karin Verena Gunnemann, *Heinrich Mann's Novels and Essays: The Artist as Political Educator*, Studies in German Literature, Linguistics, and Culture (Rochester, NY: Camden House, 2002), 52.
13 The novel's publication history illustrates clearly the dimensions of its political intervention. Serialization began auspiciously on 1 January 1914, in the Munich weekly *Die Zeit im Bild* (Time in pictures), even as

Heinrich Mann was still finishing the manuscript. The publication's editors suspended its serialization on 13 August 1914, explaining that "at the present time, a large public organ cannot express criticism of German conditions in a satirical form." Quoted in Manfred Flügge, *Heinrich Mann: Eine Biographie* (Reinbek bei Hamburg: Rowohlt, 2006), 155. The first complete German-language edition of *The Loyal Subject* came only in December 1918, just a month after Germany's defeat, selling more than 100,000 copies in the first weeks. See Ferdinando Baldessari, "Zur Enstehungsgeschichte von Heinrich Manns *Untertan*," *Quaderni di lingue e letterature* 2 (1977): 174.

14 Helmut Koopmann, *Thomas Mann – Heinrich Mann: Die ungleichen Brüder* (Munich: C.H. Beck, 2005).
15 Koopmann, *Thomas Mann – Heinrich Mann*, 8.
16 Thomas and Heinrich Mann, *Briefwechsel*, 173 (my translation).
17 Heinrich Mann, however, never publicly addressed his affiliation with this journal. See Bernd M. Kraske, "Heinrich Mann als Herausgeber der Zeitschrift Das Zwanzigste Jahrhundert," in *Heinrich Mann: Das essayistische Werk*, ed. Rudolf Wolff, Sammlung Profile (Bonn: Bouvier, 1986), 7–24; Manfred Hahn, "Heinrich Manns Beiträge in der Zetischrift Das Zwanzigste Jahrhundert," *Weimarer Beiträge: Zeitschrift für Literaturwissenschaft, Ästhetik und Kulturwissenschaften* (1967): 966–1019.
18 Simon Dentith, *Parody* (London: Taylor & Francis Group, 2000), 9.
19 Butler, *Gender Trouble*, 138.
20 Michael Grisko, *Der Untertan revisited: Vom Kaiserreich bis geteilten Deutschland*, Buddenbrookhaus-Kataloge (Berlin: Bertz + Fischer, 2007), 22.
21 Theo Buck, "Heinrich Mann: Der Untertan," in *Von Augustinus bis Heinrich Mann: Meisterwerke der Weltliteratur*, ed. Helmut Siepmann and Frank-Rutger Hausmann, Abhandlungen zur Sprache & Literatur: 16 (Bonn: Romantischer Verlag, 1989), 17.
22 See Röhl, *Young Wilhelm*, 306–24.
23 See, for instance, Wolfgang Emmerich, *Heinrich Mann "Der Untertan"* (Munich: Wilhelm Fink Verlag, 1980), 46.
24 Ariane Martin, *Erotische Politik: Heinrich Manns erzählerisches Frühwerk* (Würzburg: Königshausen & Neumann, 1993), 191–2.
25 According to a recent biography, "the one unhappy, unfulfilled love of the young Heinrich was the one to his mother." Flügge, *Heinrich Mann*, 88.
26 Krafft-Ebing, *Psychopathia Sexualis*, 12th ed. (1998), 188 (emphasis in original).
27 Martin, *Erotische Politik*, 146.
28 I borrow most of the translation for this passage from Heinrich Mann, *The Loyal Subject*, trans. Ernest Boyd and Daniel Theisen (New York: Continuum, 1998), 9–10.

29 Martin, *Erotische Politik*, 153.
30 My translation draws substantially from the English translation: Mann, *The Loyal Subject*, 21.
31 Sedgwick, *Epistemology of the Closet*, 62.
32 See chap. 1, n. 99, in this volume.
33 Charles Francis Atkinson, "Grenadier," in *The Encylopedia Britanica* (New York: Encyclopedia Britannica, Inc., 1910), 579.
34 Žižek, *The Plague of Fantasies*, 8–9.
35 Heilbut, *Thomas Mann*, 171.
36 Heilbut, *Thomas Mann*, 171.
37 My rendering of this passage draws on Mann, *The Loyal Subject*, 1.
38 Žižek, *How to Read Lacan*, 9.
39 Krafft-Ebing, *Psychopathia Sexualis*, 12th ed. (1998), 188–90. Meanwhile, sexologists and pedagogues had long expressed alarm at the sexual repercussions that could ensue from young children receiving or witnessing harsh punishments. See, for instance, Iwan Bloch, *Beiträge zur Aetiologie der Psychopathia sexualis*, vol. 1 (Dresden: H.R. Dohrn, 1902), 81–8.
40 See the unpublished letter, presumably to Fritz Freund of the Wiener Verlag: Heinrich Mann, "Autograph letter signed ("Heinrich Mann")," Munich, 19 January 1907, Kotte Autographs, accessed 28 December 2022, https://www.kotte-autographs.com/en/autograph/mann-heinrich/.
41 Heinrich Mann, *Briefe an Ludwig Ewers, 1889–1913*, ed. Ulrich Dietzel and Rosemarie Eggert (Berlin: Aufbau-Verlag, 1980), 252.
42 Helga Winter, *Naturwissenschaft und Ästhetik: Untersuchungen zum Frühwerk Heinrich Manns* (Würzburg: Königshausen & Neumann, 1994), 110.
43 Deleuze, *Coldness and Cruelty*, 99.
44 Krafft-Ebing, *Psychopathia Sexualis*, 12th ed. (1998), 133.
45 Krafft-Ebing, *Psychopathia Sexualis*, 12th ed. (1998), 139.
46 Krafft-Ebing, *Psychopathia Sexualis*, 12th ed. (1998), 139–40.
47 See Michael Stolleis, "Untertan-Bürger-Staatsbürger: Bemerkungen zur juristischen Terminologie im späten 18. Jahrhundert," in *Bürger und Bürgerlichkeit im Zeitalter der Aufklärung*, ed. Rudolf Vierhaus (Heidelberg: Verlag Lambert Schneider, 1981), 65–100.
48 As Žižek explains in response to an example involving the gallows in Kant's *Critique of Practical Reason*: "True 'passion' is not only not hindered but even encouraged and sustained by the prospect of the 'gallows' – *in other words, true 'passion' is uncannily close to fulfilling of one's duty in spite of the external threat to it.*" Žižek, *For They Know Not What They Do*, 239 (emphasis in original).
49 Žižek, *How to Read Lacan*, 55.
50 Žižek, *The Plague of Fantasies*, 35.

51 Sigmund Freud, *Totem and Taboo* (1913), in *The Standard Edition of the Complete Psychological Works of Sigmund Freud*, ed. and trans. James Strachey, vol. 13 (London: Hogarth Press, 1955), 142.
52 Slavoj Žižek, *Interrogating the Real*, ed. Rex Butler and Scott Stephens (London: Continuum, 2005), 269, 270.
53 Žižek, *The Plague of Fantasies*, 35 (emphasis in original).
54 Žižek, *The Parallax View*, 303.
55 Žižek, *How to Read Lacan*, 9.
56 Krafft-Ebing, *Psychopathia Sexualis*, 12th ed. (1998), 240–1.
57 See Deleuze, *Coldness and Cruelty*, 48.
58 Parts of this section draw on and update my arguments in Jeffrey Schneider, "'The Pleasure of the Uniform!': Masculinity, Transvestism and Militarism in Heinrich Mann's *Der Untertan* and Magnus Hirschfeld's *Die Transvestiten*," *The Germanic Review* 72, no. 3 (1997): 183–200.
59 Magnus Hirschfeld, *Die Transvestiten: Eine Untersuchung über den erotischen Verkleidungstrieb* (Berlin: Alfred Pulvermacher, 1910). Unless otherwise noted, translations are from Magnus Hirschfeld, *Transvestites: The Erotic Drive to Cross-Dress*, trans. Michael A. Lombardi-Nash (Buffalo, NY: Prometheus Books, 1991).
60 Darryl B. Hill, "Sexuality and Gender in Hirschfeld's *Die Transvestiten*: A Case of the 'Elusive Evidence of the Ordinary,'" *Journal of the History of Sexuality* 14, no. 3 (2005): 316–32.
61 Hirschfeld, *Transvestites*, 141.
62 On Wilhelm II, see Jeffrey Schneider, "The Emperor's New Uniforms: The Uniform Fantasies of Kaiser Wilhelm II and His Critics," *German Studies Review* 47, no. 1 (forthcoming, February 2024).
63 For a discussion of the ritual scarring in the *Mensur*, see Kevin McAleer, *Dueling: The Cult of Honor in Fin-de-siècle Germany* (Princeton, NJ: Princeton UP, 1994), 141–9; Lisa Zwicker, *Dueling Students: Conflict, Masculinity and Politics in German Universities, 1890–1914* (Ann Arbor: U of Michigan P, 2011), 37–60.
64 Already as a child Heßling "began to doubt the Christ child," who in German tradition brings the Christmas presents (11). Meanwhile, after he encounters the anti-Semitic thoughts of the court preacher Adolf Stöcker, he initially worries that he is supposed to go around recruiting people to Christianity, "which seemed to him a little embarrassing" (58).
65 In his letter offering Heinrich details of his short experience in the military for use in *The Loyal Subject*, Thomas concluded: "Another item for you. In connection with 'squad room,' I just remembered an incident: Someone was actually released as unfit because he announced to the Chief Reserve Commission that he was homosexual. Couldn't you weave that in?" Mann, *Letters of Heinrich and Thomas Mann, 1900–1949*, 115.

66 Hirschfeld, for instance, claims that many actors are homosexual.
67 Heinrich Mann seems to be using this scene as a lesson to his brother, for it suggests that Thomas Mann lacked the bravery of the actor to both admit his homosexuality publicly and to be secure enough in his identity to not need the military and its uniform. Though Thomas detested *The Loyal Subject*, he seems not to have given any notice that his brother might be using this scene – which is, of course, his own – to send him a message.
68 See Mann, *Letters of Heinrich and Thomas Mann, 1900–1949*, 37–42.
69 For a discussion of women's historical involvement in European armies and the consolidation of masculinity in the military that resulted from their removal under the guise of professionalism, see Cynthia Enloe, *Does Khaki Become You? The Militarisation of Women's Lives* (Boston: South End, 1983); Ruth Seifert, "Gender, Nation und Militär – Aspekte von Männlichkeitskonstruktion und Gewaltsozialisation durch Militär und Wehrpflicht," in *Allgemeine Wehrpflicht: Geschichte, Probleme, Perspektiven*, ed. Eckardt Opitz and Frank S. Rödiger (Bremen: Edition Temmen, 1994), 179–94.
70 Hirschfeld, *Transvestites*, 417.
71 Hirschfeld, *Transvestites*, 418.
72 Gunnemann, *Heinrich Mann's Novels and Essays*, 51.
73 Mann, *Betrachtungen eines Unpolitischen*, vol. 13.1, 615.
74 Mann, *Betrachtungen eines Unpolitischen*, vol. 13.1, 615.
75 Mann, *Betrachtungen eines Unpolitischen*, vol. 13.1, 615.
76 Quoted in Baldessari, "Zur Enstehungsgeschichte von Heinrich Manns *Untertan*," 174.
77 Heinrich Mann, "Bitte um Entschuldigung (Der Unterthan)," in *Essays und Publizistik*, vol. 2, *Oktober 1904 bis Oktober 1918*, ed. Manfred Hahn, Anne Flierl, and Wolfgang Klein, Essays und Publizistik: Kritische Gesamtausgabe (Bielefeld: Aisthesis Verlag, 2012), 254. For Heinrich's conciliatory letter to Thomas, see Thomas and Heinrich Mann, *Briefwechsel*, 172–4.
78 From the foreword to a new 1929 edition of *Der Untertan*, reproduced in Emmerich, *Heinrich Mann "Der Untertan,"* 120.
79 Gunnemann, *Heinrich Mann's Novels and Essays*, 69.
80 T.W. Adorno et al., *The Authoritarian Personality*, ed. Max Horkheimer and Samuel H. Flowerman, Studies in Prejudice (New York: Harper & Brothers, 1950); John Levi Martin, "*The Authoritarian Personality*, 50 Years Later: What Lessons Are There for Political Psychology," *Political Psychology* 22, no. 1 (2001): 1, 5, 3.
81 Mann, *Betrachtungen eines Unpolitischen*, vol. 13.1, 604.
82 Mann, *Betrachtungen eines Unpolitischen*, vol. 13.1, 610. During the war, Erich Mühsam also noticed that Heinrich Mann "falls into the opposite

mistake of our patriots in that he considers everything true that the *Matin* negatively reports about Germany and considers everything that appears in German papers to be a lie." Erich Mühsam, *Tagebücher*, ed. Chris Hirte and Conrad Piens, vol. 4 (Berlin: Verbrecher Verlag, 2013), 136.

83 See Martin Jay, *The Dialectical Imagination: A History of the Frankfurt School and the Institute of Social Research, 1923–1950* (Berkeley: U of California P, 1996), 227; Stephen A. Grollman, *Heinrich Mann: Narratives of Wilhelmine Germany, 1895–1925*, Studies on Themes and Motifs in Literature, vol. 64 (New York: Peter Lang, 2002), 81–2.

84 Martin, "The Authoritarian Personality, 50 Years Later," 6.

85 Quoted in Emmerich, *Heinrich Mann "Der Untertan,"* 121.

86 Randall Halle, *Queer Social Philosophy: Critical Readings from Kant to Adorno* (Urbana: U of Illinois P, 2004), 137.

87 Though Hirschfeld's first biographer claims that Heinrich Mann had been an early signatory of Hirschfeld's petition to the Reichstag against Paragraph 175, I have not located any evidence when he had signed. See Wolff, *Magnus Hirschfeld: A Portrait of a Pioneer in Sexology*, 43.

88 Willi Jasper, *Der Bruder Heinrich Mann: Eine Biographie* (Frankfurt/Main: Fischer Taschenbuch, 1994), 145.

89 Mann, *Briefe an Ludwig Ewers, 1889–1913*, 195.

90 Mann, *Briefe an Ludwig Ewers, 1889–1913*, 106–9 (emphasis in original). August von Platen-Hallermünde (1796–1835) wrote homoerotic poetry and remained one of Thomas Mann's favourite authors. Shortly before Platen's death in Italy, he fought a literary feud with Heinrich Heine, who in "The Baths of Lucca," one of three sections in *Journey to Italy*, viciously attacked the aristocratic poet's homosexuality. Heinrich Heine, *Journey to Italy*, ed. Luigi Ballerini and Andrew Wood, trans. Charles G. Leland and revised and edited by Christopher Johnson, Marsilio Classics (New York: Marsilio, 1998).

91 Heinrich Mann, "An Tommy Nach der 'Jagd nach Liebe,'" in *Essays und Publizistik*, vol. 1, *Mai 1889 bis August 1904*, ed. Peter Stein, Manfred Hahn, and Anne Flierl, Essays und Publizistik: Kritische Gesamtausgabe (Bielefeld: Aisthesis Verlag, 2013), 451.

92 Mann, "An Tommy Nach der 'Jagd nach Liebe,'" 451.

93 Mann, "An Tommy Nach der 'Jagd nach Liebe,'" 450. In recognizing that all of Thomas's male characters are really just literary versions of himself, Heinrich diagnosed what he, in response to Thomas's rejection of his peace offering at the end of 1917, would later refer to as "this furious passion for your own ego." Mann, *Letters of Heinrich and Thomas Mann, 1900–1949*, 127.

94 Sigmund Freud, "Creative Writers and Day-Dreaming (1908)," in *The Standard Edition of the Complete Psychological Works of Sigmund Freud*, trans. Joan Riviere and ed. James Strachey, vol. 9 (London: Hogarth Press, 1953), 142–53.

Epilogue: The War on Fantasy

1. Du Bois, "German Politics," 171.
2. "Postcard: 1913 January 11, Marsden Hartley to Norma Berger," Digital Collections, Yale University Library, accessed 29 December 2022, https://collections.library.yale.edu/catalog/11176992.
3. Marsden Hartley, *My Dear Stieglitz: Letters of Marsden Hartley and Alfred Stieglitz, 1912–1915*, ed. James Timothy Voorhies (Columbia, SC: U of South Carolina P, 2002), 53. Hartley's year abroad was funded by wealthy New York art patrons that Stieglitz had lined up.
4. Hartley, *My Dear Stieglitz*, 17.
5. Hartley, *My Dear Stieglitz*, 54.
6. "Postcard: 1913 August 30, Marsden Hartley to Gertrude Stein," Digital Collections, Yale University Library, accessed 29 December 2022, https://collections.library.yale.edu/catalog/2017534.
7. Magnus Hirschfeld, *Das Ergebnis der statistischen Untersuchungen über den Prozentsatz der Homosexuellen* (Leipzig: Max Spohr, 1904), 11; Hirschfeld, *The Homosexuality of Men and Women*, 784.
8. Simmel, "The Sociology of Secrecy," 465.
9. Foucault, *The History of Sexuality, Vol. I*, 35 (emphasis in original).
10. Hirschfeld, *Transvestites*; Hirschfeld, *The Homosexuality of Men and Women*.
11. Beachy, *Gay Berlin*, 140.
12. Jonathan Weinberg, *Speaking for Vice: Homosexuality in the Art of Charles Demuth, Marsden Hartley, and the First American Avant-Garde* (New Haven, CT: Yale UP, 1995), 122, 127.
13. Weinberg, *Speaking for Vice*, 124.
14. Bruce Robertson, *Marsden Hartley*, The Library of American Art (New York: Harry N. Abrams, 1995), 15.
15. Marsden Hartley, *Somehow a Past: The Autobiography of Marsden Hartley*, ed. Susan Elizabeth Ryan (Cambridge, MA: MIT P, 1997), 90.
16. Hartley, *Somehow a Past*, 87.
17. Barbara Haskell, *Marsden Hartley* (New York: Whitney Museum of American Art, 1980), 33, quoted in Townsend Ludington, *Marsden Hartley: The Biography of an American Artist* (Boston: Little, Brown and Company, 1992), 105–6.
18. Weinberg, *Speaking for Vice*, 147.
19. On Germany's colonial wars, see Hull, *Absolute Destruction*; Susanne Kiss, *German Colonial Wars and the Context of Military Violence*, trans. Andrew Smith (Cambridge, MA: Harvard UP, 2017).
20. On this dimension of militarism, see Vagts, *A History of Militarism*.
21. As a result of the steady critique of military policy from current officers, orders were issued to prevent active-duty personnel from publishing

essays without prior approval. Similarly, Wilhelm Lamszus's *Das Menschenschlachthaus* (The human slaughterhouse), a 1912 novel written for youth depicting "images of the coming war" (as the subtitle reads) in which the butchery of mass armies outfitted with machine guns and increasingly destructive artillery extinguish any form of individual heroism, was the subject of intense government scrutiny and eventually banned in 1915. See Bernhard Gleim and Dieter Richter, "'Das Menschenschlachthaus' und seine Leser. Ein Stück Wirkungsgeschichte aus den Akten der Polizei," in *Das Menschenschlachthaus: Bilder vom kommenden Krieg*, ed. Johannes Merkel and Dieter Richter, Sammlung Alter Kinderbücher (Munich: Weismann Verlag, 1980), 131–52.

22 Frevert, *A Nation in Barracks*, 212.
23 Frevert, *A Nation in Barracks*, 212.
24 Hartley, *My Dear Stieglitz*, 154.
25 Hartley, *My Dear Stieglitz*, 155.
26 Hartley, *My Dear Stieglitz*, 157.
27 Hartley, *My Dear Stieglitz*, 164–5.
28 Thomas Weißbrich, "Das Ende der Parade – Marsden Hartley und das preußische Militär," in *Marsden Hartley: Die deutschen Bilder 1913–1915*, ed. Dieter Scholz (Cologne: Verlag der Buchhandlung Walther König, 2014), 128–39.
29 Hartley wrote Charles Demuth, another homosexual American painter, that "I have not been near Potsdam since the war [began] – I don't know when I shall ever go again – there is too much to remember." Hartley to Charles Demuth, n.d., Yale Collection of American Literature, Beinecke Rare Book and Manuscript Library, Yale University, quoted in Patricia McDonnell, *Dictated by Life: Marsden Hartley's German Paintings and Robert Indiana's Hartley Elegies* (Minneapolis: Frederick R. Weisman Art Museum, 1995), 39.
30 "Von Freyburg, Carl [1913 December 3, Letter to Marsden Hartley]," Digital Collections, Yale University, accessed 29 December 2022, https://collections.library.yale.edu/catalog/17188753.
31 Weißbrich, "Das Ende der Parade – Marsden Hartley und das preußische Militär," 134.
32 Dieter Scholz, "Marsden Hartley in Berlin," in *Marsden Hartley: Die deutschen Bilder 1913–1915*, ed. Dieter Scholz (Cologne: Verlag der Buchhandlung Walther König, 2014), 28.
33 Weinberg, *Speaking for Vice*, 128.
34 Hartley, *My Dear Stieglitz*, 182.
35 Robertson, *Marsden Hartley*, 56.
36 For a key to the different elements, see Weißbrich, "Das Ende der Parade – Marsden Hartley und das preußische Militär," 138–9.

37 See Scholz, "Marsden Hartley in Berlin," 53; Alexia Pooth, "Singulär im Kollektiv. Marsden Hartley und die Tradition der amerikanischen Künstlerreise nach Europa," in *Marsden Hartley: Die deutschen Bilder 1913–1915*, ed. Dieter Scholz (Cologne: Verlag der Buchhandlung Walther König, 2014), 202–3.
38 McDonnell, *Dictated by Life*, 32.
39 Patricia McDonnell, *Marsden Hartley: American Modern* (Minneapolis: Frederick R. Weisman Art Museum, 1997), 39. McDonnell also points out that in his pursuit of "subjectivity and objectivity with equal vigor," Hartley was developing a "pictorial vocabulary" that mimics Stein's famous word portraits. McDonnell, *Dictated by Life*, 27–8.
40 Weinberg, *Speaking for Vice*, 120.
41 Weinberg, *Speaking for Vice*, 159.
42 See, for example, his letter of 15 March 1915, in Hartley, *My Dear Stieglitz*, 182.
43 McDonnell, *Marsden Hartley: American Modern*, 40. See also Weinberg, *Speaking for Vice*, 158.
44 Weinberg, *Speaking for Vice*, 162.
45 Weinberg, *Speaking for Vice*, 150. Hartley reads this image of light and white as "the sublimation of our intended relation and was without blemish, and you were therefore in this dream, immortalized."
46 Weinberg, *Speaking for Vice*, 154.
47 Magnus Hirschfeld and Andreas Gaspar, eds., *Sittengeschichte des Ersten Weltkrieges*, 2nd rev. ed. (Cologne: Komet, [1990s] [1930]), 216.
48 Crouthamel, *Intimate History of the Front*, 125.
49 Thomas Kühne, *The Rise and Fall of Comradeship: Hitler's Soldiers, Male Bonding and Mass Violence in the Twentieth Century* (Cambridge: Cambridge UP, 2017), 30.
50 Crouthamel, *Intimate History of the Front*, 140.
51 See Marhoefer, *Sex and the Weimar Republic*, esp. 112–45.
52 See Whisnant, *Queer Identities and Politics in Germany*, 193.
53 Andrew Wackerfuss, *Stormtrooper Families: Homosexuality and Community in the Early Nazi Movement* (New York: Harrington Park Press, 2015), 63.
54 See Marhoefer, *Sex and the Weimar Republic*, 158–9.
55 Hewitt, *Political Inversions*, 16.
56 Marhoefer, *Sex and the Weimar Republic*, 172.
57 Wackerfuss, *Stormtrooper Families*, 302.
58 Wackerfuss, *Stormtrooper Families*, 301, 307.
59 See Whisnant, *Queer Identities and Politics in Germany* 209–23; Geoffrey J. Giles, "Legislating Homophobia in the Third Reich: The Radicalization of Prosecution Against Homosexuality by the Legal Profession," *German History* 23, no. 3 (2005): 339–54.

60 See Geoffrey J. Giles, "The Denial of Homosexuality: Same-Sex Incidents in Himmler's SS and Police," *Journal of the History of Sexuality* 11, no. 1/2 (2002): 256–90; Geoffrey J. Giles, "The Institutionalization of Homosexual Panic in the Third Reich," in *Social Outsiders in Nazi Germany*, ed. Robert Gellately and Nathan Stoltzfus (Princeton, NJ: U of Princeton P, 2018), 233–56.
61 See, for instance, the second part of Susan Sontag, "Fascinating Fascism," in *Under the Sign of Saturn* (New York: Farrer, Strauss, Giroux, 1980), 98–105. For criticism of Sontag's approach, see Jeffrey T. Schnapp, "Fascinating Fascism," *Journal of Contemporary History* 31, no. 2 (1996): 236–7.
62 Herzog, *Sex after Fascism*, 73.
63 Herzog, *Sex after Fascism*, 156.
64 Whisnant, *Queer Identities and Politics in Germany*, 251.
65 Josie McLellan, *Love in the Time of Communism: Intimacy and Sexuality in the GDR* (Cambridge: Cambridge UP, 2011), 114.
66 Tom Smith, *Comrades in Arms: Military Masculinities in East German Culture* (New York: Berghahn, 2020), 211.
67 See Friederike Brühöfener, "Contested Masculinities: Debates about Homosexuality in the West German Bundeswehr in the 1960s and 1970s," in *Gendering Post-1945 German History: Entanglements*, ed. Karen Hagemann, Donna Harsch, and Friederike Brühöfener (New York: Berghahn, 2019), 301–3.
68 Brühöfener, "Contested Masculinities," 305–8.

Bibliography

Primary Texts

Government Publications

Bericht über die Gemeinde-Verwaltung der Stadt Berlin
Statistisches Jahrbuch für den Preußischen Staat
Stenographische Berichte

Journals, Newspapers, and Magazines

Allgemeines Literaturblatt
BZ am Mittag
Coburger Zeitung
Der Eigene
Freiburger Zeitung
Jahrbuch für sexuelle Zwischenstufen
Militär-Wochenblatt
Monatsbericht des Wissenschaftlich-humanitären Komitees
New York Times
Politisch-anthropologische Revue
Vierteljahresberichte des Wissenschaftlich-humanitäres Komitees
Volksstimme (Magdeburg)
Die Vossische Zeitung (Berlin)
Zeitschrift für Sexualwissenschaft
Die Zukunft

Books and Articles

Altmann-Gottheiner, Elisabeth. "Die deutschen politischen Parteien und ihre Stellung zur Frauenfrage." *Zeitschrift für Politik* 3 (1910): 581–98.

Anonymous. *Das perverse Berlin: Kulturkritische Gänge*. Berlin: Eckstein, 1908.
Atkinson, Charles Francis. "Grenadier." In *The Encylopedia Britannica*. Vol. 11, 579. New York: Encyclopedia Britannica, Inc., 1910.
"Aus Berliner Vororten. [Die Auflösung der bürgerlichn Demokratie.]." *Kommunale Praxis: Wochenschrift für Kommunalpolitik und Gemeindesozialismus*, 26 October, 1912, 1334–5.
"Ausbildung und Erziehung: Eine psychologische Studie (Part I)." *Militär-Wochenblatt* 78, no. 65 (1893): 1694.
Back, Dr. Georg. *Sexuelle Verirrungen des Menschen und der Natur*. 2nd and 3rd eds. Berlin: Standard-Verlag, 1910.
Below, Georg von. *Das Duell in Deutschland: Geschichte und Gegenwart*. Kassel: Max Brunnemann, 1896.
Berg, Leo. "Grausamkeit." In *Aus der Zeit – Gegen die Zeit: Gesammelte Essays*, 397–412. Berlin: Hüpeden & Merzyn, 1905.
Bergg, Franz. *Ein Proletarierleben*. Edited by Nikolaus Welter. Frankfurt/Main: Neuer Frankfurter Verlag, 1913.
"Besoldung." In *Militär-Lexikon: Handwörterbuch der Militärwissenschaften*, edited by Hermann Frobenius, 82–3. Berlin: Martin Oldenbourg, 1901.
Binet, Alfred. "Der Fetischismus in der Liebe." In *Fetischismus: Grundlagentexte vom 18. Jahrhundert bis in die Gegenwart*, edited by Johannes Endres, 226–40. Frankfurt/Main: Suhrkamp, 2017.
Bloch, Iwan. *Beiträge zur Aetiologie der Psychopathia sexualis*. Vol. 1. Dresden: H.R. Dohrn, 1902.
– *Beiträge zur Aetiologie der Psychopathia sexualis*. Vol. 2. Dresden: H.R. Dohrn, 1903.
Boguslawski, Albert von. *Der Ehrbegriff des Offizierstandes: Ein kurzes Wort zur Aufklärung*. Berlin: Schall und Grund, 1897.
Bülow, Bernhard. *Memoirs of Prince von Bülow*. Translated by Geoffrey Dunlop and F. A. Voigt. 4 vols. Vol. 4. Boston: Little, Brown, and Company, 1932.
Davis, George Breckenridge. *A Treatise on the Military Law of the United States*. 2nd ed. New York: John Wiley & Sons, 1908.
Dawson, William Harbutt. *Germany and the Germans*. 2 vols. Vol. 1. New York: D. Appleton & Company, 1894.
Du Bois, W.E.B. *The Autobiography of W.E.B. Dubois: A Soliloquy on Viewing My Life from the Last Decade of Its First Century*. New York: International, 1968.
– "Interview of W.E.B DuBois by William Ingersoll, May 24, 1960." In *The Reminiscences of William Edward Burghardt du Bois, 1963*, edited by William T. Ingersoll, 84–126. Alexandria, VA: Alexander Street Press, 2003.
– "The Present Condition of German Politics." *Central European History* 31, no. 3 (1998): 171–87.

Eulenburg, Albrecht. *Sadismus und Masochismus. Grenzfragen des Nerven- und Seelenlebens. Einzeldarstellungen für Gebildete aller Stände im Vereine mit hervorragenden Fachmännern des In- und Auslandes*. Edited by Dr. L. Loewenfeld and Dr. Hans Kurella. Vol. 19. Wiesbaden: J.F. Bergmann, 1902.
– "Zur Einführung (Introduction to Hanns Heinz Ewers's 1905 drama *Enterbt*)." In *Jasminblüte: Schwule deutschsprachige Theaterstücke um 1900*, edited by Manfred Herzer, 125–7. Hamburg: Männerschwarm, 2018

Exner, Moritz. *Der Weg zum Einjährig-Freiwilligen und zum Offizier des Beurlaubtenstandes in Armee und Marine*. 2nd ed. Leipzig: Verlagsbuchhandlung von J.J. Weber, 1897.

Field, Edward. "A Lesson from History." *United Service: A Monthly Review of Military and Naval Affairs* 7 (1892): 347–56.

Freud, Sigmund. "'A Child Is Being Beaten': A Contribution to the Study of the Origins of Sexual Perversions (1919)." In *Standard Edition of the Complete Psychological Works of Sigmund Freud*, edited and translated by James Strachey, vol. 17, 175–204. London: Hogarth Press, 1955.
– "Creative Writers and Day-Dreaming (1908)." In *The Standard Edition of the Complete Psychological Works of Sigmund Freud*, translated by Joan Riviere and edited by James Strachey, vol. 9, 142–53. London: Hogarth Press, 1959.
– "Fetishism (1928)." In *The Standard Edition of the Complete Psychological Works of Sigmund Freud*, edited and translated by James Strachey, vol. 21, 147–58. London: Hogarth Press, 1953.
– *Three Essays on the Theory of Sexuality* (1905). In *The Standard Edition of the Complete Psychological Works of Sigmund Freud*, edited and translated by James Strachey, vol. 7, 123–246. London: Hogarth Press, 1953.
– *Totem and Taboo* (1913). In *The Standard Edition of the Complete Psychological Works of Sigmund Freud*, edited and translated by James Strachey, vol. 13, 1–164. London: Hogarth Press, 1955.

Friedlaender, Benedict. "Aus der Denkschrift für die Freunde und Fondzeichner des Wissenschaftlich-Humanitären Komitees im Namen der Sezession des Wissenschaftlich-Humanitären Komitees." In *Die Liebe Platons im Lichte der modernen Biologie*, 197–230. Treptow: Bernhard Zack, 1909.
– "Schadet die soziale Freigabe des homosexuellen Verkehrs der kriegerischen Tüchtigkeit der Rasse? Ein vorläufiger Hinweis." *Jahrbuch für sexuelle Zwischenstufen* 7 (1905): 463–70.

Friedlaender, Hugo. "Der Beleidigungsprozeß des Berliner Stadtkommandanten Generalleutnant z.D. Graf Kuno von Moltke gegen den Herausgeber der 'Zukunft' Maximilian Harden." In *Interessante Kriminal-Prozesse*, edited by Hugo Friedländer, 3–203. Berlin: Hermann Barsdorf, 1919. Reprint, vol. 51 of Digitale Bibliothek, CD-ROM.

Grävell, Dr. "Die Uniform als Erzieher." *Pädagogisches Archiv: Monatsschrift für Erziehung und Unterricht* 46, no. 12 (1904): 736–45.
Handtke, Dr. H. "Sachverständigenrappel." *Der Deutsche* 7, no. 7 (10 November 1907): 193–8.
Hartley, Marsden. *My Dear Stieglitz: Letters of Marsden Hartley and Alfred Stieglitz, 1912–1915*. Edited by James Timothy Voorhies. Columbia, SC: U of South Carolina P, 2002.
– *Somehow a Past: The Autobiography of Marsden Hartley*. Edited by Susan Elizabeth Ryan. Cambridge, MA: MIT P, 1997.
Heine, Heinrich. *Journey to Italy*. Translated by Charles G. Leland and revised and edited by Christopher Johnson. Marsilio Classics. Edited by Luigi Ballerini and Andrew Wood. New York: Marsilio, 1998.
Herzer, Manfred, ed. *Jasminblüthe: Schwule deutschsprachige Theaterstücke um 1900*. Hamburg: Männerschwarm Verlag, 2018.
Hildebrandt, Paul. *Das Spielzeug im Leben des Kindes*. Berlin: G. Söhlke, 1904.
Hirschfeld, Magnus. *Berlins Drittes Geschlecht*. Edited by Manfred Herzer. Berlin: Verlag Rosa Winkel, 1991.
– *Berlin's Third Sex*. Translated by James J. Conway. Berlin: Rixdorf Editions, 2017.
– "Einiges über die Ursachen und Erscheinungsformen der männlichen (nicht erpresserischen) Prostitution." *Archiv für Kriminalanthropologie und Kriminalistik* 52 (1913): 339–63.
– *Das Ergebnis der statistischen Untersuchungen über den Prozentsatz der Homosexuellen*. Leipzig: Max Spohr, 1904.
– *The Homosexuality of Men and Women*. Translated by Michael A Lombardi-Nash. Amherst, NY: Prometheus, 2000.
– *Sappho und Sokrates: Wie erklärt sich die Liebe der Männer und Frauen zu Personen des eigenen Geschlechts?* 2nd ed. Leipzig: Max Spohr, 1902.
– *Sexualpsychologie und Volkspsychologie: Eine epikritische Studie zum Harden-Prozess*. Leipzig: Georg H. Wigand, 1908.
– *Die Transvestiten: Eine Untersuchung über den erotischen Verkleidungstrieb*. Berlin: Alfred Pulvermacher, 1910.
– *Transvestites: The Erotic Drive to Cross-Dress*. Translated by Michael A. Lombardi-Nash. Buffalo, NY: Prometheus Books, 1991.
– *Der urnische Mensch*. Leipzig: Max Spohr, 1903.
– *Von einst bis jetzt: Geschichte einer homosexuellen Bewegung 1897–1922*. Edited by Manfred Herzer and James D. Steakley. Berlin: Verlag Rosa Winkel, 1986.
– *Warum hassen uns die Völker? Eine kriegspsychologische Betrachtung*. Bonn: A. Marcus & E. Webers Verlag, 1914.
– "What People Should Know about the Third Sex." In *Berlin's Third Sex*. Translated by James J. Conway, 101–26. Berlin: Rixdorf Editions, 2017.

Hirschfeld, Magnus, and Andreas Gaspar, eds. *Sittengeschichte des Ersten Weltkrieges*. 2nd rev. ed. Köln: Komet, [1990?]. First published 1930 by Verlag für Sexualwissenschaft Schneider.

Hue de Grais, Robert. *Heer und Kriegsflotte*. Vol. 1. *Allgemeine Bestimmungen*. Berlin: Julius Springer, 1904.

Ilgenstein, Heinrich. "Mein System: Bekenntnisse von Maximilian Harden mit verbindendem Text von Heinrich Ilgenstein." *Das Blaubuch*, 31 October 1907, 1326–33.

Kant, Immanuel. "An Answer to the Question: What Is Enlightenment?" Translated by David L. Colclasure, Jeremy Waldon, Michael W. Doyle, and Allen W. Wood. In *Toward Perpetual Peace and Other Writings on Politics, Peace, and History*, edited by Pauline Kleingeld, 17–23. New Haven, CT: Yale UP, 2006.

Keller, Ernst. "Soldatenmisshandlungen." *Sozialistische Monatshefte* 14, no. 2 (1905): 130–9.

Kertbeny, Karl Maria. *Schriften zur Homosexualitätsforschung*. Bibliothek rosa Winkel. Edited by Manfred Herzer. Vol. 22. Berlin: Verlag rosa Winkel, 2000.

Korell, D.K. *Pädagogische Irrwege oder Sadismus*. Berlin: Hugo Bermühler Verlag, 1904.

Krafft, Rudolf. *Kasernen-Elend: Offene Kritik der Verhältnisse unserer Unteroffiziere und Soldaten*. Stuttgart: Verlag von Robert Lutz, 1895.

Krafft-Ebing, Richard von. *Neue Forschungen auf dem Gebiet der Psychopathia Sexualis: Eine medicinisch-psychologische Studie*. Stuttgart: Verlag von Ferdinand Enke, 1890.

– *Psychopathia Sexualis, mit besonderer Berücksichtigung der conträren Sexualempfindung: Eine klinische-forensische Studie*. 7th enlarged and rev. ed. Stuttgart: Ferdinand Enke, 1892.

– *Psychopathia Sexualis, mit besonderer Berücksichtigung der conträren Sexualempfindung: Eine klinische-forensische Studie*. 10th enlarged and rev. ed. Stuttgart: Ferdinand Enke, 1898.

– *Psychopathia Sexualis, with Especial Reference to Contrary Sexual Instinct: A Medio-Legal Study*. Translated by Charles Gilbert Chaddock, MD. 7th enlarged and rev. ed. Philadelphia: F.A. Davis, 1894.

– *Psychopathia Sexualis: With Especial Reference to the Antipathic Sexual Instinct*. Translated by Franklin S. Klaf. 12th ed. New York: Arcade, 1998.

Krickel, G., and G. Lange. *Das Deutsche Reichsheer in seiner neuesten Bekleidung und Ausrüstung*. Marzoll: Eikon-Verlag. Faksimile-Nachdruck, 1977. First published 1888/90 by H. Toussaint.

Kriegsministerium, and Geheime Kriegs-Kanzlei, eds. *Rangliste der Königlich Preußischen Armee und des XIII. (Königlich Württembergischen) Armeekorps für 1911*. Berlin: Ernst Siegfried Mittler und Sohn, 1911.

Kriegsministerium, Königlich Preußischen, ed. *Kompendium über Militärrecht*. Berlin: Ernst Siegfried Mittler und Sohn, 1900.

Kupffer, Elisarion von. *Lieblingminne und Freundesliebe in der Weltliteratur: Eine Sammlung mit einer ethisch-politischen Einleitung.* Leipzig: Max Spohr, 1899.

Liebig, Dr. Hans von. "Die Grossstadtdokumente (Review)." *Die Umschau: Übersicht über die Forschritte und Bewegungen auf dem Gesamtgebiet der Wissenschaft, Technik, Literatur und Kunst* 11, no. 47 (16 November 1907): 935–8.

Linke, Konrad. "Ich hatt' einen Kameraden – ." In *Der Eigene: Ein Blatt für männliche Kultur: Ein Querschnitt durch die erste Homosexuellenzeitschrift der Welt*, edited by Joachim S. Hohmann. Frankfurt: Foerster, 1981.

Lüders, Marie-Elisabeth. *Das unbekannte Heer: Frauen kämpfen fur Deutschland, 1914–1918.* Berlin: E.S. Mittler & Sohn, 1936.

Mann, Heinrich. "Autograph letter signed ("Heinrich Mann")," Munich, 19 January 1907. Kotte Autographs. Accessed 28 December 2022, https://www.kotte-autographs.com/en/autograph/mann-heinrich/.

– "Bitte um Entschuldigung (Der Unterthan)." In *Essays und Publizistik*. Vol. 2. *Oktober 1904 bis Oktober 1918*, edited by Manfred Hahn, Anne Flierl, and Wolfgang Klein, 254–5. Essays und Publizistik: Kritische Gesamtausgabe. Bielefeld: Aisthesis Verlag, 2012.

– *Briefe an Ludwig Ewers, 1889–1913.* Edited by Ulrich Dietzel and Rosemarie Eggert. Berlin: Aufbau-Verlag, 1980.

– *The Loyal Subject.* Translated by Ernest Boyd and Daniel Theisen. New York: Continuum, 1998.

– "An Tommy Nach der 'Jagd nach Liebe.'" In *Essays und Publizistik*. Vol. 1. *Mai 1889 bis August 1904*, edited by Peter Stein, Manfred Hahn, and Anne Flierl, 447–61. Essays und Publizistik: Kritische Gesamtausgabe. Bielefeld: Aisthesis Verlag, 2013.

– *Der Untertan.* Frankfurt/Main: S. Fischer, 2000.

– *Der Untertan.* Gesammelte Werke in Einzelbänden. Edited by Peter-Paul Schneider. Frankfurt/Main: S. Fischer, 1995.

Mann, Thomas. *Bekenntnisse des Hochstaplers Felix Krull: Der Memoiren erster Teil.* Edited by Thomas Sprecher, Monica Bussmann, and Eckhard Heftrich. Vol. 12.1. Große kommentierte Frankfurter Ausgabe. Werke, Briefe, Tagebücher. Frankfurt: S. Fischer, 2012.

– *Betrachtungen eines Unpolitischen.* Edited by Hermann Kurzke. Vol. 13.1. Große kommentierte Frankfurter Ausgabe. Werke, Briefe, Tagebücher. Frankfurt: S. Fischer, 2012.

– *Briefe, 1948–1955 und Nachlese.* Edited by Erika Mann. Vol. 3. Frankfurt/Main: S. Fischer, 1965.

– *Briefe an Otto Grautoff 1894–1901 und Ida Boy-Ed 1903–1928.* Edited by Peter de Mendelssohn. Frankfurt/Main: S. Fischer, 1975.

– "Friedrich und die Große Koalition. Ein Abriss für den Tag und die Stunde." In *Essays II*, edited by Hermann Kurzke, Jöelle Stoupy, Jörn

Bender, and Stephan Stachorski, 55–122, vol. 15.1. Große kommentierte Frankfurter Ausgabe. Werke, Briefe, Tagebücher. Frankfurt: S. Fischer, 2012.
- "Gedanken im Kriege." In *Essays II*, edited by Hermann Kurzke, Jöelle Stoupy, Jörn Bender, and Stephan Stachorski, 27–46, vol. 15.1. Große kommentierte Frankfurter Ausgabe. Werke, Briefe, Tagebücher. Frankfurt: S. Fischer, 2012.
- "Gute Feldpost." In *Essays II*, edited by Hermann Kurzke, Jöelle Stoupy, Jörn Bender, and Stephan Stachorski, 47–50, vol. 15.1. Große kommentierte Frankfurter Ausgabe. Werke, Briefe, Tagebücher. Frankfurt: S. Fischer, 2012.
- "Im Spiegel." In *Essays*, edited by Hermann Kurzke and Stephan Stachorski, 98–101, vol. 1. Frankfurt/Main: S. Fischer, 1994.
- "Lebensabriss." In *Essays*, edited by Hermann Kurzke and Stephan Stachorski, 177–222, vol. 3. Frankfurt/Main: S. Fischer, 1994.
- *Letters of Heinrich and Thomas Mann, 1900–1949*. Edited by Hans Wysling. Translated by Don Renau, Richard Winston, and Clara Winston. Berkeley: U of California P, 1998.
- *Letters of Thomas Mann*. Edited by Richard Winston and Clara Winston. Translated by Richard Winston and Clara Winston. New York: Alfred A. Knopf, 1971.
- *Reflections of a Nonpolitical Man*. Translated by Walter D. Morris. New York: Frederick Ungar, 1983.

Mann, Viktor. *Wir waren fünf: Bildnis der Familie Mann*. 3rd ed. Konstanz: Südverlag Konstanz, 1973.

Mayne, Xavier. *The Intersexes: A History of Similisexualism as a Problem in Social Life*. Naples: Privately Printed, 1908.

McAuley, Mary Ethel. *Germany in War Time: What an American Girl Saw and Heard*. Chicago: The Open Court, 1917.

Meyers Konversations-Lexikon. Vol. 5. Leipzig: Verlag des Bibliographischen Instituts, 1888.

Meyers Konversations-Lexikon. 4th ed. Vol. 6. Leipzig: Verlag des Bibliographischen Instituts, 1890.

Militär-Strafgesetzbuch vom 20. Juni 1872. Verordnung über die Disziplinar-Strafordnung für das deutsche Heer vom 31. Oktober 1872. Vorschriften über den Dienstweg und die Behandlung von Beschwerden der MilitärPersonen des Heeres und der Marine, sowie der Civilbeamten der Militär- und Marine-Verwaltung vom 6. März 1873. Kriegs-Artikel für das Heer vom 31. Oktober 1872. Amtliche Ausgabe ed. Berlin: Ernst Siegfried Mittler und Sohn, 1883.

Moll, Albert. *Ärztliche Ethik: Die pflichten des Arztes in allen Beziehungen seiner Thätigkeit*. Stuttgart: Ferdinand Enke, 1909.
- *Die konträre Sexualempfindung*. 3rd ed. Berlin: Fischers Medicinische Buchhandlung, 1899.
- *Sexuelle Perversionen, Geisteskrankheit und Zurechnungsfähigkeit*. Berlin: Leonhard Simion Nf, 1906.

Mühsam, Erich. *Tagebücher*. Edited by Chris Hirte and Conrad Piens. Vol. 4. Berlin: Verbrecher Verlag, 2013.

Näcke, Paul. "Forensisch-psychiatrisch-psychologische Randglossen zum Prozesse Dippold, insbesondere über Sadismus." *Archiv für Kriminalanthropologie und Kriminalistik* 13, no. 4 (1903).

Nightingale, Florence. *Suggestions for Thought*. Edited by Michael D. Calabria and Janet A Macrae. Philadelphia: U of Pennsylvania P, 1994.

Nordau, Max. *Degeneration*. Translated from the second edition of the German work. New York: D. Appleton and Company, 1895.

Oppenhoff, Friedrich, ed. *Strafgesetzbuch für das Deutsche Reich, mit Commentar*. 12th expanded ed. Edited by Theodor Oppenhoff. Berlin: Georg Reimer, 1891.

Ostwald, Hans. *Männliche Prostitution im kaiserlichen Berlin*. Berlin: Janssen-Verlag, 1991. First published 1906 by W. Fiedler.

Philippi. "Berlins drittes Geschlecht von Magnus Hirschfeld (Review)." *Monatshefte für praktische Dermatologie* 40, no. 4 (15 February 1905): 296–7.

Rau, Hans. *Franz Grillparzer und sein Liebesleben*. Berlin: Barsdorf, 1904.

– *Der Geschlechtstrieb und seine Verirrungen: Ein Beitrag zur Seelenkunde*. Berlin: Hugo Steinitz, 1903.

– *Die Grausamkeit mit besonderer Bezugnahme auf sexuelle Faktoren*. 3rd ed. Berlin: Hermann Barsdorf Verlag, 1913. First published 1903 by Barsdorf Verlag.

– *Liebesfreiheit! Urninge und Tribaden: Ein Aufruf an das Volk*. Oranienburg: Orania-Verlag, 1903.

– *Der Sadismus in der Armee*. Berlin: Hugo Bermühler Verlag, 1904.

– *Wollust und Schmerz: Eine psychologische Studie*. Oranienburg: Orania-Verlag, 1904.

Reddi, Franz. *Der fremde Gott: Ein Familiendrama in einem Aufzug*. Leipzig: Max Spohr, 1907.

Rehbein, Franz. *Das Leben eines Landarbeiters*. Edited by Paul Göhre. Jena: Eugen Diederichs, 1911.

Rosegger, Peter. "Im Gerichtssaal (1906)." In *Abenddämmerung: Rückblicke auf den Schauplatz des Lebens*, 229–37. Leipzig: L. Staackmann, 1919.

Schaible, Camill. *Standes- und Berufspflichten des deutschen Offizierkorps: Für angehende und jüngere Offiziere des stehenden Heeres und des Beurlaubtenstandes*. 3rd rev. ed. Berlin: R. Eisenschmidt, 1896.

Schmidt, Otto Ernst. "Soldaten oder Menschen? Ein Wort über militärische Erziehung und Soldatenmißhandlung." In *Buch der Hoffnung: Neue Folge der gesammelten Essays aus Litteratur, Pädagogik und öffentlichem Leben*, 154–203. Hamburg: Verlag von Conrad Kloß, 1896.

Schurtz, Heinrich. *Altersklassen und Männerbünde: Eine Darstellung der Grundformen der Gesellschaft*. Berlin: Georg Reimer, 1902.

Schwarzseher, von einem. *Unser Kaiser und Sein Volk! Deutsche Sorgen*. 6th ed. Freiburg: Paul Waetzel, 1906.

Simmel, Georg. "Das Geheimnis und die geheime Gesellschaft." In *Soziologie: Untersuchungen über die Formen der Vergesellschaftung*, 337–402. Leipzig: Duncker & Humblot, 1908.
- "Der Militarismus und die Stellung der Frauen." In *Aufsätze und Abhandlungen, 1894 bis 1900*, edited by Heinz-Jürgen Dahme and David P. Frisby, 37–51. Frankfurt/Main: Suhrkamp, 1992.
- "The Sociology of Secrecy and of Secret Societies." *The American Journal of Sociology* 11, no. 4 (1906): 441–98.

Soldaten-Bilderbuch für die deutsche Jugend. [Berlin?]: n.p., [1900?].

Sper, A. *Capri und die Homosexuellen*. Oranienburg: Orania-Verlag, 1903.
- *Lustmörder der Neuzeit*. Berlin: Berliner Zeitschriften-Vertrieb, 1904.

"Strafgerichts-Ordnung." *Bundes-Gesetzblatt des Norddeutschen Bundes*, no. 12 (1867): 229–82.

Thomas, Adrienne. *Die Katrin wird Soldat: Ein Roman aus Elsaß-Lothringen*. Berlin: Im Propyläen-Verlag, 1930.

Tresckow, Hans von. *Von Fürsten und anderen Sterblichen: Erinnerungen eines Kriminalkommissars*. Berlin: F. Fontane & Co., 1922.

Ulrichs, Karl Heinrich. *Forschungen über das Rätsel der mannmännlichen Liebe*. Edited by Hubert Kennedy. 12 vols. Berlin: Verlag rosa Winkel, 1994.
- *The Riddle of "Man-Manly" Love: The Pioneering Work on Male Homosexuality*. Translated by Michael A Lombardi-Nash. 2 vols. Buffalo, NY: Prometheus Books, 1994.

Verfassung des Deutschen Reichs: Gegeben Berlin, den 16. April 1871: Text-Ausgabe mit Ergänzungen, Anmerkungen und Sachregister. Edited by Ludwig von Rönne. 3rd expanded ed. Berlin: J. Guttentag, 1878.

Verzeichnis der Garnisonorte der Deutschen Armee und der Kaiserlichen Marine mit Angabe der Truppenteile, Kommandobehörden usw. sowie der Ortsklassen für sämtliche Garnisonorte. n.p.: n.p., 1910. http://reservistenkrugsammler.de/Garnisonsorte.php.

Weber, Max. *Economy and Society: An Outline of Interpretive Sociology*. Edited by Guenther Roth and Claus Wittich. Translated by Ephraim Fishoff, Hans Gerth, A.M. Henderson, Ferdinand Kolegar, C. Wright Mills, Talcott Parsons, Max Rheinstein, et al. Vol. 2. Berkeley: U of California P, 1978.

Westphal, Carl. "Die conträre Sexualempfindung, Symptom eines neuropathischen (psychopathischen) Zustandes." *Archiv für Psychiatrie und Nervenkrankheit* 2 (1870): 73–108.

Wildenbruch, Ernst von. "Das edle Blut." *Deutsche Rundschau* 73 (1892): 1–20.
- *Das edle Blut*. With Introduction, Notes, Vocabularly, and Exercises. Edited by Ashley K. Hardy. New York: Henry Holt and Company, 1906.
- *Das edle Blut*. With Introduction, Notes, Exercises, and Vocabulary. Edited by Lee M. Hollander. New York: F.S. Crofts, 1927.
- *Das edle Blut*. 24th ed. Berlin: Freund & Jeckel, 1896.

- *Das edle Blut: Eine Erzählung. Mit Zeichnungen von H. Skarbina.* 239th–240th eds. Berlin: Grote Verlag, 1969.
- *Das edle Blut: Eine Erzählung. Neue Ausgabe mit Zeichnungen von Carl Röhling.* 75th ed. Berlin: Grote Verlag, 1905.
- "Noble Blood." Translated by Muriel Almon. In *The German Classics of the Nineteenth and Twentieth Centuries: Masterpieces of German Literature Translated into English,* edited by Kuno Francke and William Howard, vol. 17, 125–53. Albany, NY: J.B. Lyon, 1913.

Wilhelm II, Ex-Emperor of Germany. *My Early Life.* London: Methuen, 1926.

Zedlitz-Trützschler, Robert von. *Twelve Years at the Imperial German Court.* Translated by Alfred Kalisch. New York: George H. Doran, 1924.

Zeydel, Edwin H., ed. *Constitutions of the German Empire and German States.* Washington, DC: Government Printing Office, 1919.

Zola, Émile. *The Ladies' Paradise.* London: Vizetelly, 1886.

Secondary Sources

Adorno, T.W., Else Frenkel-Brenswik, Daniel J. Levinson, and R. Nevitt Sanford. *The Authoritarian Personality.* Studies in Prejudice. Edited by Max Horkheimer and Samuel H. Flowerman. New York: Harper & Brothers, 1950.

Allen, Ann Taylor. *Satire and Society in Wilhelmine Germany: Kladderadatsch and Simplicissimus, 1890–1914.* Lexington: UP of Kentucky, 2014.

Alter, Reinhard. "Heinrich Mann's Untertan – Prüfstein für die 'Kaiserreich-Debatte'?" *Geschichte und Gesellschaft* 17, no. 3 (1991): 370–89.

Amin, Kadji. "Genealogies of Queer Theory." In *The Cambridge Companion to Queer Studies,* edited by Siobhan B. Somerville, 17–29. Cambridge: U of Cambridge P, 2020.

Babuscio, Jack. "The Cinema of Camp (AKA Camp and the Gay Sensibility)." In *Camp: Queer Aesthetics and the Performing Subject: A Reader,* edited by Fabio Cleto, 117–35. Edinburgh: Edinburgh UP, 1999.

Baldessari, Ferdinando. "Zur Enstehungsgeschichte von Heinrich Manns Untertan." *Quaderni di lingue e letterature* 2 (1977): 167–76.

Barkin, Kenneth. "W.E.B. Du Bois and the German *Alltag,* 1892–1894." *The Journal of African American History* 96, no. 1 (2011): 1–13.

- "W.E.B. Du Bois and the Kaiserreich." *Central European History* 31, no. 3 (1998): 155–69.
- "W.E.B. Du Bois' Love Affair with Imperial Germany." *German Studies Review* 28, no. 2 (2005): 285–302.

Bauer, Heike. *The Hirschfeld Archives: Violence, Death, and Modern Queer Culture.* Philadelphia: Temple UP, 2017.

Beachy, Robert. *Gay Berlin: Birthplace of a Modern Identity.* New York: Alfred A. Knopf, 2014.

Beddow, Michael. "Fiction and Meaning in Thomas Mann's *Felix Krull.*" *Journal of European Studies* 10 (1980): 77–92.
– "Thoughts Back in Season? Thomas Mann's First World War Essays and the Problem of German Identity." *Publications of the English Goethe Society* 64 (1996): 3–20.
Benjamin, Jessica, and Anson Rabinbach. Foreword to Klaus Theweleit, *Male Fantasies, Male Bodies: Psychoanalyzing the White Terror*, trans. Erica Carter, Chris Turner, and Stephen Conway, vol. 2, ix–xxv. Minneapolis: U of Minnesota P, 1989.
Benjamin, Walter. *The Arcades Project*. Translated by Howard Eiland and Kevin McLaughlin. Cambridge, MA: The Belknap Press of Harvard UP, 1999.
Berghahn, Volker R. "The German Empire, 1871–1914: Reflections on the Direction of Recent Research." *Central European History* 35, no. 1 (2002): 75–81.
– *Militarism: The History of an International Debate, 1861–1979*. New York: St. Martin's, 1982.
Berlant, Lauren, and Lee Edelman. *Sex, or the Unbearable*. Durham, NC: Duke UP, 2014.
Berndt, Helge. "Zur Reform der Militärstrafgerichtsordnung 1898: Die Haltung der Partein im Reichstag." *MGM* 14, no. 2 (1973): 7–29.
Bernet, Claus. "The 'Hobrecht Plan' (1862) and Berlin's Urban Structure." *Urban History* 31, no. 3 (2004): 400–19.
Blank, Lisa. "Two Schools for Secrecy: Defining Secrecy from the Works of Max Weber, Georg Simmel, Edward Shils and Sissela Bok." In *Government Secrecy: Classic and Contemporary Readings*, edited by Susan L. Maret and Jan Goldman, 59–68. Westport, CT: Libraries Unlimited, 2009.
Bohn, Robert, and Michael Epkenhans, eds. *Garnisonstädte im 19. und 20. Jahrhundert*. Edited by Robert Boh and Uwe Danker. Vol. 16. IZRG-Schriftenreihe. Bielefeld: Verlag für Regionalgeschichte, 2015.
Bösch, Frank. *Öffentliche Geheimnisse: Skandale, Politik und Medien in Deutschland und Großbritannien, 1880–1914*. Munich: R. Oldenbourg, 2009.
Bredbeck, Gregory W. "Narcissus in the Wilde: Textual Cathexis and the Historical Origins of Queer Camp." In *The Politics and Poetics of Camp*, edited by Moe Meyer, 51–74. New York: Routledge, 1994.
Brevik-Zender, Heidi. "Interstitial Narratives: Rethinking Feminine Spaces of Modernity in Nineteenth-Century French Fashion Plates." *Nineteenth-Century Contexts* 36, no. 2 (2014): 91–123.
Brooks, Peter. *The Melodramatic Imagination: Balzac, Henry James, Melodrama, and the Mode of Excess*. 2nd ed. New Haven, CT: Yale UP, 1995.
– "Psychoanalysis and Melodrama." In *The Cambridge Companion to English Melodrama*, edited by Carolyn Williams, 277–88. Cambridge: Cambridge UP, 2018.

Brühöfener, Friederike. "Contested Masculinities: Debates about Homosexuality in the West German Bundeswehr in the 1960s and 1970s." In *Gendering Post-1945 German History: Entanglements*, edited by Karen Hagemann, Donna Harsch, and Friederike Brühöfener, 295–314. New York: Berghahn, 2019.

Buck, Theo. "Heinrich Mann: Der Untertan." In *Von Augustinus bis Heinrich Mann: Meisterwerke der Weltliteratur*, edited by Helmut Siepmann and Frank-Rutger Hausmann. Abhandlungen zur Sprache & Literatur: 16, 9–26. Bonn: Romantischer Verlag, 1989.

Burroughs, Peter. "Crime and Punishment in the British Army, 1815–1870." *The English Historical Review* 100, no. 396 (1985): 545–71.

Butler, Judith. *Gender Trouble: Feminism and the Subversion of Identity*. New York: Routledge, 1990.

– *The Psychic Life of Power: Theories in Subjection*. Stanford, CA: Stanford UP, 1997.

Chickering, Roger. "Militarism and Radical Nationalism." In *Imperial Germany, 1871–1918*, edited by James Retallack, 196–218. Oxford: Oxford UP, 2008.

Clark, Christopher M. *Kaiser Wilhelm II*. Harlow, England: Longman, 2000.

Connell, R.W. *Masculinities*. 2nd ed. Berkeley: U of California P, 2005.

Conze, Werner, Michael Geyer, and Reinhard Strumpf. "Militarismus." In *Geschichtliche Grundbegriffe: Historisches Lexikon zur politisch-sozialen Sprache in Deutschland*, edited by Otto Brunner, Werner Conze and Reinhart Koselleck, 1–47. Stuttgart: Klett-Cotta, 1978.

Core, Philip. "From *Camp: The Lie That Tells the Truth*." In *Camp: Queer Aesthetics and the Performing Subject: A Reader*, edited by Fabio Cleto, 80–6. Edinburgh: Edinburgh UP, 1999.

Craig, Gordon A. *The Politics of the Prussian Army, 1640–1945*. Oxford: Oxford UP, 1955.

Craik, Jennifer. *Uniforms Exposed: From Conformity to Transgression*. Dress, Body, Culture. Edited by Joanne B. Eicher. Oxford: Berg Publishers, 2005.

Crouthamel, Jason. *An Intimate History of the Front: Masculinity, Sexuality, and German Soldiers in the First World War*. New York: Palgrave Macmillan, 2014.

Crowell, Ellen. "Queer." *Victorian Literature and Culture* 46, no. 3–4 (2018): 816–20.

Daly, Nicholas. *Ruritania: A Cultural History, from* The Prisoner of Zenda *to* The Princess Diaries. Oxford: Oxford UP, 2020.

David, Alison Matthews. "Decorated Men: Fashioning the French Soldier, 1852–1914." *Fashion Theory* 7, no. 1 (2003): 3–38.

Decker, W.C. "What Shall We Read?" *German Quarterly* 6, no. 1 (1933): 28–38.

Deist, Wilhelm. "Die Armee in Staat und Gesellschaft, 1890–1914." In *Militär, Staat und Gesellschaft: Studien zur preußisch-deutschen Militärgeschichte*, 19–41. Munich: R. Oldenbourg, 1991.

Deleuze, Gilles. *Coldness and Cruelty*. New York: Zone, 1991.
Dentith, Simon. *Parody*. London: Taylor & Francis Group, 2000.
Dickinson, Edward Ross. "Complexity, Contingency, and Coherence in the History of Sexuality in Modern Germany: Some Theoretical and Interpretive Reflections." *Central European History* 49 (2016): 93–116.
– *Sex, Freedom, and Power in Imperial Germany, 1890–1914*. Cambridge: Cambridge UP, 2014.
Dickinson, Edward Ross, and Richard F. Wetzell. "The Historiography of Sexuality in Modern Germany." *German History* 23, no. 3 (2005): 291–305.
Digitales Wörterbuch der Deutschen Sprache. Edited by Alexander Geyken. Berlin: Berlin-Brandenburgische Akademie der Wissenschaften. https://www.dwds.de/.
Doan, Laura. *Disturbing Practices: History, Sexuality, and Women's Experience of Modern War*. Chicago: U of Chicago P, 2013.
Dobler, Jens. *Zwischen Duldungspolitik und Verbrechensbekämpfung: Homosexuellenverfolgung durch die Berliner Polizei von 1848 bis 1933*. Schriftenreihe der Deutschen Gesellschaft für Polizeigeschichte e.V. Frankfurt: Verlag für Polizeiwissenschaft, 2008.
Domeier, Norman. *The Eulenburg Affair: A Cultural History of Politics in the German Empire*. Rochester, NY: Camden House, 2015.
Donovan, James M. "Culture and the Courts in France: The *Plaidoirie Sentimentale* in the Nineteenth and Early Twentieth Centuries." *Law and History Review* 35, no. 3 (2017): 789–828.
Dose, Ralf. *Magnus Hirschfeld: The Origins of the Gay Liberation Movement*. Translated by Edward H. Willis. New York: Monthly Review, 2014.
Dubout, Kevin. *Der Richter und sein Tagebuch: Eugen Wilhelm als Elsässer und homosexueller Aktivist im Deutschen Kaiserreich*. Frankfurt: Campus, 2018.
Duggan, Lisa. "The New Homonormativity: The Sexual Politics of Neoliberalism." In *Materializing Democracy: Toward a Revitalized Cultural Politics*, edited by Russ Castronovo and Dana D. Nelson, 175–94. Durham, NC: Duke UP, 2002.
Dyer, Richard. "It's Being so Camp as Keeps Us Going." In *Camp: Queer Aesthetics and the Performing Subject: A Reader*, edited by Fabio Cleto, 110–16. Edinburgh: Edinburgh UP, 1999.
Edelman, Lee. *No Future: Queer Theory and the Death Drive*. Durham, NC: Duke UP, 2004.
Eder, Franz X. "The Politics of Discourse." *Contemporary European History* 22, no. 2 (2013): 283–8.
Eley, Geoff, Jennifer L. Jenkins, and Tracie Matysik. "Introduction: German Modernities and the Contest of Futures." In *German Modernities From Wilhelm to Weimar: A Contest of Futures*, edited by Geoff Eley, Jennifer L. Jenkins, and Tracie Matysik, 1–30. London: Bloomsbury, 2016.

–, eds. *German Modernities from Wilhelm to Weimar: A Contest of Futures.* London: Bloomsbury, 2016.

Elsaesser, Thomas. "Tales of Sound and Fury: Observations on the Family Melodrama." In *Imitations of Life: A Reader on Film & Television Melodrama,* edited by Marcia Landy, 68–91. Detroit: Wayne State UP, 1991.

Emmerich, Wolfgang. *Heinrich Mann "Der Untertan."* Munich: Wilhelm Fink Verlag, 1980.

Enloe, Cynthia. *Does Khaki Become You? The Militarisation of Women's Lives.* Boston: South End, 1983.

Eribon, Didier. "Michel Foucault's Histories of Sexuality." *GLQ* 7, no. 1 (2001): 31–86.

Flintrop, Kerstin. "Die Disziplinierung des männlichen Körpers – Uniformen im historischen Vergleich von Schnittführung und Verarbeitung." In *Nach Rang und Stand*, edited by Stadt Krefeld, 28–32. Krefeld: Deutsches Textilmuseum, 2002.

Flügge, Manfred. *Heinrich Mann: Eine Biographie.* Reinbek bei Hamburg: Rowohlt, 2006.

Förster, Stig. *Der doppelte Militarismus: Die deutsche Heeresrüstungspolitik zwischen Status-Quo-Sicherung und Aggression 1890–1913.* Stuttgart: Franz Steiner Verlag, 1985.

Foucault, Michel. *The History of Sexuality, Volume I: An Introduction.* Translated by Robert Hurley. New York: Vintage Books, 1978.

Freeman, Elizabeth. *Time Binds: Queer Temporalities, Queer Histories.* Durham, NC: Duke UP, 2010.

Frevert, Ute. *A Nation in Barracks: Conscription, Military Service and Civil Society in Modern Germany.* Translated by Andrew Boreham and Daniel Brückenhaus. New York: Berg, 2004.

Fritzsche, Peter. *Reading Berlin 1900.* Cambridge, MA: Harvard UP, 1996.

– "Vagabond in the Fugitive City: Hans Ostwald, Imperial Berlin and the Grossstadt-Dokumente." *Journal of Contemporary History* 29, no. 3 (1994): 385–402.

Ganaway, Bryan. "Consuming Masculinity: Toys and Boys in Wilhelmine Germany." *Edinburgh German Yearbook* 2 (2008): 97–112.

Giles, Geoffrey J. "The Denial of Homosexuality: Same-Sex Incidents in Himmler's SS and Police." *Journal of the History of Sexuality* 11, no. 1/2 (2002): 256–90.

– "The Institutionalization of Homosexual Panic in the Third Reich." In *Social Outsiders in Nazi Germany*, edited by Robert Gellately and Nathan Stoltzfus, 233–56. Princeton, NJ: U of Princeton P, 2018.

– "Legislating Homophobia in the Third Reich: The Radicalization of Prosecution Against Homosexuality by the Legal Profession." *German History* 23, no. 3 (2005): 339–54.

Gleim, Bernhard, and Dieter Richter. "'Das Menschenschlachthaus' und seine Leser: Ein Stück Wirkungsgeschichte aus den Akten der Polizei." In *Das Menschenschlachthaus: Bilder vom kommenden Krieg*, edited by Johannes Merkel and Dieter Richter. Sammlung Alter Kinderbücher, 131–52. Munich: Weismann Verlag, 1980.

Glick, Elisa. *Materializing Queer Desire: Oscar Wilde to Andy Warhol*. Albany, NY: SUNY P, 2009.

Goldberg, Ann. *Honor, Politics, and the Law in Imperial Germany, 1871–1914*. New Studies in European History. Cambridge: Cambridge UP, 2010.

Goldman, Harvey. *Politics, Death and the Devil: Self and Power in Max Weber and Thomas Mann*. Berkeley: U of California P, 1992.

Grisko, Michael. *Der Untertan revisited: Vom Kaiserreich bis geteilten Deutschland*. Buddenbrookhaus-Kataloge. Berlin: Bertz + Fischer, 2007.

Grollman, Stephen A. *Heinrich Mann: Narratives of Wilhelmine Germany, 1895–1925*. Studies on Themes and Motifs in Literature, vol. 64. New York: Peter Lang, 2002.

Gunnemann, Karin Verena. *Heinrich Mann's Novels and Essays: The Artist as Political Educator*. Studies in German Literature, Linguistics, and Culture. Rochester, NY: Camden House, 2002.

Hahn, Manfred. "Heinrich Manns Beiträge in der Zetischrift *Das Zwanzigste Jahrhundert*." *Weimarer Beiträge: Zeitschrift für Literaturwissenschaft, Ästhetik und Kulturwissenschaften* (1967): 966–1019.

Halberstam, Jack. *The Queer Art of Failure*. Durham, NC: Duke UP, 2011.

Halle, Randall. *Queer Social Philosophy: Critical Readings from Kant to Adorno*. Urbana: U of Illinois P, 2004.

Halperin, David. *How to Do the History of Homosexuality*. Chicago: University of Chicago Press, 2002.

Hamann, Brigitte. *Bertha von Suttner: A Life for Peace*. Translated by Ann Dubsky. Syracuse: Syracuse UP, 1996.

Häntzschel, Günter. "Literatur und Krieg: Aspekte der Diskussion aus der Zeitschrift 'Das literarische Echo.'" In *Kultur und Krieg: Die Rolle der Intellektuellen, Künstler und Schriftsteller im Ersten Weltkrieg*, edited by Wolfgang J. Mommsen and Elisabeth Müller-Luckner, 209–19. Munich: R. Oldenbourg Verlag, 1996.

Harpprecht, Klaus. *Thomas Mann: Eine Biographie*. 2 vols. Reinbek bei Hamburg: Rowohlt Taschenbuch, 1995.

Harvey, David. *A Companion to Marx's Capital*. London: Verso, 2010.

Harvey, John. *Men in Black*. Chicago: U of Chicago P, 1995.

Haskell, Barbara. *Marsden Hartley*. New York: Whitney Museum of American Art, 1980.

Hayman, Ronald. *Thomas Mann: A Biography*. New York: Scribner, 1995.

Hecht, Karsten. "Die Harden-Prozesse: Strafverfahren, Öffentlichkeit und Politik im Kaiserreich." PhD diss., University of Munich, 1997.

296 Bibliography

Heilbut, Anthony. *Thomas Mann: Eros and Literature*. Berkeley: U of California P, 1995.
Hekma, Gert, Harry Oosterhuis, and James D. Steakley, eds. *Gay Men and the Sexual History of the Political Left*. New York: The Haworth Press, 1995.
Hermsdorf, Klaus. "Die Geburt eines Schelmen: Zu Thomas Manns Krull-Fragment von 1911." *Weimarer Beiträge: Zeitschrift für Literaturwissenschaft, Ästhetik und Kulturwissenschaften* (1965): 102–17.
Herwig, Holger H. "An Introduction to Military Archives in West Germany." *Military Affairs* 36, no. 4 (1972): 121–4.
Herzer, Manfred. *Magnus Hirschfeld: Leben und Werk eines jüdischen, schwulen und sozialistischen Sexologen*. Frankfurt/Main: Campus Verlag, 1992.
– *Magnus Hirschfeld und seine Zeit*. Oldenbourg: De Guyter, 2017.
Herzog, Dagmar. *Sex after Fascism: Memory and Morality in Twentieth-Century Germany*. Princeton, NJ: Princeton UP, 2005.
– *Sexuality in Europe: A Twentieth-Century History*. New Approaches to European History. Cambridge: Cambridge UP, 2011.
Hewitt, Andrew. *Political Inversions: Homosexuality, Fascism, and the Modernist Imaginary*. Stanford, CA: Stanford UP, 1996.
Hill, Darryl B. "Sexuality and Gender in Hirschfeld's *Die Transvestiten*: A Case of the 'Elusive Evidence of the Ordinary.'" *Journal of the History of Sexuality* 14, no. 3 (2005): 316–32.
Hollander, Anne. *Sex and Suits*. New York: Knopf, 1994.
Hull, Isabel V. *Absolute Destruction: Military Culture and the Practices of War in Imperial Germany*. Ithaca, NY: Cornell UP, 2005.
– *The Entourage of Kaiser Wilhelm II., 1888–1918*. Cambridge: Cambridge UP, 1982.
– "Der kaiserliche Hof als Herrschaftsinstrument." In *Der letzte Kaiser: Wilhelm II. im Exil*, edited by Hans Wilderotter and Klaus-D. Pohl, 19–30. Munich: Bertelsmann Lexikon, 1991.
– *Sexuality, State and Civil Society in Germany, 1700–1815*. Ithaca, NY: Cornell UP, 1996.
Huneke, Samuel Clowes. "Death Wish: Suicide and Stereotype in the Gay Discourses of Imperial and Weimar Germany." *New German Critique* 46, no. 1 (2019): 127–66.
Hutter, Jörg. "Die Entstehung des § 175 im Strafgesetzbuch und die Geburt der deutschen Sexualwissenschaft." In *Männerliebe im alten Deutschland: Sozialgeschichtliche Abhandlungen*, edited by Rüdiger Lautmann and Angela Taeger, 187–238. Berlin: Rosa Winkel, 1992.
Izenberg, Gerald N. *Modernism and Masculinity: Mann, Wedekind, Kandinsky through World War I*. Chicago: U of Chicago P, 2000.
Jasper, Willi. *Der Bruder Heinrich Mann. Eine Biographie*. Frankfurt/Main: Fischer Taschenbuch, 1994.
Jay, Martin. *The Dialectical Imagination: A History of the Frankfurt School and the Institute of Social Research, 1923–1950*. Berkeley: U of California P, 1996.

Jessen, Olaf. *Die Moltkes: Biographie einer Familie*. Munich: C.H. Beck, 2010.
Kay, Sarah. *Žižek: A Critical Introduction*. Key Contemporary Thinkers. Cambridge: Polity, 2003.
Keep, John. "Justice for the Troops: A Comparative Study of Nicholas I's Russia and France under Louis-Philippe." *Cahiers du Monde russe et soviétique* 28, no. 1 (1987): 31–54.
Kennedy, Hubert. *Karl Heinrich Ulrichs: Pioneer of the Modern Gay Movement*. San Francisco: Peremptory Publications, 2002.
Kiss, Susanne. *German Colonial Wars and the Context of Military Violence*. Translated by Andrew Smith. Cambridge, MA: Harvard UP, 2017.
Knötel, Herbert Jr., and Herbert Sieg. *Uniforms of the World: A Compendium of Army, Navy, and Air Force Uniforms, 1700–1937*. Translated by Ronald G. Ball. New York: Charles Scribner's Sons, 1980.
Koch, Ursula E. "Politische Bildzensur in Deutschland bis 1914." *Jahrbuch für Kommunikationsgeschichte* 16 (2014): 109–70.
Kohlrausch, Martin. *Der Monarch im Skandal: Die Logik der Massenmedien und die Transformation der wilhelminischen Monarchie*. Elitenwandel in der Moderne. Edited by Heinz Reif. Berlin: Akademie Verlag, 2005.
Kontje, Todd. *Thomas Mann's World: Empire, Race, and the Jewish Question*. Ann Arbor: U of Michigan P, 2011.
Koopmann, Helmut. *Thomas Mann – Heinrich Mann: Die ungleichen Brüder*. Munich: C.H. Beck, 2005.
– "Thomas Mann's 'Autobiographical' Stories." In *A Companion to the Works of Thomas Mann*, edited by Herbert Lehnert and Eva Wessell, 147–58. Rochester, NY: Camden House, 2004.
Kraske, Bernd M. "Heinrich Mann als Herausgeber der Zeitschrift *Das Zwanzigste Jahrhundert*." In *Heinrich Mann: Das essayistische Werk*, edited by Rudolf Wolff. Sammlung Profile, 7–24. Bonn: Bouvier, 1986.
Kühne, Thomas. *The Rise and Fall of Comradeship: Hitler's Soldiers, Male Bonding and Mass Violence in the Twentieth Century*. Cambridge: Cambridge UP, 2017.
Kurzke, Hermann. *Thomas Mann: Life as a Work of Art*. Translated by Leslie Willson. Princeton, NJ: Princeton UP, 2002.
Kurzke, Hermann, Jöelle Stoupy, Jörn Bender, and Stephan Stachorski, eds. *Thomas Mann: Essays II, 1914–1926. Kommentar*. Vol. 13.2. Große kommentierte Frankfurter Ausgabe. Werke, Briefe, Tagebücher. Frankfurt: S. Fischer, 2012.
LaCapra, Dominick. *History, Literature, Critical Theory*. Ithaca, NY: Cornell UP, 2013.
Leck, Ralph M. *Vita Sexualis: Karl Ulrichs and the Origins of Sexual Science*. Urbana: U of Illinois P, 2016.
Lehnert, Herbert H. "Fictional Orientations in Thomas Mann's Biography." *PMLA* 88, no. 5 (1973): 1146–61.

Leng, Kirsten. *Sexual Politics and Feminist Science: Women Sexologists in Germany, 1900–1933*. Ithaca, NY: Cornell UP and Cornell University Library, 2018.

Leutert, Torsten. *Ernst von Wildenbruchs historische Dramen*. Frankfurt/Main: Peter Lang, 2004.

Lewis, David Levering. *W.E.B. Du Bois – Biography of a Race, 1868–1919*. New York: H. Holt, 1993.

Lücke, Martin. *Männlichkeit in Unordnung: Homosexualität und männliche Prostitution in Kaiser und Weimarer Republik*. Frankfurt/Main: Campus, 2008.

Ludington, Townsend. *Marsden Hartley: The Biography of an American Artist*. Boston: Little, Brown and Company, 1992.

Lybeck, Marti M. *Desiring Emancipation: New Women and Homosexuality in Germany, 1890–1933*. Albany, NY: SUNY P, 2014.

Mahoney, Kristin. "Camp Modernism and Decadence." In *Decadence: A Literary History*, edited by Alex Murray, 341–60. Cambridge: Cambridge UP, 2020.

Mansfield, Nick. *Theorizing War: From Hobbes to Badiou*. Basingstoke, England: Palgrave Macmillan, 2008.

Marcus, Sharon. "Reflections on Victorian Fashion Plates." *differences* 14, no. 3 (2005): 4–33.

Marhoefer, Laurie. *Sex and the Weimar Republic: German Homosexual Emancipation and the Rise of the Nazis*. Toronto: U of Toronto P, 2015.

– "Was the Homosexual Made White? Race, Empire, and Analogy in Gay and Trans Thought in Twentieth-Century Germany." *Gender & History* 31, no. 1 (2019): 91–114.

Martin, Ariane. *Erotische Politik: Heinrich Manns erzählerisches Frühwerk*. Würzburg: Königshausen & Neumann, 1993.

Martin, John Levi. "*The Authoritarian Personality*, 50 Years Later: What Lessons Are There for Political Psychology." *Political Psychology* 22, no. 1 (2001): 1–26.

Marx, Karl. "Economic and Philosophic Manuscripts of 1844." In *The Marx-Engels Reader*, edited by Robert C. Tucker, 66–125. New York: W. W. Norton, 1978.

– "The Fetishism of Commodities and the Secret Thereof." In *The Marx-Engels Reader*, edited by Robert C. Tucker, 319–29. New York: W.W. Norton, 1978.

Matysik, Tracie. *Reforming the Moral Subject: Ethics and Sexuality in Central Europe, 1890–1930*. Ithaca, NY: Cornell UP, 2008.

Mayer, David. "Encountering Melodrama." In *The Cambridge Companion to Victorian and Edwardian Theater*, edited by Kerry Powell, 145–63. Cambridge: Cambridge UP, 2004.

McAleer, Kevin. *Dueling: The Cult of Honor in Fin-de-siècle Germany*. Princeton, NJ: Princeton UP, 1994.
McDonnell, Patricia. *Dictated by Life: Marsden Hartley's German Paintings and Robert Indiana's Hartley Elegies*. Minneapolis: Frederick R. Weisman Art Museum, 1995.
— *Marsden Hartley: American Modern*. Minneapolis: Frederick R. Weisman Art Museum, 1997.
McDowell, Colin. *The Man of Fashion: Peacock Males and Perfect Gentlemen*. London: Thames and Hudson, 1997.
McLaren, Angus. *The Trials of Masculinity: Policing Sexual Boundaries, 1870–1930*. Chicago: U of Chicago P, 1997.
McLellan, Josie. *Love in the Time of Communism: Intimacy and Sexuality in the GDR*. Cambridge: Cambridge UP, 2011.
McWilliam, Rohan. "Melodrama and the Historians." *Radical History Review* 78 (2000): 57–84.
Mertens, Lothar. "Das Privileg des Einjährig-Freiwilligen Militärdienstes im Kaiserreich und seine gesellschaftliche Bedeutung." *Militargeschichtliche Mitteilungen* 39, no. 1 (1986): 59–66.
Meyer, Moe. "Introduction: Reclaiming the Discourse of Camp." In *The Politics and Poetics of Camp*, edited by Moe Meyer, 1–22. New York: Routledge, 1994.
— "Under the Sign of Wilde: An Archeology of Posing." In *The Politics and Poetics of Camp*, edited by Moe Meyer, 75–109. New York: Routledge, 1994.
Mommsen, Wolfgang J. "Einleitung: Die deutschen kulturellen Eliten im Ersten Weltkrieg." In *Kultur und Krieg: Die Rolle der Intellektuellen, Künstler und Schriftsteller im Ersten Weltkrieg*, edited by Wolfgang J. Mommsen and Elisabeth Müller-Luckner, 1–15. Munich: R. Oldenbourg Verlag, 1996.
Moncure, John. *Forging the King's Sword: Military Education between Tradition and Modernization: The Case of the Royal Prussian Cadet Corps, 1871–1918*. New York: Peter Lang, 1993.
Mosse, George L. *Nationalism and Sexuality: Middle-Class Morality and Sexual Norms in Modern Europe*. Madison: U of Wisconsin P, 1985.
Neff, Bernhard. *"Wir wollen keine Paradetruppe, wir wollen eine Kriegstruppe ...": Die reformorientierte Militärkritik der SPD unter Wilhelm II. 1890–1913*. Cologne: SH-Verlag, 2004.
Nipperdey, Thomas. *Deutsche Geschichte 1866–1918*. Vol. 1. *Arbeitswelt und Bürgergeist*. Munich: C.H. Beck, 1993.
— "War die Wilhelminische Gesellschaft eine Untertanen-Gesellschaft?" In *Nachdenken über die deutsche Geschichte: Essays*, 172–85. Munich: C.H. Beck, 1986.
Nonn, Christoph. "Oh What a Lovely War? German Common People and the First World War." *German History* 18 (2000): 97–111.
Oosterhuis, Harry. *Stepchildren of Nature: Krafft-Ebing, Psychiatry, and the Making of Sexual Identity*. Chicago: U of Chicago P, 2000.

Ortenburg, Georg, and Ingo Prömper. *Preussisch-Deutsche Uniformen von 1640–1918*. Munich: Orbis Verlag, 1991.

Otto, Elizabeth. "Real Men Wear Uniforms: Photomontage, Postcards, and Military Visual Culture in Early Twentieth-Century Germany." *Contemporaneity* 2, no. 1 (2012): 18–43.

Otto, Uli, and Eginhard König. *"Ich hatt' einen Kameraden ...": Militär und Kriege in historisch-politischen Liedern in den Jahren von 1740 bis 1914*. Regensburg: ConBrio, 1999.

Panayi, Panikos. *Ethnic Minorities in Nineteenth and Twentieth Century Germany: Jews, Gypsies, Poles, Turks and Others*. London: Taylor & Francis Group, 2000.

Pellegrini, Ann. "After Sontag: Future Notes on Camp." In *Companion to Lesbian, Gay, Bisexual, Transgender, and Queer Studies*, edited by George E. Haggerty and Molly McGarry, 168–93. Hoboken, NJ: John Wiley & Sons, 2007.

Perry, Joe. *Christmas in Germany: A Cultural History*. Chapel Hill: U of North Carolina P, 2010.

Pfeifer, Wolfgang, ed. *Etymologisches Wörterbuch des Deutschen*. 2nd ed. Berlin: Akademie-Verlag, 1993. http://www.dwds.de/.

Pietz, William. "Problem of the Fetish, I." *Res: Anthropology and Aesthetics*, no. 9 (1985): 5–17.

Planert, Ute. "Weibliche 'Schmutzkonkurrenz' und männliche Ehre: Geschlechterbilder als Machtfaktor im deutschnationalen Handlungsgehilfenverband 1893–1918." *Internationale Wissenschaftliche Korrespondenz zur Geschichte der Deutschen Arbeiterbewegung* 34, no. 3 (1998): 441–64.

Pooth, Alexia. "Singulär im Kollektiv: Marsden Hartley und die Tradition der amerikanischen Künstlerreise nach Europa." In *Marsden Hartley: Die deutschen Bilder 1913–1915*, edited by Dieter Scholz, 193–203. Cologne: Verlag der Buchhandlung Walther König, 2014.

Puar, Jasbir. *Terrorist Assemblages: Homonationalism in Queer Times*. Next Wave: New Directions in Women's Studies. Edited by Inderpal Grewal, Caren Kaplan, and Robyn Wiegman. 10th anniversary ed. Durham, NC: Duke UP, 2017.

Ritter, Naomi. "*Death in Venice* and the Tradition of European Decadence." In *Approaches to Teaching Mann's Death in Venice and Other Short Fiction*, edited by Jeffrey B. Berlin. Approaches to Teaching World Literature, vol. 43, 86–92. New York: Modern Language Association of America, 1992.

Robertson, Bruce. *Marsden Hartley*. The Library of American Art. New York: Harry N. Abrams, 1995.

Roet, Henning. "Frankfurt als Garnisonstadt zwischen 1866 und 1914: Mit besonderem Blick auf die Kriegervereine der Stadt." In *Garnisonstädte im 19.*

und 20. Jahrhundert, edited by Robert Bohn and Michael Epkenhans, 109–18. Bielefeld: Verlag für Regionalgeschichte, 2015.

Rohkrämer, Thomas. "Heroes and Would-Be Heroes: Veterans' and Reservists' Associations in Imperial Germany." In *Anticipating Total War: The German and American Experiences, 1871–1914*, edited by Manfred F. Boemeke, Roger Chickering, and Stig Förster, 189–215. Washington, DC, and Cambridge: German Historical Institute and Cambridge UP, 1999.

Röhl, John C.G. *Wilhelm II: The Kaiser's Personal Monarchy, 1888–1900*. Cambridge: Cambridge UP, 2004.

– *Young Wilhelm: The Kaiser's Early Life, 1859–1888*. Cambridge: Cambridge UP, 1998.

Roper, Lyndal. "Beyond Discourse Theory." *Women's History Review* 19, no. 2 (2010): 307–19.

Rose, Alexander. "Clearing the Fog of War." *MHQ: Quarterly Journal of Military History* 24, no. 4 (2012): 42–7.

Rubin, Gayle S. "Thinking Sex: Notes for a Radical Theory of the Politics of Sexuality." In *The Lesbian and Gay Studies Reader*, edited by Henry Abelove, Michèle Aina Barale and David M. Halperin, 3–44. New York: Routledge, 1993.

Sagarra, Eda. *A Social History of Germany, 1648–1914*. New York: Holmes & Meier, 1977.

Salomon, Werner. "Ein Geheimbefehl Herzog Georgs von Sachsen vom Juni 1891 zur Frage der Soldatenmißhandlungen." *Militärgeschichte* 16, no. 5 (1977): 584–90.

Santner, Eric L. *My Own Private Germany: Daniel Paul Schreber's Secret History of Modernity*. Princeton, NJ: Princeton UP, 1996.

Schaffner, Anna Katharina. "Richard von Krafft-Ebing's *Psychopathia Sexualis* and Thomas Mann's *Buddenbrooks*: Exchanges between Scientific and Imaginary Accounts of Sexual Deviance." *Modern Language Review* 106 (2011): 477–94.

Schmidt, Heike I. "Colonial Intimacy: The Rechenberg Scandal and Homosexuality in East Africa." *Journal of the History of Sexuality* 17, no. 1 (2008): 25–59.

Schnapp, Jeffrey T. "Fascinating Fascism." *Journal of Contemporary History* 31, no. 2 (1996): 235–44.

Schneider, Fred, Keith Strickland, Ricky Wilson, Cindy Wilson, and Kate Pierson. "Private Idaho." In *Wild Planet*. Warner Bros. Records, 1980.

Schneider, Jeffrey. "Dueling and the Fantasmatic Specter of Male Honour in Imperial Germany: The Kaiser's Will and Theodor Fontane's *Effi Briest*." *Literature and History* 31, no. 1 (2022): 1–16.

– "The Emperor's New Uniforms: The Uniform Fantasies of Kaiser Wilhelm II and His Critics." *German Studies Review* 47, no. 1 (forthcoming, February 2024).

- "'The Pleasure of the Uniform!': Masculinity, Transvestism and Militarism in Heinrich Mann's *Der Untertan* and Magnus Hirschfeld's *Die Transvestiten.*" *The Germanic Review* 72, no. 3 (1997): 183–200.
- "Soliciting Fantasies: Knowing and Not-Knowing About Male Prostitution by Soldiers in Imperial Germany." In *After the History of Sexuality: German Interventions*, edited by Dagmar Herzog, Helmut Puff, and Scott Spector, 124–38. New York: Berghahn Books, 2012.

Scholz, Dieter. "Marsden Hartley in Berlin." In *Marsden Hartley: Die deutschen Bilder 1913–1915*, edited by Dieter Scholz, 18–64. Cologne: Verlag der Buchhandlung Walther König, 2014.

Schonfield, Ernest. *Art and Its Uses in Thomas Mann's "Felix Krull."* London: Modern Humanities Research Association, 2008.

Schreiber, William I. "[Review of *Das edle Blut*]." *The Modern Language Journal* 29, no. 6 (1945): 558.

Schumann, Andreas. "'Der Künstler an die Krieger': Zur Kriegsliteratur kanonisierter Autoren." In *Kultur und Krieg: Die Rolle der Intellektuellen, Künstler und Schriftsteller im Ersten Weltkrieg*, edited by Wolfgang J. Mommsen and Elisabeth Müller-Luckner, 221–33. Munich: R. Oldenbourg Verlag, 1996.

Scott, Joan W. *The Fantasy of Feminist History*. Durham, NC: Duke UP, 2011.
- "The Incommensurability of Psychoanalysis and History." *History and Theory* 51, no. 1 (2012): 63–83.

Sedgwick, Eve Kosofsky. *Epistemology of the Closet*. Berkeley: U of California P, 1990.

Seery, John Evan. "Political Irony and World War: A Rereading of Thomas Mann's *Betrachtungen*." *Soundings: An Interdisciplinary Journal* 73, no. 1 (1990): 5–29.

Seifert, Ruth. "Gender, Nation und Militär – Aspekte von Männlichkeitskonstruktion und Gewaltsozialisation durch Militär und Wehrpflicht." In *Allgemeine Wehrpflicht: Geschichte, Probleme, Perspektiven*, edited by Eckardt Opitz and Frank S. Rödiger, 179–94. Bremen: Edition Temmen, 1994.

"Sexual Harassment Guidance 1997." Department of Education, Office of Civil Rights, 1997. Accessed 20 July 2022, https://www2.ed.gov/about/offices/list/ocr/docs/sexhar01.html.

Shephardson, Charles. "History and the Real: Foucault with Lacan." *Postmodern Culture* 5, no. 2 (1995). http://muse.jhu.edu/journals/postmodern_culture/v005/5.2.shepherdson.html.

Showalter, Dennis E. "Army and Society in Imperial Germany: The Pains of Modernization." *Journal of Contemporary History* 18, no. 4 (1983): 583–618.

Sigusch, Volkmar. "The Sexologist Albert Moll – between Sigmund Freud and Magnus Hirschfeld." *Medical History* 56, no. 2 (2012): 184–200.

Silberman, Seth Clark. "'Youse Awful Queer, Chappie': Reading Black Queer Vernacular in Black Literatures of the Americas, 1903–1967." PhD diss., U of Maryland, 2005.

Smith, Tom. *Comrades in Arms: Military Masculinities in East German Culture*. New York: Berghahn, 2020.

Somerville, Siobhan B. Introduction to *The Cambridge Companion to Queer Studies*, edited by Siobhan B. Somerville, 1–13. Cambridge: U of Cambridge P, 2020.

Sontag, Susan. "Fascinating Fascism." In *Under the Sign of Saturn*, 71–105. New York: Farrer, Strauss, Giroux, 1980.

– "Notes on Camp." In *Essays of the 1960s & 1970s*, edited by David Rieff, 259–74. New York: Library of America, 2013. First published 1964 in the *Partisan Review*.

Sorba, Carlotta. "Melodrama in Post-revolutionary Europe: The Genealogy and Diffusion of a 'Popular' Theatrical Genre and Experience, 1780–1830." In *Leisure Cultures in Urban Europe, c.1700–1870: A Transnational Perspective*, edited by Peter Borsay and Jan Hein Furnée, 49–71. Manchester: Manchester UP, 2016.

Spector, Scott. *Violent Sensations: Sex, Crime, and Utopia in Vienna and Berlin, 1860–1914*. Chicago: U of Chicago P, 2016.

Stargardt, Nicholas. *The German Idea of Militarism: Radical and Socialist Critics, 1866–1914*. Cambridge: Cambridge UP, 1994.

Steakley, James D. *Die Freunde des Kaisers: Die Eulenburg-Affäre im Spiegel zeitgenössischer Karikaturen*. Translated by Jost Hermand. Hamburg: MännerschwarmSkript, 2004.

– *The Homosexual Emancipation Movement in Germany*. Reprints ed. Salem, NH: Ayer, 1993.

– "Iconography of a Scandal: Political Cartoons and the Eulenburg Affair." *Studies in Visual Communication* 9, no. 2 (1983): 20–51.

Sternweiler, Andreas. "Leben in der Unterdrückung." In *Goodbye to Berlin? 100 Jahre Schwulenbewegung: Eine Ausstellung*, edited by Schwules Museum and Berlin Akademie der Künste, 70–4. Berlin: Verlag Rosa Winkel, 1997.

Stolleis, Michael. "Untertan-Bürger-Staatsbürger: Bemerkungen zur juristischen Terminologie im späten 18. Jahrhundert." In *Bürger und Bürgerlichkeit im Zeitalter der Aufklärung*, edited by Rudolf Vierhaus, 65–100. Heidelberg: Verlag Lambert Schneider, 1981.

Suhr, Ernst-Friedrich. "Deutschland vor dem ersten Weltkrieg – Bilder aus einer Gesellschaft." In *Das Menschenschlachthaus: Bilder vom kommenden Krieg*. Sammlung Alter Kinderbücher, 153–74. Munich: Weismann Verlag, 1980.

Sutton, Katie. *Sex between Body and Mind: Psychoanalysis and Sexology in the German-speaking World, 1890s-1930*. Ann Arbor: U of Michigan P, 2019.

Swales, Martin. *The German Novelle*. Princeton, NJ: Princeton UP, 1977.
Theweleit, Klaus. *Male Fantasies*. Vol. 2. *Male Bodies: Psychoanalyzing the White Terror*. Translated by Erica Carter, Chris Turner, and Stephen Conway. Minneapolis: U of Minnesota P, 1989.
– *Male Fantasies*. Vol. 1. *Women, Floods, Bodies, History*. Translated by Stephen Conway in collaboration with Erica Carter and Chris Turner. Minneapolis: U of Minnesota P, 1987.
Timm, Annette F., and Joshua A. Sandborn. *Gender, Sex and the Shaping of Modern Europe: A History from the French Revolution to the Present Day*. 2nd ed. London: Bloomsbury, 2016.
Tipton, Frank B. *A History of Modern Germany Since 1815*. Berkeley: U of California P, 2003.
Tobin, Robert Deam. "The Life and Work of Thomas Mann: A Gay Perspective." In *Death in Venice by Thomas Mann*, edited by Naomi Ritter, 225–44. Boston: Bedford/St. Martin's, 1998.
– *Peripheral Desires: The German Discovery of Sex*. Philadelphia: U of Pennsylvania P, 2015.
– "Sexology in the Southwest: Law, Medicine, and Sexuality in Germany and Its Colonies." In *A Global History of Sexual Science, 1880–1960*, edited by Veronika Fuechtner, Douglas E. Haynes, and Ryan M. Jones, 141–62. Berkeley, CA: U of California P, 2017.
Vagts, Alfred. *A History of Militarism: Civilian and Military*. New York: Free Press, 1967.
Van Sant, Gus, dir. *My Own Private Idaho*. New Line Cinema, 1991.
Verhey, Jeffrey. *The Spirit of 1914: Militarism, Myth and Mobilization in Germany*. New York: Cambridge UP, 2000.
Vighi, Fabio, and Heiko Feldner. *Žižek: Beyond Foucault*. Basingstoke, England: Palgrave Macmillan, 2007.
Violette, Aurele J. "Judicial Reforms in the Russian Navy during the 'Era of Great Reforms': The Reform Act of 1867 and the Abolition of Corporal Punishment." *The Slavonic and East European Review* 56, no. 4 (1978): 586–603.
Vogel, Jakob. "Stramme Gardisten, temperamentvolle Tirailleurs und anmutige Damen: Geschlechterbilder im deutschen und französischen Kult der 'Nation in Waffen.'" In *Militär und Gesellschaft im 19. und 20. Jahrhundert*, edited by Ute Frevert, 245–62. Stuttgart: Klett Cotta, 1997.
Wackerfuss, Andrew. *Stormtrooper Families: Homosexuality and Community in the Early Nazi Movement*. New York: Harrington Park Press, 2015.
Wahl, Hans Rudolf. *Die Religion des deutschen Nationalismus: Eine mentalitätsgeschichtliche Studie zur Literatur des Kaiserreichs: Felix Dahn, Ernst von Wildenbruch, Walter Flex*. Heidelberg: C. Winter, 2002.
Walther, Daniel J. "Racializing Sex: Same-Sex Relations, German Colonial Authority, and *Deutschtum*." *Journal of the History of Sexuality* 17, no. 1 (2008): 11–24.

Webber, Andrew J. "Mann's Man's World: Gender and Sexuality." In *The Cambridge Companion to Thomas Mann*, 64–83. Cambridge: Cambridge UP, 2002.

Wehler, Hans-Ulrich. *The German Empire 1871–1918*. Translated by Kim Traynor. Leamington Spa: Berg, 1985.

Weinberg, Jonathan. *Speaking for Vice: Homosexuality in the Art of Charles Demuth, Marsden Hartley, and the First American Avant-Garde*. New Haven, CT: Yale UP, 1995.

Weinberg, Meyer, ed. *The World of W.E.B. Du Bois: A Quotation Sourcebook*. Westport, CT: Greenwood, 1992.

Weindling, Paul. *Health, Race and German Politics between National Unification and Nazism, 1870–1945*. Cambridge: Cambridge UP, 1989.

Weißbrich, Thomas. "Das Ende der Parade – Marsden Hartley und das preußische Militär." In *Marsden Hartley: Die deutschen Bilder 1913–1915*, edited by Dieter Scholz, 128–39. Cologne: Verlag der Buchhandlung Walther König, 2014.

Whisnant, Clayton John. *Queer Identities and Politics in Germany: A History, 1880–1945*. New York: Harrington Park Press, 2016.

Wiedner, Hartmut. "Soldatenmißhandlungen im Wilhelminischen Kaiserreich (1890–1914)." *Archiv für Sozialgeschichte* 22 (1982): 159–97.

Wiegman, Robyn, and Elizabeth A. Wilson. "Introduction: Antinormativity's Queer Conventions." *differences* 26, no. 1 (2015): 2–25.

Wiener, Martin J. "Treating 'Historical' Sources as Literary Texts: Literary Historicism and Modern British History." *Journal of Modern History* 70, no. 3 (1998): 619–38.

Wildenthal, Lora. *German Women for Empire, 1884–1945*. Durham, NC: Duke UP, 2001.

Williams, Linda. "Melodrama Revised." In *Refiguring American Film Genres: History and Theory*, edited by Nick Browne, 42–88. Berkeley, CA: U of California P, 1998.

Wilper, James. "Wilde and the Model of Homosexuality in Mann's *Tod in Venedig*." *CLCWeb: Comparative Literature and Culture* 15, no. 4 (2013). https://doi.org/10.7771/1481-4374.2305.

Winter, Helga. *Naturwissenschaft und Ästhetik: Untersuchungen zum Frühwerk Heinrich Manns*. Würzburg: Königshausen & Neumann, 1994.

Winzen, Peter. *Das Ende der Kaiserherrlichkeit: Die Skandalprozesse um die homosexuellen Berater Wilhelms II. 1907–1909*. Cologne: Böhlau, 2010.

– "Der erste politische Homosexualitätsskandal im Kaiserreich: Friedrich Alfred Krupp (1854–1902)." *Archiv für Kulturgeschichte* 93, no. 2 (2011): 415–50.

– *Freundesliebe am Hof Kaiser Wilhelms II*. Norderstedt: Books on Demand, 2010.

Wolff, Charlotte. *Magnus Hirschfeld: A Portrait of a Pioneer in Sexology*. London: Quartet Books, 1986.

Wysling, Hans. "Archivalisches Gewühle: Zur Entstehungsgeschichte der 'Bekenntnisse des Hochstaplers Felix Krull.'" In *Quellenkritische Studien zum Werk Thomas Manns*, edited by Paul Scherrer and Hans Wysling, 234–54. Bern: Francke, 1967.

– "Thomas Mann als Tagebuchschreiber (1987)." In *Ausgewählte Aufsätze, 1963–1996*, edited by Thomas Sprecher and Cornelia Bernini, 405–23, Thomas-Mann-Studien. Frankfurt/Main: Vittorio Klostermann, 1996.

Zarzosa, Agustin. "Melodrama and the Modes of the World." *Discourse* 32, no. 2 (2010): 236–55.

Zeeland, Steven. *Military Trade*. New York: Harrington Park, 1999.

Ziemann, Benjamin. "Militarism." In *The Ashgate Research Companion to Imperial Germany*, edited by Matthew Jefferies, 367–82. New York: Routledge, 2015.

Žižek, Slavoj. *For They Know Not What They Do: Enjoyment as a Political Factor*. 2nd ed. London: Verso, 2008.

– *How to Read Lacan*. How to Read. Edited by Simon Critchley. New York: W.W. Norton, 2006.

– *Interrogating the Real*. Edited by Rex Butler and Scott Stephens. London: Continuum, 2005.

– *The Parallax View*. Cambridge, MA: MIT, 2006.

– *The Plague of Fantasies*. London: Verso, 1997.

– *The Sublime Object of Ideology*. London: Verso, 1989.

– *Welcome to the Desert of the Real*. London: Verso, 2002.

Zwicker, Lisa. *Dueling Students: Conflict, Masculinity and Politics in German Universities, 1890–1914*. Ann Arbor: U of Michigan P, 2011.

Index

Adler Villa, 88, 89
Adorno, Theodor, 205–6; *The Authoritarian Personality*, 205
age of consent, 223
Algolagnie, 81
Amann, Paul, 160
Amin, Kadji, 11
anti-Semitism, xiii, xvi, 31, 93, 111, 135, 177, 221, 222, 245n123, 257n62, 273n64; at Harden-Moltke trial, 60
aristocrats and aristocracy, 13, 33, 42, 53, 76, 101, 127, 184, 210

Bab, Julius, 164
Babuscio, Jack, 153
Bar, Carl Ludwig von, 78
Bauer, Heike, 21
Bavaria, 22, 60, 64, 79, 80, 168, 210, 245n119
Beachy, Robert, 8, 97
Bebel, August, 64, 65, 71, 80, 115, 117, 135. *See also* Social Democratic Party
Beddow, Michael, 162, 165, 167
Benjamin, Walter, 127
Bergg, Franz, 131, 134
Berghahn, Volker, xiv, xv, 232n56

Berlin: as epicentre for *Soldatenprostitution*, 97–8, 103–4; homosexual scene of, 97, 103–4, 105, 117, 127; military nature of, 97–8, 102; number of queer establishments in, 209; police in, xii, 97, 98, 102, 103, 104, 113, 115, 120, 209, 210; size and growth of, 97. *See also perverse Berlin, Das*; Tiergarten
Berlin Guard, 102
Berlins Drittes Geschlecht (*Berlin's Third Sex*), 98, 99, 105, 110, 153
Bernstein, Max, 30, 51, 54–6, 60
Binet, Albert, 18, 99, 129; on sexual fetishes, 123, 128
bisexuality, 18, 34
Bismarck, Otto von, xiv, 214
blackmail, xiii, 40, 85, 101–2, 119, 254n22
Bloch, Iwan, 81
Blüher, Hans, 34, 148, 186, 211; *Die Rolle der Erotik in der männlichen Gesellschaft* (The role of eroticism in male society), 149
Boer War, 12
Boguslawski, Lt.-General Albert von, 125

Böhm, Ludwig, 86
Bollhardt, Johann, 50, 88, 89, 90, 91, 98, 112–13, 114, 116, 121; reaction to testimony of, 87, 113
Brand, Adolf, 164, 209, 222, 245n119
Brooks, Peter, 29, 52, 53, 56
Buck, Theo, 180
Bülow, Franz Josef von, 32
Bülow, Frieda von, xiv
Bülow, Prince Bernhard von, 26, 60, 115, 235n95, 237n14, 259n100
Bundeswehr, 223; "Lex Bundeswehr," 223
Butler, Judith, 8, 9, 10, 11; *Gender Trouble*, 9, 179
BZ am Mittag, 113–14

cadets, 69–77, 127, 133; isolation of, 249n25
camp, 25, 140, 146, 153, 155, 156, 158, 159; "camp modernism," 146; gay aesthetics of, 153, 162; in Imperial German queer culture, 153; queer failure of, 154; in Thomas Mann's writings, 150, 158, 159, 160
Caprivi, Leo von, 79
Center Party, Catholic (*Zentrumspartei*), 79, 87, 115, 174
Christmas, 51, 107, 108, 136, 150, 243n98, 273n64
Coburger Zeitung, 91, 113
Cocteau, Jean, 158
colonialism, xiii, xiv, 99, 123, 214
Community of the Special (*Gemeinschaft der Eigenen*, GdE), 165, 209, 241n78
conscription, 141, 172; laws and regulations of, 263n23; and military uniforms, 7
contrary sexual feeling (*konträre Sexualempfindung*), 17
Core, Philip, 158, 159

corporal punishment in the military, 64–5, 79, 84, 93, 102, 106, 246n2, 249n29; cruelty of, 80
corsets, 15, 232n58
cross-dressing, 20, 196–9, 211. *See also* Hirschfeld; transvestites and transvestism
Crouthammel, Jason, 220

dachshund, 184, 188, 194, 243n99
David, Eduard, 118
degeneration, 84, 114, 147–8, 191, 221
Deleuze, Gilles, 84, 191, 192
Demel, Richard, 164
Dentith, Simon, 179
Deutsche Rundschau, 68
Dionings, 17, 20, 96, 97, 100, 101, 129–30, 133, 134; coined by Ulrichs, 96. *See also* Urnings
Doan, Laura, xv
"don't ask, don't tell," 46, 59
Dose, Ralf, 33
Du Bois, W.E.B., xi–xii, 5, 21, 208–9, 211, 228n30, 234n87; *The Souls of Black Folk*, xvi; at the University of Berlin, xv–vi
Dubout, Kevin, 130
Duggan, Lisa, 108
Dyer, Richard, 153, 160

East German National People's Army (*Nationale Volksarmee*), 223
Edelman, Lee, 10, 11; and queer oppositionality, 10
effeminacy of homosexual officers, 30, 37–8, 46
effeminate homosexuals, 28, 33, 37, 55, 186, 210, 211
effeminate men, 46, 221, 224. *See also* Moltke
Ehrenberg, Paul, 139, 144–8, 149, 159, 172, 187

Eigene, Der (The special one), 34, 35, 165

Einem, Karl von, 62, 83, 88, 94, 98, 117–19, 122, 135, 136, 137, 261n150; homophobia of, 61; and homosexual "aggression," 118, 119; and Moll's sexological research, 120, 127, 136

Elbe, Lily von, 23, 53, 54, 185, 243n99, 243n102, 244n110; courtroom testimony of, 50–2, 58. *See also* Harden-Moltke trial

Eley, Geoff, xv

Ernst August III of Hanover, 209

erotic appeal of uniforms, xii, 16, 24, 117, 132

erotic attraction, 52, 140, 182, 184, 185, 186

erotic economy of militarism, 100, 120

erotic fantasies, 99, 100, 128, 129, 144, 147, 196

erotic nature of male bonds and violence in the military, 66, 67, 94

Eulenburg, Albert, 45, 81–2, 83

Eulenburg Affair (1907–9), 22, 24, 25, 46, 88, 221, 224. *See also* Harden-Moltke trial

Eulenberg-Hertefeld, Prince Philipp zu, 22–3, 46, 48, 49, 51–2, 55, 56, 60, 63, 184, 186, 235n94, 245n119

Ewers, Hanns Heinz, *Enterbt* (Disinherited), 45

Ewers, Ludwig, 191, 206

fantasy, 25; absence of in Foucault, 9; in *Felix Krull*, 152, 154, 156, 162, 179; and fetishism, 123, 129, 137; militarist, 136; *Phantasie*, 3, 12, 81, 156; power to shape and reshape reality of, 136; in response to the Real, 165–6; in sexology, 136; sexual/erotic, 99, 128, 129–30, 131, 133–4; theories of, 9–10; Thomas Mann's fantasy of military service, 139, 140, 141, 144, 147, 149, 150, 152, 171–2; and uniforms, 14, 21, 38, 128, 129, 131, 139; workings of 9. *See also* Hirschfeld; Žižek

fantasy scenarios, 25, 38, 99, 106, 110, 111, 117, 119, 133, 134

fascism, 205–6; and unconscious homosexuality, 206

fetishism, 23, 24, 26, 81, 122; coined by Binet, 18; colonial origins of the term, 123; commodity fetishism (Marx), 99, 123–4, 128; and fantasy, 123, 137; fetishistic objects, xiii, 4, 16, 123–4, 127, 209, 211; as one of Krafft-Ebing's four primary pathologies, 122; uniform fetishism of homosexuals, 100, 123, 124, 127, 128, 129, 135, 137, 223; uniform fetishism of the army, 100, 123, 134, 135, 137, 223; Žižek's conception of, 124, 128

Field, Edward, 64

First World War, 212, 215, 219, 222, 224; and Thomas Mann, 138, 140, 152, 162, 163, 164, 166, 167, 168, 174, 176

Flintrop, Kerstin, 15

Foucault, Michel, xiii, 10, 11, 18, 82, 136, 156, 210, 214; *ars erotica*, 66, 67, 76, 94; criticism of, 8–9; on fetishism, 122; *The History of Sexuality*, 8–9, 10, 66, 94, 258n90; on the homosexual as "a personage," 8, 54; and Marx, 258n90; and *méconnaissance*, 134, 213; *scientia sexualis*, 9, 66, 134

Franco-Prussian War, 4, 5, 57, 104, 141

Frederick the Great, 165, 167–8

Freeman, Elizabeth, 10–11

Freeminded People's Party (*Freisinnige Volkspartei*, FVp), 65, 78, 93, 261n150; and Ernst Müller, 93; and Eugen Richter, 65; and Otto Wiemer, 261n150; and reform of Prussian military code of criminal procedures, 79. *See also* German Freeminded Party

Freeminded Union (*Freisinnige Vereinigung*, FV), 175; and Georg Gothein, 175

Freiburger Zeitung, 91

Freikorps units, xiii, 221

Freud, Sigmund, 34, 53, 81, 99, 239n50, 243n104; and daydreams, 36–7; on men's fantasies, 207; on roots of fetishism, 128; same-sex desire and, 18; *Totem and Taboo*, 194

Freundesliebe (love of a friend), 18

Frevert, Ute, 103, 125, 131, 135, 139, 143, 214

Freyburg, Karl von, 208, 215–17, 219

Friedlaender, Benedict, 31, 32, 33, 34–5, 211

Friedrich Leopold of Prussia, Prince, 13–14; fastidiousness of, 14

Friedrich Wilhelm IV, 79

friendship (male), 8, 51, 53, 106–7, 131, 133, 217, 220

Fromm, Erich, 206

Garde du Corps, 87, 88, 91, 102, 112, 126

gays in the military, xv, 223

gender inversion, 18, 31, 122, 181, 196, 209, 220. *See also* sexual inversion

Georg, Duke of Saxony, secret order of, 78–9, 80, 83, 84

George, Stefan, 164

Georg of Prussia, Prince, 32–3

German Democratic Republic (GDR), 223

German Freeminded Party (*Deutsche Freisinnige Partei*), 65, 78, 79, 93; and Carl Ludwig von Bar, 78. *See also* Freeminded People's Party

German penal code, 20, 85, 118. *See also* Paragraph 75

German Revolution (1918), 220

German-Social Economic Coalition, 93

Goldberg, Ann, 48

Goldman, Harvey, 161, 165, 167

Goßler, General Heinrich von, 80

Gothein, Georg, 175–6

Grautoff, Otto, 139, 143, 144, 147, 156

Greece (Ancient), 18, 34

Gröber, Adolf, 79

"gute Kamerad, Der" (The good comrade), 35, 36

Halberstam, Jack, 138

Halle, Randall, 205

Halperin, David, xv, 8, 53

Hannover Anzeiger, 40

Hanover, Kingdom of, 16, 17

Harden, Maximilian, 22–3, 112, 114, 115, 117, 211, 235n94, 241n85, 244n109, 245n119; acquittal and then sentencing of, 60; *Die Zukunft*, 22, 235n94. *See also* Harden-Moltke trial

Harden-Moltke trial, 24, 25, 28, 30, 45–63, 67, 87, 104, 115, 119, 210, 121, 135, 136, 180, 184, 185, 210, 244n108, 245n119; and damaging effect on the WhK, 62; melodramatic elements of, 47–58. *See also* Bollhardt

Hartley, Marsden, 208–9, 211–19, 224, 277n29, 278n39, 278n45; and erotic fetishization of the German military uniform, 219; *Letters Never Sent*, 219; *Portrait of a German Officer*, 217, 218, 219; *The Warriors*, 211–12, 213, 214, 215

Haskell, Barbara, 212
Hasse, August, 101–2, 254n22
Hauptmann, Gerhart, 164
hegemonic masculinity, xiii, 172, 200
Heilbut, Anthony, 147, 187, 210
Hermsdorf, Klaus, 155, 158
"Hero Worship" (*Heldenverehrung*), 121
Herzog, Dagmar, 7, 101, 222
Hesse, Hermann, 164
heterosexual: "acquired heterosexuality," 187; bodies, 60; brothels, 130; cloak, 59; desire, 183; family, domesticity, marriages, 34, 107, 166, 197; masculinity, 21, 62, 159, 160, 210; men, 99, 100, 101, 107, 131, 220; relations and experiences, 101, 182; soldiers, 31, 130, 133, 134, 135
heterosexuality, 10, 180, 181. *See also* Dionings
Hill, Darryl, 197
Himmler, Heinrich, 222
Hindenburg, Paul von, 221
Hirschfeld, Magnus: and fantasy, 106, 108, 110, 111; diagnosis of Moltke, 53–5, 58, 59, 186, 197–8; on homosexuality, 33–4, 39, 54, 105; on Moltke's "emotional make-up," 63; on officers' mental and physical effeminacy, 38–9; recognition of transgender subjectivities by, 197; role in Harden-Moltke Trial, 28, 46, 52, 60, 211
Hirschfeld, Magnus, works by: *Berlins Drittes Geschlecht* (Berlin's third sex), 98, 99, 105, 110, 153; *Sappho und Sokrates*, 41, 42; *The Sexual History of the World War*, 220; *Die Transvestiten* (The transvestites), 197; "Warum hassen uns die Völker?" (Why do nations hate us?), 165. *See also* Scientific-Humanitarian Committee

Hitler, Adolf, 221–2
Hobrecht Plan (1862), 97, 254n9
Hofmannsthal, Hugo von, 164
Hohenau, General Wilhelm von, 55, 61, 62, 87, 91–3, 98, 114, 244n112, 252n94, 261n150
Hohenlohe-Schillingsfürst, Prince Chlodwig zu, 55, 79, 80
Hohenstaufe, Der, 86
Hohenzollern dynasty, 13, 33, 87, 126
homoerotic bonds among men as foundation of sociality, 34
homonationalism, 21, 108, 165, 224
homophobia, xiii, 9, 17, 28, 30, 45, 46, 54, 60, 61, 206, 211, 222; homophobic fantasy, 23, 111; homophobic oppression, 23, 27. *See also* queerphobia
homosexual activism and activists, 26, 31–45, 120
homosexual aggression, xiii, 118, 119, 120
Homosexualismus (homosexualism), 17
Homosexualität (homosexuality), 17
homosexuality: and blackmail, 40, 85, 101–2, 119; decriminalization of, 28, 31, 41, 66, 71, 105, 108, 111, 112, 114, 120, 175, 220, 221, 222, 223, 233n61; extent of in German military, 40, 131; outing, xv, 23, 43, 54, 180, 223; Paragraph 175 (1872), 20, 40, 54, 58, 59, 85–7, 105, 113, 114, 120, 135, 209, 211, 220, 222, 237n16, 245n129, 246n131, 252n80, 275n87; prosecution of, 40, 54, 220, 222, 245n129. *See also* gender inversion; Hirschfeld; same-sex; sexual inversion; *Soldatenprostitution*; uniform fetishism; Urnings
homosexual officers, 23, 28, 29, 30–1, 37, 38, 46, 61–2, 114, 210

homosexual "orgies," 23, 24, 50, 87, 112, 114. *See also* Lynar
homosexual readiness (of warrior-lovers), 34
homosexuals, closeted, xv, 23, 28, 29, 31, 38, 41, 46, 174, 210
homosexual signs and signals, 33, 44, 52, 53, 117; dress uniform as, 112–13
honour (male), 45, 48, 55, 57–8, 61, 101, 169, 170, 176, 195, 196, 199, 207, 242n92, 270n9
Hull, Isabel, 19
Hülsen, Major von, 55–6
Hussars, uniform of, 6, 126

Institute for Sexual Science, 21
Isenbiel, Hugo, 60
Izenberg, Gerald N., 161, 168

Jahrbuch für sexuelle Zwischenstufen, Das (Yearbook of sexual intermediaries), 17, 35, 40, 109, 110, 174, 237n13
Japan, 34, 35, 66
Jenkins, Jennifer, xv
Jugend, Die (Munich), 88, 89
Jünger, Ernst, 166

Kant, Immanuel, 19, 170
Kardorff, Wilhelm von, 79
Keller, Ernst, 83
Kerr, Alfred, 168
Kertbeny, Karl Maria, 17
Kessel, Lieutenant-General Gustav von, 115, 244n112
Kontje, Todd, 141, 165, 171
konträre Sexualempfindung (contrary sexual feeling or sexual inversion), 17
Koopmann, Helmut, 152, 177
Krafft, Rudolf, 64

Krafft-Ebing, Richard von, 16, 17, 18, 43, 83, 99, 122, 148, 153, 177, 190, 196; "acquired homosexuality," 181–2, 187; coins "sadism," 81; on sadism and masochism, 191–2; same-sex desire and "degeneration," 148; sexual allure of men in uniform, 127; on sexual fetishism, 128; *Psychopathia Sexualis*, 81, 106, 127, 148, 157, 191, 196
Krickel, Georg, 6, 13
Krupp, Friedrich Alfred, 114, 221, 241n85, 244n109; outed as homosexual, 54
Kühne, Thomas, 220
Kupffer, Elisarion von, 34, 37
Kurzke, Hermann, 152, 166

Lacan, Jacques, 11, 75; *jouissance*, 10, 72–3, 74, 76, 77, 193, 194; the Real, 162–3, 165–6, 214; the Symbolic, 163, 166, 194
Lacanian psychoanalysis, 10, 187, 193, 194
Leexow, Baron Karl Franz von (pseud.), 33
Lehnert, Herbert, 152
Leipzig Supreme Court, 60
Lessing, Theodor, 168
"Lex Bundeswehr," 223; Bundeswehr, 223
libidinal economy, 72, 132, 134
Lieblingminne (love of a favourite), 18
Linke, Konrad, 35; homosexual melodrama in prose form, 36–7
Literarisches Echo, 164
Lohengrin, 198
Lokal-Anzeiger (Berlin), 190, 194
Louis Ferdinand of Prussia, Prince, 67
Lübeck, 138, 142, 151, 168
Lustige Blätter, 184, 185
Lybeck, Marti, 19

Lynar, Count Johannes zu, 61, 87–92, 98, 112, 113, 114, 115, 261n150
Lynar-Hohenau trial, 87, 91–3; secrecy of, 92–3; verdicts in, 91–2

Mahoney, Kristin, 146
male soldier prostitution. See *Soldatenprostitution*
Mann, Erika, 153
Mann, Heinrich: admiration for Sacher-Masoch's work, 191; and anti-Semitism, 177; awareness of Thomas's homoerotic longings of, 177, 206, 274n67; knowledge of *Psychopathia Sexualis*, 191–2
Mann, Heinrich, works by: *Der Untertan (The Loyal Subject)*: 25, 26, 155, 174–207, 274n67; *Der Untertan* as critical portrait of Thomas, 177; *Der Untertan* as critique of military masculinity, 176, 179; *Der Untertan* as inversion of *Bildungsroman*, 176; *Der Untertan* portrayal of effeminacy in, 177, 180–1, 192, 196, 199–201, 207; *Der Untertan*, portrayal of masochism in, 188, 190–3, 194, 196; *Der Untertan*, portrayal of transvestism in, 196–203; *Der Untertan*, scene borrowed from Thomas's physical exam, 200–1; *Der Untertan*, shaming in, 179, 199–201, 207; *Der Untertan*, uniform as "instrument of martyrdom" in, 199–201; *Der Untertan*, use of parody in, 179; *Die Jagd nach Liebe*, 206
Mann, Katia (née Pringsheim), 152, 161, 187
Mann, Lula, 147
Mann, Thomas: compulsory enlistment in the military, 138, 139, 150, 151; critique of Heinrich, 164; disdain for effeminate homosexuals of, 211; early discharge from the military, 151; effects of war on, 166, 219–20; fanatical support of militarism of, 165–7; fantasies about military service of, 139, 140, 141, 144, 147, 149, 150, 152, 171–2; feelings of effeminacy of, 25, 172; homoerotic poetry of, 206; homoeroticism of, 139, 140, 144, 146–7, 151, 152, 166, 172, 177, 186, 187, 206, 211; on *The Loyal Subject*, 204, 205; marriage to Katia Pringsheim of, 148, 161, 267n93; masculinity of, 146, 150, 159, 168; Paul Ehrenberg and, 139, 144–7, 172; "private militarism" of, 139, 141, 172; tendonitis of, 150; use of gay male camp by, 140, 146–7, 153–4, 158, 160; views about his own military service of, 143, 144, 147–8, 149, 151; writes of "my sexual inversion," 149
Mann, Thomas, works by: *Die Bekenntnisse des Hochstaplers Felix Krull: Der Memoiren erster Teil* (The confessions of Felix Krull, confidence man: The early years), 140, 152–62, 163, 169, 170, 172, 179; *Die Bekenntnisse des Hochstaplers Felix Krull* as a "homosexual novel" (Mann's designation), 152; *Die Bekenntnisse des Hochstaplers Felix Krull*, Krull as Mann's own drag persona, 155; *Die Bekenntnisse des Hochstaplers Felix Krull* and queer failure, 154; *Betrachtungen eines Unpolitischen* (Reflections of a non-political man), 141, 164, 165, 170–1, 177; *Buddenbrooks*, 147 148, 151, 160; *Death in Venice*, 148, 151, 152, 167; *Friedrich und die Große Koalition* (Frederick the Great

Mann, Thomas, works by (*cont.*) and the Grand Coalition), 164, 168, 170; "Gedanken im Kriege" (Thoughts in war), 164, 166–8; "Gute Feldpost" (Good military mail), 164, 169–70; "Im Spiegel" (In the mirror), 150, 159; *Königliche Hoheit* (Royal highness), 152, 154, 161; "Lebensabriß" (A sketch of my life), 151, 159; *The Magic Mountain*, 170
Mann, Viktor, 149
Männerbund (exclusively male associations), 211, 221, 222
Mansfield, Nick, 165
Marhoefer, Laurie, 21, 221
Martin, Ariana, 181, 182, 183
Martin, John Levi, 205
Marx, Karl: concept of commodity fetishism, 99, 123–4, 126, 128; conceptualization of prostitution, 123, 124; *Economic and Philosophic Manuscripts of 1844*, 128; and Foucault, 258n90
Marxism, 122
masculinists: Adolf Brand, 164, 209, 222, 245n119; Benedict Friedlaender, 31, 32, 33, 34–5, 211; *Der Eigene* (masculinist literary journal), 34, 35, 165; Elisarion von Kupffer, 34, 37; Hans Blüher, 34, 148, 149, 186, 211; *Männerbund* (exclusively male association), 211, 221, 222
masculinity, 18, 31, 60, 132, 138; aggressive, 179; hegemonic, xiii, 172, 200; heterosexual, 21, 62, 159, 160, 210; military, 14, 25, 100, 138, 151, 166, 175, 176, 179, 203; Moltke's claim to, 58; sword-belt and, 70; of uniformed officers, 55; uniforms and, 16, 26, 100, 149, 202, 203, 210

masochism, 26, 81, 84, 107, 122, 188, 190, 191–4, 195, 196, 197; coined by Krafft-Ebing, 18, 177. *See also* sadism
masturbation, 3, 86, 128, 190, 252n80, 256n46
Matysik, Tracie, xv
McDonnell, Patricia, 217, 219
McDowell, Colin, 16
McLaren, Angus, 46, 58
McLellan, Josie, 223
McWilliam, Rohan, 29, 30
melodrama, as a response to suffering, 240n68; domestic, 43, 49, 50, 60; Harden-Moltke trial as, 30, 47–58; homophobic melodramatics, 30; homosexual, 36; origins and aesthetics of, 29–30, 35; metaphysics of, 30, 31; political function of, 44; suicide and, 23, 31, 40–1, 44, 61, 210; use in queer emancipation of, 30, 40–2, 45, 46
melodramatic: conventions, 29, 30, 57; plays and stories, 23, 29, 30, 35–6, 42–3, 48; rhetoric, 29, 30; strategies and tactics, 23, 40, 46, 60, 62
Merzbach, Georg, 37, 38–9, 44
Militair-Strafgerichts-Ordnung (MStGO), 79–80
militarism: discourse of, 136, 162; erotic economy of, 100, 120; German, xvi, 5, 27, 141, 160, 162, 169, 172, 173, 176, 177, 215; Prussian, 5, 7, 189; Prussian-German, 67, 100, 165, 211; and queerness, 108; Thomas Mann's "private militarism," 139, 141, 172
Militärstrafgesetzbuch (MStGB), 65, 93
military, German: officer corps; 5, 57, 62, 66, 76, 125–6, 127; one-year

volunteers (*Einjährig-Freiwillige*), 25, 40, 103, 138, 142–4, 146, 150, 154, 267n93; parades, 14, 126, 149, 150, 209, 214; reserve office corps, 142; soldiers' pay, 102–3
military justice: code of criminal procedure, 79–80; code of military law, 65, 93; corporal punishment in, 64–5, 79, 80, 84, 93, 102, 106, 246n2, 249n29; military courts, 65, 67, 79, 86, 87, 210; penal codes, 20, 85, 118; prosecution of homosexuality, 40, 54, 220, 222, 245n129; and secrecy, 65–6, 69, 78–9, 87, 92–4
military policies, 7, 27, 61, 64, 79, 123, 176, 210, 229n13, 276n21
military politics, and sexual/queer politics and discourse, xiii, xv, xvi, 5, 17, 21, 22, 24, 26, 174, 223, 224; sexualisation of, 25, 26
military spectacles, erotic nature of, 214
Moll, Albert, 17, 120, 127, 135, 136, 237n20, 243n104, 244n110
Moll, First-Lieutenant a.D. Erich, 32
Moltke, General Kuno Count von, 22–3, 28; alleged homosexuality of, 30, 46, 48, 49, 50, 52, 53–5, 58, 210; effeminacy of, 23, 28, 53, 57, 59, 62, 63, 210; invokes military dress (while out of uniform) during trial, 56–7; misogyny of, 50–1; trial verdict against, 58–9. *See also* Elbe; Harden-Moltke trial
Mommsen, Wolfgang, 164
Monatsbericht, 40–1, 62, 101, 113
Müller, Ernst, 93
Muskete, Die (Vienna), 120, 121

Napoleon I, 19
Napoleon III, 198
Napoleonic Code, 233n61
Napoleonic Wars, 141
National Liberal Party, 92
National Socialism (*Nationalsozialistische Deutsche Arbeiterpartei*, NSDAP), xiv, 221
Nazism and Nazi Party, xiii, 21, 221–2, 235n90, 257n62; and Adolf Hitler, 221–2; condemnation of homosexuality as degeneration by, 221; and Ernst Röhm, 221–2; and *Sturmabteilung* (SA), 221
Nazi uniforms and regalia, 222
Neff, Bernhard, 126
neue Rundschau, Die, 164
Nicolai, Lieutenant a.D., 32
Nightingale, Florence, xiv
"Nightlife in Potsdam," 115–16
Night of the Long Knives, 222
Nordau, Max, 147
Noske, Gustav, 92, 93

one-year volunteers (*Einjährig-Freiwillige*), 25, 40, 103, 138, 142–3, 144, 146, 150, 154, 267n93
Oppelt, Josef, 86–7
Oriola, Count Waldemar von, 92
Ost-Asien, 35
Ostwald, Hans, 109–12, 120; as critic of Hirschfeld, 109–10; and fantasy, 111; *Großstadt-Dokumente*, 105
Otto, Elizabeth, 14

Paragraph 175 (1872), 20, 40, 54, 58, 59, 85–7, 105, 113, 114, 120, 135, 209, 211, 220, 222, 237n16, 245n129, 246n131, 252n80, 275n87; petition to the Reichstag to repeal, 21, 24, 32, 71, 148, 174, 175, 211
parody, 107, 153, 156, 157, 202; defined, 179; of Wilhelm II, 179, 198

pederasty, 17, 34, 35, 53, 104, 153, 155
perverse Berlin, Das (Perverse Berlin), 99, 102, 118–20, 131–4
Phantasie (fantasy, imagination), 3, 12, 81, 88, 156
Phillips, Duncan, 217
Potsdam, 87, 97, 115, 208, 215, 216, 235n90, 277n29
Potsdam Guards, 50, 91, 104, 115
Potsdam scandal, 55
Prime-Stevenson, Edward (pseud. Xavier Mayne), 109
prostitution: female, 101, 108, 130; male, 23, 96, 98, 101, 102, 109, 115, 122, 127, 130, 224; semi-prostitution (*Halbprostitution*), 110. *See also* Berlin; *Soldatenprostitution*
Prussian Army, 64, 65, 67, 208; secrecy of, 76; as a secret society, 66, 67; uniforms of, 6, 59–60
Prussian criminal code, 17, 65, 84, 86, 209, 211
Prussian Guards, 97–8, 117, 122
Prussian military archives, destruction of, 21, 40, 85, 235n90
Prussian military law, 64, 71
psychoanalysis, xiii, xv, xvi, 9–10, 11, 18, 29, 53, 75, 122, 123, 128, 179, 224; Lacanian, 10, 187, 193, 194
Puar, Jasbir, 21, 165, 224

Queensbury, Marquess of, 17
queer activism, xii, xiv, 4, 21, 27, 222, 223; impediments to, 222
queer emancipation movement (in Germany), xii, xiv, xv, 5, 6, 18, 19, 23, 27, 98, 139, 141, 148, 164, 186, 209, 220, 222, 223, 224, 234n87; and Berlin, 209; and closeted homosexual officers, 28; and homonationalism, 21; medical-scientific wing of, 17; paradoxes of, 16, 21; use of melodrama in, 30, 40–2, 45, 46. *See also* Community of the Special; masculinists; Scientific-Humanitarian Committee
queerness and militarism, 108
queer oppositionality, 10
queerphobia, xiii, 179, 205
queer political fantasies emerging from wartime experiences, 220–2
queer scenes: in Berlin xii, xv, 140; in Germany, 24, 153, 209, 220, 222, 228n30
Queer Studies, 5, 8, 9, 10, 11
queer theory of Imperial Germany, xv

Rau, Hans, 83–5, 92; *Der Sadismus in der Armee* (Sadism in the army), 82–5
Reddi, Franz, 241n74; *Der fremde Gott* (The strange god), 42–5, 50, 53, 62
Reich, Wilhelm, 205
Reichsbote, Der, 113
Reichstag, debates on: military budget, 87, 92; military secrecy law, 65, 78, 80, 93; military trials, 93; petition to repeal Paragraph 175, 21, 24, 32, 71, 148, 174, 175, 209, 211, 275n87; *Soldatenmisshandlungen*, 65, 67, 78, 83, 84, 93, 94; *Soldatenprostitution*, 65, 98–9, 114
Richter, Eugen, 65, 69
Rilke, Rainer Maria, 164
Robertson, Bruce, 211
Röhm, Ernst, 221–2
Roland von Berlin, Der, 86
Rönnebeck, Arnold, 208, 215–17
Roper, Lyndal, 9,
Rosebery, Lord, 17
Rosegger, Peter, 45

Royal Bavarian Infantry
  Lifeguards, 144
Rubin, Gayle, 84, 270n4

Sacher-Masoch, Leopold von, 191, 196
Sacred Band of Thebes, 34, 36
Sade, Donatien Alphonse François,
  marquis de, 81, 84
sadism, 23, 26, 81, 122, 191; coined
  by Krafft-Ebing, 81; Eulenburg on,
  81–2; in the military, 24, 67, 80, 83,
  210; as sexological concept, 24, 94,
  174; as theoretical concept (Žižek),
  77–8. *See also* masochism; Rau;
  Soldatenmisshandlungen
Sagarra, Eda, 124–5
same-sex: activity, behaviour,
  practices, relations, 8, 17–18, 21,
  41, 53, 54, 67, 74, 105, 114, 131, 133,
  174, 175, 222, 223; attraction, 71,
  78; desire, 3, 4, 8, 17, 18–19, 23, 24,
  26, 30, 31, 41, 42, 66, 81, 99, 101,
  108, 122, 134, 148, 172, 175, 181,
  182, 196, 209, 211, 221; identity, 4,
  8, 18–19, 26, 27, 100, 139, 175, 211,
  223; love, 18, 20, 34, 220; rights, 20;
  transgressions, 136
Sandborn, Joshua, 101
satire, 26, 179, 198, 204, 207
Schaffner, Anna Katharina, 148
Schellendorff, Walther Bronsart
  von, 80
Schleswig-Holstein, Auguste
  Viktoria von, 190
Schmidt, Otto Ernst, 81
Scholz, Dieter, 217
Schrenck-Notzing, Albert von, 81;
  Algolagnie, 81
Schurtz, Heinrich, 34
schwul (or "gay"), 18
Scientific-Humanitarian Committee
  (WhK) (*das Wissenschaftlich-
  humanitäres Komitee*), 17, 20–1, 23,
  24, 29, 31–3, 35, 38, 40, 45, 46, 54,
  61–2, 85, 98, 101, 104, 109, 110, 113,
  114, 118, 130, 164, 210, 211, 219,
  220, 243n104, 246n131; founding
  of (1897), 20, 28, 32, 41, 209;
  membership of, 28, 62; petition to
  the Reichstag (to repeal Paragraph
  175) of, 21, 24, 32, 71, 148, 174,
  175, 209, 211, 275n87; secession
  of masculinists from, 28; theory
  of sexual intermediaries of, 37.
  See also Hirschfeld
Scott, Joan, 9–10, 11
Second World War, 21, 40, 85, 222
secrecy: homosexuality and, 28,
  31–2, 55, 59, 108, 133; institutional,
  23, 24, 66, 67, 76; the military
  and, 24, 65–7, 69–70, 73, 78–9, 87,
  92–4; punishment and jouissance
  and, 73–7; and Reichstag debate
  on military secrecy law, 65, 78,
  80, 93; secret order of Georg,
  Duke of Saxony, 78–9, 80, 83, 84;
  theory of 65–6, 69, 73, 74, 75, 79,
  94, 210
Sedgwick, Eve, 8, 18, 19, 28, 59, 184
Seven Years' War, 167–8
sexological, 53, 100, 114, 120, 122,
  123, 136, 156; categories, 23, 93,
  94; concepts, 24, 27, 94; circles,
  237n20, 244n110; discourse, 24,
  148, 177, 181; wing, 19, 21
sexology, xii, xvi, 8, 18, 25, 27, 49, 53,
  83, 94, 120, 122, 123, 136
sexual innocence, 31, 61, 112, 118,
  129, 131–5, 137
sexual inversion, 17, 114, 148, 149,
  156, 177, 179, 180, 181, 188, 190,
  196. *See also* gender inversion
sexuelle Zwischenstufen (sexual
  intermediaries), 17, 241n76.
  See also *Jahrbuch für sexuelle
  Zwischenstufen, Das*

shame, 74, 141, 160, 163, 179, 182, 198, 199, 200, 201, 207; shamelessness, 130, 200, 201
Shepardson, Charles, 11
Simmel, Georg, xiv, 24, 66, 69, 73, 74, 75, 79, 88, 94, 210
Sixth Congress of German Jurists (1867), 20
Smith, Tom, 223
Social Democratic Party (*Soziaidemokratische Partei Deutschlands*, SPD), 64, 67, 78, 83, 92, 115, 118, 120, 131, 175, 221, 229n13, 241n85
sodomy, 8, 17, 31, 53, 59; anti-sodomy laws, 86, 105, 109, 135
Soldatenmisshandlungen (mistreatment of soldiers), 24, 64–7, 69, 76, 77, 78, 80, 92, 93–5; debates in Reichstag about, 65, 67, 78, 83, 84, 93, 94; as an effect of militarism, 83; and military criminal code, 84; as sadism, 82–4
Soldatenprostitution (prostitution by soldiers), 24–5, 97–120, 122, 123, 127, 131, 133, 134, 135, 136, 210, 256n52, 257n63; account of in *Das perverse Berlin*, 118–19, 131–4; army's knowledge of, 115; brothels and bordellos, 24, 96, 104, 109, 130; debates in Reichstag about, 65, 98–9; economy of, 97, 100, 122, 210; Hirschfeld's account of, 105–9; low wages as impetus to, 102–3; Ostwald's account of, 109–2; prostitution by civilian men in contrast to, 24, 119; soldier bars, 103, 106, 110, 111; in Strasbourg, 104, 130; and unwelcome or mistaken advances, 85, 118, 119. *See also* Berlin; Einem; Harden-Moltke trial
Somerville, Siobhan, 17

Sonnenberg, Max Liebermann von, 93, 135
Sontag, Susan, "Notes on Camp," 153, 158; criticism of, 265n65
Sozialistische Monatshefte, 83
Spahn, Peter Joseph, 87–8, 114–15
Spector, Scott, 54
Steakley, James, 88
Stein, Gertrude, 209
Stieglitz, Alfred, 208, 215, 216, 217, 219
Sturmabteilung (SA), 221
suicide, 42, 43, 84, 85, 114, 154, 157, 159, 210, 241n76, 241n85; and melodrama, 23, 31, 40–1, 44, 61, 210
Suttner, Bertha von, xiv
Swales, Martin, 69

Thaler, Johann, 174–5
Theweleit, Klaus, *Male Fantasies*, xiii
Thiele, Friedrich, 175
Third Reich, xiv, 222
third sex, the (*das dritte Geschlecht*), 17. *See also under* Hirschfeld, works by
Tiergarten (park in Berlin), 104, 112, 122, 192
Timm, Annette, 101
transvestites and transvestism, 18, 25–6, 177, 196–203, 210; coined by Hirschfeld, 18, 177. *See also* cross-dressing; Hirschfeld
Tresckow, Hans von, 33, 98, 103–4, 112, 115, 120, 135, 244n112

Ullstein House, 114
Ulrichs, Karl Heinrich, 3–4, 6, 16–17, 24, 96–8, 100–1, 104, 105, 106, 107, 118, 128, 129, 130, 177, 181, 210, 219, 233n66, 255n40; on manliness, 133; *Memnon: The Sexual Nature of the Male-Loving Urning*, 3; *The Riddle*

of "Man-Manly" Love, 3, 20; Vindicta, 20. *See also* Urnings
uniform fetishism: of the army, 100, 123, 134, 135, 137, 223; of homosexuals, 100, 123, 124, 127, 128, 129, 135, 137, 223
uniforms, German military: and conscription, 7; dress uniform as homosexual signs and signals, 112–13; erotic appeal of, xii, 16, 24, 117, 132; as erotic fetish object for homosexual civilians, 120; and fantasy, 14, 21, 38, 128, 129, 131, 139; and female dress, 12–13; of Garde du Corps, 88, 91, 126; honour code of, 57; of Hussars, 6, 126; and masculinity, 16, 26, 100, 149, 202, 203, 210; meaning for Moltke of, 57; parade uniforms, 6, 45, 124, 215; and posture, 15–16; of Prussian Army, 6, 59–60; and self-presentation, 14; and social hierarchies, 125–7; sword-belt (*Koppel*) of, 67, 69–71, 77, 149; varieties and colours of, 6–7, 11, 12–13, 203, 212, 213, 215, 219. *See also* transvestites and transvestism
Uranian coffee social (1865), 96; Uranian love, 20; "Uranian Platform," 20; Uranians, 38
Urnings, 16, 20, 33, 96–7, 100–1, 106, 107, 122, 127, 130, 133, 153, 157, 210; attraction to soldiers of, 129; coined by Ulrichs, 4, 17; *Urningsparagraphen* (antisodomy law), 105; "Urning Union" (*Urningsbund*), 20. *See also* Dionings

Vagts, Alfred, 14
Volksstimme (Magdeburg), 91, 92, 112
Vorwärts, 78, 244n102
Vossische Zeitung, Die (Berlin), 45–6, 60, 113, 243n99

Wackerfuss, Andrew, 221, 222
Wahre Jacob, Der (Stuttgart), 89, 90, 115, 116
warme Brüder (warm brothers), 18
Weber, Max, 65
Weimar Republic, xiv, 215, 221, 224
Weinberg, Jonathan, 212–14, 217, 218, 219
Weißbrich, Thomas, 217
Werz, Friedrich, 14, 15
Westphal, Carl, 17, 181, 196
Westphalia, 65
Wiedner, Hartmut, 81
Wiegman, Robyn, 10
Wiemer, Otto, 261n150
Wiener, Martin J., 26
Wilde, Oscar, 13, 17, 140, 146, 153, 158, 228n30
Wildenbruch, Ernst von, 24, 67, 71, 87; *Das edle Blut* (Noble blood), 24, 67–78, 94, 133; *Die Quitzkows*, 68
Wilhelm, Eugen (pseud. Numa Praetorius), 109, 130, 237n13, 239n37
Wilhelm I, 32, 189
Wilhelm II, 13, 22, 24, 25, 48, 67, 80, 164, 167, 180, 183, 187, 189, 190, 192, 195–6, 204, 209; displeased by Harden's acquittal, 60; edict (1890) of, 76; favourite uniform of, 126; militaristic values of, 176; Moltke's homoerotic adulation of, 184, 186; parody of, 179, 198; religiosity of, 195
Williams, Linda, 36, 45
Wilson, Elizabeth A., 10
Winter, Helga, 191
Wolff, Kurt, 204
women's apparel, 38, 197, 199, 203

women's movement in Germany, xiv, 234n79
World War I. *See* First World War
World War II. *See* Second World War
Wysling, Hans, 148

Yearbook of sexual intermediaries. See *Jahrbuch für sexuelle Zwischenstufen, Das*

Zarzosa, Augustin, 240n68
Zedlitz-Trützschler, Count Robert, 13–14
Zeeland, Steven, 133
Ziemann, Benjamin, 139, 173
Žižek, Slavoj, 11, 72, 163, 166, 173, 190, 193; and fantasy, 26, 99, 132, 137, 214; and fetishism, 124, 128; and the "pervert," 77–8, 194; and "a shared lie," 73
Zola, Émile, 204; *La Débâcle*, 204; *The Ladies' Paradise*, 42
Zukunft, Die, 22, 235n94
Zwanzigste Jahrhundert, Das (The twentieth century), 177, 271n17

GERMAN AND EUROPEAN STUDIES

General Editor: James Retallack

1. Emanuel Adler, Beverly Crawford, Federica Bicchi, and Rafaella Del Sarto, *The Convergence of Civilizations: Constructing a Mediterranean Region*
2. James Retallack, *The German Right, 1860–1920: Political Limits of the Authoritarian Imagination*
3. Silvija Jestrovic, *Theatre of Estrangement: Theory, Practice, Ideology*
4. Susan Gross Solomon, ed., *Doing Medicine Together: Germany and Russia between the Wars*
5. Laurence McFalls, ed., *Max Weber's "Objectivity" Revisited*
6. Robin Ostow, ed., *(Re)Visualizing National History: Museums and National Identities in Europe in the New Millennium*
7. David Blackbourn and James Retallack, eds., *Localism, Landscape, and the Ambiguities of Place: German-Speaking Central Europe, 1860–1930*
8. John Zilcosky, ed., *Writing Travel: The Poetics and Politics of the Modern Journey*
9. Angelica Fenner, *Race under Reconstruction in German Cinema: Robert Stemmle's Toxi*
10. Martina Kessel and Patrick Merziger, eds., *The Politics of Humour: Laughter, Inclusion, and Exclusion in the Twentieth Century*
11. Jeffrey K. Wilson, *The German Forest: Nature, Identity, and the Contestation of a National Symbol, 1871–1914*
12. David G. John, *Bennewitz, Goethe,* Faust*: German and Intercultural Stagings*
13. Jennifer Ruth Hosek, *Sun, Sex, and Socialism: Cuba in the German Imaginary*
14. Steven M. Schroeder, *To Forget It All and Begin Again: Reconciliation in Occupied Germany, 1944–1954*
15. Kenneth S. Calhoon, *Affecting Grace: Theatre, Subject, and the Shakespearean Paradox in German Literature from Lessing to Kleist*
16. Martina Kolb, *Nietzsche, Freud, Benn, and the Azure Spell of Liguria*
17. Hoi-eun Kim, *Doctors of Empire: Medical and Cultural Encounters between Imperial Germany and Meiji Japan*
18. J. Laurence Hare, *Excavating Nations: Archeology, Museums, and the German-Danish Borderlands*
19. Jacques Kornberg, *The Pope's Dilemma: Pius XII Faces Atrocities and Genocide in the Second World War*

20 Patrick O'Neill, *Transforming Kafka: Translation Effects*
21 John K. Noyes, *Herder: Aesthetics against Imperialism*
22 James Retallack, *Germany's Second Reich: Portraits and Pathways*
23 Laurie Marhoefer, *Sex and the Weimar Republic: German Homosexual Emancipation and the Rise of the Nazis*
24 Bettina Brandt and Daniel L. Purdy, eds., *China in the German Enlightenment*
25 Michael Hau, *Performance Anxiety: Sport and Work in Germany from the Empire to Nazism*
26 Celia Applegate, *The Necessity of Music: Variations on a German Theme*
27 Richard J. Golsan and Sarah M. Misemer, eds., *The Trial That Never Ends: Hannah Arendt's* Eichmann in Jerusalem *in Retrospect*
28 Lynne Taylor, *In the Children's Best Interests: Unaccompanied Children in American-Occupied Germany, 1945–1952*
29 Jennifer A. Miller, *Turkish Guest Workers in Germany: Hidden Lives and Contested Borders, 1960s to 1980s*
30 Amy Carney, *Marriage and Fatherhood in the Nazi SS*
31 Michael E. O'Sullivan, *Disruptive Power: Catholic Women, Miracles, and Politics in Modern Germany, 1918–1965*
32 Gabriel N. Finder and Alexander V. Prusin, *Justice behind the Iron Curtain: Nazis on Trial in Communist Poland*
33 Parker Daly Everett, *Urban Transformations: From Liberalism to Corporatism in Greater Berlin, 1871–1933*
34 Melissa Kravetz, *Women Doctors in Weimar and Nazi Germany: Maternalism, Eugenics, and Professional Identity*
35 Javier Samper Vendrell, *The Seduction of Youth: Print Culture and Homosexual Rights in the Weimar Republic*
36 Sebastian Voigt, ed., *Since the Boom: Continuity and Change in the Western Industrialized World after 1970*
37 Olivia Landry, *Theatre of Anger: Radical Transnational Performance in Contemporary Berlin*
38 Jeremy Best, *Heavenly Fatherland: German Missionary Culture and Globalization in the Age of Empire*
39 Svenja Bethke, *Dance on the Razor's Edge: Crime and Punishment in the Nazi Ghettos*
40 Kenneth S. Calhoon, *The Long Century's Long Shadow: Weimar Cinema and the Romantic Modern*
41 Randall Hansen, Achim Saupe, Andreas Wirsching, and Daqing Yang, eds., *Authenticity and Victimhood after the Second World War: Narratives from Europe and East Asia*
42 Rebecca Wittmann, ed., *The Eichmann Trial Reconsidered*

43 Sebastian Huebel, *Fighter, Worker, and Family Man: German-Jewish Men and Their Gendered Experiences in Nazi Germany, 1933–1941*
44 Samuel Clowes Huneke, *States of Liberation: Gay Men between Dictatorship and Democracy in Cold War Germany*
45 Tuska Benes, *The Rebirth of Revelation: German Theology in an Age of Reason and History, 1750–1850*
46 Skye Doney, *The Persistence of the Sacred: German Catholic Pilgrimage, 1832–1937*
47 Matthew Unangst, *Colonial Geography: Race and Space in German East Africa, 1884–1905*
48 Deborah Barton, *Writing and Rewriting the Reich: Women Journalists in the Nazi and Post-war Press*
49 Martin Wagner, *A Stage for Debate: The Political Significance of Vienna's Burgtheater, 1814–1867*
50 Andrea Rottmann, *Queer Lives across the Wall: Desire and Danger in Divided Berlin, 1945–1970*
51 Jeffrey Schneider, *Uniform Fantasies: Soldiers, Sex, and Queer Emancipation in Imperial Germany*